Human Rights in Nigeria's External Relations

AFRICAN GOVERNANCE AND DEVELOPMENT

African Governance and Development identifies and elaborates on the strategic place of governance and development within the African studies. Reflecting the fact that life in Africa continues to change; particularly in political, development, and socio-economic arenas; this series explores issues focusing on the ongoing mobilization for good governance and the search for sustainable and economic development. The *African Governance and Development* series address gaps and larger needs in the developing scholarship on Africa and the African Diaspora. This series provides scholarly monographs and edited collections in the humanities, social science, and social scientific traditions. Contributors are encouraged to submit book length manuscripts that encompass, besides the above named topics, those focusing on: Africa's political economy and economic development, Africa's place in world trade development, democratization of African countries, the inclusion and representation of ethnic minorities, and the role of gender in Africa's development. Works can be focused on a single African country, a region of African countries, or the African continent's place as a global player.

Recent Titles

Pan-Africanism in Modern Times: Challenges, Concerns, and Constraints, edited by Olayiwola Abegunrin and Sabelle Ogbobode Abidde

Nigeria, Africa, and the United States: Challenges of Governance, Development, and Security, by Olayiwola Abegunrin

Human Rights in Nigeria's External Relations: Building the Record of a Moral Superpower, by Philip C. Aka

Human Rights in Nigeria's External Relations

Building the Record of a Moral Superpower

Philip C. Aka

LEXINGTON BOOKS
Lanham • Boulder • New York • London

Published by Lexington Books
An imprint of The Rowman & Littlefield Publishing Group, Inc.
4501 Forbes Boulevard, Suite 200, Lanham, Maryland 20706
www.rowman.com

Unit A, Whitacre Mews, 26-34 Stannary Street, London SE11 4AB, United Kingdom

British Library Cataloguing in Publication Information Available

Library of Congress Cataloging-in-Publication Data

Names: Aka, Philip C., author.
Title: Human rights in Nigeria's external relations : building the record of a moral superpower / Philip C. Aka.
Description: Lanham : Lexington Books, [2017] | Includes bibliographical references and index.
Identifiers: LCCN 2016042907 (print) | LCCN 2016051011 (ebook) | ISBN 9781498533553 (cloth : alk. paper) | ISBN 9781498533560 (electronic)
Subjects: LCSH: Human rights—Nigeria. | Nigeria—Foreign relations. | Nigeria—Politics and government.
Classification: LCC JC599.N6 .A45 2017 (print) | LCC JC599.N6 (ebook) | DDC 323.09669—dc23
LC record available at https://lccn.loc.gov/2016042907

∞™ The paper used in this publication meets the minimum requirements of American National Standard for Information Sciences—Permanence of Paper for Printed Library Materials, ANSI/NISO Z39.48-1992.

Printed in the United States of America

To my mother, my family, the memory of my father,
and the loving memory of Evangeline C. Aka. To all the
victims of human rights and humanitarian law abuses in Nigeria,
especially the three and a half million Igbos who died in Biafra.

Contents

Figures

Tables

Preface

This book is a broad-ranging argument for thoroughgoing reforms at home and abroad as the only antidote to the nation-building dilemmas Nigeria confronts in the first quarter of the twenty-first century. Because of its enormous material and human endowments, Nigeria is dubbed the "Giant of Africa." It is a moniker many of its leaders take seriously. These include one foreign minister who opined that there could never be a black story, "unless it is a Nigerian success story."

Yet Nigeria is a state rife with instability of every description, some of which periodically erupt into violence. Given still-ongoing national security challenges in the land, including an exceedingly bloody religion-based terrorism, the Fourth Republic since 1999, the longest period of continuous democratic rule since independence—key to the timeline of this book—has not been insulated from the spell of instability.

The main argument of this work is that internationally agreed-upon ethical standards embedded in human rights can save Nigeria. Building on the author's scholarship relating to the topic going back two decades, the book is a methodologically and theoretically grounded seminal discourse on Nigerian foreign relations from 1960 to the present time that explicitly spells out the human rights or lack thereof in those relations, including underlying and impinging domestic forces. The work is set around six issues of application embedded in a temple of Nigeria's human rights foreign policy comprising two steps and four pillars: reconstructed national interest, increased human rights at home, redesigned peacekeeping, reshaped foreign policy machinery, increased bilateralism in foreign relations, and the use of the Economic Community of West African States (ECOWAS) as a human rights tool. Although focused on the period since independence, for proper understanding of events from the past that shape the current patterns of politics in the land, the book also embodies a historical background chapter that overviews the precolonial and colonial eras.

The Dagara people in West Africa have a saying to the effect that a person can pay a debt of one cow, but dies forever in debt to his family, friend, and teachers. My problem belongs in the second category of eternal indebtedness—and to two sources. In a broad sense, this book is a congealment of my scholarship on human rights going back nearly two decades. In that respect, the first source that I owe unpayable debt here needing to be acknowledged are numerous friends and colleagues over the years who have advised me to collect my several writings into a book. Among this first source, three individuals stand out for mention: Opoku Agyeman, A.B. Assensoh, Gloria J. Browne-Marshall, Emmanuel O. Iheukwumere, and Hassan Wahab. Thank you for your encouragement going back many years. I hope you like this first effort in my attempt to translate my writings into the traditional book format.

More immediately, this book originated as a dissertation for the Doctor of Juridical Science (S.J.D.) degree at the Robert H. McKinney School of Law at Indianapolis. From this source, the debt so big it cannot be paid by a cow is owed to IU McKinney School of Law for the platform that it provided for my post-J.D. legal training. A law school means little without its faculty. Among the faculty, I express my appreciation to George E. Edwards, Anthony Page, Frank Emmert, Shawn M. Boyne, and Karen E. Bravo, for various acts of support and encouragement. The last three graciously served on my dissertation committee. I also acknowledge the editorial and production team at Rowman & Littlefield—Madhumitha Koduvalli, Kathryn Tafelsi, and Jehanne Schweitzer—for expertly shepherding this work every step of the way to production.

Through it all, my family remained an unfailing source of support—even as they engaged successfully in their own individual academic pursuits. Ellie, Phil Jr., Brad, and Amanda: I appreciate each and every one of you for your emotional encouragement, without which this project would have taken longer than it did to complete. Last but by no means least, I dedicate this book to the memory of the millions who perished in Biafra, among them two precious members of my then nuclear family.

September 2016

Abbreviations

ACHPR	African [Banjul] Charter on Human and Peoples' Rights
ACOSTA	Africa Contingency Operations Training and Assistance
ACRI	African Crisis Response Initiative
AEC	African Economic Community
AFISMA	African Union International Support Mission in Mali
AHSG	Authority of Heads of State and Government
AMIS	African Union Mission in Sudan
AMISOM	African Union Mission in Somalia
APC	All Progressives Congress
AU	African Union
AVEM I	United Nations Angola Verification Mission I
AVEM II	United Nations Angola Verification Mission II
AVEM III	United Nations Angola Verification Mission III
CCJ	Community Court of Justice
CEAO	West African Economic Community (Communauté Economique de l'Afrique de l'Quest in French)
CEN-SAD	Community of Sahel-Saharan States
CIA	Central Intelligence Agency
CID	Criminal Investigation Department
CLO	Civil Liberties Organization
CM	Council of Ministers
COMESA	Common Market for Eastern and Southern Africa
DIA	Defense Intelligence Agency
DSS	Department of State Services (also known as SSS or State Security Service)
EAC	East African Community
EBID	ECOWAS Bank for Investment and Development
ECA	Economic Commission for Africa

ECCAS	Economic Community of Central African States
ECOMICI	ECOWAS Mission in Côte d'Ivoire
ECOMIL	ECOWAS Mission in Liberia
ECOMOG	ECOWAS Monitoring Group
ECOWAS	Economic Community of West African States
FBI	Federal Bureau of Investigation
FDI	Foreign direct investment
HRVIC	Human Rights Violations Investigation Commission (Oputa Panel)
IC	Intelligence Community
ICCPR	International Covenant on Civil and Political Rights
ICESCR	International Covenant on Economic, Social, and Cultural Rights
IDPs	Internally displaced persons
IGAD	Intergovernmental Authority on Development
INEC	Independent National Electoral Commission
MINURSO	United Nations Mission for the Referendum in Western Sahara
MINUSTAH	United Nations Stabilization Mission in Haiti
MONUA	United Nations Observer Mission in Angola
MONUC	United Nations Mission in the Democratic Republic of Congo
MONUSCO	United Nations Organization Stabilization Mission in the Democratic Republic of Congo
MOPOL	Nigerian Mobile Police
MPLA	Movement for the Popular Liberation of Angola
MRU	Mano River Union
MSSD	Most-Similar-Systems Design
MTAP	Military Training Assistance Program
NAPKC	Nigeria Army Peacekeeping Center
NEPAD	New Partnership for Africa's Development
NGOs	Non-governmental organizations
NIIA	Nigerian Institute of International Affairs
NIPSS	National Institute for Policy and Strategic Studies
NPN	National Party of Nigeria
NSA	National Security Agency
NSC	National Security Council
OAU	Organization of African Unity (from 2000 renamed the African Union, AU)
ONSA	Office of the National Security Adviser
ONUC	United Nations Organization in the Congo
OPEC	Organization of the Petroleum Exporting Countries
PDP	People's Democratic Party

PKW	Peacekeeper Wing
RECAMP	Reinforcement of African Capacity to Maintain Peace
R2P	Responsibility to Protect
SADC	Southern African Development Community
TAC	Technical Aid Corps
UDHR	Universal Declaration of Human Rights
UMA	Arab Maghreb Union
UNAMID	African Union—United Nations Mission in Darfur
UNAMIR	United Nations Assistance Mission for Rwanda
UNAMSIL	United Nations Mission in Sierra Leone
UNASOG	United Nations Aouzou Strip Observer Group
UNCRO	United Nations Confidence Restoration Operation in Croatia
UNIFIL	United Nations Interim Force in Lebanon
UNIKOM	United Nations Iraq-Kuwait Observation Mission
UNIPOM	United Nations India-Pakistan Observation Mission
UNISFA	United Nations Interim Security Force for Abyei
UNITA	National Union for the Total Independence of Angola
UNITAR	United Nations Institute for Training and Research
UNMIBH	United Nations Mission in Bosnia Herzegovina
UNMIK	United Nations Mission in Kosovo
UNMIL	United Nations Mission in Liberia
UNMISMM	United Nations Multidimensional Integrated Stabilization Mission in Mali
UNMOP	United Nations Observer Mission in Angola
UNMOT	United Nations Mission of Observers in Tajikistan
UNOCI	United Nations Operation in Côte d'Ivoire
UNOHCHR	United Nations Office of the High Commissioner for Human Rights
UNOMSIL	United Nations Observer Mission in Sierra Leone
UNOSOM I	United Nations Operation in Somalia I
UNOSOM II	United Nations Operation in Somalia II
UNOSOZ	United Nations Operation in Mozambique
UNPREDEP	United Nations Preventive Deployment Force in the Republic of Macedonia (replaced UNPROFOR next below)
UNPROFOR	United Nations Protection Force (former Yugoslavia)
UNSF	United Nations Security Force in West New Guinea
UNTAES	United Nations Transitional Administration for Eastern Slovenia, Baranja, Western Sirmium in Croatia
UNTAET	United Nations Transitional Administration in East Timor
UNTAC	United Nations Transitional Authority in Cambodia
UNTAG	United Nations Transition Assistance Group (Namibia)
WCC	Within-Case Comparison

Chapter One

Introduction

SIGNIFICANCE OF THIS STUDY

This book analyzes the application of human rights in Nigeria's external relations. Nigeria is a country in West Africa overlooking the Gulf of Guinea with a landmass slightly more than twice the size of California.[1] It is bordered on the East by Cameroon, West by Benin, North by Niger, and South by the Atlantic Ocean.[2] A slight reshaping of the country's borders, reinforcing the size and population advantages of the North over the South, occurred soon after independence when, in a referendum on February 11 and 12, 1961, Northern Cameroon voted to join Nigeria, while Southern Cameroon voted to join French-speaking Cameroon. Before the referendum, Northern Cameroon was administered separately within Nigeria, while Southern Cameroon was part of Eastern Nigeria.[3] More recently, the International Court of Justice heard a land and maritime dispute between Nigeria and Cameroon in which it awarded ownership of the Bakassi Peninsula to Cameroon but a stretch of land in the area around Lake Chad to Nigeria.[4]

Nigeria is a wholesale creature of British colonialism. The country was created "by the imposition of union by an imperial power on an artificially demarcated territory containing a heterogeneous population of strangers" rather than "by a voluntary union of previously existing, closely related, and freely contracting units."[5] Following forty-six years of British control, counting from 1914 when British authorities consolidated three formerly separate holdings—the Colony of Lagos, the Northern Protectorate, and Southern Protectorate—into one unit,[6] the country became independent in October 1960,[7] and a republic three years later,[8] in a move designed to shake off residues of British control and consolidate its newly won independence.[9] For Nigeria, two major relics of the British controlled republican status removed were:

the change in the title of the governor-general of the country who represented the British monarch to the president (which under the parliamentary system that Nigeria operated was a ceremonial figurehead position since real executive power resided in the prime minister); and the Nigerian Supreme Court became the tribunal of final appeal, rather than the Judicial Committee of the Privy Council, which hitherto assumed that role.[10]

This study covers the timeline of the country's post-independence from 1960 to 2016. This is a period spanning fifty-six years during which Nigeria underwent numerous changes, most notably the ballooning of its population from nearly 56 million people to over 186 million.[11] Now, as in 1960, Nigeria remains the most populous country in Africa, but more so today in sheer size than it did fifty-six years ago, the result of a rapid growth rate in population[12] with little basis in intrinsic economic growth, even for a mineral-rich country.[13]

Administrative changes with little anchor in economic viability have also tracked the rapid growth in population. From a federation of one national government (headquartered in Lagos) and three regions at independence and four in 1963,[14] Nigerian governments have ballooned into a bureaucratic Leviathan of one national government in Abuja, 36 states, and 774 local governments.[15] All of these but the 1963 reorganization were created through military fiat.[16] In constitutional and political practice, since 1979 Nigeria has adopted the United States' presidential system of government that replaced the parliamentary system that it inherited from the United Kingdom at independence.[17] However, unlike the United States, where formerly unaffiliated territories joined the union, in the process expanding the landmass of the country,[18] state creations in Nigeria involve the breakup of a fixed and unchanging landmass into smaller entities.[19] Also unlike the U.S. Constitution, the Nigerian Constitution contains no provision on the admission of new territories as states, should such a situation arise, nor does it include any provision permitting the merger of preexisting states.[20]

Some of the changes Nigeria has witnessed since independence, such as the humanitarian convulsions of the civil war from 1967 to 1970 and the repressive experience of military rule across seven juntas for nearly three decades until 1999,[21] are negative. But others, such as the experiments in democracy, are more heartwarming. Nigeria is currently living through the longest spurt of civilian rule since independence in 1960. This bout of non-military rule since May 1999—praised at its starting point by then U.S. president William J. Clinton as "the most important democratic transition in Africa since the fall of apartheid"[22]—is referred to, somewhat oddly, as the Fourth Republic.[23] President Clinton made this statement in the course of a state visit to Nigeria in August 2000, the first such visit since President Jimmy Carter's in April 1978.

The elongated practice of democratic rule, deepened in March 2015 with the peaceful transfer of power at the center from one governing party to an opposition party,[24] provides the context for this study. Like many other countries in the world, Nigeria applies human rights in its external relations. The country participated robustly in the decolonization and anti-racialist campaigns in Africa that culminated with the achievement of majority rule in South Africa in 1994;[25] espouses "respect for international law and treaty obligations";[26] puts a premium on peace and international cooperation that it seeks to promote through peacekeeping;[27] and eschews the use of force in resolving conflicts with neighbors.[28] Nigeria also played an instrumental role in the establishment of the Organization of African Unity (OAU) and the African Union (AU) that succeeded that organization; [29] and, going back to the early days of its independence, operates a technical assistance program that in 1987 it formalized into a Technical Aid Corps (TAC) scheme.[30]

However, for a country of its size and potentials, this is barely enough. Building on auspicious foundations, such as the ones recounted in the preceding paragraph, Nigeria can do more to increase the role of human rights in its external affairs while contributing to the international human rights regime[31] in several practical terms[32] ultimately "build[ing] global governance" and "reshap[ing] the meaning of sovereignty" in a manner that includes human rights as a norm of legitimacy.[33] In the post–Cold War period, "[m]any states have made substantial progress toward a more serious incorporation of human rights into their foreign policy[,]" but many too "could readily do more."[34]

This study identifies Nigeria as one of those laggards needing to do more, outlines the justification for that assessment, but more so the extent of the deficit, and marshals several practical measures the country could use to enhance its contribution to international human rights for its own domestic well-being and to the benefit of its known aspirations for a leadership role within the sphere of its influence in West Africa and beyond. Four key questions which animate this research are:

- *Precisely* what influence do human rights have in Nigeria's external relations? Stated differently, *how far* does the country have to go to join the club of "global good citizen[s]" or "global Good Samaritan[s]"[35] who consistently apply human rights in their external affairs?
- What factors at this time make increased application of human rights in external affairs exigent for Nigeria?

- What possible *methods* could the country use to facilitate the application of more human rights in its external relations?, and
- What are the possible objections to the case for more human rights in external relations this study makes, and what are the conceivable rebuttals to those objections?

Many studies have been published on Nigerian foreign policies, across military and civilian administrations, including works focusing mainly on the Fourth Republic since 1999.[36] However, few, if any, of these studies dealt with the application of human rights to those policies,[37] save perhaps for works on peacekeeping[38] that touch human rights only incidentally or sporadically. This study fills that hole in the literature by systematically exploring the application of human rights in the country's external relations back to the period of its independence in 1960, guided by a fitting methodology and a sound theoretical framework.

In a nutshell, this book builds on three genres of literature. The first, referred to already, consists of studies on Nigerian foreign policies.[39] A second genre consists of studies on human rights in Nigeria or lack thereof, unattached to foreign policy analysis.[40] A third and final category comprises works on human rights in comparative foreign policy or the application of human rights in national foreign policies in comparative perspective.[41] Using a theoretical framework embedded in constructivism, in-between *realism* and *idealism*, based on the extent to which each theory permits introduction of human rights into external affairs, this book examines the application of human rights in Nigerian foreign relations in an attempt to improve current injection of these values both in their quality and quantity. It argues for increased integration of human rights in Nigeria's external relations, maps out the internal and external methods for achieving that application, and responds to possible objections against the argument for the adoption of a human rights–based foreign policy for Nigeria that the study makes.

This research importantly intersects law and politics. Human rights are "a matter of law" codified in international documents and interpreted by international lawyers, including regional and global treaty supervision bodies, that have also, in our time, become "a matter of diplomacy and politics as well."[42] More specifically for our purpose here, human rights-based policies "are promoted, selected, disseminated, contested, and reconstructed through political processes."[43]

Figure 1.1, the temple of Nigeria's human rights foreign policy, graphically encapsulates the achievement of this work. A Greek temple connotes religious or spiritual activities, such as prayer and sacrifice. It is a representation persuasively used in the study of democracy[44] that this work extends

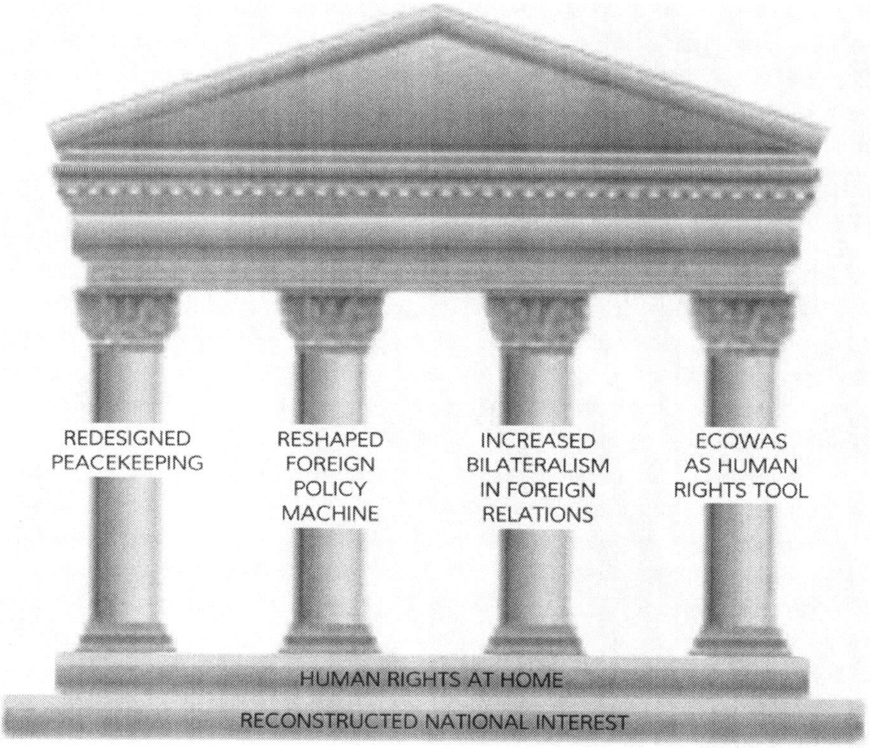

Figure 1.1. Temple of Nigeria's Human Rights Foreign Policy
Figure created by author.

to human rights. The extension is justified by the ethical character, rooted in international standards, of modern human rights.[45] The temple consists of a base of two steps and four pillars in between the foundation and the roof, each of which category is necessary for the integrity and continued maintenance of the temple structure. The demarcation between steps and pillars is simply heuristic, given that each of the two categories is *equally* important to the integrity of the structure, and neither category is superior to the other.

A STATE WORTHY OF ITS PEOPLE'S DREAMS AT HOME AND ABROAD: EXIGENCY FOR MORE HUMAN RIGHTS IN NIGERIA'S EXTERNAL RELATIONS

Several reasons make increased infusion of more human rights into Nigeria's external relations exigent. The first relates to Nigeria's origins arguably laced in human rights. Modern-day Nigeria came into being in 1914 following the melding into one whole of three estates—Northern Protectorate, Southern Protectorate, and the Colony of Lagos—each before that date held and operated separately by British colonizers.[46] The territory known today as Nigeria was once colloquially called the *Slave Coast*, in testament to the immense slave activities that took place there for hundreds of years.[47] The piecemeal occupation and subsequent colonization of Nigeria was an attempt to stop these activities and to set in motion legitimate commercial and economic activities that would replace the obnoxious trade in humans.[48] Certain dignitaries affiliated with regions that became subsumed into present-day Nigeria, such as the former Igbo slave, Olaudah Equiano, participated in this anti-slavery campaign.[49] In short, as former U.S. president Jimmy Carter once observed regarding the United States, in important respects, Nigeria is a state *invented* by human rights.[50] To whom much is given, much is expected.

Second, although colonial rule severely impeded human rights,[51] events in the later leg of British rule in Nigeria, especially after World War II and the formation of the United Nations system, helped give rise to Nigeria's non-violent independence in 1960.[52] The "protracted negotiations with British colonial power[,]"[53] short of the violent blow-out elsewhere,[54] became arguably possible due to the mellowing influence of human rights.[55] A country birthed by human rights like Nigeria can do more for human rights in external affairs than Nigeria has done so far. It can punch more within its weight, not below it, by contributing more through its word and action to international human rights.

Third, given their legendary passion for international relations,[56] increased application of human rights in external affairs will give Nigerians and their leaders the opportunity to fashion their bilateral relations with foreign countries and conduct business in multilateral settings in a more principled format than is currently the case. Human-rights policies may be "the most rapid way to improve the lives of" beleaguered citizens of foreign lands.[57] As Professors Hannum and his colleagues elaborate, using the United States as an example, the attitude of a foreign government toward a regime that is perpetrating human rights abuses "might have far more impact on the lives of people living under that regime than, for example, petitions filed with the United Nations or regional human rights bodies."[58] Such a disapproving attitude bilaterally can also reinforce initiatives at the multilateral level. For Nigeria, as for many other countries, application of these values in external affairs may be a hard-to-miss practical opportunity to contribute to the international human rights regime.[59]

Fourth, injecting more human rights into Nigeria's external relations could harmonize Nigeria's domestic and foreign policies, to the benefit of democracy at home, as it has done for countries with human rights–based foreign policies, such as Costa Rica.[60] As the partition of the Sudan in 2013 makes clear,[61] unabated abuses of human rights can have dire consequences for the integrity of a country. And should Nigeria, like Sudan, disintegrate, due to its piling human rights abuses, successor states from the ashes of the parent state will grapple with the same human rights challenges without the benefit of "a large republic"[62] that Nigeria now, for its seeming incoherence, affords.

Fifth, infusion of more human rights into Nigeria's foreign relations will also help to build a culture of the rule of law, critical for the consolidation of democracy within the country itself.[63] The rule of law is a concept encapsulated in the description of the United States' political system as "a government of laws, not of men."[64] The concept signifies two mandates: first, that all who hold the reins of power, no matter how highly placed in rank, are under the law, rather than above it; and, second, that the powers of the government to make and enforce laws are subject to legal restraints.[65] In a political system that operates under this rule, "the legal authority of the state and its officials is limited by the law, and . . . no one is above the law."[66] The connection between human rights and the rule of law is indicated by the fact, for example, that the strictures of the rule of law forbid the government from engaging in arbitrary practices that signify abuse of its powers, such as unlawful arrest, torture, kangaroo trials, corruption, and the like.[67] An independent judiciary is a critical monitor in a system based on the rule of law.[68]

Finally, Nigeria has the infrastructure to conduct a human rights–based foreign policy, if it rationalizes its resources more properly. One of these resources is a sizable population. With over 186 million residents,[69] Nigeria is the most populous country in Africa and the eighth most-populous state in the world, after China, India, the European Union (a grouping of numerous countries), the United States, Indonesia, Brazil, and Pakistan, in this order.[70] This population factor lends it "a demographic weight equal to second-ranked Egypt and third-ranked Democratic Republic of Congo combined."[71] What is more, its "population includes, in both relative and absolute terms, a large number of well-educated citizens who represent a wealth of human capital."[72] However, concededly, there are also downsides to this resource, including a low literacy rate,[73] a massive brain drain to foreign countries of a cream of its educated labor force,[74] and a population growth rate that lags behind the rate of economic growth and therefore, as indicated earlier, antithetical to economic development.[75]

Another element of infrastructure is natural resources. Nigeria is home to large quantities of hydrocarbon[76] and other mineral resources.[77] As the eighth-largest oil producer in the world, Nigeria exports over 2 million barrels of this product a day to the world economy,[78] much of which, until recently, it ships to the United States.[79] Because of its natural resource endowment, Nigeria is home to the biggest economy in Africa.[80] But, as with its labor power, there are notable downsides, some of which it shares with other petro-states and others of which are unique to Nigeria. One of the shared downsides is the "resource curse," signified in waste and corruption as well as an incompetent tax system emanating from excessive dependence on oil products.[81] A byproduct of this curse connected with taxation is that because of the incompetence of these states in collecting taxes from their nationals, these citizens tend to "feel disconnected from the state, regarding it as an alien organization force or seeing it simply as a distributor of resources."[82] There is no question that many Nigerians view their country this way.

A factor unique to Nigeria that compounds the resource curse issue is the conflict in the Niger Delta, major source of the country's oil wealth,[83] with its narratives of "environmental disaster, economic destitution, and political repression" against oil-producing communities.[84] The environmental disaster narrative goes to the damage on the ecology that oil exploration has wrought. Studies by the United Nations indicate that drinking water in some parts of the Delta region contains some 900 times the amount of benzene, a cancer-causing ingredient, deemed safe by the World Health Organization.[85] The same studies predict that cleaning the crude oil residue in the affected areas will take decades and billions in U.S. dollars.[86] An underlying issue in the Niger Delta conflict that goes to the economic destitution of the affected communities is the revenue allocation formula the Nigerian government has applied since the discovery of oil in commercial quantity which the oil-producing communities complain is unfair. From a high of 50 percent at independence, the size of allocation based on "derivation" (i.e., revenue allocation for oil found on one's land) has gyrated from 45 percent to 20 percent to 0 percent to 1.5 percent to 3 percent to its current 13 percent, reaching their lowest percentage levels during periods of military rule.[87] Political repression is indicated in the narratives because Nigerian governments at both the national and state levels use their coercive authority, including military force, to muffle protests by oil-producing communities, many of those protests peaceful, out of apprehension for the negative impact of such actions on oil production.[88] The trouble in the Niger Delta is an assault on political-civil rights and socioeconomic rights as well as a deprivation of the right to economic self-determination, contrary to the injunction of the international bill of human rights that "[i]n no case may a people be deprived of its own means of subsistence."[89] Finally, although under the Fourth Republic since 1999, the Nigerian economy has recorded important strides in service areas, such as telecommunication and entertainment,[90] it remains heavily anchored around petroleum products.

These human and natural resource impediments were probably among the reasons that Nigeria ranked low on the list of states "most likely to succeed" as "multilateral internationals" in Professor Brysk's seminal work on the small ranks of "global good Samaritans" needed to beef up the United States' slackening leadership of the international human rights movement.[91]

There is no question that the country's disabilities in infrastructure are real. Foreshadowed by colonial rule, some of the problems were evident in the early years of independence, deepened during the nearly thirty years of sustained military rule, and have witnessed little alleviation during the sixteenth years of the Fourth Republic since 1999.[92]

However, these problems are *not* destiny. The country is living through the longest stretch of civilian rule since independence. For all its unevenness, democratic rule affords a better canvas than authoritarian military rule for resolution of these issues, including the still ongoing problem of Islamic insurgency since 2009 that has killed or maimed tens of thousands of people and left millions homeless.[93] Nigeria's infrastructure for the pursuit of a human rights–based foreign policy is not limited to resources within its borders. Instead, it includes resources outside its borders, including the Economic Community of West African States (ECOWAS), an economic integration organization that Nigeria helped to found in 1975,[94] covered in chapter 10 of this work.

Nearly six decades since its independence, "Nigeria has not forged the vibrant and effective foreign policy" that matches its human and material endowments and the basis for its self-perception as the giant of Africa and the black world.[95] Nigeria should rank among the regional "tiger" from the global South that Brysk indicated are aspiring to take their place in the conduct of human rights–based foreign policies.[96] Countries like Costa Rica, which distinctively punch above their weight in international human rights, "did not require wealth or power to afford the luxury of pursuing a principled foreign policy."[97] Global good Samaritans notable for their human rights–based foreign policies are made, not born.[98] Instead, as Brysk elaborated, "although some national values and experiences harmonize readily with human rights, foreign policy projection of those norms must be learned and mobilized."[99] For Nigeria, the requisite national values harmonizing with human rights that can form the basis for learning would include its experience in peacekeeping, habit of obedience to international law, and its commitment to peaceful settlement of international disputes.[100] There is no requirement that the country punch above its weight in applying human rights in external affairs the way "global Good Samaritans" like Costa Rica have impressively done. But it needs to punch within its weight, something it has yet to do, hence this study.

In a nutshell, application of human rights in external affairs will go a long way in making Nigeria domestically and abroad a state "worthy of its people's dreams . . . [and] the world's next great opportunity to advance the cause of peace, justice, and prosperity."[101] A Nigerian military leader and politician once advised that "to survive as one political entity," Nigeria "must articulate a guiding philosophy to which [its] various peoples are committed,"[102] just as the United States did with key language in the Declaration of Independence.[103] The road to that guiding philosophy is application in external affairs of human rights norms equally internalized at home.

ORGANIZATION OF THIS BOOK

This book consists of eleven chapters divided into three parts, plus this introduction as chapter 1. Part I consists of three chapters dealing with background facts necessary for proper understanding of the work, including a methodology and theoretical framework set forth separately. Part II, comprising six chapters, deals with issues germane to the application of human rights in Nigeria's foreign relations. These issues are depicted graphically in this work (see figure 1.1) as steps and pillars in the temple of Nigeria's human rights foreign policy. Part III, the Conclusion, consists of two chapters, one of which, chapter 12, addresses objections to the argument for increased human rights in Nigeria's external affairs made in this study.

Although the entire work is devoted to addressing the four questions that drive this research, certain chapters address these questions more directly than others. For example, this chapter answers the question relating to the exigency for application of more human rights in Nigeria's external relations, while chapter 12 responds to possible objections to the argument for a human rights–based foreign policy this book makes. Chapter 2 introduces and defines the key terms of the study as well as describes its methodology rooted mainly in the comparative method of "within-case comparison."[104] Chapter 3 lays out the theoretical framework of the study anchored in *constructivism*, an approach midway between *realism* and *idealism*, defined in terms of the room it allows for interjection of human rights in external affairs. Unlike these two other worldviews, constructivism views foreign policy as essentially what a state makes of it. Chapter 4 is a historical survey that takes the story of human rights in external affairs that this book tells back into the country's colonial and precolonial past in an attempt to start the story from its proverbial beginning and to provide a holistic account that would otherwise be lacking in an extended study like this one.

Next to the issues directly tied to the application of human rights in external affairs, the steps and pillars in the temple of Nigeria's human rights policy, chapter 5 deals with the matter of how to reconstruct the country's national interest in a more human rights–sensitive direction, while chapter 6 addresses the need for increased respect for human rights at home to drive principled foreign policy. Chapter 7 focuses on the redesign of "peacekeeping" to make it more human rights compliant, while chapter 8 analyzes reshaping the Nigerian foreign policy apparatus in a more human rights–sensitive direction. Chapter 9 takes on the issue of the imperative for more symmetry between multilateral and bilateral tools in the execution of Nigeria's foreign policy, while chapter 10 discusses the use of ECOWAS as a tool for the application of human rights in the country's external relations. Last but not least, chapters 11 and 12 comprise the conclusion of the study. The first pulls together the findings of the research in a discussion that underscores the combination of reforms at home and abroad at the heart of this study, while the second is devoted specifically to the rebuttal of possible objections to the argument in this work for a human rights–based foreign policy for Nigeria.

NOTES

1. "Nigeria," *CIA World Factbook*, https://www.cia.gov/library/publications/the-world-factbook/geos/ni.html (last updated Nov. 19, 2014).
2. "Nigeria," *WorldAtlas*, http://www.worldatlas.com/webimage/countrys/africa/ng.htm.
3. "Brief Notes on Nigeria," *Online Nigeria*, http://www.onlinenigeria.com/history.asp.
4. See Land and Maritime Boundary between Cameroon and Nigeria (*Cameroon v. Nigeria: Equatorial Guinea Intervening*), Int'l Court of Justice (Oct. 10, 2002), http://www.icj-cij.org/docket/index.php?p1=3&p2=3&k=74&case=94&code=cn&p3=4.
5. Ignatius Akaayar Ayua & Dakas C.J. Dakas, "Federal Republic of Nigeria," *in* John Kincaid & George Alan Tarr, eds., *Constitutional Origins, Structure, and Change in Federal Countries* (Montreal, Canada: McGill-Queen's University Press, 2005): 242. To be sure, long before British rule, these strangers established "many economic, social, and political links among themselves," but "they did not recognize themselves as one people or as one political community." Ibid.
6. See, e.g., F.D. Lugard & A.H.M. Kirk-Greene, *Lugard and the Amalgamation of Nigeria: A Documentary Record* (London: Cass, 1968), *passim*.
7. See Nigeria Independence Act, 1960, 8 & 9 Eliz., 2 CH. 55 (July 29, 1960), www.legislation.gov.uk/ukpga/1960/55/pdfs/ukpga_19600055_en.pdf (granting the country "fully responsible status" within the British Commonwealth of Nations, effective Oct. 1, 1960).

8. See Nigeria Republican Act 1963, 1963 CH. 57 (Dec. 18, 1963), http://www.legislation.gov.uk/ukpga/1963/57 (making the country "a Republic within the Commonwealth," effective Oct. 1, 1963). See also Constitution of the Fed. Republic of Nigeria 1963 [hereinafter referred to as Nigerian Const. 1963], http://www.unesco.org/fileadmin/MULTIMEDIA/HQ/CI/WPFD2009/pdf/Nigeria%20Constitution.pdf.

9. See Nigeria (Republic) Bill, H.L., Deb. Dec. 17, 1963, Vol. 254 cc208–14 Hansard, hansard.millbanksystems.com/lords/1963/dec/17/Nigeria-republic-bill.

10. Ibid.

11. See "Nigeria Population (Live)," *Worldometers* (Apr. 26, 2016), http://www.worldometers.info/world-population/nigeria-population/ (as of Apr. 26, 2016, representing 2.48 percent of the world's population; the figure is based on United Nations estimates). The figure of 56 million refers to the 1963 census since Nigeria had its last headcount prior to independence in 1952–1953. However, accurate censuses are a rare commodity in Nigeria due to the politically sensitive nature of these headcounts tied to fear of ethnic or regional domination by groups that make such censuses controversial. Though officially accepted, the 1963 census was shrouded with "charges of inaccuracy and manipulation for regional and local political purposes[,]" and according to one account, "the official 1963 figure of 55.6 million as total national population is inconsistent with the census of a decade earlier because it implies a virtually impossible annual growth rate of 5.8 percent." See "Census History," *in* Helen Chapin Metz, ed., *Nigeria: A Country Study* (Washington, D.C.: GPO for the Library of Congress, 1991), http://countrystudies.us/nigeria/.

12. In 1960, Lagos, then capital city of the country, had little over 250,000 people. Today, 20 million people live in the city, with 6,000 new migrants arriving every day in search of job and amenities that many rural communities in the country lack. See Ryan Lenora Brown, "A Top Nigerian Export: Fervent Christianity," *Christian Science Monitor* (Sept. 28, 2015), http://news.yahoo.com/top-nigerian-export-fervent-christianity-135101567.html.

13. For all its benefits, unchecked population growth can be antithetical to economic development. Nigeria's population growth rate of about 3.2 percent, meaning that the population is projected to double about every 20 years, creates a major economic burden during periods when the rate of population growth outstrips the rate of gross domestic product (GDP), as has been the case for much of the country's history. See Elisabeth Rosenthal, "Nigeria Tested by Rapid Rise in Population," *New York Times* (Apr. 14, 2012), http://www.nytimes.com/2012/04/15/world/africa/in-nigeria-a-preview-of-an-overcrowded-planet.html?pagewanted=all&_r=0; and "Reforming Nigeria: A Conversation with Ngozi Okonjo-Iweala," *Foreign Affairs* (Mar./Apr. 2014), http://www.foreignaffairs.com/discussions/interviews/-nigeria (reporting the views of Nigeria's former finance minister to the effect that for antipoverty programs to work in the country, as it did in Asian countries like China, "we actually have to grow faster."). But a rapid population growth rate complicates the chances for any "fast" economic growth. Given the choice between faster economic growth and reduced birth rate via family planning, the latter appears to be a less painful and manageable option. However, Nigerians and their governments do not take family planning seriously. See, e.g., Mairo Mandara, "Family Planning in Nigeria and Prospects

for the Future," *International Journal of Gynecology & Obstetrics*, Vol. 117 (Feb. 20, 2012): 1–4 (positing that although "the government's population and health policies recognize family planning as a key intervention[,]" "unacceptably high unmet need for contraception exists in the country, which may indicate a lack of commitment for family planning").

14. The state was created on Aug. 9, 1963, following a referendum on Jul. 13, 1963 where 89 percent of the voters in the area approved the creation. See Rotimi T. Suberu, *Public Policies and National Unity in Nigeria* (Ibadan, Nigeria: Development Policy Center, 1999): 12.

15. See Constitution of the Fed. Republic of Nigeria 1999 [hereinafter referred to as Nigerian Const. 1999], 1st sched. Part I (listing the states, capital cities, and local governments); ibid., 1st sched., Part I (demarcating the area councils constituting the Federal Capital Territory in Abuja). The unchecked growth in population, commented upon in notes 11–13 and corresponding text, was among the factors that led the country to move its capital city to Abuja in Dec. of 1991. See "Federal Capital Abuja," *Online Nigeria* (Dec. 2, 2003 10:21:46 AM), http://www.onlinenigeria.com/links/abujaadv.asp?blurb=387 (providing background information on the logic behind the relocation to Abuja as well as the personalities that planned the relocation); Tolu Ogunlesi, "Abuja, Nigeria's Capital City, Grows and Flourishes," *Financial Times* (London) (May 4, 2014 10:59 AM), http://www.ft.com/intl/cms/s/0/68c28016-bb16-11e3-948c-00144feabdc0.html#axzz3n50kTd6W.

16. See Suberu, note 14, p. 11. These administrative exercises are the ones by General Yakubu Gowon in 1967, which replaced the four regions with twelve states; Generals Murtala Mohammed and Olusegun Obasanjo in 1976, which increased the 12 states to 19; General Ibrahim Babangida in 1987, which increased the 19 states to 21 and again in 1991 that increased the number to 30; and General Sani Abacha in 1996 that brought the number of states to its current 36-state arrangement. Ibid.

17. Constitution of the Fed. Republic of Nigeria 1979, Art. 5, § 1(a), www.constitutionnet.org/files/nig_const_79.pdf (stipulating that the executive powers of the Federation "shall be vested in the President, and may . . . be exercised by him directly or through the Vice-President and Ministers of the Government of the Federation or officers in the public service of the Federation."); Nigeria's Const. 1999, note 15, Art. 5, §1(a) (providing similarly).

18. See "States of the United States," *Statoids*, http://statoids.com/uus.html; "Statehood Dates," *50States.com*, http://www.50states.com/statehood.htm#.VoL53xUrK1s.

19. See Ayua & Dakas, note 5, p. 253 (stating that "[o]ne prominent theme of Nigeria's federal history has been an urge to subdivide.").

20. Ibid.

21. The seven regimes in chronological order are: Johnson Aguiyi-Ironsi, January–July 1966; Yakubu Gowon, July 1966–July 1975; Murtala Muhammed and Olusegun Obasanjo (two regimes usually counted as one because the latter continued the policies of the former), July 1975–1979; Muhammadu Buhari, 1983–1985; Ibrahim Babangida, 1985–1993; Sani Abacha, 1993–1998; and Abdulsalami Abubakar, 1998–May 29, 1999. For studies of Nigerian foreign policy during these military eras, see

Olayiwola Abegunrin, *Nigerian Foreign Policy under Military Rule, 1966–1999* (Westport, CT: Praeger, 2003) (covering the entire military period); Alade W. Fawole, *Nigeria's External Relations and Foreign Policy under Military Rule, 1966–1999* (Ile-Ife: Obafemi Awolowo University Press, 2003) (same); and Joe Garba, *Diplomatic Soldiering: The Conduct of Nigerian Foreign Policy, 1975–1979* (Ibadan, Nigeria: Spectrum Books, 1991) (limited to the Muhammed-Obasanjo regime). More discussion on this and their civilian counterparts can be found elsewhere in this book, such as chapter 4 containing the background history of the work.

22. William J. Clinton, "Remarks Following Discussions with President Olusegun Obasanjo of Nigeria and an Exchange with Reporters in Abuja, Nigeria, Aug. 26, 2000," *in Public Papers of the Presidents of the United States: William J. Clinton, 2000–2001* (Washington, D.C.: Best Books, 2000): 1701.

23. What makes the designation odd is that the Fourth Republic comes after two short-lived experiments in democracy, and a third that died before it had the opportunity to be born. The First Republic took place from 1960 to 1966, and the Second Republic from 1979 to 1983. A Third Republic projected for 1993 became stillborn when the military government under General Ibrahim Babangida (1985 to 1993) annulled a presidential election that year that would have ushered in that republic.

24. See "How Nigeria Won Its First Democratic Power Transfer," *Economist* (London) (Apr. 6, 2015, 23: 50), http://www.economist.com/blogs/economist-explains/2015/04/economist-explains-2; Fiyaso Soyombo, "How Will Nigeria Fare under Buhari?," *Al Jazeera* (Jun. 9, 2015 07:44 GMT), http://www.aljazeera.com/indepth/opinion/2015/06/nigeria-fare-buhari-150607105418906.html (a more measured statement wherein the author, among other things, observed that "[t]he 2015 election was about chasing out a bad government for a good one; 2019 will be about replacing a good one with a better one.").

25. Bonn O. Nwanolue & Victor C. Iwuoha, "A Reflection on Nigeria's Past: Africa as the Centerpiece of Nigeria's Foreign Policy Revisited," *Developing Country Studies*, Vol. 2 (2012): 78–79, http://www.iiste.org/Journals/index.php/DCS/article/view/1756/1709.

26. See Nigerian Const. 1999, note 15, § 19(d). Nigeria is a party to numerous global and regional human rights instruments. See University of Minnesota, Human Rights Library, Ratification of International Human Rights Treaties—Nigeria, http://www1.umn.edu/humanrts/research/ratification-nigeria.html (last visited Feb. 26, 2015) (listing various categories of instruments Nigeria ratified from 1960 to 2012). These include the six core global human rights instruments: the International Convention on the Elimination of All Forms of Racial Discrimination in 1967; the International Covenant on Civil and Political Rights (1993); the International Covenant on Economic, Social, and Cultural Rights that same year; the Convention on the Elimination of All Forms of Discrimination against Women (1985); the Convention against Torture and Other Cruel, Inhuman or Degrading Treatment or Punishment (2001); and the Convention on the Rights of the Child (1991). See ibid. Other key global human rights instruments Nigeria has ratified are: the Convention Relating to the Status of Refugees in 1967; Convention on the Prevention and Punishment of the Crime of Genocide in 2009, only following its civil war from 1967 to 1970, interestingly given

the allegation of genocide that shrouded the conflict; and the Rome Statute of the International Criminal Court in 2001. Ibid. African regional human rights instruments in Nigeria is a state party to include the African [Banjul] Charter on Human and Peoples' Right in 1983; Convention Governing the Specific Aspects of Refugee Problems in Africa (1986); and the African Charter on the Rights and Welfare of the Child (2001). See ibid. Similarly, Nigeria has ratified all four main instruments and two protocols of the Geneva Convention, all four in 1961, excepting the Geneva Convention Relative to the Protection of Civilian Persons in Time of War, which it ratified in 1988, the same year as the protocol instruments. Ibid. However, the country's 1999 constitution forbids the enforcement of treaties that have not been enacted into law by the national legislature, a process fraught with long delay, and Nigeria ratifies treaties, such as the Geneva Conventions, that it makes little effort to comply with. See, e.g., Babatunde Isaac Olutoyin, "Treaty Making and Its Application under Nigerian Law: The Journey So Far," *Int'l Journal of Business and Management Invention*, Vol. 3 (2004): 7, http://www.ijbmi.org/papers/Vol%283%293/Version-3/B033307018.pdf.

27. See Adekeye Adebajo, *Liberia's Civil War: Nigeria, ECOMOG, and Regional Security in West Africa* (Boulder, CO: Lynne Rienner Publishers, 2002); and 'Funmi Olonisakin, *Reinventing Peacekeeping in Africa: Conceptual and Legal Issues in ECOMOG Operations* (London: Kluwer Law Int'l, 2000). More information on this key tool in the implementation of Nigerian foreign policy is contained in chapter 7.

28. See Nigerian Const. 1999, note 15, § 19(d) (including peaceful "settlement of international disputes by negotiation, mediation, conciliation, arbitration[,] and adjudication" among the foreign policy objectives of the country). Constitutional provision aside or because of it, Nigeria has a reputation as a gentle giant that never uses force to settle a dispute with a neighbor, even when pushed to the point of provocation. For example, for many years, the country had a boundary dispute with Cameroon over Bakassi, an oil-rich peninsula that both countries claimed. Skirmishes erupted occasionally from the Cameroonian side that at times involved the death of Nigerians, but the country never responded in kind. Ultimately the dispute was settled via a lawsuit at the International Court of Justice that in 2002 awarded the peninsula to Cameroon. In spite of pressures from many Nigerians at home and abroad displeased with the judgment, Nigeria, under the presidency of Olusegun Obasanjo from 1999 to 2007, obeyed the judgment. See "Nigeria Cedes Bakassi to Cameroon," *BBC News* (Aug. 14, 2008), http://news.bbc.co.uk/2/hi/africa/7559895.stm. About 90 percent of the peninsula's population, estimated at about 300,000 people, is made up of Nigerian fishermen. The United Nations Secretary General, Ban Ki-Moon, praised the peaceful transfer as "a model for negotiated settlements of border disputes." Ibid. In short, Nigeria tends to limit its use of violence within its borders, rather than extend it overseas.

29. See J. Peter Pham, "Nigeria's Foreign Policy: An Inquiry into Sources and Prospects," Presentation for Int'l Conference, Lisbon, Portugal (Nov. 8–9, 2007), www.ipri.pt/eventos/pdf/JPeterPham_paper.pdf (opining that "[t]he creation of both the AU and NEPAD would have been exceedingly difficult . . . without the combined diplomatic and political efforts of" Nigeria and South Africa). The AU replaced the Organization of African Unity, the association of independent African states, set up

in May 1963. The Constitutive Act of the organization, its enabling law, stressed the determination of the AU "to promote and protect human and peoples' rights, consolidate democratic institutions and culture, and to ensure good governance and the rule of law." *Constitutive Act of the African Union (2000),* OAU Doc. CAB/LEG/23.15 (July 11, 2000), http://www.africa-union.org (preamble). NEPAD is a voluntary "peer review" tool of the organization, rooted in democratic principles and sound economic practice. "Profile: African Union," *BBC News* (Feb. 1, 2012), http://news.bbc.co.uk/2/hi/africa/country_profiles/3870303.stm; see also Philip C. Aka, "NEPAD and the Movement for Popular Participation in Development (MPPD) in Africa," *Human Rights & Globalization Law Review*, Vol. 3 (2009–2010): 81 (indicating that NEPAD presages a new kind of cooperative arrangement between African countries and outside donors, embedded in good governance, democracy, and human rights, "that embodies the vision and aspirations of African Governments and their peoples for development").

30. See, e.g., Salami B. Olawale, "The Preclude to Babangida Regime's Foreign Policy Initiatives," *Mediterranean Journal of Social Sciences*, Vol. 5 (2014): 83, http://www.mcser.org/journal/index.php/mjss/article/view/2120. More discussion on this program is contained in chapter 4 dealing with the background history of the study, particularly section III on the postcolonial era.

31. *International regimes* are "are sets of implicit or explicit principles, norms, rules, and decision-making procedures around which actors' expectations converge in a given area of international relations." Stephen D. Krasner, "Structural Causes and Regime Consequences: Regimes as Intervening Variable," *Int'l Organization*, Vol. 36 (Spring 1982): 186. See also Alison Brysk, *Global Good Samaritans: Human Rights as Foreign Policy* (Oxford University Press, 2009): 4 (defining international human rights regime as "the thin layer of international understandings, institutions, and exchanges that seek to protect individual human dignity from abuses of power").

32. As Professor Brysks explains, the influence of these states—which she variously praised as Global Good Samaritans, humanitarian internationalists, or principled states—"can be critical for framing and ratifying treaties, creating and staffing multilateral institutions, monitoring and sanctioning offenders, assisting victims, directing resources, implementing peace processes, catalyzing transnational initiatives or emerging issues, and introducing new understandings of rights to the global agenda." Ibid., p. 3.

33. Brysk, note 31, p. 4.

34. Jack Donnelly, *International Human Rights, 4th Ed.* (Westview Press, 2013): 147.

35. See Brysk, note 31, *passim*.

36. A rough sample includes: Osita C. Eze & Peter A. Egom, eds., *Foreign Policy and Nigeria's Economic Development* (Lagos: Nigerian Institute of International Affairs, 2009); Adekeye Adebajo & Abdul R. Mustapha, eds., *Gulliver's Troubles: Nigeria's Foreign Policy after the Cold War* (Scottsville, South Africa: University of KwaZulu Press, 2008); Akintola Bukola, "Nigeria and the World: A Review of Nigeria's Foreign Policy (1960–2007)," *Nigerian Army Quarterly Journal*, Vol. 3 (Dec. 2007): 438–71; Emeka A. Obi, *Fundamentals of Nigerian Foreign Policy: A Study on*

the Role of National Interest in Foreign Policy Making (Abingdon, U.K.: Bookpoint Ltd., 2006); L.E. Okogwu & A. Akpuru-Aja, *Nigerian Diplomacy and the Conflict of Laws: An Insight into the Practice of Nigeria's Foreign Policy* (Abakaliki, Nigeria: WillyRose & Appleseed Publishing Co., 2004); Steve Egbo, *Nigeria and the World: A Treatise on Foreign Policy* (Enugu, Nigeria: John Jacobs Classic Publishers, 2003); Ufot Bassey Inamete, *Foreign Policy Decision-Making in Nigeria* (Selinsgrove, PA: Susquehanna University Press, 2001); Richard A. Akindele & Bassey Ate, eds., *Selected Readings on Nigeria's Foreign Policy and International Relations* (Lagos: Nigerian Institute of International Affairs and Vantage Publishers, 2000); Mae C. King, *Basic Currents of Nigerian Foreign Policy* (Washington, D.C.: Howard University Press, 1996); G. O. Olusanya & R. A. Akindele, eds., *The Structure and Processes of Foreign Policy Making and Implementation in Nigeria, 1960–1990* (Lagos: Nigerian Institute of International Affairs, 1990); Ibrahim A. Gambari, *Theory and Reality in Foreign Policy Making: Nigeria after the Second Republic* (Humanities Press, Inc., 1989); G.O. Olusanya & R.A. Akindele, *Nigeria's External Relations: The First Twenty-Five Years* (Ibadan, Nigeria: Ibadan University Press, 1986); Ibrahim A. Gambari, *Party Politics and Foreign Policy: Nigeria under the First Republic* (Zaria, Nigeria: Ahmadu Bello University Press, 1980). For studies focused specifically on military regimes, see the three sources referenced in note 21.

37. My search uncovered Sylvester S. Shikyil, "Human Rights in Foreign Policy: Nigeria's Experience since 1979." Doctoral dissertation, Dept. of Law, University of Jos, 2000, http://datad.aau.org/handle/123456789/42302?show=full. My research departs from this in several respects. First, it spans over 55 years from 1960 to the present period, compared to the focus in Shikyil's dissertation covering 1979 to 2000 when seemingly the work was completed. Second, the goals of the two studies are also different. Although, like mine, Shikyil was concerned about human rights policies that matched the profiles of Nigeria as a rising power, his goal was "to provide the background to the discussion of human rights in contemporary international politics," specifically "the analysis of the reasons for and consequences of the internationalization of human rights, its determinants, objectives, and future perspectives." Ibid. Not to minimize his contribution, this was a diffuse goal that contrasts with the more comprehensive goal in this book that revolves around the design of a human rights policy for the country.

38. See the sources cited in note 27.

39. See note 36 and corresponding text.

40. See, e.g., Philip C. Aka, "Nigeria since May 1999: Understanding the Paradox of Civil Rule and Human Rights Violations under President Olusegun Obasanjo," *San Diego Int'l Law Journal*, Vol. 4 (2003): 209–76.

41. See, e.g., David P. Forsythe, ed., *Human Rights and Comparative Foreign Policy* (New York: United Nations University Press, 2000): 17 (stating that "[w]ith an unlimited budget and a multi-volume project, we could have added numerous states that merit study: France, Norway, Germany, *Nigeria*, Kenya, Mexico, Brazil, Pakistan, Israel, the Philippines, etc.") (emphasis added). This study fills this needed gap with respect to Nigeria.

42. Peter R. Baehr, "Foreign Policy," *in Encyclopedia of Human Rights*, Vol. 5 (New York: Oxford University Press, 2009): 237. See also Abdullahi An-Naim, "The National Question, Secession and Constitutionalism: The Mediation of Competing Claims to Self-Determination," *in* Douglas Greenberg et al. eds., *Constitutionalism and Democracy: Transition in the Contemporary World* (New York: Oxford University Press, 1993): 111, 112–13 (depicting human rights as "legal rights enforceable in a court of law" that have also immense "utility in political discourse.").

43. Brysk, note 31, p. 37. See also J. Oloka-Onyango, *Battling over Human Rights: Twenty Essays on Law, Politics[,] and Governance* (Bamenda, Cameroon: Langaa Research & Publishing, 2015), *passim* (set of essays depicting human rights as the intersection of laws, politics, and governance).

44. See Michael J. Sodaro, *Comparative Politics: A Global Introduction, 3d Ed.* (Boston, MA: McGraw-Hill, 2008): 171, fig. 7.1.

45. See Philip C. Aka, "Analyzing U.S. Commitment to Socioeconomic Human Rights," *Akron Law Review*, Vol. 39 (2006): 423 (defining human rights as "international ethical standards that uphold, as a birthright, the minimum thresholds individuals and communities everywhere require to live in dignity and to realize their potentials.").

46. See Toyin Falola & Matthew M. Heaton, *A History of Nigeria* (New York: Cambridge University Press, 2008): 85–104. The name, *Nigeria*, denominates peoples of the Niger areas, the Niger here referring to the River Niger which, with its tributary the Benue River, courses through much of the land. The name was reportedly coined in 1897 by the journalist Flora Shaw, later to become Mrs. Lugard, following her marriage to Frederick Lugard, the first governor-general of the new country. Int'l Crisis Group, *Nigeria: Want in the Midst of Plenty*, Africa Report No. 113 (Jul. 19, 2006): 2. Testimony to the little creativity in these names is the fact that Niger Republic (pop. nearly 18 million as of 2013), colonized by France, on the northern borders of Nigeria, is also confusedly named after the River Niger. "Niger," *One World Nations Online*, http://www.nationsonline.org/oneworld/niger.htm.

47. See "Slave Coast," *Encyclopedia Britannica*, http://www.britannica.com/EBchecked/topic/548212/Slave-Coast; "Slavery Fact Sheets," *Digital History*, www.digitalhistory.uh.edu/disp_textbook.cfm?smtID=11&psid=3807; and Robin Law, *The Slave Coast of West Africa 1550–1750: The Impact of the Atlantic Slave Trade on an African Society* (Oxford, U.K.: Clarendon Press, 1991).

48. See Jenny S. Martinez, *The Slave Trade and the Origins of International Human Rights Law* (New York: Oxford University Press, 2011) (tracing modern-day international human rights law to the anti-slavery movement of the nineteenth century).

49. Olaudah Equiano, *The Interesting Narrative of the Life of Olaudah Equiano: Written by Himself*, edited with an intro. by Robert J. Allison (New York: Bedford/St. Martin's Press, 1995 [originally published 1789]). Some controversy arose recently regarding whether Equiano was born in Igboland or in the United States, see Gloria Chuku, "Olaudah Equiano and the Foundation of Igbo Intellectual Tradition," *in* Gloria Chuku, ed., *The Igbo Intellectual Tradition: Creative Conflict in African and African Diasporic Thought* (New York: Palgrave Macmillan, 2013): 33–50, but none regarding whether he was Igbo.

50. Jimmy Carter, "The American Road to a Human Rights Policy," *in* Samantha Power & Graham Alison, eds., *Realizing Human Rights: Moving from Inspiration to Impact* (New York: St. Martin's Press, 2000): 49 ("In 1981, as I left the U.S. presidency, I said, 'America did not invent human rights. In a very real sense . . . human rights invented America.'"). The matter of the human rights content or lack thereof of slavery and colonialism is a complex topic, subject to careful qualification, that is revisited in the historical background portion of this study, chapter 4, under Section II dealing with the colonial era.

51. For more on this issue, see chapter 4 which chronicled the background narrative related to this topic.

52. See Louis Henkin, "Human Rights: Ideology and Aspiration, Reality and Prospect," *in* Power & Allison, eds., *Realizing Human Rights*, note 50, p. 12 (stating that "[o]ne might trace a path from the [Universal Declaration of Human Rights] to historic developments in the second half of the century," including the "end of colonialism and the proliferation of new states," and the "eradication of apartheid" and the birth of black majority rule in South Africa).

53. King, note 36, p. 16.

54. Kenya serves as an example of a violent decolonization during this period. See Martin Meredith, *The Fate of Africa: A History of the Continent since Independence*, revised and updated edition (Public Affairs, 2011): 79–87 (commenting on the Mau Mau insurgency).

55. For example, by 1954, several years before independence British authorities transferred authority for foreign affairs to Nigerians. Joseph Effiong, "Reflections on Nigeria's Foreign Policy," *Journal of Social and Psychological Sciences*, Vol. 5 (2012), www.questia.com/read/1G1-314443206/reflections-on-nigeria-s-foreign-policy.

56. "Foreign Relations," *in* Metz, ed. *Nigeria: A Country Study*, note 11 (discussing Nigeria's active participation in international organizations); Falola & Heaton, note 46, pp. 243–70 (extended discussion on "Nigeria and Nigerians in World History," including foreign policy in the period since independence in 1960).

57. Hurst Hannum et al., *International Human Rights: Problems of Law, Policy, and Practice, 5th Ed.* (Alphen aan den Rijn, Netherlands: Wolters Kluwer, 2011): 1118.

58. Ibid.

59. Otherwise, for these countries, the standard operating procedure is to pay lip service to human rights. See David P. Forsythe, *Human Rights in International Relations, 3d Ed.* (Cambridge University Press, 2012): vii (pointing out that "states continue to profess their commitment to at least some of [these human rights] standards, even as their record of compliance is often far short of what it should be.").

60. Brysk, note 31, pp. 95–118.

61. See, e.g., Jeffrey Gettleman, "After Years of Struggle, South Sudan Becomes a New Nation," *N. Y. Times* (Jul. 9, 2011), www.nytimes.com/2011/07/10/world/africa/10sudan.html?pagewanted=1&r=2&hp&adxnnlx=1310234502-5nvX4GUBg0fK28Wp4F.

62. The Federalist No. 10 (James Madison) (Nov. 22, 1787).

63. See Sodaro, note 44, p. 171, fig. 7.1 (positioning the rule of law as a foundation step in his diagram of democracy as a temple).

64. Ibid., p. 177.

65. Ibid.

66. Ibid., p. 104. As Anthony M. Kennedy, Associate Justice of the U.S. Supreme Court explains this concept in a keynote address at the annual conference of the American Bar Association in 2006, under such system, "[t]he Law rests upon known, general principles applicable on equal terms to all persons" and it is "superior to, and thus binds, the government and all of its officials." Justice Kennedy's Address, CSPAN (Aug. 5, 2006), www.c-span.org/video/?193757-1/justice-kennedy-address (Keynote Address by Justice Anthony M. Kennedy at the Meeting of the American Bar Association, Honolulu, HI).

67. Sodaro, note 44, p. 177.

68. Philip C. Aka, "Judicial Independence under Nigeria's Fourth Republic: Problems and Prospects," *California Western Int'l Law Journal* (2014): 4.

69. See note 11.

70. "Nigeria," note 1; J. Tyler Dickovick & Jonathan Eastwood, *Comparative Politics: Integrating Theories, Methods, and Cases* (New York: Oxford University Press, 2013): 578 (dubbing Nigeria "the largest society in Africa.").

71. Pham, note 29, p. 90. This does not include Nigerians in the Diaspora estimated to be anywhere from 5 to 17 million people, see "The Nigerian Diaspora," *Nigerian Diaspora*, http://www.nigeriandiaspora.com/nigerian-diaspora.php, and "Nigerians Abroad: Secret Weapon," *Economist* (London), http://www.economist.com/news/special-report/21654360-nigerias-diaspora-source-money-markets-skills-and-ideas-secret-weapon. The Nigerian Diaspora "covers practically every part of the world, but the largest populations of Nigerians can be found in the U.K., U.S.A., and South Africa." "Nigerian Diaspora," *op. cit.* Based on World Bank data, in 2013, Nigerians in the Diaspora remitted an estimated U.S. $21 billion into Nigeria, an amount said to represent about one-quarter of the country's earnings that year from oil exports. Ibid.

72. Pham, note 29, p. 90. See also William J. Clinton, "Remarks at a State Dinner Hosted by President Olusegun Obasanjo of Nigeria in Abuja, Aug. 26, 2000," *in Public Papers of the Presidents of the United States: William J. Clinton, 2000–2001*, note 22, p. 1711 (pointing out that additional to its reputation as "an important supplier of energy[,]" Nigeria deserves to be also known and honored "for its greatest energy resource," namely, its people).

73. In 2010, the most recent year for which data are available, Nigeria ranked 184 out of 194 countries in literacy, with a literacy rate of 61.3 percent (measured as persons 15 and above who can read and write), broken down into 72.1 percent for men and 50.4 percent for females). "Nigeria," note 1.

74. See David H. Shinn, "Reversing the Brain Drain in Ethiopia, Address to the Ethiopian North American Health Professionals Association" (Nov. 23, 2002), http://chora.virtualave.net/brain-drain8.htm (disclosing that "[m]ore than 2,000 Nigerian doctors work in the United States even though there continues to be a critical need for health professionals in Nigeria[,]" and that "[a]bout 10,000 Nigerian academics are employed in the United States alone."); and Anya O. Anya, "Nigeria: The Hu-

man Capital Challenge," *African Journal of Physics*, Vol. 30 (2010): 5, http://sirius-b.ncat.edu.ncat.edu/asn/afps/ajp/ajp-ISOTPAND10/Proc%20ISPD%20book5-30.pdf (lamenting Nigeria's "failure to develop her human resources," effects of which include the drain of medical professionals in its educated labor force who migrate to foreign countries).

75. See note 13 and corresponding text.

76. As of Jan. 2013, Nigeria has an estimated 37.2 billion barrels of proven crude oil reserves, the second largest amount in Africa after Libya. See U.S. Energy Information Admin., "Nigeria" (Dec. 30, 2013), www.eia.gov/contries/and/analysisbriefs/Nigeria/nigeria.pdf.

77. Other mineral resources found in commercial quantities on Nigerian soils include natural gas, coal, and numerous others like iron ore, uranium, copper, gold, and diamond. See Center for Energy Economics, "Gas Monetization in Nigeria," http://www.beg.utexas.edu/energyecon/new–era/case_studies/Gas_Monetization_in_Nigeria.pdf; Nuhu George Obaje, *Geology and Mineral Resources of Nigeria* (Berlin, Germany: Springer-Verlag, 2009): 117–19.

78. Pham, note 29, p. 90. For an overview of the country's oil industry, including the evolution of petroleum production as a mainstay of Nigeria's economy, see Jedrzej G. Frynas, *Oil in Nigeria: Conflict and Litigation Between Oil Companies and Village Communities* (Hamburg & London: Lit Verlag, 2000): 8–58.

79. Under President Barack Obama since 2009, the United States has moved to achieve "energy independence," designed to insulate the United States and its citizenry from untoward dependency on oil exports by potentially unstable political regimes abroad. See "Advancing American Energy," *White House*, https://www.whitehouse.gov/energy/securing-american-energy (particularly the section on "[r]educing [American] [d]ependence on [f]oreign [o]il."). Specifically, an immediate factor here is the "shale revolution," arising from advances in oil and natural gas production technology, notably a new combination of horizontal drilling and hydraulic fracturing (or fracking), that has stimulated tremendous production of oil and natural gas in the United States. See Edward L. Morse, "Welcome to the Revolution," *Foreign Affairs* (May/Jun. 2014), https://www.foreignaffairs.com/articles/2014-04-17/welcome-revolution. As one source explained, reporting on the negative impact of shale on Nigeria, "[a]t its peak in February 2006, the U.S. imported 1.3 m b/d from Nigeria—equal to roughly one super-tanker the size of the Exxon Valdez every day[,]" but "[b]y 2012, Nigeria was already selling just 0.5 b/d." Javier Blas, "Victim of Shale Revolution, Nigeria Stops Exporting Oil to U.S.," *Blogger* (Oct. 2, 2014, 10:12), http://blogs.ft.com/beyond-brics/2014/10/02/victim-of-shale-revolution-nigeria-stops-exporting-oil-to-us/. By early 2014 "sales dropped to a trickle of about 100,000 b/d[,]" stopping completely in July of that year. Ibid.

80. Based on the figures provided by Nigeria's office of statistics at the end of 2013, Nigeria had a gross domestic product (GDP) of $510 billion, compared to South Africa's little over $370 billion. See, e.g., "Nigeria Becomes Africa's Biggest Economy," *BBC News* (Apr. 6, 2014), http://www.bbc.com/news/business-26913497 (commenting on the rebasing of the country's GDP). The rebasing means that Nigeria included in its GDP calculations industries like telecom, information technology,

music, online sales, airlines, and film production that previously were uncounted. Ibid. Rebasing is carried out so as to give a nation's GDP statistics the most up-to-date picture of an economy as possible. It is an updating that many countries conduct about once every three years that Nigeria last did in 1990. Ibid. Although with the updating, Nigeria surpasses South Africa as Africa's largest economy, Nigerian citizens do not enjoy a higher standard of living than their counterparts in South Africa. This is because, with over 186 million denizens, Nigeria's population is more than three times larger than South Africa's 54 million persons (as of 2015). On a per-capita basis, South Africa's GDP numbers are three times larger than Nigeria's. Ibid. Little wonder why one Nigerian financial analyst quoted in the BBC news story called the revisions "a vanity" in that for average Nigerians, their country's surpassing South Africa "doesn't put more money in the bank, more food in their stomach. It changes nothing." Ibid.

81. Terry Lynn Karl, *The Paradox of Plenty: Oil Booms and Petro-States* (Berkeley, CA: University of California Press, 1997): 189–220.

82. Dickovick & Eastwood, note 70, pp. 54–55.

83. See Frynas, note 78, *passim*; Int'l Crisis Group, note 46.

84. Larry Diamond, *Foreword*, *in* Rotimi T. Suberu, *Federalism and Ethnic Conflict in Nigeria* (Washington, D.C.: United States Institute of Peace, 2001): xv.

85. See Patrick H. O'Neil et al., *Cases in Comparative Politics, 4th Ed.* (New York: W. W. Norton & Co., 2012): 724.

86. Ibid.

87. See Ayakeme Whisky, "The South-South Position: A Stitch in Time Saves Nine," *Vanguard* (Lagos) (Jun. 5, 2014), http://www.vanguardngr.com/2014/06/south-south-position-stitch-time-saves-nine/.

88. See Frynas, note 78, *passim*.

89. Int'l Covenant on Civil and Political Rights, Dec. 16, 1966, S. Treaty Doc. No. 95–20, 6 I.L.M. 368 (1967), 999 U.N.T.S. 171, Art. 1, §§1–2; Int'l Covenant on Economic, Social and Cultural Rights, Dec. 16, 1966, S. Treaty Doc. No. 95–19, I.L.M. 360 (1967), 993 U.N.T.S. 3, Art. 1, §§1–2.

90. Dickovick & Eastwood, note 70, p. 585. On telecommunication, one source assesses that "[t]he Nigerian telecommunications sector is among the best performing sectors of the Nigerian economy and one of the fastest growing employers of labor in the country." Lanre Adedeji, "Telecommunications and the Nigerian Economy," *Lawyers Chronicle*, http://thelawyerschronicle.com/telecommunications-and-the-nigerian-economy/ (last visited Mar. 23, 2015). On entertainment, Professors Dickovich and Eastwood observe that the Nigerian film industry, Nollywood, "distributes movies across Africa at a rate faster than Hollywood itself." Dickovick & Eastwood, note 70, p. 585.

91. Brysk, note 31, pp. 8–17 (table 1.1, with countries that meet the threshold for potential global good citizenship highlighted in light gray); ibid., p. 232–34 (characterizing the United States as the "deadbeat dad of global governance."). See also Michael Ignatieff, *Is the Human Rights Era Ending? in* Allan J. Cigler ed., *Perspectives on Terrorism: How 9/11 Changed U.S. Politics* (Boston, MA: Houghton Mifflin Co., 2002): 103–6 (lamenting that due to the war against terror, "[t]he new element

in determining American foreign policy is what assets—bases, intelligence[,] and diplomatic leverage—it can bring to bear against Al Qaeda[,]" rather than the needed U.S. leadership on international human rights).

92. See Aka, note 68, *passim*, although its focus is limited to the challenges of judicial (in)dependence under the Fourth Republic since 1999.

93. See Farouk Chothia, "Who Are Nigeria's Boko Haram Islamists?" *BBC News Africa* (May 4, 2015), http://www.bbc.com/news/world-africa-13809501.

94. Olufemi A. Babarinde, "Regionalism and African Foreign Policies," *in* Stephen Wright, ed., *African Foreign Policies* (Boulder, CO: Westview Press, 1999): 215–36.

95. Pham, *supra* note 29, at 91.

96. Brysk, note 31, p. 230. These tigers, none of them from Africa, are Argentina, Brazil, Chile, and South Korea. Ibid.

97. Ibid., p. 118. Judging by population size alone, Costa Rica has 3 million people, compared to Nigeria's 135 million denizens as of 2009 when the Brysk study was published. Ibid., pp. 8–17.

98. Ibid., p. 221. Brysk creatively built the theme of her work on the biblical parable of the Good Samaritan, Luke 10: 25–37 (New International Version).

99. Brysk, note 31, p. 221.

100. See notes 28–33 and corresponding text.

101. Clinton, note 22, p. 1701.

102. Emeka Odumegwu Ojukwu, "Nigeria: The Truths Which Are Self-Evident," *Sunday Magazine* (Lagos) (Mar. 6, 1994): 18. Ojukwu (1933–2011) served as military governor of Eastern Nigeria and, subsequently, Head of State of the Republic of Biafra from 1967 to 1970. Biafra was the former Eastern Region of Nigeria that sought unsuccessfully to break away from Nigeria. The secession failed and the region was re-annexed to Nigeria in 1970 after nearly three years of exceedingly bloody war. See, e.g., Chinua Achebe, *There Was a Country: A Personal History of Biafra* (New York: Penguin Press, 2012): *passim* (memoir on the war).

103. For General Ojukwu, the applicable language in the Declaration of Independence is "We hold these truths to be self-evident that all men are created equal, that they are endowed by their Creator with certain unalienable rights, that among these are Life, Liberty, and the pursuit of Happiness." Ojukwu, note 102, p. 15.

104. See Dickovick & Eastwood, note 70, p. 19.

Part I

STARTING POINTS

Chapter Two

Conceptual Framework

This chapter deals with two disparate but interlinked issues: definitions of key terms in the study and methodology. The ensuing discussion takes these two issues in turn.

DEFINITION OF KEY TERMS IN THIS STUDY

Because concepts are "abstract mental images"[1] that, by their nature, are "fuzzy and imprecise,"[2] the definition of key terms is critical in any study. Concern for precision was what the Chinese thinker Confucius (551–479 B.C.) had in mind when he once famously indicated that the beginning of wisdom is to call things by their proper names.[3] Pressed on regarding how this injunction related to public policy, Confucius elaborated that "[i]f language be not in accordance with the truth of things, [public] affairs cannot be carried on to success."[4] Because he believed that social disorder stemmed from failure to call things by their right names,[5] Confucius advised individuals in society vested with certain roles or positions, including "rulers," to act in ways appropriate to those names.[6]

To restate, the topic of this work is "Human Rights in Nigeria's External Relations: Building the Record of a Moral Superpower." The vector of key terms in the study is the main title. Consistent with the injunction to call things by their right name, key terms embedded in that main title that the reader would like defined in this study are *human rights* and *foreign policy* (standing for external relations) plus the *relationship between the two* as a third term.

Human Rights

Human rights are guarantees of freedom, such as life, liberty, security, and subsistence to which people as humans have rights.[7] They are generally understood as claims against the state (the government) or society held equally by all persons simply because they are human beings.[8] These claims are made both against repressive regimes and even good, meaning democratic, governments.[9] Although non-governmental entities, such as individuals and organizations, can also abridge these guarantees, human rights "are usually taken to have a special reference to the ways in which states treat their own citizens."[10] No genuine development takes place at the expense of human rights. Instead, in our time, the "true standard" of a society is measured by the extent to which its leaders respect human rights,[11] and the level of a country's development is measured "by the extent to which its citizens enjoy human rights in all their ramifications."[12] There are over three dozen of these rights distilled from the international bill of human rights.[13] The values codified in international human rights instruments "are at the core of what it means to lead a complete and fulfilled human life."[14]

Many discussions on human rights echo the tenets of Western liberalism, embedded in Mill's famous proposition that "[o]ver himself, over his own body and mind, the individual is sovereign."[15] However, *human rights* are not limited to individual rights but rather also encompass collective (or group) rights, among them the right to self-determination, equally contained in the international bill of human rights.[16] Although for analytic convenience, classifiable into civil and political (or political-civil) rights and economic, social, cultural (or socioeconomic) rights,[17] all human rights are indivisible, interdependent, and interrelated guarantees that all governments must treat with equal emphasis.[18] Political-civil rights and socioeconomic rights are individual rights that may also be enjoyed by groups; and collective rights, like the rights to peace, development, a clean environment, and the right to self-determination, are group rights that individuals may also enjoy.[19] Safeguarding minority rights and affording all citizens the opportunity "to participate in the national life in a climate of justice and peace" have become, in our time, the mark of "a morally adult society."[20] Moreover, because abusive state policies in Nigeria and other Africa countries put groups at risk,[21] "[n]o strategy for human rights promotion in Nigeria will succeed that does not pay strong attention to group rights."[22]

For this reason or in spite of it, collective rights "have always been critical in Nigeria" where fear of majority domination by minority groups was the factor that led to the enshrinement of "fundamental rights" in the country's 1960 Constitution and subsequent ones.[23] In the words of one germane study, "[p]romoting increased access to state power for all groups is a human rights issue in Nigeria" [and] "[a]ccomplishing this purpose can also minimize opportunities for conflict that could result in human rights violations."[24] During his visit to Nigeria in August 2000, then-U.S. president William J. Clinton commented on the need for Nigerian leaders to create a country "worthy of its *people's* dreams."[25] Given the multiethnic character of Nigeria and its still-loose integration as one nation, the advice can equally pass as a challenge for Nigerian leaders to create a country worthy of its *peoples'* dreams.[26]

Foreign Policy

Foreign policy is colloquially and laconically the "interplay between the outside and the inside."[27] Specifically, it is "the formulation, implementation, and evaluation of external choices within one country, viewed from the perspective of that country."[28] Fundamentally speaking, the foreign policy of a state comprises the two key elements of "national *objectives* to be achieved and the *means* for achieving them[,]" as well as the interaction between objectives and means."[29] To put the matter simply, foreign relations are a continuation of domestic policy by other means,[30] or, alternatively, engagements abroad to support the work of security and economic development at home.[31] The lesson conductors of Nigeria's foreign policy need to draw from the interlocking connection between domestic and foreign policies is that they cannot *weaken* at home the very same thing they are trying to *strengthen* abroad.[32]

To reduce monotony, the term *foreign policy* is used interchangeably in this work with expressions like *Nigeria's external relations*, *Nigerian external relations*, *Nigeria's external affairs*, *Nigerian external affairs*, and *principled foreign policy*. Interchanging these terms with *foreign policy* is a technique meant to inject variety and facilitate the flow of discussion; it should not be read to mean that these terms are identical to or even technically equivalent with *foreign policy*.

Relationship between Human Rights and Foreign Policy

Different scholars have commented on the essentially "national character of human rights."[33] Given this occurrence, how does a country apply human rights in its external relations? Stated differently, what features make the application of human rights in external relations different from its application domestically, and why should the distinction matter? Applying human rights in foreign relations means adoption of a *human rights policy*, a term itself used interchangeably in this study with *principled foreign policy*. No universal definition of such a policy exists. Instead, different analysts posit different requirements with more or less connection to human rights for such policy. For Professor Sikkink, a state has a human rights policy when the state in question "has explicit mechanisms for integrating human rights concerns into foreign policy and when those mechanisms have modified foreign policy decisions in some cases."[34] For Professor Donnelly, for states that chose to apply human rights in their external relations, "we can reasonably demand that human rights actually enter into calculations balancing competing interests, with a weight that roughly matches their stated place in the hierarchy of national interests."[35] This configuration is not as stringent as it looks on the surface. This is because, as Professor Donnelly pointed out elsewhere, commenting on U.S. foreign policy, the key point is to assess "the impact of the full range of . . . foreign policy behavior on international human rights practices, not just those initiatives that explicitly address human rights."[36] In Donnelly's view, "a moral add-on after the 'real' foreign policy decisions have been made" isn't enough.[37]

For Professor Brysk, an external activity rises to a human-rights foreign policy when such activity "seek[s] to protect and empower citizens of other countries in order to secure the" key rights embodied in the international bill of human rights—the Universal Declaration of Human Rights, the International Covenant on Civil and Political Rights, and the International Covenant on Economic, Cultural, and Social Rights.[38] Specifically, an international activity qualifies as a human rights policy when, keeping aside the ultimate impact and effectiveness of that activity, "(1) its primary announced goal is humanitarian protection or empowerment, and (2) the resources and strategies used correspond to a reasonable outside observer's standard of humanitarian orientation."[39] Finally for David Gilles, pursuit of a human rights–based foreign policy involves some measure of opportunity cost defined to mean "any action which, to a significant extent, will be likely to disrupt normal diplomatic relations, limit commercial opportunities, inflict domestic economic hardship, strain alliance structures, or provoke retaliation by a target state."[40]

In short, application of human rights in external affairs spells the adoption of a human rights policy embedded in global human rights instruments along with complimentary regional human rights instruments in the case of an African country like Nigeria also subject to those instruments.[41] States who apply human rights in their foreign affairs are what Alison Brysk calls "global good Samaritans,"[42] who, in their foreign relations, project a "kindness of strangers"[43] driven by the biblical injunction to "love your neighbor as yourself."[44] While application of human rights in external relations comes in "a variety of cooperative, value-oriented" international activities broadly subsumable under "aid, diplomacy, the use of force, and sometimes migration,"[45] these values, for an African country like Nigeria subject to both global and regional human rights instruments, may be reduced to the indicators encapsulated in table 2.1 below.

To both recapitulate and conclude this statement on the relationship between human rights and foreign policy, three observations are in order. The first is that, although important in that it can lay the foundation for principled foreign policy, application of human rights in external affairs in the sense we define it in this work is a more deep-seated concept that rises beyond sheer emergence of human rights in world politics found in some portion of the literature.[46] Second, although important for the background insight moral values introduce into the conversation[47] as well as the capacity of these values to inform the foreign policy decisions of an affected country,[48] the application of human rights in external affairs in the sense we define it in this work rises beyond occasional interjections of ethical values into external affairs. Instead, it "is a pattern of persistent principled politics" rising beyond "episodic altruism"[49]—"an interconnected congeries of beliefs about our duty to protect strangers[,]"[50] tied, as shown above, into the provisions of applicable global and regional human rights instruments.

The third and final observation is that interjecting moral principles embedded in human rights does *not* violate the principle of non-interference in the domestic affairs of another state. The principle here involved is the requirement in the United Nations Charter that forbids member-states from intervening into "matters which are essentially within the domestic jurisdiction of any state."[51] Because "breaches of human rights, especially gross breaches, are taken out of domestic jurisdiction[,]" concern for human rights does not negate the principle of non-interference.[52] Human rights emerged in world politics (distinguished from its distinct application in external affairs by way of a human rights policy)[53] as a counterweight against the unrestrained *exercise* of sovereignty fingered as a factor in the atrocities of World War II. Because Adolf Hitler and his National Socialist German Workers' Party (known for short as the Nazi Party) persecuted and murdered 6 million Jews, Slavs, Gypsies, and other supposedly "inferior" peoples, during World War II, the atrocities they perpetrated during this period "gave sovereignty a bad name."[54] The felt need to moderate the raw exercise of sovereignty in the interest of human rights became evident even while World War II was still raging. The Allied powers built their opposition against the Nazis on human rights grounds, citing the Declaration of the United Nations, precursor to the U.N. Charter of 1945, that these Allied Powers adopted in January of 1942, in which document they claimed that "complete victory over their enemies is essential to defend life, liberty, independence and religious freedom, and to preserve human rights and justice in their own lands as well as in other lands."[55]

Table 2.1. Conceivable Tools for the Application of Human Rights in External Relations

Serial No.	*Tool of Engagement*	*Bilateral or Multilateral?*
1.	Commitment to international human rights, indicated by activities, such as the number of treaties ratified, "founding, funding, and joining international human rights bodies; drafting, sponsoring, and supporting human rights treaties and resolutions; [and] promoting the development of international law"[a]	More multilateral than bilateral
2.	Peacekeeping and related engagements[b]	More multilateral than bilateral
3.	Economic, military, and diplomatic assistance to foreign countries (foreign aid)[c]	More bilateral than multilateral
4.	Assisting victims of human rights abuses through policy relating to refugees[d]	More bilateral than multilateral
5.	Publishing reports on human rights, such as the U.S. State Department's *Country Reports on Human Rights Practices*[e]	More multilateral than bilateral
6.	Promoting democracy in another country	More bilateral than multilateral
7.	Paying a price for commitment to human rights, indicated by factors such as loss of economic, military, or diplomatic assistance[f]	More bilateral than multilateral[g]
8.	Miscellaneous exchanges and contacts related to human rights, such as private and public diplomacy, sanctions, mediations, as well as cultural and scholarly engagements[h]	More bilateral than multilateral

[a]Brysk, note 38, p. 20 (defining multilateralism). These acts of multilateralism can be channeled through regional or global institutions in various ways, including voluntary funding for the United Nations Office of the High Commissioner for Human Rights (UNOHCHR), and diplomatic support for the International Criminal Court (ICC). Founded in December 1993, in the aftermath of the World Conference on Human Rights in Vienna earlier in June of the same year, the UNOHCHR "act[s] as the principal focal point of human rights research, education, public information, and advocacy activities in the United Nations system." "What We Do," United Nations Human Rights Office of the High Commissioner, http://www.ohchr.org/EN/AboutUs/Pages/WhatWeDo.aspx. The office assists national governments to realize their human rights obligations domestically as well as internationally through various means, including "expertise and technical trainings in the areas of administration of justice, legislative reform, and electoral process. . . ." Ibid. For a book-length work on this organization, see B.G. Ramcharan, *The United Nations High Commissioner for Human Rights: The Challenges of International Protection* (Leiden, Netherlands: Martinus Nijhoff Publishers, 2002). Regarding the ICC, see below.

[b]These other activities include "weapons control, conflict prevention, and post-conflict reconstruction efforts, especially activities "that focus on the protection of civilians and vulnerable populations," as well as "financial support for demining," given the danger that this weapon poses to civilians and other vulnerable groups. Brysk, note 38, p. 21.

[c]Keeping in mind the U.N.'s recommendation of .7 percent of a country's gross domestic product (GDP) to foreign aid, the requisite assistance exists when that assistance "is sufficient in quantity, not unduly tied to donor interests, directed to grassroots groups and basic human needs, and fosters improvements in the rule of law and the empowerment of marginalized sectors." Ibid.

[d]Sheltering refugees, "needy foreigners" often with "no natural constituency within host nations," is viewed as "the single most direct and immediate measure states can take to assist the victims of human rights abuses." Brysk, note 38, p. 22.

[e]A valid question is whether materials like the Human Rights Record of the United States published by the Chinese government would qualify. See Philip C. Aka, "The Country Reports on Human Rights Practices and U.S. Human Rights Policy in a Changing World," *Perspectives on Global Development & Technology*, Vol. 14 (2015): 243–44. The answer would be probably no for various good reasons. Begun in 1998, the Record is focused specifically on the United States and, less impressively still, as tit-for-tat for the United States' practice of criticizing China in the Country Reports on Human Rights Practices, criticisms that the Chinese leadership considered as an interference into China's domestic affairs. Second, much of the Chinese chronicle is propagandistic, confined as it is to U.S. domestic socioeconomic issues such as poverty, crime, and racial discrimination. Ibid., p. 244.

[f]An example that comes to mind here would be refusal to sign bilateral immunity agreement. Since the Second World War, the international community has favored the establishment of a permanent judicial tribunal for punishment of heinous offenses: genocide, war crimes, and crimes against humanity. When the International Criminal Court (ICC) finally came into existence in July 2002, the United States under George W. Bush was unalterably opposed to it, even though American officials participated in the drafting of the Rome Statute that established the Court. The U.S. government voiced the fear that American nationals could be tried by the Court, impelling the Bush administration to negotiate so-called bilateral immunity agreements (BIAs) with countries designed to exempt U.S. peacekeepers from the ICC's jurisdiction. See Jason Ralph, *Defending the Society of States: Why America Opposes the International Criminal Court and Its Visions of World Society* (New York: Oxford University Press, 2007), *passim*. As of Dec. 2006, the State Department reported the signature of 102 of such agreements. Coalition for the International Criminal Court, Status of U.S. Bilateral Immunity Agreements, http://www.iccnow.org/documents/CICCFS_BIAstatus_current.pdf. (last modified Dec. 11, 2006). Countries which failed to sign these agreements risked reduction or loss of U.S. assistance. Id. Human Rights Watch, Bilateral Immunity Agreements (June 25, 2003), http://www.hrw.org/legacy/campaigns/icc/docs/bilateralagreements.pdf.

Seven African countries which suffered these fates are Kenya, Lesotho, Mali, Namibia, Niger, South Africa, and Tanzania. Deborah H. Cotton & Godfrey O. Odongo, "The Magnificent Seven: Africa's Response to U.S. Article 98," *African Human Rights Law Journal*, Vol. 7 (2007): 1–34, http://www.ahrlj.up.ac.za/cotton-d-h-odongo-g-o. Under President Barack Obama, the U.S. government has expressed an intention to reduce its hostility toward the ICC and has removed some of the sanctions attached to the BIAs but has yet to make a formal policy decision on the ICC or the status of the BIAs. See Mark Kerstein, "The U.S. and the ICC: Towards a Closer Relationship?" *Justice in Conflict* (Apr. 10, 2011), http://justiceinconflict.org/2011/04/10/the-us-and-the-icc-towards-a-closer-relationship/.

[g]For example, Nigeria's intervention in Sierra Leone to restore a democratic government was multilateral (given that it was done under the auspices of ECOWAS). Simultaneously, the intervention was also a bilateral attempt by the then military government under Sani Abacha to promote democracy in Sierra Leone while, strangely, maintaining military rule in Nigeria. See Norimitsu Onishi, "What War Has Wrought: Sierra Leone's Sad State," *New York Times* (Jan. 31, 1999), http://www.nytimes.com/1999/01/31/world/what-war-has-wrought-sierra-leone-s-sad-state.html?pagewanted=all.

[h]Donnelly & Liang-Fenton, note 36, p. 10; and Debra Liang-Fenton, "Conclusion: What Works?," in Liang-Fenton ed., *Implementing U.S. Human Rights Policy*, note 36, pp. 436–48.

Sources: Table created by the author, drawing on multiple sources, including Brysk, note 35, pp. 24–26; Gilles, note 37, p. 49; Donnelly & Liang-Fenton, note 33, p. 10; and Debra Liang-Fenton, *Conclusion: What Works?, in* Liang-Fenton, ed., *Implementing U.S. Human Rights Policy*, note 33, pp. 435, 436–48.

In a word, as one African human rights scholar noted, "[t]he shock of the Second World War led very quickly to the realization that it was no longer appropriate or possible to leave the business of protecting human rights to the sovereign state alone."[56] Underscoring the role of the atrocities of World War II as a key factor in the emergence of human rights as a counterweight to abuses in the unrestrained exercise of sovereign powers, the Convention on the Prevention and Punishment of the Crime of Genocide (the Genocide Convention) was adopted one day before the adoption of the Universal Declaration of Human Rights on December 10, 1948.[57] Before the Second World

War, explicit interjection of moral values into international affairs was "historically unusual."[58] Following the War, such application came into vogue, reaching a high point with the Carter administration in the United States from 1977 until 1981.[59] Pursuit of a human rights policy requires a state conducting that policy to "transgress the norm of non-interference and sacrifice short-term gains to safeguard long-range values."[60] Thus, although human rights cannot be an excuse for unwarranted intervention into the affairs of other countries,[61] in the period since World War II, "a normatively robust global human rights regime has developed[,]" even though States "largely retained for themselves the responsibility—and the sovereign right—to implement these rights in their own territories."[62]

This said, there is no intention to minimize the injunction of non-interference in international law. "Human rights exist within a set of hegemonic ideas constituting the reigning mantra of world politics."[63] High on that list is the norm of sovereignty, which doctrine still exerts a lingering influence on the behavior of powerful states like the United States and China.[64] A state's national self-image is not "exhausted by a commitment to human rights."[65] Instead, as Professor Donnelly posited, "in addition to human rights, sovereignty and non-intervention are vital norms of international society."[66] To use China as an example, in its human rights action plan for 2000–2010, the country confessed its fidelity to human rights. Yet that did not prevent the Chinese leadership from linking human rights with the country's identity as a socialist state, asserting unpersuasively that "the task of our party is to establish the rule of law and construct a socialist country with the rule of law."[67]

METHODOLOGY

Methodology is "the science of finding out"[68] and an integral part of scientific social science research.[69] Many human rights studies are inherently comparative in nature.[70] This one is no exception. Additionally, explicitly, the method for collecting and analyzing data in this study is the comparative method,[71] specifically a mixture of the Most-Similar-Systems Design (MSSD)[72] and Within-Case Comparison (WCC)[73] complemented with comparative checking.[74] MSS design is a research technique wherein the researcher compares cases that are similar with respect to a number of factors but with distinct outcomes.[75] It is predicated on the logic that two cases, e.g., two countries, similar in a variety of ways, would have similar political outcomes, and where that is not the case, but, instead variations in outcome occurred, the researcher will seek explanation regarding the dissimilarity.[76] One concern about this design relates to the premium that it places on identifying the differences between cases, rather than the similarities: "If two cases are most similar, what is remarkable about comparing them?"[77] As Professors Dickovick and Eastwood explain, "[w]hat is remarkable is *where* most similar cases differ. Differences in outcomes between similar cases are noteworthy, and differences in possible causes are what will help us explain them."[78]

WCC involves the study of one country at different points in time and space. Under this technique, "the researcher look[s] more carefully within [his or her] own case(s) to examine the variations there[in]," the logic being that "[l]ooking at different moments in time or in space may allow us to dig deeper into a case to better understand our evidence."[79] WCC is often associated with "process-tracing" by which "the researcher examines histories, archival documents, interview transcripts and other sources to see whether the causal process a theory hypothesizes or implies in a case is in fact evident in the sequence and values of the intervening variable in that case."[80]

Unlike MSSD and WCC, comparative checking is *not* a distinctive technique, but a device the comparative analyst uses to cross check whatever technique the researcher chooses to guard against possible errors of interpretation. It is the process of testing the researcher's conclusions "from a set of comparisons against additional cases or evidence,"[81] bearing in mind that any single design or set of designs that is chosen forms "the foundation for initial comparison," not basis to preclude further examination.[82]

Although the whole book is guided by the two main components of the comparative method identified above, the following is the breakdown of the balance of each component in the main chapters of the work (i.e., excluding chapter 3 on theoretical framework and chapters 11 and 12, the two concluding chapters):

- Chapter 4 laying out the historical backdrop of the study (mostly WCC),
- Chapter 5 on reconstructing Nigeria's national interest (mostly WCC),
- Chapter 6 on increased respect for human rights within Nigeria (MSSD and WCC),
- Chapter 7 on redesigning peacekeeping (mostly WCC),
- Chapter 8 on reshaping Nigeria's foreign policy machinery (MSSD and WCC),
- Chapter 9 on the need for more symmetry between multilateral and bilateral activities in Nigerian external relations (MSSD and WCC), and
- Chapter 10 on ECOWAS as a tool for applying human rights in external affairs (MSSD and WCC).

Although legal research focuses on "what is and why," it may also legitimately delve into what should be in instances when agreed-upon criteria exist "for deciding what makes one thing better than another."[83] By its nature, this research combines the best of what is and what should be, *describing* the application of human rights in Nigerian foreign policy the way it is now while *prescriptively* incorporating suggestions on the ideal way forward. Most extended research needs a theoretical framework to complement and complete the conceptual framework. Chapter 3 focusing on the theoretical framework of the study takes on that topic.

NOTES

1. Michael G. Maxfield & Earl R. Babbie, *Research Methods for Criminal Justice and Criminology, 7th Ed.* (Stamford, CT: Cengage Learning, 2015): 110–11.
2. Ibid., p. 112 (under the definition of "conceptualization" last three lines of the left portion of the page); see also ibid., p. 239 (stating that "there are no ultimately true meanings for any of the concepts we typically study in social science").
3. "The Rectification of Names," *Cultural China*, http://www.cultural-china.com/chinaWH/History/en/165History878.html.
4. James Legge, *Confucian Analects, The Great Learning, and the Doctrine of the Mean* (Mineola, N.Y.: Dover Publications, 1971): 263–64 (translating *Analects*, Book XIII, chapter 3, verses 4–7).
5. He stated:

> If names be not correct, language is not in accordance with the truth of things. If language be not in accordance with the truth of things, affairs cannot be carried on to success. When affairs cannot be carried on to success, proprieties and music do not flourish. When proprieties and music do not flourish, punishments will not be properly awarded. When punishments are not properly awarded, the people do not know how to move hand or foot. . . . What the superior man requires is just that in his words there may be nothing incorrect.

Ibid.

6. "Rectification of Names," note 3.
7. Jack Donnelly, *International Human Rights, 4th Ed.* (Boulder, CO: Westview Press, 2013): xvii; R.J. Vincent, *Human Rights and International Relations* (Cambridge University Press, 1986): 9–11 (discussing five features of human rights).
8. Donnelly, note 7, p. 19. The distinguished human rights scholar, Louis Henkin, called human rights "claims of rights, not by grace, or love, or charity, or compassion" that "society is morally, politically, even legally obligated to respect, ensure, and realize." Louis Henkin, "Human Rights: Ideology and Aspiration, Reality and Prospect," *in* Samantha Power & Graham Allison, eds., *Realizing Human Rights: Moving from Inspiration to Impact* (New York: St. Martin's Press, 2000): 5.
9. Henkin, note 8, p. 5.
10. Donnelly, note 7, p. xvii; Int'l Committee of the Red Cross (Jan. 1, 2004), https://www.icrc.org/eng/resources/documents/misc/5kzmuy.htm (explaining that the

"principal goal" of human rights "is to protect individuals from arbitrary behavior by their own governments.").

11. U. Oji Umozurike, *The African Charter on Human and Peoples' Rights* (Leiden, Netherlands & Boston, MA: Brill, 1997): 5.

12. Ibid., p. 7.

13. See Donnelly, note 7, p. 7. Instruments comprising the international bill of human rights are the Universal Declaration of Human Rights, UDHR (1948), the International Covenant on Civil and Political Rights (ICCPR), and the International Covenant on Economic, Social, and Cultural Rights (ICESCR). The last two came into force in 1976. Some commentators include the United Nations Charter (1945), the first instrument ever to use the language of human rights, among the documents of the international bill of human rights. The UDHR sets forth "common standards of achievement for all peoples and all nations" that the two human rights covenants, as binding multilateral treaties, then elaborated. Additionally, over the years, the UDHR garnered such authoritativeness that today some international law scholars appropriately consider it as customary international law. See Henkin, note 8, p. 12.

14. Kenneth Roth, "Human Rights Organizations: A New Force for Social Change," *in* Power & Allison, eds., *Realizing Human Rights*, note 8, p. 230 (referring to the Universal Declaration of Human Rights).

15. *The Basic Writings of John Stuart Mill: On Liberty, the Subjection of Women, and Unilateralism* (New York: Modern Library, 2002): 3–97.

16. Two instruments of the international bill of rights that "guarantee" the right to self-determination are the ICCPR, and the ICESCR. See International Covenant on Civil and Political Rights, Dec. 16, 1966, S. Treaty Doc. No. 95–20, 6 I.L.M. 368 (1967), 999 U.N.T.S. 171, Art. 1; International Covenant on Economic, Social and Cultural Rights, Dec. 16, 1966, S. Treaty Doc. No. 95–19, 6 I.L.M. 360 (1967), 993 U.N.T.S. 3, Art. 1.

17. *Civil rights* include the right to life; right to liberty and security of person; protection against slavery; protection against torture and cruel and inhuman punishment; right to equality of rights without discrimination; right to equal protection under the law; access to legal remedies for rights violations; protection against arbitrary arrest or detention; hearing before an independent and impartial judiciary; presumption of innocence until proved guilty; protection against *ex post facto* (or retroactive) laws; right to privacy; freedom of thought, conscience, and religion; freedom of opinion, expression, and the press; and freedom of assembly and association, among others. An example of a source that embodies many of these rights is the ICCPR. See International Covenant on Civil and Political Rights, G.A. Res. 2200A (XXI), U.N. GAOR, Supp. No. 16, U.N. Doc. A/6316 (1966). *Political rights*, also contained in the ICCPR, include the right of political participation. See ibid., art. 25. Civil-political rights that may not be derogated, i.e., suspended, by states during periods of emergency include the right to life, protection against torture and cruel and inhuman punishment; and protection against retroactive laws. *Economic rights* include the right to food, clothing, and housing; the right to work under favorable conditions; the right to healthcare and social services; and the right to social security, among others. One typical human rights instrument that collects these rights is the ICESCR. See

International Covenant on Economic, Social, and Cultural Rights, G.A. Res. 2200, U.N. GAOR, 21st Sess. Supp. No. 16, at 49–52, U.N. Doc. A16316, 993 U.N.T.S. 3, 6 I.L.M. 360 (1966). *Social rights*, also embodied in this instrument, include the right to education. Ibid., Arts. 13–14. *Cultural rights*, also equally embodied in the same instrument, include the right to participate in one's cultural life. Ibid., Art. 15.

18. Vienna Declaration and Program of Action (Jun. 25, 1993), Office of the United Nations High Comm'r for Human Rights, ¶ 5, http://www.ohchr.org/EN/ProfessionalInterest/Pages/Vienna.aspx.

19. Philip C. Aka, "Human Rights as Conflict Resolution in Africa in the New Century," *Tulsa Journal of Comparative & Int'l Law*, Vol. 11 (Fall 2003): 186.

20. Emilio J. Cárdenas & María Fernanda Cañás, "The Limits of Self-Determination," *in* Wolfgang Danspeckgruber, ed., *The Self-Determination of Peoples: Community, Nation, and State in an Interdependent World* (Boulder, CO: Lynne Rienner, 2001): 101 (quoting Pope John Paul II).

21. Philip C. Aka, "Nigeria since May 1999: Understanding the Paradox of Civil Rule and Human Rights Violations under President Olusegun Obasanjo," *San Diego Int'l Law Journal*, Vol. 4 (2003): 273–74.

22. Ibid.

23. Aka, note 21, p. 274. In the 1950s, as Nigeria moved inexorably toward independence, minority groups in each of the country's three regions voiced the concern that the dominant ethnic group in each region, the Igbo in the East, the Yoruba in the West, and the Hausa-Fulani in the North, would dominate them once the country became independent from Britain. These groups demanded their own separate states to prevent that occurrence or minimize its effect. In response, in 1957, the British colonial authority set up a commission of inquiry to look into their claim. With independence just three years away, the commission left the regional structure unchanged the way it was, but recommended the equivalent of a bill of basic rights that it adapted from the European Convention on Human Rights of 1950, to be inserted in the country's independence constitution. The colonial government accepted the recommendations. See *Report of the Commission Appointed to Inquiry into the Fears of Minorities and the Means of Allaying Them* (London: Her Majesty's Stationery Office, 1958), *passim*.

24. Aka, note 21, p. 274.

25. William J. Clinton, "Remarks Following Discussions with President Olusegun Obasanjo of Nigeria and an Exchange with Reporters in Abuja, Nigeria, Aug. 26, 2000," *in Public Papers of the Presidents of the United States: William J. Clinton, 2000–2001* (Washington, D.C.: Best Books, 2000): 1701.

26. See Emeka Odumegwu Ojukwu, "Nigeria: The Truths Which Are Self-Evident," *Sunday Magazine* (Lagos) (Mar. 6, 1994): 18 (positing that "the *peoples* of Nigeria have not . . . had, the same or similar benefits and privileges from the Nigerian polity[,]" but that, instead, "whilst some have experienced joy, others experienced pain.") (emphasis added).

27. F.S. Northedge, "The Nature of Foreign Policy," *in* F.S. Northedge, ed., The Foreign Policies of the Powers (Westport, CT: Praeger, 1969): 15. See also Mae C. King, *Basic Currents of Nigerian Foreign Policy* (Washington, D.C.: Howard Uni-

versity Press, 1996): 237 (observing that "[f]oreign policy defines our relations with strangers[,]" and that "[i]t is also an extension of domestic policy.").

28. James E. Dougherty & Robert L. Pfaltzgraff, *Contending Theories of International Relations: A Comprehensive Survey, 3d Ed.* (New York: Harper & Row, 1990): 15.

29. Cecil V. Crabb Jr., *American Foreign Policy in the Nuclear Age, 3d Ed.* (New York: Harper & Row, 1972): 1.

30. See J. Peter Pham, "Nigeria's Foreign Policy: An Inquiry into Sources and Prospects." Presentation for an Int'l Conference, Lisbon Portugal (Nov. 8–9, 2007), www.ipri.pt/eventos/pdf/JPeterPham_paper.pdf (defining foreign policy as "a dynamic process involving the interaction between a country's internal and external environments.").

31. See Larry Berman & Bruce Allen Murphy, *Approaching Democracy, 8th Ed.* (New York: Pearson Education, Inc., 2013): 514 (defining U.S. foreign policy as "actions the U.S. government takes on behalf of its national interests abroad to ensure the security and well-being of Americans and the strength and competitiveness of the U.S. economy.").

32. The material in chapter 6 on increased human rights at home continues and completes this line of argument.

33. See, e.g., Donnelly, note 7, pp. 14–16 (commenting on the system of national implementation that mark the global human rights regime); Henkin, note 8, p. 8 (defining *international human rights* as "an international movement to promote and protect and assume and assert international responsibility for *national* human rights, that is, rights within national societies."); and Louis Henkin, "The Universal Declaration and the U.S. Constitution," *PS: Political Science & Politics*, Vol. 31 (Sept. 1998): 512–13 (characterizing "international human rights as national rights").

34. Kathryn Sikkink, "The Power of Principled Ideas: Human Rights Policies in the United States and Western Europe," *in* Judith Goldstein & Robert O. Keohane eds., *Ideas and Foreign Policy: Beliefs, Institutions, and Political Change* (Ithaca, NY: Cornell University Press, 1993): 143.

35. Donnelly, note 7, p. 146.

36. Jack Donnelly & Debra Liang-Fenton, "Introduction," *in* Debra Liang-Fenton ed., *Implementing U.S. Human Rights Policy* (Washington, D.C.: United States Institute of Peace Press, 2004): 6.

37. Donnelly, note 7, p. 146.

38. Alison Brysk, *Global Good Samaritans: Human Rights as Foreign Policy* (New York: Oxford University Press, 2009): 5.

39. Ibid.

40. David Gilles, *Between Principles and Practice: Human Rights in North-South Relations* (Montreal, Canada: McGill-Queen's University Press, 1996): 50.

41. These regional instruments include the African [Banjul] Charter on Human and Peoples' Rights, which Nigeria ratified in 1983; the Convention Governing the Specific Aspects of Refugee Problems in Africa, ratified in 1986; and the African Charter on the Rights and Welfare of the Child, ratified in 2001. See University of Minnesota,

Human Rights Library, Ratification of International Human Rights Treaties—Nigeria, http://www1.umn.edu/humanrts/research/ratification-nigeria.html (last visited Feb. 26, 2015). One key regional instrument Nigeria is yet to ratify is the Protocol to the African Charter on Human and Peoples' Rights on the Establishment of an African Court on Human and Peoples' Rights. Ibid. The Court came into being on Jan. 25, 2004, following ratification by fifteen states necessary to bring it into existence.

42. Brysk, note 38, pp. 28–30, 42–219. Seven Good Samaritans this book surveyed, six of them states, and each of which applied human rights in external affairs in varying degrees, are Sweden, Canada, Costa Rica, The Netherlands, Japan, South Africa, and a set of transnational human rights organizations, "coalitions of the caring," such as the Organization for Security and Cooperation in Europe (OSCE), the Human Security Network, Community of Democracies (Club Dem), the International Institute for Democracy and Electoral Assistance (IDEA), the Organization for Economic Cooperation and Development (OECD) Donor Assistance Committee, and the Network of National Human Rights institutions (Team Gov).

43. Brysk, note 38, book's frontispiece (poem on "The Kindness of Strangers.").

44. Brysk built the theme of her work on the biblical parable of the Good Samaritan, Luke 10: 25–37 (New Int'l Version).

45. Brysk, note 38, p. 5.

46. For examples of this latter category, see, e.g., Donnelly, note 7, pp. 3–16 (sketching the emergence of human rights as an issue in world politics); David P. Forsythe, *Human Rights in International Relations, 3d Ed.* (New York: Cambridge University Press, 2012), *esp.* pp. 3–33 (commenting on "human rights in international relations"); and Vincent, note 7, p. 7 ("The idea that human beings have rights as humans is a staple of contemporary world politics.").

47. See chapter 4 on the historical backdrop of this study.

48. For example, the theologian John C. Bennett noted that moral values contribute to public policy debates on foreign policy goals by providing "ultimate perspectives, broad criteria, motives, inspirations, sensitivities, warnings, moral limits." John C. Bennett, *Foreign Policy in Christian Perspective* (New York: Scribner's, 1966): 36.

49. Brysk, note 38, p. 3.

50. Ibid., pp. 34–35.

51. Charter of the United Nations (1945), 59 Stat. 1031, T.S. 993, 3 Bevans 1153, Art. 2, ¶ 7 (stipulating that "nothing contained in the present Charter shall authorize the United Nations to intervene in matters which are essentially within the domestic jurisdiction of any state . . .").

52. Umozurike, note 11, p. 7.

53. See note 46 and corresponding text.

54. Forsythe, note 46, p. 31.

55. Donnelly, note 7, p. 4.

56. J. Oloka-Onyango, *Battling over Human Rights: Twenty Essays on Law, Politics[,] and Governance* (Bamenda, Cameroon: Langaa Research & Publishing, 2015): 12.

57. Donnelly, note 7, p. 191 (noting that the occurrence both marked "the central role of the Holocaust in crystallizing international concern with human rights, as well

as "the creation of a separate legal regime[,] genocide, largely divorced from the global human rights regime" until the 1990s).

58. See Donnelly, note 7, p. 16 (under 1 in the list of "discussion questions.").

59. Jimmy Carter, "The American Road to a Human Rights Policy," *in* Power & Allison, eds., *Realizing Human Rights*, note 8, pp. 49–61 (commenting on the sources of increased human rights awareness in the United States and abroad along with the road to a human rights policy that the United States treaded under his leadership from 1977 to 1981).

60. Gilles, note 40, p. 50.

61. As Professor Gutmann points out, human rights being universal does not mean that support for coercive enforcement of these norms will be equally universal. Amy Gutmann, "Introduction," *in* Michael Ignatieff, *Human Rights as Politics and Idolatry* (Princeton, N.J.: Princeton University Press, 2001): xvi. This means, she said, that intervention to enforce human rights "must be used sparingly lest it become[s] an unintended excuse for human rights violations on the part of intervening states." Ibid.

62. Donnelly, note 7, p. 14.

63. David P. Forsythe, "Human Rights Fifty Years after the Universal Declaration," *PS: Political Science & Politics*, Vol. 31(3) (Sept. 1998): 507, 508.

64. See ibid., p. 510.

65. Jack Donnelly, *An Overview*, *in* David P. Forsythe, ed., *Human Rights and Comparative Foreign Policy* (New York: United Nations University Press, 2000): 315.

66. Ibid., p. 318. Because "[a]ll states, in fact, have a deeper and more enthusiastic commitment to sovereignty than to human rights," Professor Donnelly advised policymakers not to "overestimate either human rights or sovereignty" in the external behavior of states. Ibid.

67. See Philip C. Aka, "Introductory Note to the Human Rights Action Plan for China (2009–2010)," *Int'l Legal Material*, Vol. 48 (2009): 842.

68. Maxfield & Babbie, note 1, p. 7.

69. See Anol Bhattacherjee, *Social Science Research: Principles, Methods, and Practices* (Scholar Commons Textbooks Collection, 2012): 5 (describing the "scientific method.").

70. See Philip C. Aka, review of Lutz Oette, ed., *Criminal Law Reform and Transitional Justice: Human Rights Perspectives for Sudan* (Burlington, VT: Ashgate, 2011), *Africa Today*, Vol. 59(4) (Summer 2013): 134 (pointing out that "[g]iven the appeal to international standards, . . . much human-rights scholarship already inherently embeds a measure of comparative analysis."); Frank L. Wilson, *Concepts and Issues in Comparative Politics: An Introduction to Comparative Analysis* (Upper Saddle River, N.J.: Prentice Hall, 1996): 4 (noting that "[b]y tradition, most American scholars of comparative politics direct their attention to foreign countries while making at least implicit contrasts with U.S. politics.").

71. See J. Tyler Dickovick & Jonathan Eastwood, *Comparative Politics: Integrating Theories, Methods, and Cases* (New York: Oxford University Press, 2013): 13–19 (breaking down the elements and features of the comparative method). Unlike physical and biological scientists, who "use laboratories to reproduce experiments in their

search for scientific laws and factors," social scientists "cannot conduct such laboratory experiments in their search for generalizations about politics." Wilson, note 70, at p. 4. The closest to lab experiments these social scientists settle for is the comparative method. Ibid. "Through comparative studies, [these non-physical scientists] can compensate for the lack of laboratory experiments by comparing political experiences and phenomena in one setting with those in other settings." Ibid.

72. See Dickovick & Eastwood, note 71, pp. 14–16.

73. See ibid., p. 19.

74. See ibid., pp. 17–19.

75. Ibid., p. 14.

76. See ibid., pp. 14–16 (including the illustration with Ghana and Togo).

77. Ibid., p. 16.

78. Ibid.

79. Ibid., p. 19.

80. Alexander L. George & Andrew Bennett, *Case Studies and Theory Development in the Social Sciences* (Cambridge, MA: MIT Press, 2005): 6.

81. Dickovick & Eastwood, note 71, pp. 18, 609 (glossary).

82. Ibid., p. 17.

83. See Maxfield & Babbie, note 1, pp. 32–33 (commenting on social scientific theory); Jonathan E. Adler & Catherine Z. Elgin, eds., *Philosophical Inquiry: Classic and Contemporary Readings* (Indianapolis, IN: Hackett Publishing Co. Inc., 2007): 449 (contrasting empirical judgments based on description and moral judgments embedded in prescription); James N. Danziger, *Understanding the Political World: A Comparative Introduction to Political Science, 11th Ed.* (New York: Pearson, 2013): 5–7 (including description and prescription, along with an explanation of three types of political knowledge).

Chapter Three

Theoretical Framework

Theory is part of the "foundations of social science" research.[1] It is the ingredient that makes the world of analysis go round; a theory helps the researcher make sense of and order the phenomenon under observation, explain it, and, where appropriate, make predictions, among other salient functions.[2] Broadly speaking, this chapter builds on the conceptual framework presented in chapter 2. More specifically, it introduces and justifies *constructivism*, the theoretical framework that animates this study. Three components to the presentation in this chapter are: an overview of eight theories of international relations, including constructivism, with more or less tie to human rights; juxtaposition of constructivism to two of those eight theories in an attempt to further draw it out; and overall justification of the framework as the theory for this study.

A PARADE OF EIGHT INTERNATIONAL RELATIONS THEORIES

Eight theories of international relations, each of which, with constructivism, spots an explanatory equal chance as a candidate in this study, are realism, idealism (or liberalism),[3] constructivism, Marxism, feminism, environmentalism, postmodernism, and radical Islamism.[4] Although the appellation *theory* suggests a unity, this can be misleading, given that, as will become obvious shortly in this discussion, many of these theories have variants, in some cases several.[5]

Realism is a school of thought in international relations that stresses the primacy of power, security, and survival in political life.[6] Its basic premise is that individuals, along with the states that represent them, are self-centered.[7] Given this attribute, made no less urgent by the situation of anarchy in the international system (meaning lack of a world government), supposedly impelling states to rely on self-help, realists advise that states neither base their domestic or foreign policies on universal moral principles nor use those principles in evaluating state actions.[8] Prisoners' dilemmas and game theories are all spinoff of classic realist theory.[9] Additionally, variants exist within the theory. For example, while classic realists insist on absolute gain in power, neo-realists contend that states pursue relative gains.[10]

Idealism is the flipside of realism. Taking the basic goodness of human nature as its starting point, the theory contends that individuals and the states that represent them are altruistic (rather than always self-centered) and cooperative.[11] Idealism posits that states "have different preferences and internal structures that lead them to behave in different ways."[12] Accordingly, the theory "pays greater attention to the role of domestic institutions in international relations, and it makes efforts to explain cooperation and peace between some states while also accounting for conflict in other circumstances."[13] Because states have many goals they pursue at home and abroad, "aggressive, power-maximizing behavior is not inevitable."[14] For idealists, vis-à-vis realists, it is possible to create an international system wherein well-designed institutions facilitate cooperative behavior among all actors, whether state or non-state, wherein no one loses and actually some win (positive sum), rather than a zero-sum scenario where "an increase in power for one actor results in an equivalent decrease for others."[15]

Constructivism is the school of international relations which holds that states and other actors "interpret the structural conditions in which they find themselves, based on their own experiences, norms, and values."[16] It stresses the need "to recognize that actors develop" these distinctive "understandings of events[.]"[17] The theory is isolated for closer examination in the two sections below following this one. *Marxism* is the theory of socialism according to German social scientist Karl Marx (1818–1883). The framework "emphasizes the role of social classes in shaping politics and highlights the role of capitalist accumulation as a prime driver in international affairs."[18] Specifically, Marxism holds that "society is composed of competing classes based on economic power, that class struggle and change are inevitable, and that the desired goal" in society should be "the equal distribution of welfare[.]"[19] Just like idealism, with other variants of socialism, Marxism takes a positive view of human nature.[20] Along with other variants of socialism, it works to achieve fulfillment of human needs, including satisfying work and fair share of the worker's work product.[21] For Marxists, the obstacles blocking realization of this goal are false consciousness, class divisions, economic inequalities, and unequal life chances.[22]

Feminism is a school of international relations which posits, generally speaking that, due to their differential socialization, or differential brain wiring, women have different political orientations than men.[23] One indication of that differentness feminists point to is that women "are more inclined toward cooperative interactions and nonviolent solutions"; that "if more such women were in positions of power, states would interact somewhat less aggressively."[24] Feminists seek equality of opportunity for women.[25] For them (which includes men who work for women equality), the obstacles blocking this goal are legal and institutional discrimination.[26] These impediments include patriarchy, rule of men as a social group over women as a social group in intellectual, cultural, religious, or political traditions and practices.[27] Feminism is not a monolithic entity; instead it has liberal, social, radical, and diversity perspectives.[28]

Environmentalism is a school of international relations which posits that humans should act as stewards of nature and expand the concept of political obligations to include obligations to preserve ecosystems.[29] The theory makes several important claims, including: the proposition that the use of nature should be conducted in a manner that supports sustainable development, owning natural resources does *not* imply complete discretion over use of those resources, and economic value is not the only value to consider when calculating the worth of natural resources.[30] Environmentalism rejects the belief that humans are the center of the universe and masters of nature.[31] Because destruction of natural resources threatens human communities no less than war, civil disorder, and other issues that political ideologies recognize as important, this theory adjudges ecosystem integrity to be a political issue.[32] Environmentalists aim to achieve survival and flourishing of all species.[33] For them, one key obstacle blocking this goal is anthropocentrism,[34] "[t]he mistaken belief that human beings are self-sufficient and sovereign masters of nature."[35] Environmentalists pinpoint anthropocentrism as a factor that underlie the disregard by many people "for the delicate and interconnected web of life."[36]

Postmodernism is a school of international relations which forbids putting forward absolute statements as timeless truths but instead views such supposedly timeless truths with profound skepticism.[37] It questions or abjures "metanarratives," meaning any system of thought that identifies its own explanation of reality as an undeniable truth.[38] Metanarratives present themselves as descriptions of and prescriptions regarding an independently existing reality, when in fact they are not.[39] Postmodernism "is often associated with relativism" in that "[i]n denying any ideology's claim to absolute truth, postmodernism suggests that what we consider true is inevitably a product of our own individual frame of reference."[40] Put differently:

> A recurrent theme of the theory is the celebration of the diversity of thinking that logically follows from rejecting orthodox belief. If metanarratives are groundless, if truth is relative, then widely divergent notions of ethics, politics, and social relations—previously represented by metanarratives that closed off all unorthodox explanations of reality—gain credibility as competing options.[41]

Because some commentators equate postmodernism's positioning of all claims of absolute truth as a call for dismissing the existence of the world itself, these critics find the theory's relativism to be troubling and intellectually dubious.[42]

Radical Islam is "a rigid and conservative interpretation of" the Islamic religion that "encourages active, even violent opposition against any[one] who undermine[s] its beliefs about the appropriate way of living, both public and private."[43] Dubbed "political Islam" because of its features that span beyond religion, this school of thought is "directed not only against the West but also against Muslims who subscribe to 'Western' ideas and aspirations that would allegedly make Islam into a more open and tolerant religion."[44] Radical Islam spots a view of human nature and freedom derived not just from its idiosyncratic reading and interpretation of the Koran but also from its idiosyncratic understanding of the long history of encounters between Muslims and Christians, particularly Christians from Western nations.[45] Radical Islam shares with other monotheistic religions (such as Judaism and Christianity) the premise that humans are by nature weak and prone to sin, but departs from these religions with its belief that, to overcome temptation, faith Muslims must engage in jihad, the struggle against evil, at both individual and collective levels.[46] Radical Islamists work to establish Islamic states based on Islamic law.[47] For them the obstacles blocking the realization of the goal are liberalism, secularism, modernity, as well as Western economic and military power, including support for Israel.[48]

JUXTAPOSING CONSTRUCTIVISM WITH ITS TWO RIVAL THEORIES

Although all of the eight theories surveyed in the last section are supposedly international relations theory with some degree of ties to human rights, several of the theories barely made the cut. In some cases, the tie to human rights or even their status as international relations theory is dubious. A case under this category is radical Islamism. As Professor Ball and his colleagues noted, focusing on the relationship between the ideology and democracy, radical Islam tends to be suspicious of, if not hostile to, democracy, particularly the secular strand known as liberal democracy, where "different factions, parties, and interest groups vie for political power with little apparent concern for some shared or greater good."[49]

Another theory smacking of dubious connection to human rights or international relations but for wholly different reasons is Marxism. Before the end of the Cold War in 1991,[50] the theory provided an influential "explanation for the behavior of actors in the international system[,]" reaching the apogee of its appeal during the ideological struggle.[51] The situation changed with the demise of socialism in the Soviet Union and the end of the Cold War that followed that historic event. The result is that today, although it still "persists in diagnosing how the global political economy functions," including "who gains and who loses in this system[,]" the framework has lost much of its appeal especially for developing societies.[52] In a word, radical Islamism and Marxism are *not* appropriate frameworks in this study. So too do feminism, environmentalism, and postmodernism, for all the merit in their postulations. The occurrence leaves us with realism, idealism, and constructivism as the three frameworks still standing. (Co)incidentally, the three also happen to rank among the leading schools of thought today in international relations.[53]

Comparing a phenomenon the researcher is attempting to understand with its opposite(s) can facilitate knowledge of that phenomenon. Accordingly, to build on the survey in the last section on the roadwork to justification of constructivism as the choice approach for this study, this section juxtaposes the theory with the two remaining major schools of thought in international relations—in-between *idealism* on the left of the political spectrum and realism on the *right* (see table 3.1).[54] Several salient and interrelated features and concepts of international relations conveniently used to draw out the three theories here at issue are teachings related to human nature, the nature of the state, anarchy, war, national interest, balance of power, and the role of diplomacy (table 3.1).

All of the other theories evolved in response to realism, and it is only natural that we begin with the framework.[55] Also known as realpolitik or power politics, *realism* takes a negative view of human nature. For realists, human beings are self-centered species whose behaviors are essentially driven by self-interest.[56] On the nature of the state, realists regard states as the primary and most important actors in international relations,[57] an orientation that puts a heavy accent on sovereignty.[58] They also view the world as *anarchic*, meaning absence of centralized authority at the world level necessary to enforce compliance among states.[59] The "condition" of anarchy results in a "security dilemma" leading sometimes to war,[60] which states seek to overcome through various self-help measures meant to promote security and survival, including maximizing their power, promoting national interests defined in terms of power resources,[61] and engaging in balance of power

Table 3.1. Narratives of Realism, Idealism, and Constructivism on Key Concepts of International Relations

Serial No.	*Feature or Concept*	*Theories*		
		Idealism	*Constructivism*	*Realism*
1.	View of human nature	Inherently positive	Could be positive or negative, depending on a state's construction of a situation	Inherently negative
2.	Nature of the state	Accent on individuals and private groups alongside the state	Accent on norms, identities, and interests	State sovereignty and the corollary of national interest (two rows below) defined in terms of power and security
3.	Anarchy	Posits that international cooperation is still possible, resulting in "positive sum"[a] outcomes, despite this "condition"	Anarchy is what a state makes of it, meaning it does not have to unrelievedly lead to conflict	Heavy accent on the "condition" and its negative consequence for state behavior
4.	National interest	Recognizes concept but does *not* limit it to survival and security	National interest is what the state makes it to be	Ties concept unrelievedly to survival and security
5.	War	Recognizes concept but stresses that cooperation is still possible regardless	War is not imminent or even inevitable unless states choose to make it so	Points to international conflicts as one of the unavoidable consequences of anarchy
6.	Balance of power	Recognizes concept but doesn't see it as preventing cooperation	Puts the *least* stress on concept, compared to idealism and realism	Depicts concept as a variable impelled by anarchy
7.	Role of diplomacy	Assigns diplomacy an enhanced role not limited to the imperatives of anarchy	Puts the *most* stress on concept, compared to idealism and realism	Diplomacy is important but subject to the imperatives of anarchy

[a]"Positive sum" outcomes are occurrence where all parties gain and no one loses. They are contrasted with "zero-sum" scenarios where, in the case of power for realists, "an increase in power for one another results in an equivalent decrease for others." Danziger, note 3, p. 286.

Source: Table created by author

politics, to ensure that no state or group of states dominates the international system.[62] Diplomacy is critical under this model, but only as a secondary issue subject to the imperatives of anarchy.[63]

In contrast to realism, *idealism* takes a decidedly positive view of human nature. For idealists, human beings can be intrinsically selfless entities capable of altruistic and cooperative behaviors.[64] On the nature of the state, idealists finger individuals and private groups, rather than the state all by itself, as primary actors in international relations.[65] Perceiving the dominant international role of states to be weakening, the result of various international forces that include globalization, idealists posit that, alongside states, other forces, such as international law and institutions, today contribute importantly to an evolving international community that, together with the state, deserve analytic attention.[66] Idealists concede anarchy and the other concepts associated with it, such as war, national interest, and balance of power, to the point that some within this school accept war as a legitimate means of settling international disputes.[67] However, consistent with the theory's positive view of human nature, their narrative related to anarchy and its consequences for international relations is much less thorough-going, compared to realists. Also vis-à-vis realists and consistent with their much broader view of international relations not limited to the role of states, idealists espouse wider possibilities for cooperation among states. Finally, idealists perceive a much broader role for diplomacy in international relations than the limited role dictated by the imperatives of anarchy that realists bestow this tool.

Constructivism takes a middle ground between realism and idealism that straddles the views of these two contending and competing theories regarding human nature,[68] as opposed to depicting it categorically as positive or negative. On the nature of the state, constructivism stresses the impact of norms, interests, and identities on state behavior.[69] Specifically, constructivists argue "that states come to accept norms and ideas through a process of socialization and internationalization."[70] Where realists "seem to take the goal of power as a given" and idealists imagine broader possibilities within the security dilemma of anarchy permitting international cooperation among states, constructivists "question[] the underlying goal of seeking power or, minimally strive[] to explain why states pursue certain goals to obtain social acceptance within the community of nations."[71] Finally, compared to the two previous theories, constructivism spots the least extreme narrative on anarchy and the consequences of this "condition" for international relations. For example, constructivists posit that the absence of a world government with authority to enforce compliance among states need not automatically lead to conflict, given that "anarchy is what states make of it."[72] Similarly, "foreign policy is what states make of it."[73]

In sum, on international affairs and foreign policy, constructivism is a theory in the middle that consciously seeks to overcome some of the embedded weaknesses of realism and idealism. The theory's location within these two rival theories calls to mind the answer of former Secretary of State Madeleine Albright responding to the question, "[h]ow often in the world of politics do reality and pragmatic considerations step on moral ideals?"[74]

> I think that I am somebody who has a good moral basis, foundation—an idealist, but also at various times pragmatic and realistic. That's why I've never liked the division between idealist and realist . . . because the two have to combine. So I sometimes call myself an idealistic realist or a realistic idealist. I believe that you have to have an overall set of goals and principles. But ultimately politics and foreign policy have to have compromise in it, because you're dealing with more than just what you want. Foreign policy is trying to get some other country to do what you want. But you do have to figure out what is acceptable, what is doable.[75]

More than its competitors, constructivism holds the key to the compromise former Secretary Albright talked about.

THREE JUSTIFICATIONS FOR THE CHOICE OF CONSTRUCTIVISM OVER REALISM AND IDEALISM AS THE THEORETICAL FRAMEWORK FOR THIS STUDY

Building on the discussion in the last section, there are three justifications for the choice of constructivism over realism and idealism as appropriate framework for the study of human rights in Nigeria's external relations. They are that: compared to its two famous rivals, constructivism affords the most scope for interjecting human rights in external affairs; more than liberalism, the theory stands a better chance of correcting the moralistic excesses of realism; and there are a growing number of studies that have successfully used constructivism in their own works.

Most-Scope Argument

The first justification supporting the preference of constructivism over its two famous rivals is that constructivism affords the most scope for interjecting human rights in external affairs. Realism sees little utility in bringing moral principles into international relations;[76] accordingly, realists counsel states to forswear such integration.[77] And with its stress on opportunities for cooperative behavior and by multiple actors on the international stage besides just states, idealism represents a welcome improvement on realism. However, the theory still takes as given some of the supposed consequences arising from the "condition" of anarchy, such as war and the necessity for balance of power, whether in its classic form or as collective security.

These inadequacies of realism and idealism leave constructivism as the only plausible explanatory alternative. Constructivists perceive the contexts in which states interact to range from competitive to cooperative, in a manner that permits states to respond in many different ways.[78] It treats national identity, whether essentialist or aspirational, as a primary site of political contestation and "constant process" that is "continuously shaped by various actors and communities both domestically and internationally."[79] Under the framework, states display their inclinations to human rights norms, including the application of those norms in external relations, based on identities and mutually constitutive interests that are continuously shaped through social interaction. Constructivism regards foreign policy as a means through which a state all at once achieves several goals, including expressing its national identity and interest, projecting a self-image that differentiates it from other states or political communities, providing a forum for political contestation, and interacting with other international actors, both state and non-state actors alike, in the process of socialization.[80]

In short, quite unlike any other, the framework adopts "a wider remit of how interests are defined."[81] If national interests are viewed as "intersubjective understanding of what it takes to advance power, influence, and wealth," then constructivism "is equipped to show how national interests are born, how they acquire their status of general political understandings, and how such understandings are politically selected in through political processes."[82] Under the theory, foreign policy is what a state makes of it, and the "condition" of anarchy in international relations poses no barriers to the pursuit of a human rights–based policy unless a state so chooses. This is in contradistinction to realism which equates these interests narrowly with power and security and assumes them a priori.[83]

Given the foregoing reasons, constructivism "offers a valuable way of studying how shared beliefs, rules, organizations, and cultural practices shape the behavior of states and other actors as well as their identities and interests."[84] As an explanatory tool, these factors add up to lend constructivism a realistic quality that its two competitors lack.[85] Constructivism embodies elements beyond the limited confines of its rivals, especially realism, that takes international relations and foreign policy, including the influence of human rights in these fields, "into new areas of inquiry."[86] By exploring the ever-evolving identities and interests that drive state behavior, constructivism "provide[s] unique insight into the underlying motivations of states international human rights policies."[87]

Correcting the Moralistic Excesses of Realism

Professor Donnelly presents one of the most broad-ranging criticisms of realist teaching related to human rights,[88] one revolved around the concern that realists may have "wildly exaggerated" "[a] valuable caution against moralistic excesses" "into a general principle of politics."[89] First, he concedes "a kernel of truth" to realists regarding the possibility that the demands of morality may conflict with the national interest defined in terms of power.[90] The problem, however, he noted is that "all objectives of foreign policy, not just moral ones, may compete with the national interest thus defined."[91] Second, "most moral objectives," including human rights goals, "can be pursued at a cost far less than national survival[]" critical to realism.[92] Third, nothing prevents a country, if it wishes, from including moral concerns, such as human rights, in its configuration of the national interest.[93] True, "[s]ecurity, independence, and prosperity may be unavoidable necessities of national political life."[94] However, governments need not limit themselves to just these concerns. "Even if the primary obligation of governments must be to the national interest defined in terms of power, this need not be their sole, or even ultimate, obligation."[95] Fourth, Donnelly takes issue with realist suggestion that moral behavior in foreign policy is not possible without the existence first of "an effective government that can deter and punish illegal actions."[96] He argues that "[j]ust as individuals may behave morally without government to enforce moral rules, so moral behavior is possible in international relations."[97] Finally, Donnelly concedes the point regarding the possible costs of moral behavior. Notwithstanding those costs, he said, "states often can act on moral concerns without harm, and sometimes with success. There may be good policy reasons to pursue amoral, or even immoral, policies in particular instances. There are, however, no good theoretical reasons for requiring amoral policies, or even accepting them as the norm."[98]

Given the plasticity embedded in its notion that foreign policy is what states make of it, more than idealism, constructivism holds a better explanatory chance of correcting the moralistic excesses of realism. Realism provided the dominant explanation for international politics for much of the period during the era of the Cold War, the ideological competition between East and West that ended in 1991 with the breakup of the Soviet Union.[99] But because of sea changes in world politics since then, including the expanded multilateralism globally within the United Nations and regionally as well as the increased advocacy for human rights by non-governmental organizations (NGOs)—events unanticipated by realism—the consensus is that the theory has become an inadequate framework for analyzing world politics, including the influence of human rights in external affairs.[100] The inadequacy leaves an explanatory hole that, because of its plasticity and robustness vis-à-vis idealism, constructivism has stepped up to fill.[101]

The Growing Number of Studies Using Constructivism That This Book Joins

The third and final justification for the choice of constructivism over its two rival theories revolves around the growing number of studies that have successfully applied the framework in their own works—that this book joins. These studies include *Why Canada Cares: Human Rights and Foreign Policy in Theory and Practice* by Andrew Lui,[102] and *Global Samaritans: Human Rights as Foreign Policy* by Alison Brysk.[103] To this list, arguably, should be added *Human Rights and Comparative Foreign Policy*, edited by David P. Forsythe,[104] even though the volume did not explicitly use the term *constructivism*.

In *Why Canada Cares*, Andrew Lui argued that while, on the one hand, Canada has rarely shown a willingness to sacrifice material advantages for international human rights causes, on the other hand, the country has pursued human rights in a broader attempt to cement individual rights as the cornerstone of Canadian federalism as well as to mitigate friction between the country's diverse social groups.[105] The book includes a postscript on the conservative administration of Stephen Harper, prime minister from 2006 to 2015, under whose government Canada managed to maintain its human rights foreign policy, even though initial indications, including failure to adopt a government White Paper on Canadian foreign policy released by the previous government, suggested otherwise.[106] In tracing and testing the influence of constructivism on Canadian policy, Liu began with realism as a baseline in Part 1, "interests all the way down," encompassing two chapters,[107] before delving into Part 2, "ideas all the way down," in an analysis, in three chapters, devoted specifically to constructivism.[108]

Overall, Lui takes the position that in examining Canadian policies, "realist and constructivist accounts should be regarded as complementary rather than as competing and mutually exclusive."[109] Because both realism and constructivism offer useful, albeit "immoderate and incomplete," insights on Canadian foreign policies,[110] Lui advised adoption of a "theoretical eclecticism" that "bridge both perspectives," instead of each in its pure form,[111] assuming that pure form exists for constructivism.

In *Global Samaritans*, Alison Brysk enquires into factors that impel political communities to pay prices, including the risk of lives, treasure, and diplomatic repercussions, to promote human rights in their external relations.[112] Using six states—Canada, Costa Rica, Japan, The Netherlands, South Africa, and Sweden[113]—along with a coalition of equally six groups, some of them states,[114] as case study, Professor Brysk illustrated how, even in a world of realist security dilemmas, some political communities reconstruct their national interests as a long-term common good to embed human rights in their foreign relations.[115] The book closed with a set of recommendations, instructively titled, "The World Needs More Canada,"[116] including nine learned lessons.[117] Eight of these lessons relevant here are: the reward in goodness; identity politics can be constructive; good citizens are made, rather than born; good Samaritans need only to be good enough, not perfect; different strokes for different folks, meaning that countries can and should specialize in projecting areas of domestic strength; it takes a global village; size is not everything as even small countries can punch above their weight when that weight is well developed and well distributed; and eternal vigilance is the price of global citizenship, given that the adoption of human rights foreign policies is progressive, rather than permanent.[118] The theoretical framework of the book anchored in constructivism revolved around the reconstruction of national interest necessary for a human rights–based foreign policy.[119]

Compared to Lui's work, as suggested already in the previous statement, the application of constructivism in Professor Brysk's book was an indirect one that synonymized or integrated constructivism and reconstructing the national interest. Principled foreign policy evident in constructivism "is possible," she said, "but it requires the continuous reconstruction of national interest through the constitution and projection of norms of cosmopolitan interdependence."[120] Brysk posited that, compared to states which do not consistently apply human rights in external relations, global Good Samaritans "have a broader, long-term vision of national interest. Global good citizens have reconstructed their national identity in accordance with universalist norms, roles, and expectations."[121] For these states, "the principled pursuit of human rights is a consciously constructed alternative pathway of enlightened self-interest."[122] More than rival theories, constructivism "draws our attention to the active and political work of putting ideas into practice";[123] for Brysk "[a] constructivist theory of foreign policy can help us to understand how cosmopolitan political cultures like human rights values make sense—and how such cultures are learned."[124] Moreover, a human rights–based foreign policy need not preclude realism.[125] "Ideas matter, but constructivism tells us that human rights norms are always competing with alternative discourses of security threat, parochial nationalism, and narrowly material, short-term calculation."[126] In fact, "the interplay of moral and material interests can help to explain the selectivity and targeting of principled foreign policy."[127] Brysk's theoretical framework embedded in constructivism includes a showing of "identities as interests."[128] Because "[s]tates are political communities that seek values and identity[,]"[129] in contradistinction to realist teaching, under constructivism "what interests a nation is not always state security."[130] Instead, "[n]ations also expend scarce resources in pursuit of identity, which is often formed in international relationships."[131]

In *Human Rights and Comparative Foreign Policy*, Professors Forsythe and his colleagues examined the influence or lack thereof of human rights in the foreign policies of a wide range of contemporary states, using a common framework of analysis consisting of an intersection of domestic and foreign factors for the ten political communities covered in their work.[132] The authors made several important points relating to the subject matter. First is an increased salience to human rights in the foreign policies of many contemporary states. However, secondly, many states who interject human rights in their external affairs, including even liberal-democratic ones, such as the United Kingdom and the United States, much of the time fail to accord human rights issues the same level they assign traditional security and economic concerns. Related to this second factor, due to factors, such as national political culture and perceived national interests, different states bring different emphases to their human rights diplomacy. A fourth and final issue is the matter of inconsistency that arises when human rights are balanced against competing foreign policy when, for example, states treat comparable human rights violations in different countries differently.[133]

Though the introduction unveils some useful conceptual ideas that frame the work, the theoretical chapter of the volume by Jack Donnelly, modestly titled "An Overview," is chapter 12.[134] Professor Donnelly's discussion covers four separate issues, two of which—the influence of national identity on human rights, and self-image[135]—are germane to this chapter which unveils constructivism and justifies the choice of the theory as an appropriate framework for this study on human rights in Nigeria's external relations. In statements that smack of constructivism, Donnelly posited that a state's national interest "is a matter of what [that] state values," based partly on "how that state sees itself, both nationally and internationally[,]"[136] and that many states' human rights policies are largely "identity based," in that "they reflect the extent to which (national and international) human rights values have shaped or re-shaped understandings of who they are and what they value."[137] Next on self-images, Donnelly indicated that a state's national self-image is not "exhausted by a commitment to human rights."[138] Instead, "in addition to human rights, sovereignty and non-intervention are vital norms of international society."[139] And because "[a]ll states, in fact, have a deeper and more enthusiastic commitment to sovereignty than to human rights," he indicated, it is foolhardy to "overestimate either human rights or sovereignty" in the external behavior of states.[140] He depicted on a quadrant based on "orientation toward international society" from "nationalist" on the left to "internationalist" on the right, the range of national attitudes toward international human rights of ten states covered in the volume.[141]

SUMMATION

This chapter is a discussion on the justification of constructivism as theoretical framework for this work entailing, as background issue, a survey of eight theories; juxtaposition of constructivism to two other leading theories in an attempt to better understand it; and a review of previous works that successfully applied constructivism the study here now joins. Weissbrodt and his colleagues observe that constructivism may "suffer from a lack of sincerity on the part of the state actors."[142] But rather than a flaw as such, this may be a compliment that speaks to the theory's plasticity. And assuming, for the sake of argument, that the theory is not a strong connection, it may be the best under the circumstances where no other theory comes close. The fact of the matter is that vis-à-vis its two rival theories, constructivism is more "adequately sensitive to the socially constructed nature of the identities and norms that shape beliefs and guide actions taken by" states and other actors in international relations.[143] For their seminal volume, Professor Forsythe and his team could not include numerous states like Nigeria that deserve examination because of budgetary constraints.[144] This study fills that gap with a study on the country that tests the theory of constructivism using the country.

Some studies limit the applications embedding a scientific enterprise to the four elements of: a set of well-formulated research questions, conceptual framework, a methodology, and theoretical framework.[145] Others include a historical background.[146] This work falls into the latter category and includes a historical backdrop on human rights in Nigeria's external relations that forms the topic of chapter 4.

NOTES

1. Michael G. Maxfield & Earl R. Babbie, *Research Methods for Criminal Justice and Criminology, 7th Ed.* (Stamford, CT: Cengage Learning, 2015): 31–32.
2. Ibid., p. 14.
3. *Liberalism* is sometimes interchanged in the literature with *idealism*. See James N. Danziger, *Understanding the Political World: A Comparative Introduction to Political Science, 11th Ed.* (New York: Pearson, 2013): 286; and Jack Donnelly, *International Human Rights, 4th Ed.* (Boulder, CO: Westview Press, 2013): 29. This researcher chose *idealism* to keep things simple, given the several variants within this

ideology that can confuse all but the most initiated reader. See Terence Ball et al., *Political Ideologies and the Democratic Ideal, 9th Ed.* (Boston, MA: Pearson, 2014): 44–93 (highlighting three divisions—classical liberalism, neoclassical liberalism, and reformist (or welfare)—within this one school of thought).

4. My research turned up a ninth theory, *institutionalism*, which, however, is not included in this survey. See David Weissbrodt et al., *International Human Rights: Law, Policy, and Process, 4th Ed.* (San Francisco, CA: LexisNexis, 2009): 28 (including institutionalism as the second of four explanations as to why states agree to and often obey international human rights). As Professor Weissbrodt and his colleagues elaborate, "Institutionalists start from a similar set of assumptions as do realists," the only difference being that, unlike realists, "institutionalists focus on the gains that states obtain by cooperating with other nations in the context of inter-governmental relationships created by membership in international organizations." Ibid. Sometimes, as in the last statement, the description of institutionalists calls to mind idealism. Because of the fussy demarcation from other theories, institutionalism is *not* among the set of theories surveyed in this section.

5. See also note 3.

6. Donnelly, note 3, p. 29; see also J. Tyler Dickovick & Jonathan Eastwood, *Comparative Politics: Integrating Theories, Methods, and Cases* (New York: Oxford University Press, 2013): 400.

7. Danziger, note 3, p. 286. A *state* is the tool for control over a specific territory that comes in a range of sizes with some, such as China, big (pop. over 1.3 billion people) and others, such as Andorra (pop. over 79,000 people), small. "What Is a 'State,'" *Global Policy Forum*, https://www.globalpolicy.org/nations-a-states/what-is-a-state.html. Altogether, there are 196 states in the world, all of which, but Kosovo, Taiwan, and the Vatican, are members of the United Nations. "Member States," United Nations, http://www.un.org/depts/dhl/unms/cms.shtml; Matt Rosenberg, "Non-Members of the United Nations," *About.com*, http://geography.about.com/od/politicalgeography/a/nun.htm.

8. Donnelly, note 3, p. 29. "To pursue a moral foreign policy," realists contend, "would not only be foolishly unsuccessful, but also leave one's country vulnerable to the power of self-interested states." Ibid.

9. See Dickovick & Eastwood, note 6, pp. 400–2. *Prisoner's dilemma* is a game model wherein two actors would benefit from cooperation, but where both parties have individual incentives that lead them to ultimately defect from cooperation. *Game theory* consists of strategic interactions between actors, rooted in mathematical modeling, wherein the "players" respond rationally to incentives and to the expected actions of other players. Ibid., p. 400.

10. Weissbrodt et al., note 4, p. 26. Incidentally, neo-realism appears to be little different from institutionalism which framework Professors Weissbrodt and his colleagues include among their theories of why states ratify and enforce human rights treaties and accept other human rights norms. See note 4.

11. Danziger, note 3, p. 286.

12. Dickovick & Eastwood, note 6, p. 402.

13. Ibid.

14. Danziger, note 3, p. 286.

15. Ibid. For idealists, "[i]f a state's actions reduce the welfare of people in any country or increase interstate conflict and war, it is usually because of poorly designed institutions (e.g., governments, economic systems, and legal systems), not because people and states are evil or selfish." Ibid.

16. Danziger, note 3, p. 287.

17. Ibid.

18. Dickovick & Eastwood, note 6, p. 404.

19. Danziger, note 3, p. 40. See also Dickovick & Eastwood, note 6, p. 404.

20. Ball et al., note 3, p. 134. Marxists deny the view coming from the likes of realism that individuals are by nature competitive and self-centered. If per chance they seem to be so, they argue, it is because of social conditions which encourage and reward these traits. Otherwise, they are by nature potentially caring and cooperative, and able and willing to work for the common good. Ibid., p. 135.

21. Ibid., p. 136, Fig. 5.1 (diagramming the socialist view of freedom)

22. Ibid.

23. Danziger, note 3, p. 287.

24. Ibid.

25. Ball et al., note 3, p. 244 (diagramming the liberal feminist view of freedom).

26. Ibid.

27. Ellen Grisby, *Analyzing Politics: An Introduction to Political Science, 5th Ed.* (Belmont, CA: Wadsworth Cengage Learning, 2012): 142.

28. Ibid., pp. 142, 147–52.

29. Ibid., p. 160.

30. Ibid., p. 153.

31. Ibid.

32. Ibid., p. 160.

33. Ball et al., note 3, p. 292, Fig. 9.2 (diagramming the "green" view of freedom).

34. Ibid.

35. Ibid., p. 291.

36. Ibid.

37. Grisby, note 27, p. 159.

38. Ibid.

39. Ibid.

40. Ibid.

41. Ibid., p. 160.

42. Ibid.

43. Danziger, note 3, p. 40.

44. Ball et al., note 3, p. 302.

45. Ibid., p. 305.

46. Ibid.

47. Ibid., p. 308, fig. 10.1 (diagramming the radical Islamist conception of freedom).

48. Ibid.

49. Ibid., pp. 310–11.

50. Regarding this ideological rivalry between East and West, led by the now defunct Soviet Union and the United States, respectively, see, e.g., Edward H. Judge & John W. Langdon, *The Cold War: A Global History with Documents, 2d Ed.* (Upper Saddle River, N.J.: Prentice Hall, 2010).

51. Dickovick & Eastwood, note 6, p. 404.

52. Ibid.

53. See ibid., pp. 400–44.

54. *Left* and *right* on the political spectrum is a manner of classifying political positions, ideologies, and parties, with *left* signifying radicalism and *right* conservatism. The terms take their origins from the seating order in the first National Assembly following the French Revolution of 1789. Supporters of the revolution sat on the left, while lawmakers supporting the king (or the status quo) sat on the right. See Marcel Gauchet, "Right and Left," *in* Pierre Nora & Lawrence D. Kritzman, eds., *Realms of Memory: Conflicts and Divisions* (New York: Columbia University Press, 1997): 242–45.

55. The theory dates back to the fifth century BCE. See "Political Realism in International Relations," *Stanford Encyclopedia of Philosophy* (Jul. 26, 2010, rev. Apr. 2, 2013), http://plato.stanford.edu/entries/realism-intl-relations/ (sketching the roots of the realist tradition to include Thucydides' thesis on the importance of power, Machiavelli's critique of the moral tradition, and Hobbes's concept of the state of nature).

56. See Danziger, note 3, p. 286; Donnelly, note 3, p. 29; Hans J. Morgenthau, *Politics Among Nations: The Struggle for Power and Peace, 5th Ed.* (New York: Alfred A. Knopf, 1978): 6 (warning that "[w]e cannot conclude from the good intentions of a statesman that his foreign policies will be either morally praiseworthy or politically successful.").

57. Weissbrodt et al., note 4, p. 26; Danziger, note 3, p. 286.

58. Sovereignty "requires independence from any outside power and final authority over men who live within certain boundaries." Joseph R. Strayer, *On the Medieval Origins of the Modern State* (Princeton, NJ: Princeton University Press, 2005): 58. It also forbids intervention into "matters which are essentially within the domestic jurisdiction of any state . . ." Charter of the United Nations (1945), 59 Stat. 1031, T.S. 993, 3 Bevans 1153, Art. 2 (7). The doctrine implies two things: control over a territory, and source of legitimate authority.

59. See Brian C. Schmidt, *The Political Discourse of Anarchy: A Disciplinary History of International Relations* (Albany, N.Y.: State University of New York Press, 1998), *passim*.

60. This does not necessarily mean that realists like war. To the contrary, many realists study the causes of war in an attempt to reduce the chances of future conflicts. See Robert Jervis, "Realism in the Study of World Politics," *in* Peter J. Katzenstein et al., eds., *Explorations and Contestation in the Study of World Politics* (Cambridge, MA: MIT Press, 1999): 334.

61. See Morgenthau, note 56, p. 5 (positing that "[t]he main signpost that helps political realism to find its way through the landscape of international politics is the concept of interest defined in terms of *power*"—in the same manner that economics, for example, defines interest in terms of *wealth*).

62. See, e.g., John A. Vasquez & Colin Elman, eds., *Realism and the Balance of Power: A New Debate* (Upper Saddle River, N.J.: Prentice Hall, 2005); and Michael Sheehan, *Balance of Power: History and Theory* (New York: Routledge, 1996).

63. See Paul Sharp, *Diplomatic Theory of International Relations*, Cambridge Studies in International Relations No. 111 (New York: Cambridge University Press, 2009): 53–73 (discussing diplomacy and diplomats in realist theory).

64. See Danziger, note 3, p. 286. For example, idealists see no reason why the nonviolent principles and cooperative techniques, key to nonviolent resolution of disputes at the domestic level, should not be extended to the international level. See Jonathan Schell, *The Unconquerable World: Power, Nonviolence, and the Will of the People* (New York: Henry Holt & Co., 2003): 265–79.

65. Weissbrodt et al., note 4, p. 29.

66. For example, for idealists, state power matters, but it is a power exercised within a framework of international rules and institutions capable of facilitating cooperation—or stimulating conflict. See Karen A. Mingst & Margaret P. Karns, *The United Nations in the 21st Century, 4th Ed.* (Westview Press, 2012): 10. Similarly, for idealists, states are pluralistic (not unitary actors as realists see them) who, because their goals vary and their interests change, do not apply one single definition of national interests. Ibid.

67. To be sure, the position of idealists on the consequences for international relations arising from the "condition" of anarchy is more complex than I have sketched here. On the one hand, there are the so-called liberal hawks who accept war as a legitimate means for settling international disputes. See Joseph S. Nye, Jr., *Understanding International Conflicts: An Introduction to Theory and History, 7th Ed.* (New York: Longman, 2008): 4. On the other hand, consistent with the vision of Woodrow Wilson, many idealists espouse a collective security arrangement in place of the balance of power. See Margaret MacMillan, *Paris 1919: Six Months That Changed the World* (New York: Random House, 2003): 3–16 (focusing on Woodrow Wilson).

68. Emanuel Adler, "Seizing the Middle Ground: Constructivism in World Politics," *European Journal of Int'l Relations,* Vol. 3 (1997): 319–63 (situating constructivism as a "middle ground" between realism and idealism).

69. See Weissbrodt et al., note 4, p. 30; Alison Brysk, *Global Good Samaritans: Human Rights as Foreign Policy* (New York: Oxford University Press, 2009): 33–4.

70. Weissbrodt et al., note 4, p. 29.

71. Ibid.

72. Alexander Wendt, "Anarchy Is What States Make of It: The Social Construction of Power Politics," *Int'l Organization*, Vol. 46 (1992): 391–425.

73. Steve Smith, "Foreign Policy Is What States Make of It: Social Construction and International Relations Theory," *in* Vendulka Kubálková, ed., *Foreign Policy in a Constructed World* (Armonk, N.Y.: M.E. Sharpe, 2001): 38–55.

74. "Madeleine Albright Extended Interview," PBS (May 19, 2006), http://www.pbs.org/wnet/religionandethics/2006/05/19/may-19-2006-madeleine-albright-extended-intreview/2838/.

75. Ibid.

76. See Donnelly, note 3, p. 28 (observing that for realists, "there is no significant independent international community, let alone an international body with the right to act on behalf of human rights."). In realists' view, the only permissible guide to foreign policy should be considerations of the national interest, defined in terms of power and security. Ibid., p. 29.

77. George Kennan, a contemporary realist thinker and an architect of U.S. post–World War II foreign policy, argued that "[t]he process of government . . . is a practical exercise and not a moral one." Opining that misgovernment has been and will always remain "the common condition of most of mankind," Kennan likened the U.S. government's attempt to correct "the political habits of large parts of the world's population" to "tilting against the windmills." Donnelly, note 3, pp. 29–30 (citing three works Kennan published from 1954 to 1986).

78. See Alexander Wendt, *Social Theory of International Politics* (New York: Cambridge University Press, 1999), *passim.*

79. Andrew Lui, *Why Canada Cares: Human Rights and Foreign Policy in Theory and Practice* (Montreal, Canada: McGill-Queen's University Press, 2012): 117.

80. See Lui, note 79, p. 117.

81. Ibid., p. 116.

82. Adler, note 68, p. 337.

83. Lui, note 79, p. 116.

84. Mingst & Karns, note 66, p. 11.

85. See Daniel C. Thomas, *The Helsinki Effect: International Norms, Human Rights, and the Demise of Communism* (Princeton, N.J.: Princeton University Press, 2001): 15 (reasoning that the more salient the identity specified by an international norm, "the more the actor will seek to fulfill its obligations under that norm.").

86. Lui, note 79, p. 112.

87. Ibid.

88. See Donnelly, note 3, pp. 29–30.

89. Ibid., p. 30.

90. Ibid., p. 30.

91. Ibid.

92. Ibid.

93. Ibid.

94. Ibid.

95. Ibid.

96. Ibid.

97. Ibid., p. 30.

98. Ibid.

99. See note 50.

100. Mingst & Karns, note 66, p. 10.

101. Lui, note 79, p. 112.

102. Lui, note 79, *passim.*

103. Brysk, note 69.

104. David P. Forsythe, ed., *Human Rights and Comparative Foreign Policy* (New York: United Nations University Press, 2000).

105. See generally Lui, note 79; ibid., p. 7.
106. Ibid., pp. 177–81.
107. Ibid., pp. 21–95.
108. Ibid., pp. 99–176.
109. Ibid., p. 164.
110. Ibid., p. 168.
111. Ibid., p. 169. On this issue, Lui's argument begins to sound confusing. Dismissing a "middle ground" between the extremes of realism and constructivism, he contended that "theoretical eclecticism is more useful than (1) adopting either realism or constructivism or (2) attempting to synthesize them." *Id.* 168. But how can one configure an eclectic theory that does not synthesize the two models? Lui conveyed that "[r]ather than favoring one theoretical perspective over another or calling for a conceptual synthesis between the two, however, [he] stress[es] the need for theoretical pluralism." Ibid., p. 8. What makes a *theoretical pluralism* different from *conceptual synthesis*, in the context of the two theories used in his study?
112. See Brysk, note 69, *passim*.
113. Ibid., pp. 42–196.
114. This set of transnational human rights organizations which Brysk dubs "Coalitions of the Caring" are: the Organization for Security and Cooperation in Europe (OSCE), the Human Security Network, the Community of Democracies (Club Dem, comprising 10 states), the International Institute for Democracy and Electoral Assistance (IDEA), the Organization for Economic Cooperation and Development (OECD) Donor Assistance Committee (comprising 30 developed northern states), and the Network of National Human Rights Institutions (Team Gov). Brysk, note 70, pp. 197–219.
115. See Brysk, note 69, *passim*.
116. Brysk, note 69, pp. 220–34.
117. Ibid., pp. 220–24.
118. Ibid.
119. Ibid., pp. 31–40.
120. Ibid., p. 40.
121. Ibid., p. 31.
122. Ibid., p. 32.
123. Ibid.
124. Ibid., p. 31.
125. See ibid., p. 32 (pointing out that "[a]n emphasis on normative change can be combined with a recognition of rationalist parameters or structural dialectics of foreign policy.").
126. Ibid., p. 40.
127. Ibid., p. 33.
128. Ibid., pp. 33–37.
129. Ibid., p. 33.
130. Ibid.
131. Ibid.
132. Forsythe, ed., *Human Rights and Comparative Foreign Policy*, note 104, *passim*. The ten political communities covered in the book are the United States, the

Netherlands, the United Kingdom, and Japan, classified under "liberal democracies," along with Russia, India, Iran, Central Europe (consisting of Hungary, the Czech Republic, and Poland), South Africa since 1994, and Latin America. Ibid., pp. 21–309.

133. Forsythe, ed., *Human Rights and Comparative Foreign Policy*, note 104, *passim*. See also Donnelly, note 3, p. 145 (discussing the charge of inconsistency in international human rights policies).

134. Jack Donnelly, "An Overview," *in* Forsythe, ed., *Human Rights and Comparative Foreign Policy*, note 104, pp. 310–34.

135. Ibid. The two not relevant here are his comments relating to the intensity of human rights commitments, ibid., pp. 321–24, and evaluation of international human rights policies, ibid., pp. 324–31.

136. Ibid., p. 311.

137. Ibid.

138. Ibid., p. 315.

139. Ibid., p. 318.

140. Ibid.

141. Ibid., p. 320 (fig. 12.1). Six of the countries—South Africa, Hungary, Japan, Netherlands, Costa Rica, and the U.K.—are clustered on the "international" end of the quadrant with the last three close to the right-hand margin. Three of the countries, Russia, India, and the United States, are placed around the center of the quadrant with Russia and India much closer to the "nationalist" end, compared to the United States. Iran stood alone under the "nationalist" end of the diagram. Ibid.

142. Weissbrodt et al., note 4, p. 29.

143. Danziger, note 3, p. 287.

144. See David P. Forsythe, "Introduction," *in* Forsythe, ed., *Human Rights and Comparative Foreign Policy*, note 104, p. 17 (indicating, "[w]ith an unlimited budget and a multi-volume project, we could have added numerous states that merit study: France, Norway, Germany, Nigeria, Kenya, Mexico, Brazil, Pakistan, Israel, the Philippines, etc.").

145. See generally Thomas Kuhn, *The Structure of Scientific Revolutions, 3d Ed.* (Chicago, IL: University of Chicago, 1996).

146. See, e.g., Peter R. Baehr, "Trials and Errors: The Netherlands and Human Rights," *in* Forsythe, ed., *Human Rights and Comparative Foreign Policy*, note 104, pp. 50–52 (providing a "historical background" preceding his analysis).

Chapter Four

Activities That Shape the Current Patterns of Politics

Historical Backdrop on Human Rights in Nigeria's External Relations

This study critically assesses the influence of human rights in Nigeria's external relations from the timeline of the country's independence from the United Kingdom in 1960 to the present time. Altogether, there are five periods involved: the First Republic from 1960 to 1966, the first round of military rule from 1966 to 1979, the Second Republic from 1979 to 1983, the second round of military rule from 1983 to 1999, and the Fourth Republic since 1999[1] (see table 4.1 below). However, the story of human rights in Nigeria's external relations will be incomplete without the era(s) before independence in 1960. Awareness "of a country's past" is necessary "to fully understand the nature and issues of [its] contemporary politics," and it is imperative that the researcher look at the politics of a state in question in tandem with "many other activities that have shaped the current pattern of politics."[2] Accordingly, although the main focus in this chapter is on the era since 1960, the ensuing discussion also includes two past eras—the precolonial and colonial timeframes—that before 1960 shaped the current patterns of politics in Nigeria.

There are some advantages in including the pre-independence past. First, doing so starts the story of human rights in Nigeria's external relations from its proverbial beginning and provides useful insights related to the topic. Second, including the pre-independence past fits in with and feeds well into the methodology of this work anchored in within-case comparison (WCC).[3] WCC involves the study of one country at different points in time and space. Under this technique, "the researcher look[s] more carefully within [his or her] own case(s) to examine the variations there[in]," in the hope that "[l]ooking at different moments in time or in space may allow us to dig deeper into a case to better understand our evidence."[4] Including the pre-independence period affords more canvas in time duration for comparative analysis.

This chapter complements, completes—and valorizes—the conceptual and theoretical underbrushes laid out in chapters 2 and 3. Ethics is an element of normative analysis involving the "examination, justification, and critical analysis of morality."[5] And back in time, ethical considerations, presaging what today we might call human rights, play a role in the foreign policy of many nations.[6] Different ways through which moral norms influence international relations include the conscience of decision makers, the influence of domestic public opinion, and the influence of international reputation.[7] As the experience of the United States exemplifies, ethical considerations in the foreign policy of a nation can go on for a long time, all the while lacking in systematization as far as meets the eyes, before congealing into "a pattern of persistent principled politics" going beyond "episodic altruism" that defines the adoption of a human rights policy.[8] Accordingly, a common streak that runs through the three timeframes analyzed below—the precolonial, colonial, and postcolonial eras—is the influence of ethical considerations, short and shorn of any full-blown human rights policy, in Nigeria's external relations.[9]

PRECOLONIAL ERA

Modern-day Nigeria came into existence in 1914 when three territories previously maintained separately by Britain—the northern protectorate, southern protectorate, and the colony of Lagos—were consolidated into one entity in a process Nigerians call "the amalgamation."[10] Nigeria is a "new state" superimposed on numerous "old societies";[11] the period before then, dating back more than 5,000 years, constitute the country's precolonial era.[12] Specifically, present-day Nigeria is a multinational state with over 250 ethnic groups, and language groups double that number.[13] Therefore, discussion on human rights in precolonial Nigeria boils down ultimately to ethical practices prevalent among ethnic groups, conveniently the major ones, within the areas that formed modern-day Nigeria. Three of the most populous groups are the Igbo in the East, the Yoruba in the West, and the Hausa-Fulani in the North.[14] This "ethnic triumvirate" makes up about two-thirds of the country's population.[15] Many of the remaining more than 200 groups are small, some of them numbering only in the tens of thousands.[16] The Hausa-Fulani had a highly centralized system centered on Emirs who combined political and religious powers in a system characterized by few checks and balances.[17] In contrast, Igbo societies were kingless communities, who organized themselves into over two thousand villages, marked by decentralized political powers.[18] "[M]onarchical and hierarchically structured and centralized with some measure of republicanism," the Yoruba represented a midpoint between the Hausa-Fulani and the Igbo.[19]

As with the composition of the areas stitched together to form modern-day Nigeria, complexity surrounds the search for human rights in precolonial Nigeria, an inquiry complicated by paucity of available data related to this era.[20] A temptation is to regard this period as an era of pre-rights when humans lived "in small tribes" isolated from outsiders whom they perceived as a possible threat to survival.[21] After all, as the human rights scholar Chidi Odinkalu points out, some African languages lack the term *human rights*.[22] Add to these the fact that understanding of human rights in the sense we know it today as "the rights of all people, and of all people equally,"[23] is an occurrence of recent vintage that goes back to the end of World War II with the inauguration of the United Nations organization.[24] As Pope Francis averred in a different context, "it is difficult to judge the past by the criteria of the present."[25] However, the matter is more complicated than it seems at first sight. "Although in some African languages there is no direct equivalent to the phrase 'human rights,'" both the notion of justice that underlies human rights and the experience of struggle to realize these rights are well known to Africa.[26] This is because with or without the formal language of human rights, individuals and communities "will struggle for their rights."[27] Accordingly, some societies in the areas subsequently brought together as Nigeria promoted as well as violated approximations or simulacrums of these rights.[28]

Take the Igbo as example.[29] On the one hand, precolonial Igbo communities "organized themselves into village democracies, over 2,000 in all, where they practiced a direct democracy characterized by a system of checks and balances, the pursuit of consensus through protracted discussion, the use of religious sanctions, and political institutions designed to combine popular participation with weighting for experience, among other features."[30] As the historian Elizabeth Isichei recounted in her work on Igbo history, "[o]ne of the things that struck the first Western visitors to Igboland, was the extent to which democracy was truly practiced."[31] And although in precolonial Igbo societies, elderly males ran affairs, "there was also much scope for individual mobility, and political participation was open to many, including women."[32] On the other hand, these societies also perpetrated practices that today would militate against human rights. These derogations include human sacrifice, trial by ordeal, rampant kidnapping, twin killings, and maintenance of the *osu* caste system.[33]

Of the last, one commentator observed elaborately that the practice "involves inequality in freedom of movement and choice of residence, inequality in the right of peaceful association, inequality of residence, in[e]quality in the right of peaceful association, inequality in the enjoyment of the right to marry and establish a family, [and] inequality in access to public office."[34] The practice was abolished in Eastern Nigeria in 1956, though the law did not change attitudes in some communities where the discrimination lingered.[35] However, Nigeria's 1999 Constitution forbids discrimination against individuals based on circumstances of birth, by interpretation including any caste system.[36]

The reader should keep in mind that *not* all Igbo communities perpetrated these derogations.[37] Moreover, some of these practices, such as human sacrifice, trial by order, and rampant kidnapping, were occurrences associated with the slave trade.[38] In sum, using the Igbo as example, it is fair to conclude with the assessment of Professor Eze that, while societies in precolonial Nigeria, like elsewhere in Africa, "witness[ed] some measure of *concern* for human rights," they "did not go far enough" in *protecting* these rights.[39]

COLONIAL ERA

British control of Nigeria took place from the late nineteenth century until the country's independence in 1960. Although European colonial authorities justified some of their imperialist activities in Africa on human rights grounds,[40] colonial control marked a frontal assault on every category of human rights—political and civil (or political-civil) rights; economic, social, and cultural (or socioeconomic) rights; and collective (or group) rights.[41] Repressive practices like forced labor, forced taxation, and the use of sedition laws as a weapon designed to stamp out opposition to foreign rule and impede the evolution of a free press marked its negation of political-civil rights.[42] Colonial governance was also an attack on socioeconomic rights because foreign rule is inconsistent with any meaningful notion of economic development.[43] In Nigeria and other dependent territories, European colonialism sowed the seed for the distortion of economic life that until that date many of these societies had yet to overcome.[44] As Professor Isichei observed concerning the paucity of British socioeconomic human rights benefits in Eastern Nigeria, "the important thing to the historian of Igboland is the sobering reflection that after half a century of colonial rule and mission, over 80 [percent] of the population was illiterate."[45] Lastly, colonial rule contradicted collective rights because foreign rule violated the right of people to determine their destiny for themselves rather than have foreigners do so for them.[46] During World War II, British Prime Minister Winston S. Churchill opposed extending to Nigeria and other British colonies the self-determination concept embedded in the Atlantic Charter of 1941,[47] on the ground that these colonies were not "sovereign," compared to countries like Poland occupied by Nazi-ruled Germany, which were accorded the right.[48] In contrast, President Franklin D. Roosevelt, with whom Churchill signed the Atlantic Charter, seemed committed to the dismantling of all colonial empires, including those held by the United Kingdom, because of the conditions that lead to war the colonial system represented.[49] Therefore, the "wind of change" in nationalism that ultimately reached the shores of these British colonies in Africa[50] occurred *in spite of* British opposition.

In a nutshell, as opposed to being vehicles for promoting human rights, European colonial institutions were primarily "structures of exploitation, despotism, and degradation";[51] colonialism, wherever it existed in Africa, was something "imposed by violence, and maintained by its potential capacity for violence."[52] Europe had little in the way of a human rights plan for its colonies in Africa beyond their use as sources of raw materials for European industrialization and as markets for excess outputs. Instead, in the apt language of one analyst, "[t]he entire architecture of colonial rule, like that of military rule down the road in [Africa], was built and maintained solely and completely on naked force designed to *crush* any and every 'native' resistance to external domination."[53]

But this is not to say that every aspect of British rule in Nigeria was unrelievedly evil, given the existence of certain positive features with ramifications for human rights from that experience. First, British rule injected a "capitalist mode of production and the principles of liberal democracy" that inspired subsequent economic and political developments in Nigeria and other British colonies.[54] Secondly, British rule eliminated precolonial practices, with negative ramifications for human rights, such as human sacrifices, trial by ordeal, rampant kidnapping, twin-killings, and the operation of a caste system,[55] some of which, like the first three, are traceable to the slave trade,[56] which the colonial system replaced. Thirdly, uniquely for Nigeria, the benefits of colonial rule included the creation of a big state with the potential to play a major role in international relations, including international human rights. Thanks to British effort and ingenuity, at independence in 1960, Nigeria had all the features and trappings of a democratic state that, for many commentators, made it "a beacon of hope for democracy" in Africa.[57] These features included a federal constitution, one of few in Africa, that guaranteed a measure of autonomy to three regions, increased to four in 1963; a parliamentary democracy on the British Westminster model, based on majority rule; bill of rights embedded in a constitutional document that calls to mind the American constitution; and a regional, multiparty system that set the country apart from many African countries that adopted a one-party system soon after independence.[58] Finally, under British tutelage, Nigeria made important strides in constitutionalism,[59] including the growth of political parties,[60] some of which, interestingly, had their origins in opposition to British foreign rule.

But there were also several downsides to colonial rule that over time has defied easy resolution. First, following the forced amalgamated of incompatible ethnic groups with no prior history of living together, British colonial authorities made little attempt to create a coherent country out of these disparate groups.[61] Professor Ayoade described Nigeria's birth in 1914 variously as an "amalgamation without integration" aimed mainly at "freeing the British treasury of the financial responsibility for Northern Nigeria" in a manner that invokes the analogy of a "prisoner pa[ying] for his own handcuffs."[62] He likened the British indirect rule experiment in the country to a "LEGO, a line of construction toys consisting of colorful interlocking plastic blocks[,]" so un-tightly "assembled to require more than a child's effort to separate and re-assemble to make other objects."[63] Second, related to this first factor, British rule engendered domination by the north.[64] Implementation of British "indirect rule" in Nigeria created a system that insulated the Islamic North from the "corruption" of the South. The insulation included restriction of missionary activities with the accompanying educational benefits those activities brought along, an occurrence which stunted educational growth in the North vis-à-vis the South. More than this, British rule engendered preferences for Fulanis, which reeked of racism, and that some analysts called "British-supervised indigenous or internal colonialism."[65] British writers and administrators repeatedly referred to the Fulani as a ruler race in glowing terms that included "capable race," "European in form," "races higher than the negroid type," and "races born to conquer."[66] With British support and encouragement, in the lead up to independence, northern leaders in two conferences (one at Ibadan in 1950 and another in London in 1953) made demands for autonomy, inconsistent with a federal system of government, all of which were granted to stave the threat of northern secession and keep them in an independent Nigeria. These concessions, which reinforced northern domination in an independent country, included assignment of 50 percent of the seats in the national legislature and a separate public service. The advantages were codified in the Littleton Constitution of 1954 which created a federal arrangement for the country wherein the Northern Region had more seats in the national legislature than the Eastern and Western Regions combined.[67] Since independence, northern leaders have striven hard to maintain these advantages, to the detriment of nation-building and national integration.[68]

Even the positive contributions of colonial rule over time turned out to be dubious. For example, some commentators, including surviving British public servants who saw colonial service in Nigeria, have wondered whether the experiment of forcibly transmuting disagreeable ethnic groups into one mega-state as the United Kingdom did in Nigeria was a good idea.[69] Similarly, the model of constitutional development bequeathed to Nigeria from British colonial rule has come under question because of its slowness in generating the habit of constitutionalism and the culture of the rule of law among the citizenry of the country.[70] For these various reasons, while there is no question regarding "the influence of human rights ideas" at home and abroad in dismantling the British colonial system,[71] ultimately making way for Nigeria's independence, in the final analysis, given its abstruse and diffuse nature, that influence seems more apparent than real.

POSTCOLONIAL ERA: SURVEY OF FIVE PERIODS AND FIFTEEN GOVERNMENTS

Dependency status is inconsistent with the conduct of foreign policy. Nigeria shed that status when it gained independence on October 1, 1960, sealing the achievement with admission into the United Nations on October 7, 1960, as the 99th member of the organization.[72] Accordingly, compared to the colonial era, the postcolonial era—ushered in by independence in 1960, and capped by severance of the ligament of ties to the British monarchy through the achievement of republican status three years later—afforded Nigerian leaders the opportunity, previously lacking, to design and implement an indigenous foreign policy.[73] To restate, five periods mark this era: the First Republic spanning over five years from 1960 to 1966, the first round of military rule spanning thirteen years from 1966 to 1979, the Second Republic lasting little more than four years from 1979 to 1983, the second round of military rule spanning over fifteen years from 1983 to 1999, and the Fourth Republic since 1999 going on now for more than sixteen years (table 4.1). Within these five periods, fifteen administrations (see table 4.1, under "leader" column) have piloted Nigeria's foreign policy. Four of the periods comprised multiple political chief executives, while two, the brief First Republic and the even shorter Second Republic, featured only one leader each.

Three concentric circles, flowing from inside to outside, drive Nigerian foreign policy endeavors (see figure 4.1).[74] These three circles of Nigerian diplomacy, powered by events at home, are West Africa, Africa, and the larger world (or international community). Although some of these circles predated the event, the circles mirror lessons about foreign policy from the civil war from 1967 to 1970 that successive Nigerian regimes took to heart: first, the survival of the country as one entity should be the primary purpose of foreign policy, not something taken for granted; second, the need to secure its backyard in West Africa to limit the influence therein of extra-African powers like France whose close allies there, at France's instigation, backed the Biafrans who tried to break away from Nigeria; third, strong pan-African institutions were neces-

Table 4.1. Five Periods in Nigerian Foreign Policy since Independence in 1960

Serial No.	*Periods*	*Leader*	*How Rule Ended*
1.	First Republic, 1960–1966	Abubakar T. Balewa	Successful military coup
2.	First installment of military rule, 1966–1975	Johnson Aguiyi-Ironsi, 1966–1966	Successful countercoup
		Yakubu Gowon, 1966–1975	Successful military coup
		Murtala Mohammed, 1975–1976	Death during an unsuccessful coup
		Olusegun Obasanjo, 1979–1979	Transferred power to civilian government
3.	Second Republic, 1979–1983	Shehu Shagari	Successful military coup
4.	Second installment of military rule, 1983–1999	Muhammadu Buhari, 1983–1985	Successful countercoup
		Ibrahim Babangida, 1985–1993	Forced resignation impelled by the ruckus from an annulled presidential election
		Ernest Shonekan, 1993–1993	Resumption of power by military junta following sack of interim government
		Sani Abacha, 1993–1998	Death in office
		Abdulsalami Abubakar, 1998–1999	Transferred power to a civilian government

Serial No.	*Periods*	*Leader*	*How Rule Ended*
5.	Fourth Republic, 1999 to the Present	Olusegun Obasanjo, 1999–2007	Termed limited
		Umaru Yar'Adua, 2007–2010	Died in office
		Goodluck Jonathan, 2010–2015	Electoral defeat
		Muhammadu Buhari	2015–

Source: Table created by author.

sary to support the country's national security; and, fourth, the need to cultivate extensive ties with all major power blocs, Western as well as Eastern.[75]

Now to the circles, the West African sub-region reflects a recognition or assessment that Nigeria's security is tied to that of its neighbors,[76] beginning with its five immediate neighbors—Cameroon, Chad, Niger, Benin, and Togo—[77] and encompassing other ECOWAS countries.[78] The logic behind deepening relations with immediate neighbors, as one Nigerian ambassador recently put it, is that "while we can choose our friends, we cannot choose our neighbors."[79] To the extent that it featured at all in Nigerian foreign policy, before 1975, the West African sub-region was subsumed within the Africa circle.

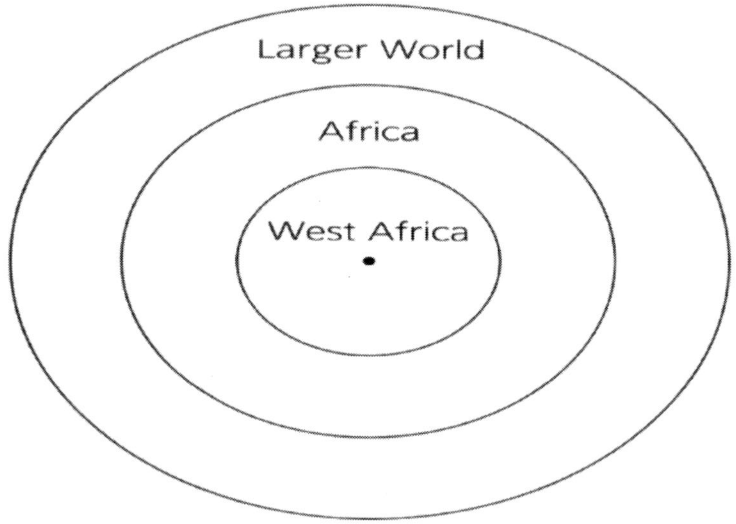

Figure 4.1. Three Concentric Circles of Nigerian Foreign Policy: Africa, West Africa, and the Larger World

Figure created by author.

The next concentric circle in Nigerian foreign policy is Africa. The common expression used to convey this notion is Africa as "centerpiece" of Nigerian foreign policy,[80] meaning that the country's "engagement in the international system will be looked at through the binoculars of Africa."[81] It is a concept borne out of the related notion of Nigeria as the "giant" of Africa, meaning that as the most populous country in Africa and the entire black world, Nigeria perceives itself as the potential leader of the black world.[82] It is a position the early shapers of Nigerian foreign policy, civilian and military alike, agreed on. These shapers include Prime Minister Abubakar T. Balewa and Jaja Wachuku, later to become the country's foreign minister. Balewa declared that "[o]n the question of colonialism and racial discrimination, I am afraid that we in Nigeria will never compromise."[83] Wachuku reportedly remarked that "the whole black continent is looking up to this country to liberate it from thralldom. The whole negroid race is looking up to Nigeria to be free from slavery."[84] But the "expectation" witnessed its most robust expression by General Johnson T. Aguiyi-Ironsi, military Head of State who proclaimed in 1966 that "[i]n the whole sphere of Nigeria's external relations, the Government attaches the greatest importance to our African policy," added:

> We are aware that because of our population and potentials, the majority of opinion in the civilized world looks up to us to provide responsible leadership in Africa; and we realize that we shall be judged, to a very great extent, by the degree of success or failure with which we face up to this challenge which this expectation throws on us. We are convinced that whether in the political, economic or cultural sphere, our destiny lies in our role in the continent of Africa.[85]

Several issues which give practical expression to this worldview include "the remnants of colonialism [in Africa], apartheid in South Africa, liberation war, [as well as] ideological and proxy conflicts."[86] The decolonization of formerly dependent portions of Africa—initially the Lusophone territories of Angola and Mozambique, Zimbabwe, and subsequently Namibia followed by the attainment of Black-majority rule in South Africa in 1994—raises question regarding what is still left of this field of concentration of Nigerian foreign relations.[87] At the risk of over-simplification, emphasis in recent policies on "economic diplomacy," "citizen diplomacy," and related slogans may properly be seen as attempts by different administrations to answer this question.[88]

Last but not least is the concentric circle made up of the larger international community. This circle covers everything else that is not encompassed in the first two categories. In addition to the United and its affiliated agencies, this category includes Eastern Europe, the Middle East, North America, and Western Europe. On this category, Nigerian foreign policymakers initially focused narrowly on relations with West European countries but subsequently broadened the focus of this category to encompass countries in the former Soviet orbit as Nigeria, after the First Republic, but particularly following the civil war from 1967 to 1970, which became more non-aligned in its foreign relations. With the fall of the Soviet Union and demise of what used to be the Eastern bloc, there is pressure for attention in this field of concentration to extend to a much broader spectrum that includes influential players in the global economy, such as Argentina, Brazil, China, India, Mexico, Singapore, and South Korea.[89]

Over the years, various policy tools Nigerian foreign policymakers have used in implementing these concentric circles include peacekeeping and technical assistance. Beginning with the 1979 Constitution, some of the tools of Nigerian foreign policy have been codified in the Nigerian charter document.[90] The ensuing discussion recounts key events that drove Nigerian foreign policies during each of the five phases delineated in table 4.1.

First Republic, 1960–1966

This period featured only one chief executive, Abubakar T. Balewa, who combined his role as prime minister[91] with foreign minister until July 1961 when he ceded the latter position to Jaja Wachuku,[92] who held the position until 1965.[93] As first political chief executive, Balewa helped shape the early foreign policy of the country.[94] Under him, Nigeria operated a low-quality democracy at home[95] that drove a diplomacy of "uncertainty and timidity" abroad,[96] including a "low-keyed, hesitant, and often apologetic approach to African affairs."[97] On the major issues of the day, Nigeria "did not speak with one voice and when she spoke she leaned toward the West."[98] These issues included a secret defense agreement between the Nigerian government which the Nigerian masses opposed when it came to their notice, the crisis in the Congo, and the Arab-Israel conflict, among others.[99] During this period, because what passed for the national government was "a weak coalition of regional and ethnic-based political parties" where the prime minister did not have the power to override divergent groups' encroachments upon Nigeria's foreign policy, the country lacked a "national ideology or even nationwide political consciousness" to guide the formation and implementation of foreign policy.[100]

Given these policymaking disabilities, Nigeria operated "a nonaligned policy that was in reality pro-West."[101] As Professor Gambari illustrated with some key issues of Nigerian foreign policy, Nigerian ratified then abrogated but later retained the basic elements of a contentious defense agreement with Britain; "sent troops to the Congo under the United Nations umbrella without fully supporting Patrice Lumumba, who requested the troops; opted for a weak Organization of African Unity; negotiated and signed but did not ratify an agreement with the European Economic Community; and professed a 'neutral' federal policy toward the Arabs and Israelis in the Middle East that was actually inoperative in northern Nigeria."[102] Additionally, strange for a supposedly independent state, Prime Minister Balewa reportedly had a practice of asking the British High Commissioner in Nigeria to brief him on foreign policy questions, to the chagrin of opposition groups in the country.[103] Few of the many signals of the country's pro-Western orientation included Prime Minister Balewa's pledge of the country's eternal friendship with Britain in his inaugural address[104] and the fact that the official title of the head of the foreign ministry was Minister of Foreign Affairs and Commonwealth Relations.[105]

Operating under the then-available two concentric circles of Africa and the global community, the Balewa government conducted peacekeeping operation in the Congo (later Zaïre),[106] participated in the anti-apartheid campaign in South Africa,[107] and help found the Organization of African Unity (OAU).[108] During Balewa's period, Nigeria was the first African country to enshrine elaborate fundamental human rights guarantees in its constitution.[109] The occurrence followed the work of the Willink's Commission.[110] However, more accurately, this was an accomplishment predating Balewa that was part of the negotiations in the lead up to independence.

The First Republic ended on January 15, 1966, the result of a bloody coup which claimed the life of Balewa as well as those of a number of the country's other leaders, including ministers and regional leaders.[111] The overthrow of the Balewa government culminated a succession of crisis that buffeted the country, almost from the moment of independence, that included the persistent troubles and violence in the Western Region, controversies over the accuracy of census figures, a devastating workers' general strike in June of 1964, and a dispute over the rigging and other electoral irregularities that marred the conduct of the general elections in 1964, among others.[112] An overarching factor in the demise of the First Republic "was the disproportionate power of the north" in what should have been a federal system of more balanced federating units.[113] "The departing colonial authority had hoped that the development of national politics would forestall any sectional domination of power, but it underestimated the effects of a regionalized party system in a country where political power depended on population."[114]

First Round of Military Regimes, 1966–1979

Vis-à-vis the First Republic from 1960 until 1966, this period featured multiple leaders—Johnson A. Aguiyi-Ironsi, Yakubu Gowon, Murtala Mohammed, and Olusegun Obasanjo (see table 4.1)—testimony to a longer timeframe double that earlier period, even though it does not justify it. Two interrelated developments marked this period. First was a reassessment of Nigeria's diplomacy of uncertainty and timidity under the First Republic. The second, building on the reassessment, was the implementation of an assertive foreign policy that commentators praise as the golden era of Nigerian foreign policy.[115] Despite its brevity, Aguiyi-Ironsi regime's set the tone for the important changes in Nigeria's foreign policy. In June 1966, under Aguiyi-Ironsi's watch, the country hosted a six-day Ambassadors' Conference in Lagos, the first of its kind since the country's independence in 1960, to re-examine the premises and directions of Nigeria's foreign policy.[116] Evidently informed by General Aguiyi-Ironsi's expressed position that "in the whole sphere of external relations, the Government attached greatest import to our African policy,"[117] the conference rededicated Nigeria to the total emancipation of all African territories still under colonial control.[118]

Under Gowon, Nigeria fought a bloody civil war, from 1967 to 1970, conducted *outside* the strictures of the Geneva Conventions on the treatment of noncombatants during a war.[119] The occurrence led to unsurpassed abuses of the individual and collective human rights of Easterners about which till date a fierce debate still rages in Nigeria.[120] Throughout the period of the war, Nigerian foreign policy "was defensive, aimed at limiting Biafra's penetration of the international system" by, among other means, prevailing on African governments "to maintain a solid front of diplomatic support as a means of discouraging intervention that would foster Biafran independence."[121] Abroad, the Nigerian government under Gowon became more truly non-aligned,[122] drawing from the lessons during the war of undependable support from Western countries vis-à-vis the military support of the Soviet Union and other East European countries.[123] The war taught the Nigerian leadership a lesson regarding the necessity to spread the range of its bilateral and multilateral relations beyond the traditional West European countries. But with the war over, Nigerian foreign policy experienced a loss of momentum that tracked the deteriorating domestic political situation which reached an all-time high in October 1974 when Gowon assessed as unrealistic his promise to return the country to civilian rule.[124] In a nutshell, for all its shortcomings, the Gowon regime made notable contributions to Nigerian foreign policy at the West African sub-regional circle via its efforts in the formation of ECOWAS and to the Africa concentric circle manifested in support for liberation movements in Africa.[125] The foreign policy achievements were facilitated by increased earnings from hydrocarbon products, which, in the aftermath of the civil war, replaced exports of agricultural products as the mainstay of Nigeria's economy.[126]

The reassessment of Nigeria's timid policy under the First Republic leading to evolution of true nonalignment reached its highest point under Murtala Mohammed, head of state from 1975 until his assassination during a failed military coup in February 1976. Domestically, Mohammed developed a robust transition-to-civilian rule program[127] that his successor, General Olusegun Obasanjo, successfully completed, finally keeping the promise Aguiyi-Ironsi made in 1966 to return power to civilians that, in the end, took thirteen years to accomplish.[128] Abroad, Mohammed's most notable act was the recognition of the Movement for the Popular Liberation of Angola (MPLA) "as the sole legitimate representative of the people and government of Angola," a recognition that ultimately garnered OAU support for the organization.[129] His regime backed this up with increased "diplomatic, financial, and material support to the liberation movements in Southern Africa."[130] As indicated by a speech in Addis Ababa, Ethiopia, at a summit meeting of the OAU in January 1976, General Mohammed was not afraid to call out Western powers when the occasion warranted it.[131] In the speech, instructively titled, "Africa Has Come of Age," Mohammed declared:

> Africa has come of age. It's no longer under the orbit of any extra continental power. It should no longer take orders from any country, however powerful. The fortunes of Africa are in our hands to make or to mar. For too long have we been kicked around: for too long have we been treated like adolescents who cannot discern their interests and act accordingly. For too long has it been presumed that the African needs outside "experts" to tell him who are his friends and who are his enemies. . . . The time has come when we should make it clear that we can decide for ourselves; that we know our own interests and how to protect those interests; that we are capable of resolving African problems without presumptuous lessons in ideological dangers which, more often than not, have no relevance for us, nor for the problem at hand.[132]

In other words, Africa would no longer be a pawn in the cold war struggle between East and West, the downtrodden grass in the fight between two elephants.[133] The speech was triggered by a private letter from then United States president Gerald Ford to many African leaders, warning them against the Soviet-Cuban role in Angola and calling for support of the U.S. position in Southern Africa.[134] Not only did the Nigerian government reject the request, it also as well published the private letter to the approval of informed public opinion in the country.[135] Building on the foundations laid by Mohammed, Obasanjo contributed to the liberation struggle in Southern Africa, reaching a high point with the nationalization of the assets of British Petroleum, the British oil and gas mega-company, over the British government's position in Rhodesia, later Zimbabwe.[136] However, a discernable soft-pedaling in the pursuit of an activist foreign policy occurred under General Obasanjo, due partly to a slowdown in Nigeria's oil-based economy.[137] Reflecting on the leverage of cartel power to some developing countries arising from export of a precious mineral resource, the London *Economist* observed in August 1979 that "a world outside the old Euro-American heartland has developed its own centers of power: its Arabias, Brazils, and Nigerias."[138] The credit is due much more to Mohammed than to Obasanjo.

Second Republic, 1979–1983

Like with the First Republic, President Shagari was the only leader during this period. His tenure was even shorter than the First Republic, lasting only until December 1983 when it was cut short by a military coup. The logical assumption was that a civilian administration would build on the momentum in foreign policy activism established during the first round of military rule from 1966 to 1979. Unfortunately, things did not pan out that way. Instead, Shagari turned out to be an ineffective leader whose administration drew comparison with the First Republic[139] under which coincidentally he served.[140] During his watch, the wheels figuratively came off the train of Nigerian foreign policy in that "[t]he innovativeness and assertiveness" of the Mohammed-Obasanjo era evaporated, and was "replaced with a lack of forthrightness and excessive caution in approaching issues."[141] This was ironic given the enormous executive power of the president under the presidential system of government patterned on the United States that Shagari's regime inaugurated, compared to the parliamentary system under the First Republic where the prime minister, by definition, wielded less power,[142] with important ramifications for foreign policies.[143] At home, massive corruption and bad management of the economy at a time of declining oil prices[144] destroyed the domestic base for creative foreign policymaking. Abroad, under Shagari, Nigeria witnessed little progress in both the Africa and West Africa circles of its foreign policy. On the first, the country failed to translate its resources and power position in Africa into reality by bringing its weight to bear creatively and constructively in solving African problems.[145] On the latter, faced with economic difficulties at home, the Shagari government unwisely embarked on the expulsion of undocumented foreign workers from West Africa,[146] whom his administration made the hapless scapegoats of Nigeria's economic troubles.

Second Round of Military Regimes, 1983–1999

Like Round One, Round Two of military rule in Nigeria encompassed multiple leaders—Muhammadu Buhari, Ibrahim Babangida, Ernest Shonekan,

Sani Abacha, and Abdulsalami Abubakar—and lasted more years, six longer, to boot. Buhari's regime failed to contribute to the tradition for assertive foreign policy laid down during the first installment of military rule in the country.[147] Instead, save for a campaign against corruption domestically, his rule intriguingly appeared to clone the discredited NPN government that he overthrew.[148] His regime was also, even by military standards,[149] a repressive one that did not commit itself to return the country to civilian rule.[150] In the final analysis, Buhari was a leader of insular dispositions who expressed distinct aversion for matters of external affairs that would take away from his focus on the Nigerian economy battered by corruption that he inherited,[151] and whose regime continued the anti-ECOWAS initiatives of the Shagari administration that detracted from the energized Africa-centered policy of the Mohammed-Obasanjo regimes.[152]

Babangida equally operated a repressive regime, albeit less blatantly,[153] that also dubiously set a new standard for political corruption.[154] He set the record for a convoluted return to a civil rule program that some commentators legitimately likened to a permanent transition, inconsistent with popular expectation, dating back to Aguiyi-Ironsi, that counseled return of power to civilians after the army has fixed the problem that brought them into office.[155] Despite these domestic failures, his regime managed to chalk in some innovative accomplishments in two concentric circles—West Africa sub-region and Africa—that resonate with the assertive foreign policy program associated with the latter leg of the first round of military rule. For West Africa, Babangida gave the integration impetus of ECOWAS, stalled under Shagari and Buhari, a proverbial shot in the arm. Among other initiatives, he donated land in Abuja for the building of the ECOWAS Secretariat and contributed $4.5 million toward its construction.[156] It was also during this period, in July 1986, that the community's Protocol on Free Movement of Citizens, enacted in 1979, took effect.[157] Also via his formalization of technical assistance under the Technical Aid Corps (TAC),[158] Babangida carved a new arrow in the quiver of Nigeria's external relations, with ramifications for all three concentric circles in Nigerian foreign policy since the scheme exported Nigerian expertise to various corners of the world, including West Africa, Africa, and the Caribbean.[159]

With a lifespan of under three months, the interim government under Shonekan, a Yoruba, had hardly settled down before it was sacked. From every indication, his government was little more than a ploy by the Babangida regime to douse the earth-rending protests which accompanied his invalidation of the June 12, 1993, presidential election believed by many to have been won by another Yoruba, businessman Moshood Abiola.[160] Abacha held the all-time record for human rights disrespect and atrocities. Under him, dissidents were routinely tortured, political prisoners were tried in camera before military tribunals that hardly set them free, and execution for offenses, such as armed robbery, were commonplace. His massive abuses of human rights drew widespread condemnation, including suspension of Nigeria's membership in the Commonwealth of Nations following the hanging death in October 1995 of Keni Saro-Wiwa, along with 9 other Ogoni activists.[161] Under him, the pariah status of the country in the international community, instigated by Babangida's annulment of the 1993 presidential election, reached a new low. Nigerian peacekeeping efforts in Liberia and Sierra Leone, the first to end a raging civil war and the latter to restore an elected leader forced out of office in a military coup,[162] in no way mitigated Abacha's failures in domestic and foreign policies. Imagine, for example, the solecism of a military regime leading an interventionist force to restore democracy in Sierra Leone. Part of the legacy of Abacha was the unprecedented spike in corruption that occurred under his regime.[163] In the observation of one Nigerian political scientist, during his period, corruption moved from being part of Nigeria's government to being "the object of government."[164]

A key element of the assault on individual and group human rights in the military years, especially during the Abacha regime, was an elaborate international public relations campaign "by which tyranny was defended abroad, paid for with assets that should have been used to meet the needs of Nigerians at home."[165] By the time of Abacha's death on June 8, 1993—after three continuous decades in office, only interrupted by four years of civilian rule under the Second Republic—it was obvious that a Nigerian army "[c]onsumed with fear, factionalism, and greed" "could hardly any longer be viewed as a potential source of rescue for democracy."[166] It is foolhardy "to weaken at home what one is trying to strengthen abroad."[167] The moment came to rebuild Nigeria's image battered by prolonged military rule. This was the setting in which Abubakar emerged[168] to start the process of the repair of Nigeria's sick image abroad needing to be preceded by a genuine transition to civil rule program.[169] Abubakar was Chief of Defense under Abacha before the ruling junta selected him as Head of State.[170] He was chosen because "he was seen a professional soldier without political ambitions of his own," but also equally because, although an Abacha loyalist, Abubakar believed that "the survival of the country depends on a rapid and peaceful transition to a lasting democracy."[171] He dismantled Abacha's transition program together with the five political parties, "five fingers of a leprous hand" as one Nigerian politician derisively called them, each of which unanimously adopted Abacha as its sole presidential candidate,[172] and finally completed the return-to-civil-rule agenda that the Nigerian army initiated in 1986 under Babangida, orchestrating the soldiers' long-overdue retreat to the barracks.[173]

Fourth Republic, 1999 to the Present

Four heads of state—Olusegun Obasanjo, Umaru Yar'Adua, Goodluck Jonathan, and Muhammadu Buhari—have featured in Nigeria's long-running period of civilian rule since independence. The fact that two of these individuals, Obasanjo and Buhari, are former military leaders, speaks to the continuing influence of the army in the political system 17 years after the Nigerian army retreated to the barracks. Testimony further to that lingering influence is the fact that the two leaders who succeeded Obasanjo, like him members of the People's Democratic Party (PDP), until March 2015, Nigeria's ruling party, were handpicked by Obasanjo.[174]

Obasanjo continued the rehabilitation of Nigeria's international image that Abubakar initiated.[175] He equally made important strides in domestic politics that included reduction of Nigeria's external debt and laid the groundwork for expansion of telecommunication services that caught fire in the country after he left office.[176] However, after two terms in office which he sought unsuccessfully to extend into a third term,[177] there was little evidence of "democratic dividend" for the citizenry,[178] a large segment of whom remained mired in poverty.[179] Next to external relations, while certain gains were made in all concentric circles of Nigerian foreign policy, those achievements lacked the sharpness the country witnessed during his first time around for a variety of reasons that includes the inability to reshape the country's Africa-centered prong in the architecture of the country's foreign policy to reflect a changed world. In a speech in 2005, Obasanjo indicated why he "believe[d] that Africa should remain the centerpiece of our foreign policy."[180] His justification was a defensive one that evinced poverty of imagination on how to reshape Nigeria's Africa-centered policy in the wake of the decolonization in Africa capped by the achievement of majority rule in South Africa in 1994, several years before he took office.[181]

Given a chronic health condition that kept him hospitalized for long periods, Yar'Adua remained a transitional leader for much of the less than three years he served in office before his death on May 5, 2010, three months of which period from February 9, 2010, vice-president Jonathan filled in acting capacity while Yar'Adua received treatment in Saudi Arabia.[182] Like Jonathan after him, Yar'Adua had no military background. Jonathan won his own separate term in 2011 and left office in 2015 after he lost his bid for reelection.[183] Like Yar'Adua before him, Jonathan's government created a truly civilian atmosphere, a departure from the military approach to non-military issues that marked Obasanjo's civilian years in office.[184] Although the best educated of Nigeria leaders since independence,[185] and although he maintained momentum on the three concentric circles in the architecture of Nigerian foreign policy, Jonathan was an effete leader.[186] One singular issue more any other which manifested this want of strong leadership skill—and a major factor in his failure to win a second term in office—was his ineffective response to the crisis of terrorism by the insurgency group, Boko Haram, that rocked the northeast of the country under his watch.

Boko Haram stands for the notion that "Western education is evil," which evilness these terrorists are convinced can be resolved by turning Nigeria into an Islamic state in the mold of Iran or Saudi Arabia. Populated by retired and serving soldiers, policemen, and immigration personnel from Nigeria and foreign nationals from Niger, Chad, and Sudan, the group has conducted relentlessly bombings and gun attacks on ordinary citizens and more well-known ones, such as politicians, and religious leaders. It has also targeted government infrastructure of all types within and outside the epicenter of its operation in north-eastern Nigeria, including police stations, army barracks, the United Nations office in Abuja, churches, and recreation centers, among other seeming symbols of Western education. Since inaugurating its violent phase in 2009, the group has killed or maimed over 20,000 people, displaced millions of others from their homes, kidnapped hundreds, including school girls, and blew off public and private property running into millions of dollars. The group is linked to al-Qaeda, the global terrorist group founded by Osama bin Ladin, and professes allegiance to another terrorist organization, the Islamic State of Iraq and Syria (ISIS).[187] Because the group aims to make Nigeria an Islamic theocracy in the model of Iran, the conflict appears to cap the continued salience of religion in Nigerian politics under the Fourth Republic that began with the institution of sharia as legal code in twelve northern states between 2000 and 2001.[188]

Although Buhari has made progress in stemming the problem, the national security dilemma lingers, joined by a range of new challenges all across the land, including agitations for self-determination in the Southeast and campaigns for control over oil resources in the Niger Delta, at a time of economic difficulties. But the jury is still out on this new government, an occurrence that counsels against any premature analysis.[189]

SUMMATION

This chapter caps the background presentations necessary for understanding this study, begun with the conceptual framework (chapter 2) and continued with the theoretical framework (chapter 3). Although mainly focused on the period since Nigeria's independence from the United Kingdom in 1960 at the heartbeat of this research, the discussion also included a pre-independence timeline consisting of the precolonial and colonial eras. Including the pre-independence period affords more canvas in time duration for comparative analysis beneficial to the methodology of this research anchored in within-case comparison (WCC). WCC involves the study of one country, here Nigeria, at different points in time and space, poring over a wealth of relevant sources, including histories, archival documents, and transcripts of interviews.

Several lessons emerge from this chapter, particularly the material on the postcolonial era. First is the interrelatedness of domestic and foreign policies. Second is the instability in the Nigerian political system with ramifications for the conduct of domestic and foreign policies. Fifteen administrations have governed Nigeria in the nearly fifty-six years since its independence. This comes to a lifespan of 3.67 years for each administration or 3.92 years if one excludes the interim government of Ernest Shonekan whose tenure lasted only 84 days. Third is the influence of military rule in Nigerian politics. Only seven of the fifteen administrations surveyed (47 percent) are civilian, down to six or 40 percent when one excludes the Shonekan regime. Nothing speaks to the lingering influence of military rule in the Nigerian system better than the fact that two of the four administrations under the Fourth Republic are headed by former military generals. One of those leaders, Olusegun Obasanjo, also handpicked the only two non-soldier leaders.

With the methodological and background issues of Part I now over, this work is poised to enter Part II of the research, dealing with six issues related to the application of human rights in Nigeria's foreign policy, which issues are encapsulated earlier in chapter 1 as a temple of two steps and four pillars. The first of those issues, and the first of two steps in the temple, which chapter 5 tackles, is the redesign of the country's national interest.

NOTES

1. Any reader with basic understanding of arithmetic will notice from this enumeration that a Third Republic in between the Second Republic and the Fourth Republic is missing in action. A Third Republic projected for 1993 became stillborn when the military government under General Babangida (1985–1993), on June 23, cancelled a presidential election that year that would have ushered in that republic. It did so on the implausible ground that a profusion of legal disputes swirling the election made a "ridiculous charade" of the election likely to "culminate in judicial anarchy" and that General Babangida needed to save the Nigerian judiciary "from being ridiculed and politicized locally and internationally." Kenneth B. Noble, "Nigerian Military Rulers Annul Election," *New York Times* (Jun. 24, 1993), http://www.nytimes.com/1993/06/24/world/nigerian-military-rulers-annul-election.html. The real reason for the cancellation, however, was ethnic politics: Nigeria's northern-dominated mili-

tary did not want power being transferred to a southerner. See Larry Diamond, "Nigeria: The Uncivic Society and the Descent into Praetorianism," *in* Larry Diamond et al., *Politics in Developing Countries: Comparing Experiences with Democracy, 2d Ed.* (Boulder, CO: Lynne Rienner, 1995): 456 (recounting how "Babangida and his fellow ruling officers debated deep into the night how to handle the one outcome they had not anticipated—a decisive victory by the southern, Yoruba, S[ocial] D[emocratic] P[arty] candidate," Moshood K.O. Abiola). The fallouts from the annulment impelled Babangida to step down and transfer power to an interim national government. A less arithmetically confusing approach that Nigerian constitutionalists could have adopted but failed to use would have been to denominate the period since 1999 the Third Republic, rather than the Fourth.

2. Frank L. Wilson, *Concepts and Issues in Comparative Politics: An Introduction to Comparative Analysis* (Upper Saddle River, N.J.: Prentice Hall, 1996): 17.

3. J. Tyler Dickovick & Jonathan Eastwood, *Comparative Politics: Integrating Theories, Methods, and Cases* (New York: Oxford University Press, 2013): 13, 19.

4. Ibid., p. 19.

5. Mark R. Amstutz, *International Ethics: Concepts, Theories, and Cases in Global Politics* (Lanham, MD: Rowland & Littlefield Publishers, 1999): 2.

6. See ibid., pp. 1–25 (commenting on the influence on morality in foreign policy); pp. 47–69 (analyzing "the role of ethical traditions"); and p. xv (identifying the role of moral values in foreign policy, and the ethical foundation of the rules and structures of global society as two dimensions of international political morality).

7. Robert W. McElroy, *Morality and American Foreign Policy* (Princeton, N.J.: Princeton University Press, 1992): 30.

8. Alison Brysk, *Global Good Samaritans: Human Rights as Foreign Policy* (New York: Oxford University Press, 2009): 3. It was not until 1976, under the presidency of Jimmy Carter, backed by a Congress controlled by the Democratic Party and public support from a country, chastened by the turbulence of the United States' involvement in the long war in Vietnam, and the Watergate scandal, that these ethical concerns crystallized into full-scale human rights policy. Philip C. Aka, "The *Country Reports on Human Rights Practices* and U.S. Human Rights Policy in a Changing World," *Perspectives on Global Development & Technology*, Vol. 14 (2015): 240.

9. The focus on ethics is consistent with the definition of human rights as ethical precepts. See Philip C. Aka, "Analyzing U.S. Commitment to Socioeconomic Human Rights," *Akron Law Review*, Vol. 39 (2006): 423 (defining human rights as "international *ethical* standards that uphold, as a birthright, the minimum thresholds individuals and communities everywhere require to live in dignity and to realize their potentials") (emphasis added).

10. See Dapo Fafowora, "Lord Lugard and the 1914 Amalgamation of Nigeria," *Nation* (Feb. 28, 2013), http://thenationonlineng.net/lord-lugard-and-the-1914-amalgamation-of-nigeria-2/; F.D. Lugard & A.H.M. Kirk-Greene, *Lugard and the Amalgamation of Nigeria: A Documentary Record* (London: Cass, 1968).

11. Clifford Geertz, ed., *Old Societies and New States: The Quest for Modernity in Asia and Africa* (New York: Free Press of Glencoe, 1963). Prior to European engagement, societies in Nigeria and other parts of Africa witnessed the emergence of

states as well as attained a certain level of technological development and capacity. See Osita C. Eze, *Human Rights in Africa: Some Selected Problems* (Lagos: Nigerian Institute of Int'l Affairs and Macmillan Nigeria, 1984): 10; Ignatius Akaayar Ayua & Dakas C.J. Dakas, "Federal Republic of Nigeria," *in* John Kincaid & George Alan Tarr, eds., *Constitutional Origins, Structure, and Change in Federal Countries* (Montreal, Canada: McGill-Queen's University Press, 2005): 240 (observing that "[p]recolonial Nigeria consisted of a bewildering variety of communities and entities of varying sizes, levels of political and social development, and degrees of independence and autonomy . . . At no time before the British arrived was Nigeria even loosely ruled by one government."); Int'l Crisis Group, *Nigeria: Want in the Midst of Plenty*, Africa Report No. 113 (Jul. 19, 2006): 5 (pointing out that "[t]he boundaries of present-day Nigeria contain a prodigious variety of historical political units, social orders, economies, and cultures."). Little wonder some scholars consider the independence of African countries in the second half of the twentieth century as "reestablishment" of an original independence lost following European "conquest" of these societies. See Herbert Ekwe-Ekwe, *Biafra Revisited* (Dakar, Senegal: African Renaissance, 2006): 18 (viewing Nigeria's independence in 1960 as "the reestablishment of independence for its various peoples, after 60 years of British conquest and occupation[.]"); and Ibrahim A. Gambari, *Party Politics and Foreign Policy: Nigeria under the First Republic* (Zaria, Nigeria: Ahmadu Bello University Press, Ltd., 1980): 7 (depicting a cluster of indigenous independent states at the point of contact which "experienced the advent of the Europeans first as traders, then as explorers and missionaries, and finally as rulers.").

12. See Elizabeth Isichei, *A History of the Igbo People* (New York: Palgrave Macmillan, 1976): 3 ("[M]en have been living in Igboland for at least [5,000] years. One of the most notable factors of Igbo history is its length and continuity."); Toyin Falola & Matthew M. Heaton, *A History of Nigeria* (New York: Cambridge University Press, 2008): 16–38 (discussing "the early history of human habitation and the development of states in the territories of modern-day Nigeria, from the period of the earliest archeological findings in the Late Stone Age (LSA) to the coming of European traders in the late fifteenth and sixteenth centuries CE").

13. See "Nigeria," *in* M. Paul Lewis, ed., *Ethnologue: Languages of the World, 17th Ed.* (SIL Int'l, 2010), http://www.ethnologue.com/country/NG (last visited Nov. 17, 2014) (listing the number of individual languages in the country as 527, of which 514 are living and 11 extinct).

14. See A. Carl LeVan & Oladimeji Aborisade, "Politics in Nigeria," *in* G. Bingham Powell Jr. et al., eds., *Comparative Politics Today: A World View, 11th Ed.* (New York: Pearson 2014): 633–34; Donald Terfa Gaadi, "Ethnic Groups and Geo-Political Regions in Nigeria," *Eagle Reporters* (Abuja) (Dec. 28, 2013 1:49 PM), http://eaglereporters.com/2013/12/28/ethnic-group-and-geo-political-region-in-nigeria-by-donald-terfa/.

15. Diamond, note 1, p. 419. Each of these groups has a population that runs into tens of millions. See Larry Diamond, "Nigeria: Pluralism, Statism, and the Struggle for Democracy," *in* Larry Diamond et al., eds., *Democracy in Developing Countries: Africa, Vol. 2* (Boulder, CO: Lynne Rienner Publishers, 1988): 35, table 2.1 (listing

the populations of ten major ethnic groups alphabetically: Edo, Fulani, Hausa, Ibibio-Efik, Igbo, Ijaw, Kanuri, Nupe, Tiv, and Yoruba).

16. See Philip C. Aka, "Prospects for Igbo Human Rights in Nigeria in the New Century," *Howard Law Journal,* Vol. 48 (Fall 2004): 180, n.87.

17. Oyediji O. Babatunde, "Hausa/Fulani Pre-Colonial Political System in Nigeria," *WordPress* (Mar. 30, 2014), http://www.profseunoyediji.wordpress.com/2014/03/30/hausafulani-pre-colonial-political-system-in-nigeria (characterizing the Emir as an "absolute ruler" who exercised his authority unrestrained by any "principle of checks and balances.").

18. See Elizabeth Isichei, *The Ibo People and the Europeans: The Genesis of a Relationship—to 1906* (New York: St. Martin's Press, 1973): 47; Elizabeth Isichei, *A History of Christianity in Africa: From Antiquity to the Present* (Grand Rapids, MI: Wm. B. Eerdmans Publishing, 1995): 155.

19. Mojeed Olujinmi A. Alabi, "Law Making in Pre-Colonial Yorubaland," *in* Toyin Falola & Ann Genova, eds., *The Yoruba in Transition: History, Values, and Modernity* (Durham, NC: Carolina Academic Press, 2006): 122.

20. Part of the reason for the occurrence, as Professor Eze points out, is that, except for societies that came under Islamic influence, African customary law is oral, rather than written. Eze, note 11, p. 9. Related to this factor, much of what available information that exists is derived from colonial laws and practices that either confirm or abrogate precolonial practices. Ibid.

21. Chip Pitts, "'Mobilizing Shame' Can Bring Abuses Up Short," *Topeka Capital-Journal* (Mar. 11, 2005), http://cjonline.com/stories/031105/opi_pitts.shtml (tribute to Peter Benenson, founder of Amnesty International, upon his death that year).

22. Chidi A. Odinkalu, "Why More Africans Don't Use Human Rights Language," *Human Rights Dialog,* Vol. 2 (Dec. 1999), www.carnegiecouncil.org/publications/archive/dialogue/2_01/articles/602.html (stating that "in some African languages there is no direct equivalent to the phrase 'human rights.'").

23. R.J. Vincent, *Human Rights and International Relations* (New York: Cambridge University Press, 1986): 136.

24. See Karen A. Mingst & Margaret P. Karns, *The United Nations in the 21st Century, 4th Ed.* (Boulder, CO: Westview Press, 2012): 197–246 (commenting on the role of the United Nations in human rights); Louis Henkin, *Human Rights: Ideology and Aspiration, Reality and Prospect, in* Samantha Power & Graham Allison, eds., *Realizing Human Rights: Moving from Inspiration to Impact* (New York: St. Martin's Press, 2000): 17–18 (including the United Nations as one of six forces responsible for the emergence, survival, and flourishing of international human rights "as a shared ideology in the latter half of the twentieth century.").

25. Pope Francis, Text of Address to a Joint Session of the U.S. Congress (Sept. 24, 2015 10:30 AM EDT), http://www.politico.com/story/2015/09/pope-francis-speech-to-congress-transcript-text-video-214016 (commenting on the (mis)treatment of Native Americans, of whom His Holiness observed that "[t]ragically, the rights of those who were here [in the U.S.] long before us were not always respected[;]" instead, "[t]hose first contacts were often turbulent and violent.").

26. Odinkalu, note 22.

27. Ibid.

28. See Eze, note 11, *passim*.

29. For more on this group, see Aka, note 16, pp. 177–84 (discussing "[t]he Igbo People and Nation").

30. Ibid., p. 177 (internal quotes omitted).

31. Isichei, note 12, p. 21.

32. Aka, note 16, pp. 177–78 (internal quotes omitted).

33. See Eze, note 11, pp. 9–14 (covering the precolonial period); Isichei, *The Ibo People and the Europeans*, note 18, pp. 59–60.

34. Tony Uchenna, "Osu Caste in Igboland," *Vanguard* (Lagos) (Oct. 9, 2010; 7:35 PM), http://www.vanguardngr.com/2010/10/osu-caste-in-igboland/; see also Andrew Walker, "The Story of Nigeria's 'Untouchables,'" *BBC News* (Apr. 7, 2009 10:30 UK), http://news.bbc.co.uk/2/hi/africa/7977734.stm.

35. See E.I. Nwogugu, *Family Law in Nigeria* (Ibadan, Nigeria: HEBN Publishers, 2014): 65.

36. Ibid. (citing Art. 42(2) which provided that "no citizen of Nigeria shall be subjected to any disability or deprivation merely by reason of the circumstances of his birth").

37. Eze, note 11, p. 13. Some Igbo communities killed twins in the superstitious belief that their existence brings evil or back luck. Ibid. But there were also Igbo communities who did not. Such was the case in Enugu-Ezike, a town near Nsukka in northern Igbo, whose indigenes regarded twin and multiple births "as symbol of good luck and fortune." Gloria Chuku, "Olaudah Equiano and the Foundation of Igbo Intellectual Tradition," *in* Gloria Chuku, ed., *The Igbo Intellectual Tradition: Creative Conflict in African and African Diasporic Thought* (New York: Palgrave Macmillan, 2013): 62, n.64.

38. Isichei, *The Ibo People and the Europeans*, note 18, pp. 59–60.

39. Eze, note 11, p. 228.

40. One such ironic occurrence was the Berlin Conference in 1885 where European countries formally partitioned African territories among themselves, with the United States as witness. What made the conference and the partition that it occasioned ironic were that they were premised on human rights embedded in the abolition of the slave trade. See Matthew Craven, "Between Law and History: The Berlin Conference of 1884–1885 and the Logic of Free Trade," *London Review of Int'l Law*, Vol. 3 (2015): 31–59; U. Oji Umozurike, *The African Charter on Human and Peoples' Rights* (Leiden, Netherlands: Brill, 1997): 20; and Frederick J.D. Lugard, *The Dual Mandate in British Tropical Africa* (London: Frank Cass & Co., 1922) (self-serving narrative by Nigeria's former governor-general and major brain behind the creation of the country that recounts the supposed benefits of British rule in Nigeria).

41. For definitions of these three categories of human rights, see chapter 2 of this study, specifically the section titled "Definition of Key Terms in This Study."

42. Philip C. Aka, "The Military, Globalization, and Human Rights in Africa," *Journal of Human Rights*, Vol. 18 (2002): 380, 382.

43. Ibid., p. 381.

44. See Eze, note 11, p. 228 (observing that European colonialism in Africa left in place "[i]nstitutional structures [designed] to serve the predatory interests of the colonial powers" which until today "continue to impose major obstacles" to economic development of many African states).

45. Isichei, note 12, p. 199.

46. Aka, note 42, p. 381; see also Eze, note 11, p. 228 (observing that "[t]he civilizing mission of colonialism was . . . antithetical to human rights" and "[i]ts racist overtone compounded other forms of discrimination that existed in Africa.").

47. The Atlantic Charter is an eight-point agreement between Churchill and U.S. president Franklin D. Roosevelt regarding the goals of their two countries (and the Allied Group) for World War II and their collective vision of the world after that conflict. See "Atlantic Charter" (Aug. 14, 1941), http://avalon.law.yale.edu/wwii/atlantic.asp. The third of these "common principles" was "respect[ing] the right of all peoples to choose the form of government under which they will live" and restoring "sovereign rights and self-government" "to those who have been forcibly deprived of" these guarantees. Ibid.

48. Henkin, note 24, p. 7 (noting that "[t]he ideology of rights was not encouraged in, and did not spread to, the colonies of the British and French empires"); J.A.A. Ayoade, "Nigeria: Positive Pessimism and Negative Optimism: A Valedictory Lecture," *Nigerian Voice* (Sept. 17, 2010): 5, http://www.thenigerianvoice.com/print/34992/1/nigeria-positive-pessimism-and-negative-optimism-a.html. Lord Moyne, British Colonial Secretary, took the position that self-determination applied only to territories occupied by the Germans because these territories were "not in need of political tutelage." Ibid.

49. For FDR, the colonial system took wealth from dependent territories without putting anything back into those territories by way of education, healthcare, or jobs, among other guarantees people need for a life of dignity, a deprivation that creates the conditions that lead inevitably to war. Ayoade, note 48, p. 5.

50. This refers to a speech at the South African Parliament in Cape Town on Feb. 3, 1960, wherein Harold Macmillan, British prime minister from 1957 to 1963, indicated that his government recognized the "growth of national consciousness" sweeping through Africa as "a political fact." Harold Macmillan, Speech at the South African Parliament, Cape Town, http://www.bbc.co.uk/archive/apartheid/7203.shtml (video). Macmillan declared, "The wind of change is blowing through this continent. Whether we like it or not, this growth of national consciousness, is a political fact." Ibid. A highlight of his tour of British colonies in Africa starting Jan. 6 of that year, including stopovers in Ghana, and Nigeria, the speech, acknowledged, *inter alia*, that the campaigns for self-rule by still-dependent Africans were legitimate and that the British government had a responsibility to promote the creation of societies that uphold the rights of citizens. "'Wind of Change' Speech," *About.com*, http://africanhistory.about.com/od/eraindependence/a/wind_of_change1.htm.

51. Robert Fatton Jr., "Liberal Democracy in Africa," *Political Science Quarterly*, Vol. 105 (1990): 457.

52. Isichei, note 12, p. 119.

53. Aka, note 42, p. 379 (emphasis added).

54. Eze, note 11, p. 229.

55. Isichei, *The Ibo People and the Europeans*, note 18, pp. 59–60; Eze, note 11, p. 229.

56. Isichei, *The Ibo People and the Europeans*, note 18, pp. 59–60.

57. "First Republic," *in* Helen Chapin Metz, ed., *Nigeria: A Country Study* (Washington, D.C.: GPO for the Library of Congress, 1991).

58. See ibid.

59. Under British rule, Nigeria witnessed the production and unveiling of five constitutional documents. These constitutions, each named after the British administrator who introduced it, are the Lugard Constitution of 1914 amalgamating the country, Clifford's Constitution of 1922, the Richard's Constitution of 1946, the McPherson Constitution of 1951, and the Littleton Constitution of 1954 setting up the country's federal system of government. Anthony Kirk-Greene, "The Remedial Imperatives of the Nigerian Constitution, 1922–1992," *in* Larry Diamond et al., eds., *Transition without End: Nigerian Politics and Civil Society under Babangida* (Boulder, CO: Lynne Rienner, 1997): 31.

60. See Richard L. Sklar, *Nigerian Political Parties: Power in an Emergent African Nation* (Princeton, N.J.: Princeton University Press, 1963), *passim*.

61. See Ayoade, note 48, pp. 2–3.

62. Ibid., p. 2.

63. Ibid., p. 3.

64. See Eghosa E. Osaghae, *The Crippled Giant: Nigeria since Independence* (Bloomington, IN: Indiana University Press, 1998): 6.

65. Ayoade, note 44, p. 12.

66. Ibid.

67. See Osaghae, note 64, p. 6; Adisa Adeleye, "The Old and the New: Which Way Forward?," *Vanguard* (Lagos) (Nov. 15, 2013), http://www.vanguardngr.com/2013/11/old-new-way-forward/ (enumerating the eight-point demand of northern leaders in 1953).

68. See Osaghae, note 64, p. 6.

69. See Idowu Ajanaku, "Ex-Colonial Officer Faults Amalgamation of Nigeria," *Guardian* (Lagos) (Apr. 28, 2005); *cited in* Ekwe-Ekwe, note 11, p. 18, n.1 (reporting the confession of Peter Smithers, a former colonial official to the effect that, in retrospect, the amalgamation "was a grave mistake which has cost many lives and will probably continue to do so," including the conviction of this official that "[i]t should have been better to establish several smaller states in a free trade area.").

70. See Kirk-Greene, note 59 (contrasting the "remedial" system consisting of the unveiling of numerous constitutions that are created and quickly discarded utilized in the country with the U.S. system of one document with piecemeal amendments as the need arises for change); Ayoade, note 48, p. 3 (noting that Nigerian constitutionalism "did not match the growth of the Nigerian territory" and that "most of the colonial constitutional reforms de-emphasized the essence of corporate existence of Nigerians.").

71. Jack Donnelly, "An Overview," in David P. Forsythe, ed., *Human Rights and Comparative Foreign Policy* (New York: United Nations University Press,

2000): 313 (attributing the dismantling of the British colonial empire partly to "the influence of human rights ideas" in both the home country and the colony); Neta C. Crawford, *Argument and Change in World Politics: Ethics, Decolonization, and Humanitarian Intervention* (New York: Cambridge University Press, 2002): 2, 388 (pinpointing human rights as a factor in the demise of slavery and colonialism which prompted "the biggest change in the structure and practice of international relations in the last 500 years.").

72. S. O. Akinboye, "Beautiful Abroad but Ugly at Home: Issues and Contra[di] ctions in Nigeria's Foreign Policy," University of Lagos Inaugural Lecture Series, 2013, www.unilag.edu.ng/opendocnew.php?.

73. The opportunity to design an indigenous policy calls to mind Dr. Kwame Nkrumah's notion of "African Personality." Nkrumah declared, "For too long in our history, Africa has spoken through the voices of others. Now, what I have called an African Personality in international affairs will have a chance of making its proper impact and will let the world know it through the voices of Africa's own sons." Quoted in Olayiwola Abegunrin, *Africa in Global Politics in the Twenty-First Century: A Pan-African Perspective* (New York: Palgrave Macmillan, 2009): 1.

74. The notion of "concentric circles" in Nigeria's foreign policy was developed under Okoi Arikpo, external affairs minister from 1967 to 1975. Keith Campbell, Nigerian Foreign Policy and the Economic Community of West African States (ECOWAS), Occasional Paper, South African Institute of Int'l Affairs 1 (Sept. 1978). Different authors sketch these circles differently. See, e.g. Ibrahim Gambari, "From Balewa to Obasanjo: The Theory and Practice of Nigeria's Foreign Policy," *in* Adekeye Adebajo & Abdul Raufu Mustapha, eds., *Gulliver's Troubles: Nigeria's Foreign Policy after the Cold War* (Scottsville, South Africa: University of Kwazulu-Natal Press, 2008): 58–80 (sketching four concentric circles comprising: a first circle of four immediate neighbors; a second circle revolved around relations with the Economic Community of West African States, ECOWAS; a third circle focused on Africa; and a fourth with states and organizations outside Africa); "Foreign Relations," *in* Metz, ed., *Nigeria: A Country Study*, note 57 (sketching four, without explicitly using the term *concentric circles*, comprising relations with neighboring states, relations with the rest of Africa, relations with major powers, and relations with international organizations.). To keep things simple, this study will stay with three concentric circles.

75. J. Peter Pham, Nigeria's Foreign Policy: An Inquiry into Sources and Prospects, Paper Prepared for Presentation at an Int'l Conference in Lisbon, Portugal (Nov. 8–9), at 95, www.ipri.pt/eventos/pdf/JPeterPham_paper.pdf.

76. Campbell, note 74.

77. Nigeria shares 1,500 km of land border in the North with Niger and Chad, about 1,000 km in the West with Benin, 1,700 km in the East with Cameroon, and 700 km of Atlantic coastlines in the South. Victor A.O. Adetula, "Between National Security Considerations and the Challenge of Cross-Border Crime in West Africa," *in* Celestine Oyom Bassey & Oshita D. Oshita, eds., *Governance and Border Security in Africa* (Lagos: Malthouse Press Ltd., 2010): 300.

78. Only the last three states are members of ECOWAS; the first two, Cameroon and Chad, are not. The community is covered in chapter 10.

79. Ambassador Olugbenga Ashiru, Seminar to Review Nigeria's Foreign Policy (Jul. 28, 2011), http://www.mfa.gov.ng/news_one.php?article=41.

80. See Adebayo Adedeji, Report of the Committee on the Review of Nigerian Foreign Policy, Including Economic and Technical Cooperation (Lagos: Government Printer, 1976), *passim*.

81. Atah Pine, "Nigerian Foreign Policy, 1960–2011: Fifty Years of Conceptual Confusion," *Modern Ghana* (Oct. 4, 2011), http://www.modernghana.com/print/354264/1/nigeria-foreign-policy-1960-2011-fifty-one-years-o.html.

82. "Foreign Relations," *in* Metz, ed., *Nigeria: A Country Study*, note 57.

83. Quoted in Abegunrin, note 73, p. 5. In retrospect, the focus on Africa was an outlook that predated Nigeria's independence and an accent that many other African leaders shared. For example, in his "midnight" address to mark the achievement of Ghana's independence on March 5, 1957, Dr. Kwame Nkrumah stated that "our [Ghana's] independence is meaningless unless it is linked up with the total liberation of the African continent." "Kwame Nkrumah's Vision," *BBC World Service* (Sept. 14, 2000), www.bbc.co.uk/worldservice/people/highlights/000914_nkrumah.shtml. Subsequently, this principle found its way into the Charter of the Organization of African Unity (OAU). One of the principles of the organization is "absolute dedication to the total emancipation" of still dependent African territories. Charter of the Organization of African Unity, 479 U.N.T.S. 39 (entered into force Sept. 13, 1963), http://www1.umn.edu/humanrts/africa/OAU_Charter_1993.html, Art. III.6. The idea goes even further back to pan-Africanism, an ideology which stresses the solidarity and common destiny of black people, irrespective of where they make their home. See Pine, note 81 (opining that "the ideals of pan-Africanism . . . lubricated the wheels of this foreign policy conceptualization."); P. Olisanwuche Esedebe, *Pan-Africanism: The Idea and Movement 1776–1991, 2d Ed.* (Washington, D.C.: Howard University Press, 1994) (tracing the roots of pan-Africanism from the period of the American revolution in 1776 to the early 1990s).

84. Federal Parliamentary Debate Reports, Independence Motion (Jan. 4, 1960 at 89), quoted in Gambari, note 11, p. 68.

85. Johnson T. Aguiyi-Ironsi, Remarks by the Head of State to the Regional Conference of Heads of Missions in Africa, Lagos, Jun. 9, 1966, Cn 1/21/I, 114; cited in John J. Stremlau, *The International Politics of the Nigerian Civil War, 1967–1970* (Princeton University Press, 2015): 3.

86. Pine, note 81.

87. See, e.g., John Danfulani, "The End of Apartheid: A Redefinition of Nigerian Foreign Policy," *IQSRJ Journal of Humanities & Social Science*, Vol. 19 (2014): 53–57, http://iosrjournals.org/iosr-jhss/papers/Vol19-issue11/Version-3/I0191135357.pdf (arguing for the "imperatives of [a] paradigm shift" in Nigeria's Africa-centered foreign policy, given the end of apartheid and the emergence of Black-led governments in South Africa).

88. Developed in 1987 by General Ike Nwachukwu, foreign minister from 1987–1989 and 1990–1993, *economic diplomacy* emerged as a foreign policy theme during the period of General Ibrahim Babangida, Head of State from 1985 to 1993. Under this formula, Nigeria's foreign policy is said to serve the purpose of economic development at

home, in a calculated attempt to tackle the parlous state of Nigeria's oil-based economy. See C.N. Ajaebili, "The Option of Economic Diplomacy in Nigeria's Foreign Policy," *Int'l Journal of Humanities & Social Science*, Vol. 1 (2011): 277–80, http://www.ijhssnet.com/journals/Vol_1_No_17_Special_Issue_November_2011/30.pdf. Several practical issues the concept embeds include a focus "on export promotion, encouragement of direct foreign investment, debt rescheduling, [and] embracing of neo-liberal economic measures[,]" among others. Pine, note 81. Developed by Ojo Maduekwe, foreign minister from 2007–2010 under the administration of Umaru Yar'Adua (2007–2010), *citizen diplomacy* stands for the proposition that "Nigeria's foreign policy will henceforth be focused on . . . Nigerian citizens at home and in [the] [D]iaspora." Monday Dickson, "Citizen Diplomacy in President Umaru Musa Yar'Adua's Nigeria, 2007–2009: An Assessment," *Int'l Journal of Politics & Good Governance,* Vol. 1 (2010): 1, http://onlineresearchjournals.com/ijopagg/art/59.pdf (suggesting that the president's concept of "citizen diplomacy" in foreign relations lacks substance). Under this worldview, "[t]he country will strive for a synergy between foreign policy and domestic affairs in such a way that the citizen is taken as the focus of foreign policy." Ibid. In proposing this accent, foreign minister Maduekwe quipped, "[W]here is the citizen in our foreign policy?" Ibid., p. 5. The concept also appears to embody the concept of Nigeria as "giant of Africa." For example, Maduekwe opined that there could never be a black story, "unless it is a Nigerian success story." Ibid.

89. See Dapo Fafowora, "Review of Nigeria's Foreign Policy," *Nation* (Jun. 14, 2015), http://thenationonlineng.net/review-of-nigerias-foreign-policy/.

90. See Constitution of the Fed. Republic of Nigeria 1979, http://www.constitutionnet.org/files/nig_const_79.pdf, Art. 19 (spelling out the "foreign policy objectives" of the country); and Constitution of the Fed. Republic of Nigeria 1999, www.nigeria-law.org/constitutionofthefederalrepublicofnigeria.htm, Art. 19 (a)-(3). The latter is more elaborate and spells out the objectives to include: promoting and protecting the national interest; promoting African integration and support for African unity; promoting international cooperation for consolidating universal peace and mutual respect among nations; eliminating all forms of discrimination; respect for international law and treaty obligations as well as seeking pacific settlement of international disputes; and promoting a just world economic order.

91. Under the parliamentary system of government modelled after the United Kingdom's that Nigeria practiced during the First Republic, a fusion of legislative and executive powers existed wherein the prime minister, as leader of the party that won the most or majority seats in the legislature, participated in legislative business in a manner not possible in a presidential system of government (such as the United States), marked by strict separation of the powers of the legislative and executive branches. See, e.g., Michael J. Sodaro, *Comparative Politics: A Global Introduction, 3d Ed.* (Boston, MA: McGraw-Hill Higher Education, 2008): 194–205 (juxtaposing features of the parliamentary and presidential systems).

92. Courtney Faal, "Balewa, Sir Abubakar Tafawa (1912–1966)," *Blackpast.org*, http://www.blackpast.org/gah/balewa-sir-abubakar-tafawa-1912-1966.

93. "Wachuku, Jaja Anucha," *S9.com Biographical Dictionary*, http://www.s9.com/Biography/Wachuku-Jaja-Anucha.

94. Faal, note 92. Following the first military coup in January of 1966, Nigeria abandoned the parliamentary system of government, blamed for some of the instability of the First Republic years, in place of the presidential system of government which it has used in the Second Republic (1979–1983) and in the still ongoing Fourth Republic. See "Nigeria: Past, Present[,] and Future," Embassy of the Fed. Republic of Nigeria, Washington, D.C., http://www.nigeriaembassyusa.org/index.php?page=nigeria-past-present-and-future.

95. See Diamond, note 15, p. 40 (assessing Nigeria under the First Republic as a "quasi-democracy struggling to establish fully democratic government[,]" given "the shallow commitment of political elites to democratic norms of tolerance and fair play" which made "it difficult to classify Nigeria at independence as a democracy.").

96. Ibrahim A. Gambari, *Theory and Reality in Foreign Policy Making: Nigeria after the Second Republic* (Atlantic Highlands, N.J.: Humanities Press Int'l, Inc., 1989): 6.

97. Ibid., p. 7.

98. Ibid., p. 6.

99. Professor Gambari examined these and other issues in some detail in his *Party Politics and Foreign Policy: Nigeria under the First Republic*, note 11, pp. 33–131 (covering the Anglo-Nigerian Defense Pact, the Congo crisis and relations with Ghana, relations with South Africa and then Rhodesia, the Arab-Israeli conflict and Nigeria's relations with the then European Economic Community).

100. Gambari, note 99, pp. 6–7.

101. Ibid., p. 7.

102. Ibid.

103. Gambari, note 11, pp. 50–51.

104. See "Independence Day Speech by Tafawa Balewa," https://www.facebook.com/notes/fela-durotoye/dreams-of-our-founding-fathers-independence-day-speech-by-tafawa-balewa-october-/10150259870812185 (specifically Balewa's expression that his government is "grateful to the British officers whom we have known, first as masters, and then as leaders, and finally as partners, but always as friends.").

105. "Wachuku, Jaja Anucha," note 93.

106. "The Gowon Regime," *in* Metz, ed., *Nigeria: A Country Study*, note 57 (observing that "[b]y 1964 Nigerian army units, under General Johnson Aguiyi-Ironsi's command, formed the backbone of the UN force.").

107. His government lodged a vocal protest of the massacre in Sharpeville, South Africa, and, working with other countries in the British Commonwealth, attempted to expel South Africa from the Commonwealth because of its apartheid policies. Faal, note 92.

108. Ibid.

109. See "The First Republic," *in* Metz, ed., *Nigeria: A Country Study*, note 57.

110. Minority ethnic groups in the country expressed the fear that majority groups in their regions would dominate them once the country became independent from the United Kingdom. To look into this fear, in 1956, the British government appointed a commission head by Sir Henry Willink. Rather than recommend the separate regions these minority groups requested as antidote, the Commission took the seemingly

middle ground of fundamental guarantees in a constitutional document, which the British authorities, desirous of avoiding any delay in the road to independence, readily accepted. See *Report of the Commission Appointed to Inquire into the Fears of the Minorities and the Means of Allaying Them* (London: Her Majesty's Stationery Office, 1958). In sum, the inclusion of fundamental guarantees, a bill of rights, in the 1960 and subsequent constitutions of Nigeria, including the 1963, 1979, and 1999 constitutions, were a result of the Willink Commission which recommended guarantees of human rights, adapted from the European Convention on Human Rights of 1950, in lieu of the separate regions the minority ethnic groups requested.

111. Literature on the first coup, some by participants in the act, include: Adewale Ademoyega, *Why We Struck: The Story of the First Nigerian Coup* (Ibadan, Nigeria: Evans Brothers Ltd., 1981) (participant); and Ben Gbulie, *Nigeria's Five Majors: Coup d'état of 15th January 1966, First Inside Account* (Lagos: Africana Educational Publishers, 1981) (participant); Olusegun Obasanjo, *Nzeogwu: An Intimate Portrait of Major Chukwuma Kaduna Nzeogwu* (Ibadan, Nigeria: Spectrum Books, 1987); and Robin Luckham, *The Nigerian Military: A Sociological Analysis of Authority and Revolt, 1960–1967* (New York: Cambridge University Press, 1971).

112. Aka, note 16, p. 206.

113. "The First Republic," *in* Metz, ed., *Nigeria: A Country Study*, note 57.

114. Ibid.

115. Ufot Bassey Inamete, *Foreign Policy Decision-Making in Nigeria* (Selinsgrove, PA: Susquehanna University Press, 2001): 103.

116. Stremlau, note 85, p. 3.

117. See note 85.

118. Stremlau, note 85, p. 3.

119. See Aka, note 16, pp. 196–209 (commenting on the "Conduct of the Biafran War," including assessment of allegations of genocide against the Igbo, the major ethnic group in Biafra). The Geneva Conventions comprise international treaties dating back to 1864 and amplified by numerous changes, some as recent as 1978, dealing with a multiplicity of topics, including the treatment of civilians during wars, humane treatment of prisoners of war, and treatment rules relating to care of the wounded and sick. See, e.g., Emily Crawford & Alison Pert, *International Humanitarian Law* (New York: Cambridge University Press, 2015): 1–27.

120. See Chinua Achebe, *There Was a Country: A Personal History of Biafra* (New York: Penguin Press, 2012): 209–11, 228–39 (memoir on the war by a famous writer who supported the secessionist side); Chimamanda N. Adichie, *Half of a Yellow Sun* (New York: Alfred A. Knopf, 2006) (work of fiction based on the war by an Easterner born after the conflict).

121. Stremlau, note 85, pp. 3–4.

122. Indicators of this posture include "warmer attitude toward the Soviet Union," recognition of the People's Republic of China, stepped-up condemnation of the activities and policies of Western powers toward Southern Africa, and increased financial and other support for the liberation movements in Southern Africa. Gambari, note 96, p. 7. See also "The Gowon Regime," *in* Metz, ed., *Nigeria: A Country Study*, note 57 (stating that the regime committed itself to eliminating the policy of apartheid in

South Africa, and, under the auspices of the Organization of African Unity, channeled financial and military assistance to liberation movements in Africa).

123. See note 75.

124. Ifeoma Azikiwe, *Nigeria: Echoes of a Century: 1914–1999, Vol. 1* (Bloomington, IN: AuthorHouse, 2013): 217.

125. For example, at the time of his overthrow in July of 1975, General Gowon was attending an OAU meeting in Kampala, Uganda, over the Angolan civil war. Terry M. Mays & Mark W. Delancey, *Historical Dictionary of International Organizations in Sub-Saharan Africa* (Lanham, MD: Scarecrow Press, 2002): 161.

126. Gambari, note 96, p. 7.

127. See Diamond, note 15, pp. 45–49 (commenting on "[t]he [t]ransition to the Second Republic").

128. See ibid.

129. Gambari, note 96, p. 8.

130. *Id.* Under Mohammed and subsequently Obasanjo, Nigeria earned the honor of unofficial or informal membership in the Frontline States (FLS). Abba Mahmood, "Nigeria's Africa Policy in Perspective," *Leadership* (Dec. 26, 2013), leadership.ng/columns/Thursday-column/343/nigerias-africa-policy-in-perspective. The FLS was an organization of independent African states formed in 1975 designed to achieve majority rule in South Africa. Its members included Angola, Botswana, Lesotho, Malawi, Mozambique, Swaziland, Tanzania, Zambia, and Zimbabwe. These countries, all led by black majority governments, formed a ring around South Africa. Nigeria was the only such member of the group that was not geographically located in Southern Africa. See *The Legacy of the Frontline States, Building Security in Southern Africa*, Monograph No. 43 (Nov. 1999), https://www.issafrica.org/pubs/Monographs/No43/TheLegacy.html.

131. Gambari, note 96, p. 8.

132. Murtala Mohammed, "Africa Has Come of Age, Speech to the OAU Extraordinary Summit Conference," Addis Ababa, Jan. 11, 1976, Africa Youth Union (Dec. 3, 2013), https://www.facebook.com/Africanyouthunion/posts/726490580710778.

133. Joseph G. Healey, "African Proverb of the Month Nov. 2001," *Afriprov.org*, http://www.afriprov.org/african-proverb-of-the-month/27-2001proverbs/172-nov2001.html.

134. Gambari, note 96, p. 8.

135. The speech is a perfect example of an outcome that would not have occurred but for the stroke of serendipity. Mohammed initially planned to send his second-in-command, General Obasanjo, to attend this meeting, but changed his mind after a letter he received from U.S. president Gerald Ford, hand-delivered on Jan. 3, 1976, through Donald Easum, U.S. ambassador to Nigeria, regarding the conflict in Angola where the U.S. government supported UNITA, the Portuguese acronym of the National Union for the Total Independence of Angola, and opposed the Marxist-oriented MPLA. The Mohammed regime considered the letter a "gross insult." Africa Youth Union, note 132. This was among the setting in which Mohammed decided to attend the OAU conference himself rather than send an emissary. Ibid.

136. See Gambari, note 96, pp. 8–9.

137. Ibid.

138. Ibid., quoting *Economist* (London) (Aug. 4, 1979): 11.

139. See Gambari, note 96, p. 11 (stating that under Shagari, "it was as if Nigeria had rapidly slipped back into the policies of subservience to the West and hesitancy in African affairs, closer to the situation in the 1960s"); Diamond, note 15, p. 65 (positing that this time around, though ethnic polarization failed to metamorphose into conflict, "politics were not significantly less violent, vituperative, and chaotic in the Second Republic than they had been in the First Republic.").

140. Appointed parliamentary secretary to future Prime Minister Abubakar T. Balewa in 1959, Shagari went on to hold several positions in the Cabinet, including minister of economic development in 1959, minister of internal affairs in 1962, and minister of labor in 1965. "Biography of Alhaji Shehu Usman Aliyu Shagari," *The Biography*, http://thebiography.us/en/shagari-alhaji-shehu-usman-aliyu.

141. Steve Egbo, *Nigeria and the World: A Treatise on Foreign Policy* (Enugu, Nigeria: John Jacobs Classic Publishers, 2003): 78. See also A.I. Pogoson, "Leadership Roles and Foreign Policy: A Study of President Shehu Shagari's Foreign Policy Posture," *Africabib*, http://www.africabib.org/rec.php?RID=170748693 (stating that, despite the promise of "a vigorous and active foreign policy," Shagari is generally acknowledged to have been weak and indecisive," judging by the positions of his government on a range of major foreign policy issues, including "decolonization, Namibian independence, [and] racism in South Africa.").

142. See Sodaro, note 91, pp. 194–205 (juxtaposing features of the parliamentary and presidential systems).

143. See generally Gambari, note 11.

144. See Diamond, note 15, pp. 65–63 (commenting on "Why the Second Republic Failed").

145. Gambari, note 99, p. 13.

146. See Associated Press, "Expelled Foreigners Pouring Out of Nigeria," *New York Times* (May 4, 1985), http://www.nytimes.com/1985/05/05/world/expelled-foreigners-pouringout-of-nigeriaby-the-associated-press.html?pagewanted=print; Micah Bump, "Ghana: Searching for Opportunities at Home and Abroad," *Migration Info Source* (Mar. 1, 2006), http://www.migrationpolicy.org/article/ghana-searching-opportunities-home-and-abroad (section commenting on "expulsion from Nigeria.").

147. Diamond, note 15, pp. 55–7.

148. "Return to Military Rule," *in* Metz, ed., *Nigeria: A Country Study,* note 57.

149. See Diamond, note 15, pp. 56–57 (commenting on several controversial decrees unleashed by the regime permitting trials by military tribunals, curtailing expression, and detentions without trial).

150. "Political Transition," *in* Metz, ed., *Nigeria: A Country Study*, note 57 (pointing out that "political transition has been on the agenda of every military government since Ironsi's, with the probable exception of that of Buhari.").

151. Seyi Gesinde, "Nigeria's Foreign Policy in the Eye of Global Challenge," *Tribune Online* (Lagos) (May 28, 2015), http://tribuneonlineng.com/content/nigeria%E2%80%99s-foreign-policy-eye-global-challenge. Under him, in Dec. of 1984, Nigeria signed a tripartite security agreement with Benin, Togo, and Niger,

to deal with the challenges of national security arising from drugs and psychotropic substances, smuggling in small arms, human trafficking, and currency trafficking. See Hugo Odiogor & Abiodun Alade, "I Cannot Rest When the World Is Being Terrorized—Prof. Ibrahim Gambari," *Vanguard* (Lagos) (Jun. 21, 2015 1:44 AM), http://www.vanguardngr.com/2015/06/i-cannot-rest-when-the-world-is-being-terrorised-prof-ibrahim-gambari/ (interview with Professor Gambari). While this agreement could go as foreign policy achievement for Buhari, it also reinforces the need for a stronger action, lacking under his regime, in the sub-regional circle or prong of Nigerian foreign policy.

152. See "Return to Military Rule," *in* Metz, ed., *Nigeria: A Country Study*, note 57.

153. One incident that easily comes to mind is the death by letter bomb of the investigative journalist Dele Giwa in October 1986. See Diamond, note 1, pp. 486, n.100 (enumerating evidence tying the Babanginda regime to the murder).

154. See Diamond, note 1, p. 449 (recounting reasons why "[i]ncreasingly, Babangida was seen as the most massively corrupt ruler in Nigerian history.").

155. See Diamond et al., eds. *Transition without End,* note 59, *passim* (providing a critical analysis of Babingida's insincere transition to democracy program).

156. John N. Shagaya, *Governance in Nigeria: The IBB Era: An Insider's View* (Lagos: Viewpoint Communications Ltd., 2003): 86. Despite these marked achievements, the Babangida regime did not represent a high point for Nigeria's foreign policy given that, in the words of one analyst, "rhetorics, emptiness, inaction, policy somersault, and indecision . . . mark[ed] the second half of his tenure." Egbo, note 141, at 95.

157. See Comfort Asaa Mantey, "Ensuring Free Border Movements in ECOWAS Integration: Challenges to National Security," M.A. thesis, University of Ghana (Jul. 2013). The multiparty agreement eliminated travel restrictions, such as visa, among members of the community. Ibid.

158. Egbo, note 141, p. 95. More information on the TAC program is saved for chapter 9 on increased bilateralism in Nigerian foreign relations.

159. Egbo, note 141, p. 95.

160. Babangida's Decree No. 61 establishing the Interim National Government stated that Sani Abacha, Chief of Defense Staff under Babangida and a member of the Armed Forces Ruling Council, the country's highest policymaking body, shall be "Vice President, Defense Secretary, and Senior Minister." Ibid., quoted in "Ernest Shonekan, Nigeria's Most Fugacious Leader," *Nairaland Forum*, http://www.nairaland.com/1336063/ernest-shonekan-nigerias-most-fugacious. Taking advantage of this decree, on Nov. 17, 1993, Abacha eased Shonekan out of power and became head of state. "Nigerian Military Leader Ousts Interim President," *New York Times* (Nov. 18, 1993), http://www.nytimes.com/1993/11/18/world/nigeria-military-leader-ousts-interim-president.html.

161. See Howard W. French, "Nigeria Executes Critic of Regime; Nations Protest," *New York Times* (Nov. 11, 1995), http://www.nytimes.com/1995/11/11/world/nigeria-executes-critic-of-regime-nations-protest.html?pagewanted=all; "Nigeria Suspended from Commonwealth," CNN (Nov. 11, 1995), http://www.cnn.com/WORLD/9511/nigeria/11-11/.

162. See Adekeye Adebajo, *Building Peace in West Africa: Liberia, Sierra Leone, and Guinea-Bissau* (Boulder, CO: Lynne Rienner Publishers, 2002): 43–78 (Liberia); ibid., pp. 79–110 (Sierra Leone).

163. See James Rupert, "Corruption Flourished in Abacha's Regime," *Washington Post* (Jun. 9, 1998): A01, http://www.washingtonpost.com/wp-srv/inatl/longterm/nigeria/stories/corrupt060998.htm. See also "U.S. Freezes $458 m Stolen by Sani Abacha," *Vanguard* (Lagos) (Mar. 6, 2014 9:09 AM), http://www.vanguardngr.com/2014/03/us-freezes-458-mn-stolen-nigeria-dictator-abacha/ (story includes a quote attributed to a U.S. Department of Justice official who called the freeze "the biggest civil forfeiture action to recover the proceeds of foreign official corruption ever brought by" the department). In addition to the usual kickbacks, under General Abacha avenues for corruption included subsidies of refined petroleum products imported from abroad (leaving the country's refineries underutilized), creating artificial scarcity of fuel that negatively impacted Nigeria's economy. Rupert, *op. cit.*

164. Quoted in Rupert, note 163.

165. Richard Joseph, "Nigeria and the Challenge of Leadership," *Tell* (Lagos) (Jul. 5, 1999): 50.

166. Diamond, note 1, p. 464.

167. Thomas E. Patterson, *The American Democracy, 8th Ed.* (New York: McGraw-Hill, 2008): 513–14 (discussing the economic dimension of national security policy, citing the warning of former U.S. president Dwight D. Eisenhower against "the unwarranted influence" and "misplaced power" of the military-industrial complex, the coalition of military establishment, industries that manufacture weapons, and members of Congress from constituencies that depend heavily on the arms industry that mutually benefit from a high level of defense spending).

168. Gerald E. Ezirim, "Fifty Years of Nigeria's Foreign Policy: A Critical Review," *Sacha Int'l Academic Journal* (2011), http://www.academia.edu/345652/Fifty_Years_of_Nigeria_s_Foreign_Policy_A_Critical_Review.

169. Ibid.

170. "Abdulsalam Abubakar," *Online Nigeria*, http://www.onlinenigeria.com/abubakar.asp.

171. Ibid.

172. Abacha's fake transition program aimed at self-succession before the dictator's death on Jun. 8, 1998. See, e.g., 'Kunle Amuwo, "Introduction: Transition as Democratic Regression," *in* 'Kunle Amuwo et al., eds., *Nigeria during the Abacha Years (1993–1998)* (Lagos: IFRA-Nigeria, 2001): 1–56.

173. The occurrence calls to mind the ignominious humiliation in 1982 arising from the defeat of the Argentine army by British forces over control of the Falkland Islands, which both countries claimed, that eased it out of partisan politics. See Jack Donnelly, *International Human Rights, 4th Ed.* (Boulder, CO: Westview Press, 2013): 65 (observing that "[h]aving attacked its own people, brought the economy to the brink of ruin, and then embarrassed itself and the country before the entire world, the Argentine military had little choice but to permit a return to civilian government.").

174. Robyn Dixon, "Umaru Yar'Adua Dies at 58; Nigerian President," *Los Angeles Times* (May 7, 2010), http://articles.latimes.com/2010/may/07/local/la-me-umaru

-yaradua-20100507; Christine Purefoy, "Goodluck Jonathan: By Name and Nature?" *CNN* (Apr. 17, 2011 10:36 pm EDT), http://www.cnn.com/2010/WORLD/africa/05/06/nigeria.jonathan/.

175. Ezirim, note 168. Commentators dubbed his approach "shuttle diplomacy" reminiscent of former U.S. Secretary of State Henry Kissinger, testimony to the numerous travels Obasanjo undertook as president aimed at securing that repair.

176. See, e.g., "The Obasanjo Years: His Legacy," *Lawyers Chronicle*, http://thelawyerschronicle.com/the-obasanjo-years-his-legacy/ (including his period as military Head of State from 1976 to 1979); Emmanuel Ojameruaye, "A Tentative Analytical Evaluation of President Obasanjo's Performance (May 1999–May 2007)," *Gamji.com*, http://www.gamji.com/article6000/NEWS7024.htm (finding his overall performance "barely satisfactory," yet "better than most other past Nigerian presidents" based on promises and results on a range of domestic issues, including human development, corruption, healthcare, and education as well as foreign policy).

177. See Darren Kew & Peter Lewis, *Nigeria, in* Mark Kesselman, ed., *Introduction to Politics of the Developing World: Political Challenges and Changing Agendas* (Boston, MA: Cengage Learning, 2013): 214; Ofeibea Quist-Arcton, "Nigeria Rejects Term-Limit Change in Constitution," *N[ational] P[ublic] R[adio]* (May 17, 2006 6:00 AM ET), http://www.npr.org/templates/story/story.php?storyID=5410582; Craig Timberg, "Bid to Allow Nigerian a Third Term Hits Snag," *Washington Post* (May 13, 2006), http://www.gpo.gov/fdsys/pkg/CHRG-105shrg48230/html/CHRG-105shrg48230.htm.

178. See, e.g., Philip C. Aka, "The 'Dividend of Democracy': Analyzing U.S. Support for Nigerian Democratization," *Boston College Third World Law Journal*, Vol. 22 (2002): 215.

179. Ojameruaye, note 176 (finding that on human development, "about 60 percent to 70 percent" of Nigerians still live below the poverty line, defined as less than $1 per day.).

180. Obasanjo, quoted in Ezirim, note 168.

181. Obasanjo declared that "[t]he renewed determination of African leaders, our strengthening of regional economic communities, the restructuring of the OAU into the AU, and a better global disposition toward Africa, the AU and the AU's program, NEPAD, are indicators that we are indeed in a new Africa."

182. See "Obituary: President Yar'Adua," *BBC News* (May 6, 2010 02:33 UK, updated at 01:33), http://news.bbc.co.uk/2/hi/africa/6187249.stm; Ademola Bello, "Umaru Yar'Adua: A Mediocre Administrator, the Least Prepared Nigerian President since Shehu Shagari," *Huffington Post* (May 13, 2010 2:11 pm. EDT, updated May 25, 2011, 4:30 pm EDT), http://www.huffingtonpost.com/ademola-bellow/umaru-musa-yaradua-a-medi_b_575125.html (noting that under Yar'Adua, "Nigeria's celebrated peace-keeping roles, leadership of ECOWAS, and the country's Giant of Africa status all took a back seat.").

183. See Will Ross, "Nigeria Elections: Buhari Scores Historic Win," *BBC News* (Apr. 1, 2015), http://www.bbc.com/news/world-africa-32141703; Damian Zane, "Nigeria's Goodluck Jonathan: Five Reasons Why He Lost," *BBC News* (Mar. 31, 2015), http://www.bbc.com/news/world-africa-32136295.

184. See Philip C. Aka, "Nigeria since May 1999: Understanding the Paradox of Civil Rule and Human Rights Violations under President Olusegun Obasanjo," *San Diego Int'l Law Journal*, Vol. 4 (2003): 237–55 (commenting on Obasanjo's handling of four crises, including the military reprisals at Odi and Benue State).

185. Jonathan earned a Ph.D. in zoology from the University of Port Harcourt. See Amy McKenna, "Goodluck Jonathan, President of Nigeria," *Encyclopedia Britannica*, http://www.britannica.com/biography/Goodluck-Jonathan.

186. See Fisayo Soyombo, "Why Is Nigeria's Jonathan Worried?" *Al Jazeera* (Nov. 27, 2014, 14:39 GMT), http://www.aljazeera.com/indepth/opinion/2014/11/why-nigeria-jonathan-worried-20141123104313818965.html (opining that "[a] Jonathan win in 2015 will not invalidate the fact that his first-term performance was underwhelming.").

187. For a sample of the numerous commentaries in academic and popular media on this terrorist group, see John Ford, "The Origins of Boko Haram," *Nat'l Interest* (Jun. 6, 2014), http://nationalinterest.org/print/feature/the-origins-boko-haram-10609; and Farouk Chothia, "Who Are Nigeria's Boko Haram Islamists?" *BBC News* (May 4, 2015), http://www.bbc.com/news/world-africa-13809501.

188. See Philip C. Aka, "Judicial Independence under Nigeria's Fourth Republic: Problems and Prospects," *California Western Int'l Law Journal*, Vol. 45 (Fall 2014): 42, n.170 (indicating that "the bloody campaign since 2009 by Boko Haram" "amplifies the upgrading of sharia into legal code in Northern Nigeria").

189. More discussion on the problems that the new administration confronts is saved for chapter 6 on the need for increased human rights at home to drive a human rights–oriented foreign policy.

Part II

TEMPLE OF NIGERIA'S HUMAN RIGHTS FOREIGN POLICY

(SIX KEY ISSUES RELATING TO THE APPLICATION OF HUMAN RIGHTS IN NIGERIA'S FOREIGN POLICY)

Chapter Five

Reconstructing Nigeria's National Interest in a More Human Rights–Sensitive Direction

Part II of this work is devoted to analysis of six issues regarding the application of human rights in Nigeria's foreign relations. This chapter is the first of those issues and one of two steps in the temple of Nigeria's human rights foreign policy, unveiled in chapter 1, comprising four pillars and two steps. The other step, covered in chapter 6, is increased respect for human rights in Nigeria. The pillars—redesigned peacekeeping, reshaped foreign policy machine, increased bilateralism in foreign relations, and the Economic Community of West African States (ECOWAS) as a human rights tool—are covered in chapters 7, 8, 9, and 10 of the work, respectively. Individually, each step or pillar performs a necessary and unique role in the temple of Nigerian human rights foreign policy. Collectively, the steps and pillars are of equal importance, with neither category being superior nor inferior to the other.

This chapter canvasses ideas on how to reconstruct Nigeria's national interests in a more human rights–sensitive direction. Questions regarding the application of human rights in external relations "reflect[] a fundamental redefinition of the national interest[,]"[1] and reconstructing the national interest is a requisite first step for any country that chooses to adopt a human rights–based policy.[2] Three questions this chapter seeks to answer are: (1) What are "national interests"? (2) How have these interests developed in Nigeria over the post-independence period at the focus of this book?, and (3) How does one reconstruct Nigeria's national interest to make it human rights compliant?

DEFINING NATIONAL INTERESTS

There is no universally agreed-upon definition of national interest(s). Instead, different writers define the term differently. To use three examples, the realist scholar, Hans J. Morgenthau, defined national interest in terms of survival,[3] the political scientist Vernon Von Dyke as "desires on the part of sovereign states,"[4] and the think tank Brookings Institution as "the general and continuing ends for which a nation acts."[5] A common element that arguably brings these definitions together is that national interests are "the claims, objectives, goals, demands[,] and interests which a nation always tried to preserve, protect, defend and secure in relations with other nations."[6] There are other points of common or emerging agreement. These include that: a state has the *right* to promote its national interest, the national interest is *the* principle by which every state justifies its actions in international relations and conditions its behavior,[7] and a litmus test, so to speak, of every foreign policy decision is whether it serves the national interest.[8]

National interests may be classified into two categories, based on whether or not a state is willing to go to war to protect those interests.[9] These categories are vital (or necessary) interests, such as territorial identity (physical identity), political-economic benefits (political identity) and historical values that a nation upholds as part of its cultural heritage (cultural identity). They are values over which a country will be willing to go to war, if necessary, to protect.[10] Protecting these vital interests brings to mind Walter Lippman's elegant definition of *security* as "the extent to which it is not in danger of having to sacrifice core values if it wishes to avoid war, and is able, if challenged, to maintain them in such a war."[11] In contrast to vital interests, non-vital or variable interests are "other" interests outside the vital category—such as peace, justice, and prestige—sometimes dictated by the necessity of securing the vital interests that a state would like to see realized but over which it will not go to war.[12] Other systems for classifying these interests exist. For example, for the United States, former Congressman Hamilton identified the following components: preserving the territorial integrity of the United States and the safety and security of its people; sustaining United States' economic prosperity, e.g., through free markets and reacting to financial crises abroad to minimize their domestic impact; to promote democratic values; to promote basic human rights, including economic rights (freedom from starvation), political-civil rights (religious freedom and freedom of expression), and group rights (freedom from genocide); and protecting the health and welfare of Americans.[13] Popular means through which states seek to secure their national interests in the international system include: diplomacy, propaganda, economic means, alliances and treaties, and coercive means as a last resort.[14] *Diplomacy* "involves the presentation of the goals and objectives of national interest in such a way as can persuade others to accept these as just and rightful demands of the nation."[15] It is the tool through which "the foreign policy of a nation travels to other nations."[16] *Propaganda* is the art of salesmanship by which the nation using this tool seeks to convince the target nation(s) "about the justness of the goals and objectives or ends" that the nation using this tool seeks to accomplish.[17] *Economic means* consist of economic tools, such as aid and loans as a means for promoting interests in another country or countries by the nation using that tool.[18] *Alliances and treaties* are agreements concluded by two or more states for achieving common interests.[19] *Alliances* can be either military or economic in nature.[20] Though discouraged in modern international relations, states can use force (such as war) to secure their national interests, but more advisedly coercive means short of war, such as intervention, embargoes, boycotts, reprisals, etc.[21] One exception that makes the rule here is international terrorism against which threat today world public opinion permits the use of military power.[22]

The national interest has two usages revolved around what is *best* for an affected state in foreign affairs.[23] These two usages are as: an *instrument of political action* in justifying, denouncing, or proposing policies; and *political analysis* (or *analytic tool*) in describing, explaining, or evaluating the sources or adequacy of a nation's foreign policy.[24] The term's function as an instrument of *political action* goes back a long time to the sixteenth century in Italy and the seventeenth century in England.[25] In this first sense, the evolution of the term coincided with the emergence of the nation-state as a new form of political organization and allegiance, in replacement of the existing feudal order.[26] The use of the term in *political analysis* evolved much latter in the twentieth century, particularly to evaluate the policies of certain European states—England, France, and the United States on the one hand and Germany on the other hand—leading to World War II. In this latter sense, the term is contrasted with the *public interest* at the domestic level.[27]

Because it lends itself to opportunistic use in political action[28] and given the inherent limitations that bedevil its use in political analysis,[29] some scholars paint a mixed picture regarding the future of national interest in political inquiry.[30] In one such commentary, Professor Rosenau predicted that "[a]s political inquiry becomes more systematic and explicit, the concept is . . . likely to be used less and less[,]" a process that he expected to accelerate with "[t]he ever greater interdependence of nations and the emergence of increasing number of supranational actors."[31] At the same time, complicatedly, Rosenau posits that the term "cannot be entirely abandoned" because "[p]olitical actors will no doubt continue to make extensive use of the national interest in their thinking about foreign-policy goals and in their efforts to mobilize support for them. And, to the extent that they do, political observers must take cognizance of the national interest."[32] Put differently, "while the national interest has little future as an analytic concept, its use in politics will long continue to be a datum requiring analysis."[33] It is for the same reason—the continued use of the concept as an instrument of political action, in turn mandating its cognizance in political analysis—that the term is deemed helpful for this study.

To recapitulate based on the three theories surveyed in chapter 3, dealing with the theoretical framework for this study, the national interest ineluctably calls to mind the teachings of the realist school, which suggests that the pursuit of human rights concerns in external relations does not promote the national interest of a state and goes as far as to advise against such interjection of ethical values on the ground that it may impede protection of a country's vital interests.[34] Realists advocate a concept of national interest defined in terms of power in which human rights is relegated to "a (merely) moral concern."[35] For them, ethical concerns like human rights may be appropriate at the domestic level but *not* at the international level.[36] Next to idealism, although this school emphasizes cooperation in international relations among a larger group of actors other than states, it embraces the anarchic view of international politics, centered around the absence of centralized authority at the world level necessary to enforce good behavior and compliance among errant states,[37] at the heartbeat of realist theory. In contrast to these two contending and competing theories, constructivism, favored for this study, takes the most middle position, viewing foreign policies as what states make of them,[38] thereby permitting the pursuit of human rights as national interest should a state so choose.

TRACING THE DEVELOPMENT OF NIGERIAN NATIONAL INTEREST SINCE INDEPENDENCE IN 1960

A productive way to approach this discussion, conceivably, is to inquire whether Nigeria has national interests that drive its relations with other countries. Several factors necessitate or form the basis for this question. First, a flush of analyses in academic and popular forums by Nigerians take the more or less explicit position that the country's foreign relations *lack* the compass of national interests. A sample of recent commentaries illustrates this point. The first is by Jonathan Ajere who depicted (and pejoratively dismissed) Nigerian foreign policy since independence as "regional voluntarism" and "Afrocentrism."[39] Ajere posited, among other things, that "Nigeria's self-assumption of African interest promotion responsibility is indicative of the role of a volunteer[,]" a posture he said is inconsistent with realist theory.[40] However, Ajere maintained that Nigeria's "commitment[] to African security and development" and the "achievement of its national interests are *not* incompatible[,]" *if* the country improves its "local politics and economic management."[41]

Another commentary suggesting the lack of national interests in Nigerian foreign policies is by Atah Pine who highlighted the "conceptual confusion" in those policies.[42] Four slogans in Nigeria's foreign policy that Pine singled out for criticism were dynamic foreign policy, Africa as the centerpiece of Nigeria's foreign policy, economic diplomacy, and citizen diplomacy.[43] Pine opined that what Nigeria needs but currently lacks "is a foreign policy that will contain the crisis of underdevelopment, the challenges of poverty, leadership, political development, and a host of other maladies and launch her as a modern state in the twenty[-]first century in order to realize her full potentials and cravings for continental and global leadership."[44] Instead, what currently passes for policies are regime-specific pronouncements that are "not grounded in deep philosophical thought, visionary imagination[,] and broad[-]based considerations of long-lasting benefits to the *national interests*."[45] According to Pine, Nigeria's foreign policies since independence may be summed up as "change and continuity, motion without movement, dynamism without surge."[46]

A third commentary suggesting a lack of national interests in Nigerian foreign policies is by Stevens Okoro who maintained that "in most countries, Nigeria is represented by diplomats who have no idea of their functional responsibilities[,] hence they cannot protect Nigeria's *national interest* feverishly even in the face [of] violations."[47] As solution to the problem, he recommends that Nigerians "experiment with new and different tactics in the fervent pursuits of [their] *national interest*."[48]

Last but not least among these critics is Hadi Y. Al-Hassa who opined that the "omnibus nature" of the country's Africa-centered foreign policy "does not appear to be well aligned to the country's *national interests* or has not served the *national interest* in a commensurate measure."[49] After extensive reviews of the country's numerous engagements and commitments in Africa since independence, he posited, "[i]t seems that there is apparent disconnect between *national interest* and Nigeria-African relations. It is apparent that the nation is doing too much in the African continent without corresponding positive outcome."[50] He advised that the country's "attention should be more focused toward achieving our *vital national interests*[,] such as the socio-economic growth and development so as to improve the standard of living of the populace."[51] Al-Hassa called for the convention of a foreign policy summit on a range of issues, including "redefining our *national interest*, refocusing our foreign policy in such a way that we will minimize loss and increase gains as well as tying it to the socio-economic growth and development of our great country."[52]

A second factor forming the basis for the question as to whether Nigeria's external relations are guided by national interests is the fact that Nigeria has ceded territory, something which works against territorial integrity and a value which many definitions of the national interest will classify as vital interest, in defense of which a country would be willing to go to war, if necessary.[53] As indicated in chapter 1, the Nigeria government obeyed an unfavorable 2002 judgment against it by the International Court of Justice that awarded the Bakassi peninsula, a territory rich in oil located in the boundary between Nigeria and Cameroon, to Cameroon in a long-standing dispute between the two countries over ownership of the territory.[54] Nigeria complied with the ruling despite the fact that 90 percent of the peninsula's estimated 300,000 people are Nigerians.[55]

A third and final factor forming the basis for the question as to whether a sense of national interest(s) guides Nigeria's external relations revolves around the instability of the country. Nigeria is a land rife with frequent changes in government. As the human rights scholar Chidi A. Odinkalu put it in 1996, "in its 36 years as an independent state, Nigeria has had seven military rulers, six military inspired changes of government (five of which have been successful military coups), four constitutions (including one that was never used!), four constitution drafting processes, at least four programs of transition from military to civilian government, at least three unsuccessful coup attempts, three national censuses, two civilian regimes, two constituent assemblies, one civil war[,] and one successful transition program."[56]

In the nineteen years since he wrote these words, the country has undergone five other changes in government, made up of one successful transition to civil rule in 1999 and four administrations under the Fourth Republic since 1999. As chapter 4 shows, altogether fifteen administrations have run Nigeria and managed its foreign policies since its independence in 1960. As the same chapter also indicates, this comes down to a lifespan of less than four years for each administration. The number drops down to less than two years when one divides the years since independence by the number of foreign ministers over the period in question—twenty-eight altogether as of 2015 (see table 8.2 in chapter 8). Rather than administrations in a general sense, in gauging national interest or lack thereof, foreign ministers are a more reliable tool of measurement, given the "direct[] responsib[ility] for foreign policy formulation and implementation[]" that the Ministry of External Affairs, headed by the foreign or external minister, has in the Nigerian system.[57] Specifically, "[b]ecause matters were usually left in the hands of the minister and his officials, foreign policy positions could change radically from one minister to another, depending on the minister's orientation."[58]

The foregoing positions contribute important points to the discussion and are well taken. Nonetheless, Nigeria has national interests that guide its external relations. First, every state that conducts external relations has a national interest that animates those relations. Nigeria is no different. Because as a leading oil producer, the country—a non-autarkic state born in international relations through British colonialism[59]—conducts relations designed to facilitate export of its energy resources to the capitalist world economy, among other reasons it is fair to say that it has a national interest that drives those external relations.

Secondly, several times in the post-independence life of the country, Nigerian leaders have convened conferences or empaneled committees to review the country's foreign policies and map the way forward. These initiatives include: the Ambassadors' Conference in 1966 under General Aguiyi-Ironsi, the Adedeji Panel in 1976 under the Mohammed-Obasanjo regime, and a conference in 1986 under General Babangida to "review the country's foreign policy and recommend broad policy frameworks for the 1990s and beyond."[60] In each of these instances, covered in chapter 4, dealing with the historical background of the study under the post-colonial era, the conferees recommitted the country to the principle of Africa as centerpiece of Nigeria's foreign relations laid down in the early days of the country's independence.

In addition to these reviews, various Nigerian governments have created think tanks to help them formulate foreign policies. The most notable of these institutions are: the Nigerian Institute of International Affairs (NIIA), formed in 1961,[61] and the National Institute for Policy and Strategic Studies (NIPSS) established in 1979.[62] The NIIA avowedly "seeks to promote a deeper understanding of Nigeria's foreign policy, international relations, and global cultures and peoples," through "painstaking research, national and international conferences and seminars, workshops[,] and public lectures on crucial issues in world affairs."[63] The Institute is modeled after Chattam House of the Royal Institute of International Affairs in London.[64] The NIPSS touts itself "as a high[-]level center for reflection, research[,] and dialog" where "academics of excellence, seasoned policy initiators and executors and other citizens of mature experience and wisdom, drawn from all walks of life, meet to reflect and exchange ideas on the great and critical issues of society, particularly as they relate to Nigeria and Africa, within the context of a constantly changing world."[65] To add to these deliberate energies, beginning from 1979 Nigerians codified the country's foreign policy objectives by including them in their governing document, the constitution.[66]

Rather than assailments directed at the national interest as such, critics who complain that Nigerian foreign policy lacks national interest direct their anger at what they consider the excessive emphasis on Africa in Nigerian foreign policy—not sufficiently rooted in "enlightened self-interest or deliberate search for sustainable advantages."[67] Accordingly, Ajere saw no conflict between Nigeria's commitment to Africa and its national interest, *if* the country implements the necessary reforms in domestic politics that should form the basis for an African-centered foreign policy.[68] Atah argued similarly with his view that, for all its benefits and Nigeria's laudable energies in this respect, the focus on Africa in Nigerian foreign policy soon took a life all its own, "reproduc[ing] itself, like the ever[-]recurring mathematical decimal," without regard to any merit rooted in economic or other tangible benefits.[69] Atah cited Nigeria's interventions in Liberia and Sierra Leone on humanitarian missions whose interventions in the aftermath of the conflicts earned the country no reckonable economic rewards.[70] To overcome this problem, he said, the country needs a coherent foreign policy, *not* regime specific, that will stem its hosts of "maladies," including "the crisis of underdevelopment" and poverty at home that it must overcome to realize its potentials for leadership in Africa and the world.[71] And to create the strong economic base that it needs to use its economy as an "instrument of diplomatic engagement," Nigeria must build its still "grossly underdeveloped" economy.[72]

For Okoro, the main concern is a lack of sync between domestic and foreign policies, contradictions evident in a "false generosity" abroad and "penury at home," as well as in the country's "stupidly overstretching [itself] to maintain peace in other countries while at home there is fire on the mountain" run, run, run.[73] Last but not least is Al-Hassa the gravamen of whose argument is that the Africa-centered orientation takes an "omnibus nature" that puts it out of alignment with the country's national interests.[74]

A resolution by the Nigerian Senate in December 2015 mirrored these popular sentiments.[75] The resolution pled with the Nigerian government to review the objectives of the country's foreign policy to ensure that its relationship with other countries produce tangible benefits for Nigeria.[76] More specifically, it advised the national government to "imbibe Nigeria's economic interest as vital component of our foreign policy objectives in countries where the nation invested her enormous human and material resources to restore security, peace, stability[,] and democracy[.]"[77] In addition, activities that critics view as altruism may be, in actuality, undergirded by considerations of national interest. An example would be the decision in 1974 by the Gowon regime (1966–1975) to extend subsidy on oil to some African countries by selling crude oil to them at concessionary rates, provided they had their own refineries and would not re-export the oil to third countries.[78] The decision came in spite of Nigeria's role as a member of the Organization of the Petroleum Exporting Countries (OPEC), which role impels it to favor higher oil prices.[79] However, there was a substantial dose of national interest embedded in this seemly altruistic policy. As one perceptive source explained, "[p]roviding subsidies for African countries was a safe move for Nigeria" for a number of good reasons, including that "it enhanced [the country's] position and influence in Africa while building African solidarity," "protected security interests by preventing economic decline[,]" and "aided Nigeria in its efforts to create ECOWAS."[80]

Another example not focused directly on Africa would be the importance that Nigeria placed on international organizations anchored on its commitment to peace and international cooperation. On the surface this does not sound like promotion of national interest. But more critically examined, it *is*, given that "in the cases of the OAU and ECOWAS, these organizations also served to increase African unity," a key goal in Nigeria's foreign relations.[81] Besides the right, states also have the *duty* to protect their national interests. Based on the foregoing, including the continuity across leaderships in the emphasis on Africa in Nigerian foreign policy, there is no *prima facie* evidence that Nigerian decision makers failed in their duty to protect the national interest.

RECONSTRUCTING NIGERIA'S NATIONAL INTEREST TO MAKE IT HUMAN RIGHTS COMPLIANT

A reconstructed national interest is *the* desideratum for a human right–based foreign policy. Such a change occurs when a state remakes its "national identity in accordance with universalist norms, roles, and expectations[,]" and views itself "as [an] interconnected member[] of a global community that works best for everyone when human rights are respected."[82] States who apply human rights in their external relations do *not* do so at the expense of their national interests.[83] To the contrary, they are following their national interests, the only difference being that, unlike states who define their national interest based on power, as realist theory counsels, states with a human-rights-based policy spot "a broader, longer-term vision of national interest."[84] What is more, pursuit of a human rights policy need not spell abandonment of complementary material interests. Instead, "the interplay of moral and material interests can help to explain the selectivity and targeting of principled foreign policy" by states who apply human rights in their external affairs.[85]

Inertia is bliss,[86] but the pains arising from transition to "a new order of things"[87] is made more manageable—or even palatable—when there is a small or scalable gap between where we are now and where we need to be. Nigeria is arguably in this fortunate position. Given that, as the discussion in the preceding section bears out, the country's foreign policy since independence has not conformed strictly to realist teaching, Nigeria should experience little difficulty making the transition to a human rights–based foreign policy. The discussion so far has provided information on *why* Nigeria should reconstruct its national interest and the factor that makes that job less painful, but has yet to answer the *how* element of what to do to make its national interest human-rights compliant. There are two answers to that question.

The first is to make the national interest of Nigeria whatever the country and its citizens are interested in.[88] Under the constructivist worldview that informs this work, "what interests a nation is not always state security."[89] Accordingly, if Nigeria "feel[s] that it is in [its] interest to expend some of [its] foreign policy resources and attention on the rights of foreigners, there is no reason [it] should not[,]"[90] and for intrinsically human rights reasons, rather than on instrumental ground(s).[91] A few examples should draw out this point. Let's say the issues the country pursues in its foreign policy is divisible into the two categories of vital interests and non-vital interests as analyzed above in the first section of this chapter. In that case human rights concerns should sometimes make it into the vital category, rather than be forever relegated to the non-vital category as would normally be the case for a case steeped in realist thinking. For another example, say the goals the country seeks to achieve in its foreign policies are divided into security, economic, and "other" classes and that the country ranks these classes of goals in roughly this order.[92] In such a scenario, human rights would occasionally occupy the first and second categories, where they had in the past stayed put in the last class if the country were following the commandments of realism.

Such elevation of human rights in the scheme of things does *not* dictate that human rights win all the time. The national interest and the objectives of foreign policy are "not reducible to human rights," but instead can and often include other components.[93] This last statement calls to mind the various definitions of a human-rights policy set out in chapter 2 dealing with the conceptual framework of this study, one of which, provided by Professor Donnelly, deserves to be quoted in full:

> Setting priorities among various national interests is an essential part of the process of defining the national interest. International human rights law leaves states considerable latitude with respect to the weight they attach to human rights objectives in their foreign policy. There is no requirement that they include international human rights goals. . . .
>
> For those states that have included international human rights in their foreign policies, however, we can reasonably demand that human rights actually enter into their stated place in the hierarchy of national interests.[94]

And this standard is not as onerous as it seems on the surface given that, as Professor Donnelly clarified elsewhere, the main point is to assess "the impact of the full range of . . . foreign policy behavior on international human rights practices, not just those initiatives that explicitly address human rights."[95] It is also all right if a mixture of moral and material interests occurs, as Professor Brysk observed in her profile of a set of states and other political communities that consistently apply human rights in their external relations—whether the material interests are prominent as in the case with trade in Canadian policy and migration in Dutch policy or subdued in the case of Swedish policy aimed at strengthening civil society organizations in Africa.[96] Still on this matter of the national interest of the country being whatever the country and its citizens are interested in, using a decision-making formula that assigns human rights a weight that roughly matches their stated place in the hierarchy of national interest,[97] it does not hurt if the country puts things in writing. One good place to start, apart from the promotional materials of the Ministry of External Affairs, would be in a national security strategy document of the type adopted by U.S. presidents.[98]

SUMMATION

This chapter is the first port of call on a journey of six issues encapsulated in a temple of Nigeria's human rights foreign policy unveiled in chapter 1. Nigeria has national interests that drive its relations with other countries that, however, lack proper implementation, largely due to an over-concentration on Africa by a plethora of fifteen administrations and external ministers nearly double that number. A necessary first step in the transition to a human rights foreign policy is a reconstructed national interest. It is the only one among the six tools of application isolated for this study not specific to Nigeria but instead common to all countries who adopt a principled foreign policy. Such a reconstruction occurs when a state remakes its national identity to conform to international standards and requirements. The transition does not require that the country abandon pursuit of complementary material interests. Applying human rights in external affairs is predicated on a set of national interests in dealing with other countries that includes human rights concerns, but is also not limited to just these concerns. Rather, as Professor Donnelly observed, "in addition to human rights, sovereignty and non-intervention are vital norms of international society."[99]

Getting Nigeria ready for a human rights foreign policy ultimately means making the national interest of the country whatever the country and its citizens are interested in, consistent with the constructivist framework set forth in chapter 2 of this study—using a decision-making formula that assigns human rights a weight that roughly matches their stated place in the hierarchy of national interest. To promote more deliberateness going beyond the commendable codification of foreign policy goals in its national constitution, it does not hurt if the country adopts a national security strategy. Since its independence in 1960, Nigeria follows a foreign policy footwork removed from realist teaching. Accordingly, there is a small gap between where the country is now and where it needs to be that makes a transition to human rights–based foreign policy relatively pain-free.

Disaggregating national interest into its constituent parts elicits the problem with the term for a country like Nigeria. *Interest* stands for the selfish pursuit of one's own welfare[100] and *nation* is a group of people, with or without territorial control, who share common customs, origins, history, or language.[101] While with Nigeria the first property exists, there is uncertainty regarding the latter, given the multi-national character of the country as a land of over 250 ethnic groups, each of which in its own right qualifies as a nation. To be sure, the dilemma is not unique to Nigeria, given the fact that few states in the world are ethnically or racially homogenous.[102] However, compared to many of these states, Nigeria has a particularly low sense of nationhood.[103] The country is a living example of the problems of aggregation in the use of the concept of national interest in political analysis.[104] Nigerian leaders such as Olusegun Obasanjo attempt to get around this dilemma by aggregating the values of the various groups within the country. For example, Obasanjo's once defined Nigeria's national security as "the aggregation of the security interests of all individuals, communities, ethnic groups, political entities, and institutions which inhabits the territory" of Nigeria.[105] The contention lacks persuasiveness. With a population of over 186 million people and over 250 ethnic groups, to use just these two variables, the work of aggregation needing to be accomplished is daunting. Another topic that complements this discussion, the other step in the temple of Nigeria's human rights foreign policy that this study sketches, is increased human rights at home. That topic forms the focus of chapter 6.

NOTES

1. Jack Donnelly, *International Human Rights, 4th Ed.* (Boulder, CO: Westview Press, 4th ed., 2013): 139.

2. See, e.g., Alison Brysk, *Global Good Samaritans: Human Rights as Foreign Policy* (New York: Oxford University Press, 2009): 31–41.

3. See Morgenthau, quoted in "National Interest: Meaning, Components[,] and Methods," *Dinesh Int'l Politics*, http://www.yourarticlelibrary.com/international-politics/national-interest-meaning-components-and-methods/48487/ (stating that "[t]he meaning of national interest is survival—the protection of physical, political[,] and cultural identity against encroachments by other nation-states.").

4. See Vernon Von Dyke, quoted in "National Interest," note 3 (stating that "[n]ational interest is that which states seek to protect or achieve in relation to each other[,]" i.e., "desires on the part of sovereign states.").

5. See Brookings Institution, quoted in "National Interest," note 3 (defining national interest as "[w]hat a nation feels to be necessary to its security and wellbeing" that "reflects the general and continuing ends for which a nation acts.").

6. "National Interest," note 3.

7. Ibid.

8. Lee H. Hamilton, "Defining National Interest," *Christian Science Monitor* (Mar. 30, 1998), http://www.csmonitor.com/1998/0330/033098.opin.opin.2.html (commenting on the United States' national interest).

9. Ibid.; "National Interest," note 3.

10. Hamilton, note 8; "National Interest," note 3.

11. Walter Lippman, *U.S. Foreign Policy: Shield of the Republic* (Boston, MA: Little Brown, 1943): 5.

12. "National Interest," note 3.

13. Hamilton, note 8.

14. "National Interest," note 3.

15. Ibid.

16. Ibid.

17. Ibid.

18. Ibid.

19. Ibid.

20. Ibid.

21. See ibid.

22. Ibid.

23. James N. Rosenau, "National Interest," *Int'l Encyclopedia of the Social Sciences* (1968), http://www.encyclopedia.com/doc/1G2-3045000855.html.

24. Ibid.

25. *The Idea of National Interest: An Analytical Study in American Foreign Policy* (New York: Macmillan, 1934): 22–24.

26. Ibid.

27. Rosenau, note 23. In his perspicacious essay, Professor Rosenau identified two schools regarding the use of national interest as political analysis. The first are the "objectivists" because of their interest in analyzing the contents of foreign policy, including their underlying assumption that the national interest can be objectively determined. Hans J. Morgenthau, *Politics Among Nations: The Struggle for Power and Peace, Revised 5th Ed.* (New York: Alfred A. Knopf, 1978), first published in 1948, exemplifies this first school. The second school consists of "subjectivists" is so called because of their interest in explaining why nations do what they do when they engage in international action—or the decision-making approach to international politics. Rosenau, note 23. There are weaknesses with each school, which speak to the inherent limitations of national interest as political analysis. For the objectivists, it is the premise that the national interest can be objectified. For the subjectivists, it is the notion that the national interest is a reflection—and aggregation—of the individual and sometimes conflicting preferences of many groups within a nation. Ibid.

28. One infamous abuse of the term that comes quickly to mind is Adolf Hitler's invocation of "German national interests" to justify his expansionist policies before

and during World War II. "National Interest," note 3. On a much less extreme note, one analyst lists national interest among several most-abused clichés in foreign policy. Paul J. Saunders, "The Five Most Abuses Foreign-Policy Clichés," *Nat'l Interest* (retrieved Jan. 20, 2016), http://nationalinterest.org/commentary/the-five-most-abused-foreign-policy-cliches-9978. The four others are isolationism, someone "must" do something, the international community, and on the right/wrong side of history. Ibid.

29. See Rosenau, note 23 (discussing "[l]imitations of the concept"). Note 27 above summarizes some of those limitations.

30. See Rosenau, note 23 (commenting on the "[f]uture of the concept").

31. Ibid.

32. Ibid.

33. Ibid.

34. Realists make a sharp distinction between *high politics*, denoting issues supposedly vital to the survival of a state, such as sovereignty, national security, and warfare; and *low politics*, matters supposedly secondary to core security interests, such as trade, finance, migration, and social welfare. Russell Bova, *How the World Works: A Brief Survey of International Relations* (New York: Longman, 2010): 211.

35. Donnelly, note 1, p. 139. While under this formula, "states may choose to pursue international human rights objectives, out of a sense of compassion or justice," such objectives "must be rigorously subordinated to vital material national interests." Ibid.

36. See Morgenthau, note 27, p. 11 (positing that "[p]olitical realism refuses to identify the moral aspirations of a particular nation with the moral laws that govern the universe[,] because "[t]o know that nations are subject to the moral law is one thing, while to pretend to know with certainty what is good and evil in the relations among nations is quite another."); Hans J. Morgenthau, "The Pathology of American Power," *Int'l Security,* Vol. 1 (Winter 1977): 20 (warning, as President Jimmy Carter poised to take office in 1977, that "[t]o establish and maintain stability in an existentially unstable world requires of necessity an anti-reformist and anti-revolutionary foreign policy.").

37. See Brian C. Schmidt, *The Political Discourse of Anarchy: A Disciplinary History of International Relations* (Albany, N.Y.: State University of New York Press, 1998), *passim*.

38. Steve Smith, "Foreign Policy Is What States Make of It: Social Construction and International Relations Theory," *in* Vendulka Kubálková, ed., *Foreign Policy in a Constructed World* (Armonk, N.Y.: M.E. Sharpe, 2001): 38–55.

39. Jonathan Ajere, "Regional Voluntarism: The Sustainability of Nigerian Afrocentrism," *E-Int'l Relations* (Jul. 19, 2012), *passim*, http://www.e-ir.info/2012/07/19/regional-voluntarism-the-sustainability-of-nigerian-afrocentrism/.

40. Ibid., p. 4.

41. Ibid., p. 9 (emphasis added).

42. Atah Pine, "Nigerian Foreign Policy, 1960–2011: Fifty One Years of Conceptual Confusion," *Modern Ghana* (Oct. 4, 2011), *passim*, http://www.modernghana.com/print/354264/1/nigeria-foreign-policy-1960-2011-fifty-one-years-o.html.

43. Ibid.

44. Ibid.

45. Ibid. (emphasis added).

46. Ibid.

47. Stevens Okoro, "Nigeria and the Concept of National Interest," *Daily Independent* (Lagos) (Jul. 2012), http://dailyindependentnig.com/2012/07/nigeria-and-concept-of-national-interest/ (emphasis added).

48. Ibid. (emphasis added).

49. Hadi Y. Al-Hassa, "Evaluating Nigerian Foreign Policy at 50," *Gamji.com* [no date included, but probably published in 2010], http://www.gamji.com/article9000/news9139.htm (emphasis added).

50. Ibid. (emphasis added).

51. Ibid. (emphasis added).

52. Ibid. (emphasis added).

53. See notes 9–11.

54. See chapter 1, footnote 25.

55. Chapter 1, footnote 25, citing "Nigeria Cedes Bakassi to Cameroon," *BBC News* (Aug. 14, 2008), http://news.bbc.co.uk/2/hi/africa/7559895.stm.

56. Chidi A. Odinkalu, "The Management of Transition to Civil Rule by the Military in Nigeria (1966–1999)," *in* 'Kunle Amuwo et al., eds., *Nigeria during the Abacha Years* (Lagos: IFRA Nigeria, 2001): 57.

57. "Foreign Relations," *in* Helen Chapin Metz, ed., *Nigeria: A Country Study* (Washington, D.C.: GPO for the Library of Congress, 1991), http://countrystudies.us/nigeria/80.htm.

58. Ibid.

59. Inspiration for this idea comes from Hanes Walton Jr. & Robert C. Smith, *American Politics and the African American Quest for Universal Freedom, 5th Ed.* (Longman, 2010): 283 (depicting African Americans as a people "born in foreign affairs through African slavery and the slave trade.").

60. "Foreign Relations," note 57.

61. "Director-General's Message," http://niianet.org/dgmessage.htm; *About Us*, http://niianet.org/aboutus.htm.

62. "Objectives," http://nipsskuru.gov.ng/index.php/similar-tags.html.

63. "Director-General's Message," note 61.

64. Ibrahim A. Gambari, *Theory and Reality in Foreign Policy Making: Nigeria after the Second Republic* (Atlantic Highlands, N.J.: Humanities Press Int'l, Inc., 1989): 11.

65. "Objectives," note 62.

66. See Constitution of the Fed. Republic of Nigeria, 1999 [hereinafter referred to as Nigerian Const. 1999], Art. 19 (enumerating the five objectives of the country in foreign policy, instructively including as the very first, "promotion and protection of the national interest.").

67. Reuben Abati, "The President as Chief Diplomat," *YNaija.com* (Apr. 17, 2016), http://ynaija.com/president-travel-reuben-abati/.

68. Note 41.

69. See Atah, note 42.

70. Ibid.

71. Notes 43–44.

72. Atah, note 42.

73. Okoro, note 47. Fire on the Mountain, Run, Run, Run is an age-old children's singing game where children follow the command to run when told there is fire on the mountain.

74. Note 49.

75. See "Senate Asks Buhari to Review Nigeria's Foreign Policy," *Premium Times* (Lagos), http://www.premiumtimesng.com/news/top-news/194812-%E2%80%8Bs%E2%80%8Benate-asks-buhari-to-review-nigerias-foreign-policy.html.

76. Ibid.

77. Ibid.

78. "Foreign Relations," note 57.

79. Ibid.

80. Ibid.

81. Ibid.

82. Brysk, note 2, p. 31.

83. See ibid.

84. Ibid.

85. Ibid., p. 33.

86. See Mark Twain, quoted in Nancy M. Lorenzi & Robert T. Riley, "Managing Change: An Overview," *Journal of American Medical Informatics Association*, Vol. 7 (Mar.–Apr. 2000): 116 (stating that "[i]t's not the progress I mind, it's the change I don't like"); and Niccollo Machiavelli, quoted in ibid., p. 110 (stating that "[t]here is nothing more difficult to take in hand, more perilous to conduct, or more uncertain in its success, than to take the lead in the introduction of a new order of things.").

87. Machiavelli, quoted in Lorenzi & Riley, note 86.

88. See Donnelly, note 1, p. 139.

89. Brysk, note 2, p. 33.

90. Donnelly, note 1, p. 140.

91. Ibid. (e.g., living in a more just world, rather than that, for example, "rights-protective regimes are more peaceful or better trading partners.").

92. Ibid., p. 145.

93. Ibid.

94. Ibid., p. 146.

95. Jack Donnelly & Debra Liang-Fenton, *Introduction, in* Debra Liang-Fenton ed., *Implementing U.S. Human Rights Policy* (Washington, D.C.: United States Institute of Peace Press, 2004): 6.

96. Brysk, note 2, p. 33.

97. Donnelly, note 1, p. 146.

98. As its name suggests, U.S. National Security Strategy is a coherent document, not a promotional brochure on the policy of an affected U.S. administration that sets the priorities of a particular U.S. administration and communicates those priorities to Congress, the American people, and the world. Karen DeYoung, "Obama Redefines National Security Strategy, Looks Beyond Military Might," *Washington Post* (May 27, 2010; 4:46 PM), http://www.washingtonpost.com/wp-dyn/content/

article/2010/05/27/AR2010052701044.html. The document is prepared annually, pursuant to the Goldwater-Nichols Act of 1986, Pub. L.99–433, which mandates the president to submit to Congress an annual strategic statement. National security is something that presidents do whether or not they report to Congress, but by requiring the White House to make its policy explicit, Congress asserts greater control over the military while affording itself an opportunity to exert greater influence on the president's national security strategy. "National Security Strategy, United States," *Encyclopedia of Espionage, Intelligence & Security* (2004), http://www.encyclopedia.com/doc/1G2-3403300516.html.

99. Jack Donnelly, "An Overview," *in* David P. Forsythe, ed., *Human Rights and Comparative Foreign Policy* (New York: United Nations University Press, 2000): 318. Donnelly legitimately warned that it will be foolhardy to "overestimate either human rights or sovereignty" in the external behavior of states. Ibid.

100. See *Oxford American Dictionary and Thesaurus* (New York: Oxford University Press, 2003): 781. Realists tie such pursuit of selfish interest to power which they, however, concede is ever-changing. See Morgenthau, note 27, pp. 9–10 (commenting on the definition and features of power).

101. See Daniel S. Papp, *Contemporary International Relations: Frameworks for Understanding, 6th Ed.* (Upper Saddle River, N.J.: Pearson, 2001): 38.

102. See, e.g., "Ethnicity and Race by Countries," *Infoplease*, http://www.infoplease.com/ipa/A0855617.html; James D. Fearson, "Ethnic and Cultural Diversity by Country," *Journal of Economic Growth*, Vol. 8 (Jun. 2003): 195–212, https://web.stanford.edu/group/fearon-research/cgi-bin/wordpress/wp-content/uploads/2013/10/Ethnic-and-Cultural-Diversity-by-Country.pdf; and Max Fisher, "A Revealing Map of the World's Most and Least Ethnically Diverse Countries," *Washington Post* (May 16, 2013), https://www.washingtonpost.com/news/worldviews/wp/2013/05/16/a-revealing-map-of-the-worlds-most-and-least-ethnically-diverse-countries/.

103. See Alade Rotimi-John, "The Nigerian Question and Its Resolution," *Guardian* (Lagos) (Nov. 18, 2015 4:20 am), http://www.ngrguardiannews.com/2015/11/the-nigerian-question-and-its-resolution/ (harping on the need to "set the country on the path of true nationhood" that it currently lacks); Kwasi Kwarteng, "Nigeria's Current Troubles and Its British Colonial Roots," *The Globalist* (Mar. 9, 2012), http://www.theglobalist.com/nigerias-current-troubles-and-its-british-colonial-roots/ (conveying that Nigeria lacks the "strong sense of nationhood" found in countries like the United Kingdom and the United States).

104. See note 27.

105. Quoted in Victor A.O. Adetula, "Between National Security Considerations and the Challenge of Cross-Border Crime in West Africa," *in* Celestine Oyom Bassey & Oshita D. Oshita, eds., *Governance and Border Security in Africa* (Lagos: Malthouse Press Ltd., 2010): 299.

Chapter Six

Charity Begins at Home

Increased Respect for Human Rights in Nigeria

Increased respect for human rights is the second of two key steps in the temple of Nigeria's human rights foreign policy unveiled in chapter 1 of this study; the other is reconstructed national interest analyzed in chapter 5. This chapter marshals and presents ideas on how Nigeria can generate the increased respect for human rights at home that is desideratum for the successful conduct of a human rights–oriented foreign policy. As indicated in chapter 1, Nigeria is a party to numerous global and regional human rights instruments, consistent with a proclamation of "respect for international law and treaty obligations" in its Constitution.[1] Despite this pledge, the country remains a hotbed of human rights abuses of every category, individual and group, both during military dictatorships and civilian governments alike.[2] Consequently, the ensuing discussion is animated by an essentialist instinct for a transition from inspiration to impact in realizing human rights that rises beyond verbal commitment to human rights ideals.[3]

EXPLAINING THE IDIOM ABOUT CHARITY BEGINNING AT HOME

Charity begins at home is an idiom which stands for the proposition that a person should be generous first to his family before extending the same to others.[4] Realistically, the do-gooder "should begin at himself."[5] Or else, "how shall we expect charity towards others, when we are uncharitable to ourselves?"[6] How can a person be "beautiful abroad but ugly at home"?[7] Another way of expressing this wisdom in the context of this study is that foreign policy begins at home.[8] "It is folly to weaken at home what one is trying to strength abroad."[9] Instead, as Professor Brysk indicates in her case study of global "Good Samaritan" states and political communities who apply human rights consistently in their external affairs, a country's own human rights records is the basis for projection of human rights abroad.[10] Put differently, democracy at home "provides an incentive, model, and rationale for" a human rights foreign policy,[11] and projecting human rights abroad must be rooted in and reflect respect of human rights at home.[12] Former Nigerian president Goodluck Jonathan arguably expressed a similar idea when he indicated that the country's foreign policy should be the tool for externalizing the "domestic priorities and the aspirations of [Nigerian] citizens, including the values of democracy within the country."[13] In the final analysis, foreign policy initiatives, including demonstrations of national sovereignty in international relations, amount to little if a state is unable to protect the basic rights of its citizens, beginning with the right to life.[14]

JUSTIFYING INCREASED HUMAN RIGHTS AT HOME

Nigeria can perform important service for international law just by getting its human rights house in order. Because of its status as the most numerous black state in the world, human rights peace in Nigeria is a boon for international human rights. The reverse is true when violations are rife. For example, the tragic humanitarian fallouts of the Nigerian civil war from 1967 to 1970 vastly occupied the attention of the international community and generated debate about excessive use of force by the Nigerian central government, in its attempt to suppress the secession of Eastern Nigeria, that until today still rages within the country.[15] A similar human rights crisis today, in a country that has more than doubled its population in the forty-five years since the war and within the context of a post–Cold War world marked by increased globalization, would divide the world and occupy its attention more.

In addition to the gains for international human rights law, there are benefits inuring to Nigeria that justify increased respect for human rights at home. First, more human rights at home will help to remove or minimize the contradiction of "beautiful abroad but ugly at home"[16] that marks the country's external behavior. Second, increased human rights at home will ensure that the leadership role in international affairs that Nigeria aspires to abroad is credible, as well as lends increased credibility to the country's external relations now mostly anchored around peacekeeping and a fledgling technical aid corps program. Because foreign policy is an expression of a country's national interest, Nigeria's foreign relations cannot be isolated from the domestic context of the country.

SEVEN STEPS TO INCREASED HUMAN RIGHTS AT HOME

Given the reality summarized above that foreign policy begins at home, how does Nigeria generate the human rights at home necessary for the pursuit of a human rights–oriented foreign policy? A conceivable answer is the seven steps to the haven of increased human rights in Nigeria that this section analyzes, namely: (1) maintaining civilian rule; (2) extending the "dividend of democracy" under the Fourth Republic since 1999 to economic rights; (3) taking collective rights seriously, including punishment for human rights violations, and reparations for past abuses; (4) taking political restructuring, defined as decentralization and devolution of power, seriously; (5) stemming the influence of religion in politics; (6) electing competent governments able and willing to handle tasks 2 to 5; and (7) external support or assistance. Before delving into the steps, several observations are in order. The first is that the list is illustrative, rather than exhaustive,[17] and mirrors the recommendations of other scholars, though on matters different from this topic.[18] Second, for the best result, many of these steps must be synchronized, rather than implemented sequentially. Because steps 1 and 7 are predicates, the applicable steps needing synchronization are the five in-between those two factors. Third, as the ensuing discussion makes clear, these steps are not exclusive but instead overlap at various points. The fourth relates to the expression "increased respect for human rights at home" in the title of this chapter. The phraseology raises the question regarding the depth of concern that is appropriate.[19] The appropriate respect is not an inchoate desire to treat citizens "fairly and seek to realize their interests";[20] instead, it is solicitude of a more general or universal nature embedded in "recognized *rights* of subject (citizens) that can be exercised against their rulers."[21]

Maintaining Civilian Rule

Nigeria is a land paved with the instability of military rule. Until 1999, the only government many Nigerians grew up in, back to 1966 when the military seized power for the first time, was a military dictatorship. Accordingly, civilian rule, practiced only three times in the entire history of Nigeria with the period since 1999 as the longest of the three periods, is the flipside of military rule. Another name for civilian rule would be *democracy*, "government of the people, by the people, for the people," as Abraham Lincoln famously defined the term.[22] But people-centered governance, in the sense Lincoln used the term, has yet to take root in Nigeria, hence the preference for the term *civilian rule*. Although important, procedures, such as elections, are not the only constituent features of a democracy; instead, *quality* is also a key ingredient in the definition of any democracy.[23] In theory as in practice, democracy is a dynamic notion that entails progressive and widespread application of democratic principles that proceed apace until democracy becomes the "only game in town,"[24] through routinization and internalization "in social, institutional, and even psychological life, as well as in political calculations for achieving success."[25]

Maintaining civilian rule is the foundation for any sustained progress in human rights in Nigeria. True, many of the country's political institutions, such as the 36-state structure,[26] transfer of the country's national capital from Lagos to Abuja,[27] and adoption of the presidential system of government in place of the parliamentary system, occurred during the years of military rule.[28] Similarly, some of the gains in Nigerian foreign policy, including the evolution of peacekeeping as a niche in the implementation of the country's external affairs, covered in chapter 7, took place during military rule. However, these changes are little more than a testament to military domination of the political system. First, abuses of human rights in the country reached their apogee during periods of military rule.[29] Secondly, prolonged military rule has a severely negative effect on many political values necessary for the growth of the rule of law, including judicial independence.[30] Third, political corruption, the use of public offices and trusts for private ends,[31] reached dubiously new heights during the two long stretches of military rule for nearly thirty years.[32] Fourthly, unlike their counterparts in East Asia (China, Hong Kong, Singapore, South Korea, and Taiwan), said to have used authoritarianism to build the economy, Nigerian military dictators produced slow or negative economic progress.[33]

Concededly, the quality of civilian rule under the Fourth Republic has been distinctively low.[34] Several reasons account for this development, including the unrelieved rifeness of corruption in the land; domination of the political system by former military leaders of a kind that raises questions regarding the civilian content of the political system; widespread poverty in the land of a kind that points to an absence or failure of an anti-poverty program; and limited progress on cohesion or sense of nationhood necessary for successful conduct of foreign relations. The first two reasons are dealt with in this section, while the last two are dealt with in the sections below. Regarding the rifeness of corruption, two scandals involving General Olusegun Obasanjo (1999–2007) and Goodluck Jonathan (2010–2015), whose two administrations span most of the 16 years of the Fourth Republic, typify the scale of this problem. In the first, Obasanjo expended about U.S. $16 billion during the period of his eight years in office with no tangible improvement in the country's energy power situation as electricity supply remained unreliable as it did when he took office.[35] A House of Representative Committee which looked into the matter discovered about 2,500 containers of imported power equipment worth about $5 billion abandoned at Lagos ports.[36] In the second, still unraveling, a key adviser to Jonathan is accused of stealing over $2 billion meant to purchase weapons to combat the Boko Haram insurgency that has ravaged the country since 2009.[37] Plato taught in his allegory of the Cave that "the well-governed city is impossible" where "beggars hungry for private goods go into public life, thinking that the good is there for the seizing[.]"[38] This feature appears to characterize Nigerian governments under the Fourth Republic since 1999. And although various legal measures have been unveiled designed to deal with this problem,[39] these laws lack vigorous enforcement for various reasons, including lack of political will.[40] Meanwhile, the Nigerian state continues to rank dubiously high on many perceptions-of-corruption indicators.[41] Corruption has a negative effect on the country's image abroad, complicates foreign relations, impedes foreign direct investment (FDI) into the country,[42] and because, by its laws and examples, the government sets the tone for behavior in society, stimulates a culture of graft in the larger community.[43] If not stemmed, corruption has the potential to delegitimize the Fourth Republic like it did the Second Republic from 1979 to 1983.[44]

In addition to the intractable problem of continued corruption, to the extent it has unfolded under the Fourth Republic since 1999, civilian rule has also been heavily dominated by former military generals. These former military officers include Olusegun Obasanjo (1999–2007) and Muhammadu Buhari since 2015. Each of these individuals also served as former military heads of state, Obasanjo from 1976 to 1979 and Buhari from 1983 to 1985. Finally, each was a participant on the federal side in the Nigerian civil war from 1967 to 1970. Domination of the political system by former military personnel was a tendency in the making for a while[45] that reached a high point with Buhari's election in spring of 2015.[46] To get a sense of the real extent of the continued military domination of the Nigerian political space since 1999, General Obasanjo completed two full terms in office and tried to change the constitution to give him a third term. When the attempt failed,[47] he handpicked two candidates who succeeded him: the first, Umaru Yar'Adua as president and the second, Goodluck Jonathan as vice-president.[48] These were the only individuals without a military background who have come to the presidency under the Fourth Republic. The first served for only three years when he died in office in 2010. The second completed his predecessor's remaining one year in office before winning election in his own right and serving four years, bringing his total period in office to five years. Because it raises questions regarding the civilian content of a supposedly democratic regime, domination of the political system by former military generals appears to negate civilian control of the military and the police, a key element of democracy.[49] Civilian control of the military is present when there is supremacy of elected officials of state over appointed officers at all levels but is lacking where, instead, security forces control the civilian population.[50] In addition, the domination throws up issues about leadership styles. As president, time and again, Obasanjo adopted military solutions to non-military issues,[51] an inflexible orientation that, from early indications, Buhari also appears to share to an even greater degree.[52] These mindsets for individuals who participated in the bloody campaign during the civil war (1967–1970) to keep Nigeria one has ramifications for a range of national issues, such as political restructuring, discussed later.

Despite the low quality of civilian rule recounted above, civilian governments are preferable because of the opportunity they afford, vis-à-vis repressive military regimes, for experimentation in self-governance necessary for the growth of the rule of law.[53] Military regimes and safeguard of human rights are an oxymoron. Military rule was among the key factors that impeded progress in human rights after independence. "All eight military regimes that ruled Nigeria since independence have put the constitution on hold."[54] Agitation for human rights in the country coincided with the harshness of military rule during the second installment of military rule from 1984 to 1999, with the birth of the Civil Liberties Organization (CLO), a key human rights organization, in 1987.[55] "[A]s the military effectively silenced, co-opted, or intimidated all other pressure groups in the polity, including the trade union, professional associations, and religious organizations," non-governmental organizations (NGOs) formed the only entity that the population looked up to as alternative voice.[56] Conscious of the repression of military regimes and convinced that civilian rule provides a more conducive environment for human rights, many of these NGOs fought for a return to democracy, mobilizing local and international support for this purpose.[57] Compared to military regimes, civilian rule affords an atmosphere conducive for safeguarding all categories of human rights in Nigeria. To play on Winston Churchill's famous dictum about democracy as the worst form of government,[58] for human rights and the rule of law, the worst civilian government in Nigeria is better than the most benevolent military rule.[59] Moreover, the immense diversity of Nigeria makes the country hard to manage by military means.[60]

In a nutshell, vis-à-vis military regime, civilian rule affords more room for ventilation and rectification of historically unjust relationships.[61] A key feature of the post–Cold War landscape in Africa is that, to be effective, any system of governance in the region must be *more* democratic than in the past. This is because in the age of globalization, the Internet, and the Worldwide Web, political techniques used in the past to maintain non-democratic governments, including adherence to artificial boundaries, have eroded to the point of no return.[62] Human rights foreign policy is hardly built on a "tenuous" democratic base.[63] Instead, because foreign policy is the product of a self-governing people that also mirrors their values and interests at home, by definition military rule is inconsistent with foreign policy. The stability of civilian rule over military dictatorship as a political system is indicated by the fact that under the presidential system of government that Nigeria practices, General Buhari is guaranteed four years in office, a protection that a military regime lacks—considering that in his first outing, Buhari was schemed out of office by his colleagues in a "palace coup" after only 20 months in office. Little wonder that consensus for democracy as a basis for the political and human rights process is growing in the country.[64] Yet the impediments to democracy are real in Nigeria and should not be minimized. These deficiencies are the reason why although a necessary condition, maintaining civilian rule in and of itself is insufficient. Instead, those deficiencies counsel the "auxiliary precautions" embedded in a backup of the other six factors,[65] considering that no government in the world, not even the United States', perfectly respects human rights.[66]

Extending the Supposed Dividend of Democracy to Socioeconomic Rights

With civilian rule as predicate, Nigeria needs progress in individual rights, particularly economic, social, and cultural (or socioeconomic) rights to increase human rights at home. Under the Fourth Republic since 1999, Nigerians enjoy more freedom than they did during military rule.[67] But there should be more to it than that. A free society must "help the many who are poor[;]"[68] as then U.S. president Bill Clinton advised in his address to the Nigerian National Assembly in August of 2000, "in the end, successful political change must begin to improve people's daily lives. That is the democracy dividend Nigerians have waited for."[69] Despite the advice, civilian rule is shorn of the "dividend of democracy" for the masses of Nigerian citizens.[70] Nigeria is a country of "abundant human and natural resources [that] still struggles with mass impoverishment."[71] Although continuously under civilian rule now for nearly two decades, Nigeria remains a rich country of many poor people.[72] The country is a stalwart of NEPAD that has yet to live up to the poverty-alleviation mission of the organization.[73] Instead, about two-thirds of Nigerians still live below the poverty line.[74] Civilian rule must mean more for the average Nigerian than the freedom to make fun of a "litany of social ills and troubles," monuments of low-quality governance, evident in "daily blackouts, long lines at gas stations" or protection from the ravages of an ongoing religion-based terrorism in the northeastern portion of the country.[75] Nigerian leaders should keep in mind the injunction of the World Conference on Human Rights that "[t]he existence of widespread extreme poverty inhibits the full and effective enjoyment of human rights," an occurrence that makes the "immediate alleviation and eventual elimination" of such poverty "high priority."[76]

To increase the attachment of the masses of the Nigerian people to democracy,[77] civilian rule must, in addition to "clean government" touched upon under step 1. above, produce improved living standards, including more jobs and better public service.[78] Nigeria's constitution enumerates both political and civil (political-civil) and socioeconomic rights.[79] Political-civil rights are guarantees of freedom with which governments must not interfere. These guarantees include the right to life, personal liberty, fair hearing, privacy and family life, the right to freedom of thought, conscience, and religion; freedom of expression and the press, peaceful assembly and association; and freedom of movement. Socioeconomic rights are material-based guarantees of freedom that require governmental preparation for the enjoyment of these rights. Without such preparation, the realization of these rights is made difficult or impossible. These guarantees include access to education, healthcare, food, shelter, and clean water; the right to work, including protection against unemployment; right to form and join trade unions; and the right to social security, among others.[80] Global and regional human rights instruments that the Nigerian government ratified, pledging as a matter of international law to protect these rights for its citizens, include the International Covenant on Civil and Political Rights (ICCPR); the International Covenant on Economic, Social, and Cultural Rights (ICESCR); and the African [Banjul] Charter on Human and Peoples' Rights (ACHPR).[81]

However, while it protects political-civil rights, Nigeria's constitutions make socioeconomic rights non-justiciable, meaning that these rights are merely aspirations that individuals, as a matter of law, cannot sue on when these "guarantees" are violated.[82] One way to stir Nigerian governments from their slumber on economic rights would be to make these rights—access to education, healthcare, food, shelter, clean water, and so forth—justiciable under the Nigerian constitution. This would give citizens a legal reference point, currently non-existent, to bring lawsuits for breaches of these rights when they are violated, as has repeatedly been the case since the country's independence in 1960. States are obligated under international human rights law to create conditions favorable for the "full and effective enjoyment of human rights," including eliminating all impediments to such enjoyment.[83] They must give high priority to alleviating, if not eliminating, "widespread extreme poverty" of the type that can impede "full and effective enjoyment of human rights."[84] How can Nigeria be so rich while its citizens are so poor?[85]

Appeals by leaders to the masses for patience and continued sacrifice are unwarranted and less likely to be heeded if citizens believe that their contributions to democracy are not leading to any improvement in their economic circumstances.[86] Consistent with the injunction of the Vienna Declaration and Program of Action, the Nigeria government has a duty to "promote and protect *all* human rights and fundamental freedoms" for all its citizens,[87] as well as create favorable conditions "to ensure the full and effective enjoyment of human rights," including eliminating "all violations of human rights and their causes, as well as obstacles to the enjoyment of these rights."[88] Given these enjoinments, Nigerian government must protect both categories rather than privilege one category of right over the other as it does now.

To stem the high level of unemployment that bedevils its economy, especially among the youth,[89] Nigeria "need[s] a job strategy, not just a growth strategy."[90] Still on economic progress, Nigeria needs to redress the imbalance between a high rate of fertility and a low rate of GDP growth. True, Nigeria got its giant-of-Africa status from "endowments" that include its big population. But population growth must have some basis in intrinsic economic growth, even for a mineral-rich country. Nigeria must build up the economic dimension of its national security by diversifying its economy beyond oil products.

Taking Collective Rights Seriously, Including Punishment for Human Rights Violations, and Reparations for Past Abuses

Adding to the two steps analyzed above and building on them, to create the increased respect for human rights at home that Nigeria needs to drive its external relations, the country's leaders must also, as a matter of law, protect collective or group rights. These guarantees, appropriately denominated by some writers as "solidarity rights,"[91] necessarily complement individual rights (both political-civil and socioeconomic rights).[92] They are guarantees which the individual may enjoy as a member of a particular society. These rights which, like political-civil rights and socioeconomic rights, are contained in global and regional human rights multilateral treaties, which, as indicated before, Nigeria is a state party to—and therefore obligated under international law to comply with—include the equality of peoples, the right to existence and self-determination, the right to free disposal of natural wealth and resources, the right to development, the right to international peace and security, and the right to a clean environment. The enjoinment for states to "promote and protect *all* human rights and fundamental freedoms" for all citizens,[93] arguably, encompasses collective rights. "Political-civil rights and socioeconomic rights are individual rights that may also be enjoyed by groups; and solidarity rights, like the rights to peace, development, a clean environment, and the right to self-determination, are group rights that individuals may also enjoy."[94] Given the interconnectedness, and indivisibility of all categories of human rights, privileging individual rights over group rights makes little sense.[95]

Group rights have always been critical in Nigeria. In fact, the fear of majority domination by minority groups was the factor that led to the enshrinement of "fundamental rights" in the country's 1960 constitution and subsequent ones.[96] Yet Nigeria has a poor record of respect for these collective rights. Using the right to self-determination as case in point, under the Fourth Republic since 1999, Nigeria has responded inadequately to campaigns for this right,[97] vis-à-vis similarly situated countries.[98] For ethnic peace in the Niger Delta (the developmentally neglected source of Nigeria's oil wealth) and other trouble spots in the country, the Nigerian national government must heed the injunction in the international bill of human rights, regarding economic self-determination, that "[i]n no case may a people be deprived of its own means of subsistence."[99]

Although human rights "are usually taken to have a special reference to the ways in which states treat their own citizens," it is not only governments (standing for states) that violate these rights.[100] Instead, life, liberty, security, property, and other freedoms to which people have human rights may also as well be denied by an array of non-state actors, including individuals and organizations.[101] What this means for the issue here at hand is that in addition to respecting individual and collective human rights, the government has an obligation to ensure that individuals and groups (including corporate entities) in society also respect these rights and that they are held accountable for abuses of human rights that they perpetrate. Unfortunately, this is not the case in Nigeria where, instead, the government time and again tolerates the violations by individuals and groups of the human rights of politically powerless or disfavored groups. One such group, going back to the early history of the country, but especially since the end of the Biafra war in 1970, is the Igbo.[102] "Nigeria violates the human rights of all its inhabitants, but much more so the human rights of Igbos."[103] Or as one Igbo sociocultural group put it, the Igbo "enjoy *less* protection of the law than any other ethnic group in Nigeria."[104] The reason for this occurrence is because Nigerian governments have a history and practice of *not* holding abusers of Igbo human rights—whether private citizens, government officials or organizations—accountable.[105] Better attention to collective attention in Nigeria must include eschewal of impunity by taking more seriously punishment for human rights violations by individuals and public officials who violate the rights of individuals from politically powerless or disfavored groups. The country (un) wittingly sets the ground for conflicts that detract from the national cohesion necessary for effective conduct of foreign relations when it fails to hold individuals and officials accountable for the abuses of the human rights of all Nigerians, Igbo and non-Igbo.

Taking punishment for human rights violations seriously includes reparations for past human rights abuses. Reparation means to repair a victim or put that victim back, as much as possible, to his or her pre-damage condition. The principle also mandates restitution or the return to a victim of something wrongfully taken from that victim. However, like with punishment for human rights violations, and again as the Igbo experience evinces, Nigeria has a poor history of reparations for past human rights abuses.[106] Reparations "for past violations will compel individuals or groups to think twice before they violate other people's individual and collective human rights. Conversely, the lack of reparation for past human rights abuses in Nigeria is probably among the reasons these abuses recur."[107] In 1999, the Obasanjo administration (1999–2007) established a commission, the Human Rights Violations Investigation Commission (HRVIC), to investigate past human rights abuses in the country and make recommendations on how to redress those abuses and deter future atrocities.[108] However, the Commission submitted a report that the government never released, much less enforced.[109] To prevent impunity, human rights abuses, whether by state or non-state entities, must be punished, regardless of which entity perpetrated the violations. Given the point made earlier that life, liberty, security, property and other freedoms to which people have human rights may also as well be denied by non-state actors,[110] the governments fails in its obligation toward human rights when abuses by non-state entities go unpunished.

Taking Political Restructuring Seriously

To generate the human rights at home that it needs for a human rights foreign policy, along with the preceding steps and reinforcing those measures, Nigerian leaders need to take political restructuring seriously. At issue is the "national question" revolved around "how to structure the state so that every ethnic or religious group and every Nigerian as an individual becomes a stakeholder."[111] Nigeria was not created "by a voluntary union of previously existing, closely related, and freely contracting political units[.]"[112] Instead, union was "forced on the country in 1914" by British colonial authorities.[113] Ever since, "the question of whether the [forced fusion into one country] should continue has never been freely and openly discussed among all nationalities."[114] It was in an attempt to address this national question that Nigeria adopted federalism in 1954.[115]

Paradoxically, going back to the days of the civil war in 1967, Nigeria's leadership, for the most part dominated by northern Muslims, has operated the country's federal system in a unitary format—much to the chagrin of many non-northerners.[116] Under the Fourth Republic since 1999, "[a] recurring theme in Nigerian federalism is the federal government's dominance vis-à-vis the state and local governments," evidenced by various provisions in the 1999 Constitution, including exclusive control of the police and the armed forces, a sizable listing of subject areas over which only the national government can legislate, and judicial powers for the national government that extends to state courts.[117] To put the matter in proper perspective, Nigeria is a country of 36 states, one federal capital territory at Abuja, and 774 local governments[118] underlain by six geo-political zones not reflected in the constitution.[119] However, the 1999 Constitution allocates 68 powers to the national government;[120] 12 others which it shares with the states,[121] some smattering of residual powers, nothing spelled out like the reserved powers of the states under the Tenth Amendment of the U.S. Constitution;[122] and two for the numerous local governments.[123]

Pressed by repeated appeals for a return to "true federalism,"[124] General Olusegun Obasanjo (1999–2007) and Goodluck Jonathan (2010–2015), two leaders whose combined 13 years in office spanned most of the Fourth Republic, made feeble moves toward power devolution, signified by more or less self-serving national conferences, each of which produced laborious reports that were never implemented.[125] This was in spite of findings by a presidential committee the Obasanjo administration set up in 1999, which reviewed the Fourth Republic Constitution.[126] The committee observed that "[o]ne of the dominant issues which featured in a large number of submissions and representations is the preferred political structure for Nigeria."[127] It found that "so strong is the concern and agitation for the desired restructuring that Nigerians cannot seem to wait longer for them to witness the emergence of a True Federation with more powers, responsibilities[,] and resources . . . decentralized and devolved in favor of the lower tiers of Government."[128] One measure of the size of a government is the proportion of money it controls.[129] Under Nigeria's revenue allocation formula since 1999, the national government based in Abuja keeps 56 percent of all revenues, leaving only 44 percent for the sub-national governments made up of 36 states and 774 local governments.[130]

The Nigerian government needs to decentralize powers. Such devolution is critical, given the status of Nigeria as a patchwork of numerous ethnic groups,[131] some of which, like the Igbo, Hausa-Fulani, and Yoruba, with populations running into tens of millions, are sizable enough to form their own separate countries. For how much longer can the country continue to buck the global trend toward power sharing and devolution? Why would a country like Nigeria, included in the comparative politics literature among examples of a federal system,[132] continue to *operate*, as it has done since the end of the civil war in 1970, like a unitary system, at a time unitary systems like China and the United Kingdom, through extensive devolution of power to constituent units, are "seek[ing] the benefits of decentralized government without necessarily establishing federalism[?]"[133]

How will a Nigerian political system that is properly decentralized and devolved look? Drawing on insights shaped by multiple sources, including the contributions of Ojukwu and Anyaoku referenced above,[134] such a system will be a cross between a federal and con-federal systems,[135] with ingredients designed to promote the economic viability of each "federating" unit within the political system. It should have six units, whether named regions, provinces, or zones, based on the six geopolitical zones, either each by itself in place of the current 36 states or as "a cluster of states put together on the basis of ethnic homogeneity."[136] Second, similar to the practice during the First Republic from 1960 until 1966, each geopolitical zone should have its own constitution. Third, each zone should be responsible for its own census. Fourth, each should have control of its own resources, specifically revenue allocation based on a principle of ownership rooted on the proposition that "everybody owns all that is [on] one's land or under it."[137] Fifth, each zone should recruit and control its police force, and, to minimize the known propensity of the Nigerian army to stage coups, the armed forces should be decentralized along the lines of the Aburi Accord.[138] Sixthly, taking a cue from the Ethiopian constitution adopted one year after Ojukwu's speech, the Constitution should integrate a secession clause to give any zone that wants to leave the union the opportunity to do so.[139] Finally the Constitution of the national government should be mandatorily reviewed about every twenty years.[140] Now as in 1954, the goal should be to assign to the central government as few subjects as it needs to preserve unity[141]—foreign affairs, defense, and coordination of economic activities among the states. This would translate into an exclusive legislative list of no more than ten items, compared to the current 68.[142] As a corollary, "[t]he funds for running the Federal account shall be allocated to reflect the duties of the Federal Government."[143]

For readers not versed in the intricacies of Nigerian politics, the formula for restructuring laid out in the preceding paragraph is redolent of the Swiss model,[144] a configuration that, given its known history of political instability, for some stands the risk of ending the Nigerian state as we know it.[145] There are two responses to such assessment. First, given that the Nigerian state is not sustainable in its current shape, the argument for human rights in external affairs made in this study is dependent on reforms in various sectors, domestic as well as foreign, that include the reshaping of the state itself, as chapter 11 of this study elaborates. Left as it is, the current excessively powerful center is an albatross that, to borrow the words of Atiku Abubakar, vice president of Nigeria from 1999 until 2007, makes Nigeria's "unity more fragile, [its] government more unstable and [the] country more unsafe."[146] Related to this first point, under Buhari since May of 2015, calls for restructuring have approached a din, with pressures to do something that few governments in a democratic setting can successfully resist, even in the short run. A sample of three opinions by three Nigerians in the summer of 2016 illustrates this point. In addition to former Vice President Abubakar,[147] the contributors are the commentators Reuben Abati[148] and Alabi Williams.[149]

Abubakar, who, instructively, is also an influential member of President Buhari's political party, All Progressives Congress (APC), opines that an excessively powerful center militates against (rather than facilitates), national unity, and that the country must renegotiate its union to make it stronger.[150] He contended that "no federal system is set for all time[,]" and that "the rising tide of agitations" in the country, some of them "militant and violent," mandate "a reset in our relations as a united nation."[151] Agitations for restructuring in the land have become so wide-spread, ranging beyond the traditional "regional, ethnic[,] and religious groupings[,]" to encompass "labor and professional groups[,]" and many, such as unemployed youths, increasingly feel that "their voices are not being heard or that they are unable to hold those in power to account."[152] While the government has in the past responded to these agitations through certain measures, such as creation of new states, these measures have proven inadequate or in some cases, such as concentrating power at the federal level, even contradictory.[153] Abubakar believes that there is no point in the government waiting to resolve the governance and economic challenges the country faces to implement restructuring.[154] He opines that restructuring is good for *every* section of the country, including the North which has held political powers for much of the period since independence, and advised Nigerians to refrain from the habit of assuming that anyone calling for restructuring the country means to break it up.[155] Abubakar proposed several measures to achieve political restructuring, including: a smaller, leaner federal government with reduced responsibilities; a tax-centered revenue base; common citizenship for all, based on residency, rather than ethnic group of birth; and state police forces to augment federal law enforcement.[156]

Building on the views of Abubakar, Abati maintained that Nigeria "is in urgent need of a . . . redesign" away from the nominal federalism it has operated since the first military coup in the country in 1966.[157] This is the only antidote against the present situation where Nigerians "feel excluded from the current power-sharing arrangement . . . marginalized, treated unfairly and alienated by a compromised state that is in need of reinvention."[158] His proposal for change includes the following. First, organization of the current 36 states "on a zonal basis, to reflect the existing six geopolitical zones, with each zone having its own government, and responsible for its own development."[159] Second, each of the six autonomous zones will make financial contributions to the coffers of "a central government whose functions will be limited to defense, foreign affairs, national security" and other mutually-agreed-upon functions that must be spelled out in a new constitution.[160] Third, institution of a unicameral legislature at the center with equal number of members from each of the six zones, and presidential power at the center rotated "from one geo-political zone to the other, for a single term each of about six years."[161] Fine details of the new order, he said, "can be negotiated once there is a commitment to change and a broad consensus on what exactly will work for Nigeria."[162]

Williams posited that the centripetal rumblings in the land today that include deadly clashes between Fulani herdsmen and farmers in various parts of the country over access to grazing lands "are direct responses of aggrieved nationalities to the attitude of today's government in conceptualizing issues of restructuring the polity."[163] However, he observed, "[o]n many occasions, President Buhari has exhibited lack of interest in debates, just like it was under military regimes. He would rather deploy arms to deal with certain issues, while he feigns disinterest in others."[164] But given the magnitude of the national security challenges Nigeria faces that, in addition to deadly conflicts over access to grazing lands, include agitation for Biafra, and bombing of oil installations in the Niger Delta by militants advocating for resource control, "this is the best time to review Nigeria,"[165] he posited.

Stemming the Influence of Religion in Politics

A fifth step Nigeria can use to increase human rights at home on the road to a human rights foreign policy is to stem the influence of religion in politics. A disquieting issue in Nigerian politics under the Fourth Republic since 1999 is the increased salience of religion in politics and public life. While fundamentalism is a problem for all religions in Nigeria,[166] Islamic extremism is particularly troubling because of the intertwining of Islam and ethnicity in northern Nigeria.[167] Until Nigeria's independence in 1960, Islamic (or sharia) law formed the legal system in northern Nigeria.[168] On the eve of independence, under an agreement some commentators refer to as "the Settlement of 1960," application of sharia law was confined to family and personal issues, such as marriage, divorce, child custody, and inheritance.[169] Supported by the departing British colonial authorities, the agreement was necessary to protect basic rights for all citizens and to promote economic relations in the new nation.[170]

Contrary to the letter and spirit of the Settlement of 1960, some northern Nigerian leaders worked diligently in the post-independence period to expand the role of sharia law in the Nigerian public square. The campaign for more sharia began somewhat modestly in 1979 when northern Muslims staged a walk-out during the drafting of the Constitution for the Second Republic, following the defeat of their proposal to include a Federal Sharia Court of Appeal in the constitution. The impasse was resolved by then Head of State General Olusegun Obasanjo, a Christian from the Yoruba ethnic group, only following agreement by the Constituent Assembly, which wrote into the new constitution provisions for Sharia Court of Appeal "for any state that requires it," and, in the same manner, Customary Court of Appeal, "for any state that requires it."[171] Successive military rulers, all of whom were Muslims, did not approach the sharia issue with the same even-handedness. For example, in 1986, General Ibrahim Babangida, Head of State from 1985 to 1993, clandestinely enrolled the country into the Organization of the Islamic Conference, backing off only following a deafening public outcry from Christians in all parts of the country.[172]

Two events that have unfolded under the Fourth Republic since 1999 speak to the increased salience of religion into Nigerian politics. The first is the upgrading of sharia law into criminal code by 12 states in northern Nigeria in 2000–2001, beginning with Zamfara.[173] Going further, Nigeria's sharia states created *hisbah* organization (sharia police), charged with responsibility for prosecuting a range of offenses, including "social vices" like prostitution, mixing of the sexes, and drinking in public places. Taken together, these actions had the effect of restoring sharia law in northern Nigeria "to a state of completeness and a degree of autonomy" never seen before in the country "for over a century."[174] Another event under the Fourth Republic, coming from northern Nigeria, that lent testimony to the growing salience of religion in politics is the insurgency group known as Boko Haram, which colloquially means "Western education is a sin."[175] The group works feverishly to turn Nigeria into an Islamic state.[176] In pursuit of its bigoted goal, Boko Haram members have waged war on any target—police stations, rival Muslim clerics, politicians, public institutions, ordinary citizens, name it—which they consider insignia of Western education, using every terroristic tool of violence within their reach, including arson, fire-bombing, suicide bombing, kidnapping, raping, and maiming.[177] The group has killed about 20,000 people, maimed an untold number, engaged in incalculable destruction of private and public property, and rendered millions of citizens homeless both within their area of operation in northeastern Nigeria and beyond.[178] Dubious highlights of the group's terroristic campaign include the kidnapping of over 200 schoolgirls in April 2014, and the bombing in August 2011 of a United Nations building in Abuja.[179]

Electing Competent Governments Able and Willing to Handle the Preceding Four Tasks

Although political restructuring, covered in the penultimate section, is important, a political system is only as good as the men and women who run it.[180] This is where competent governments able to discharge the four tasks highlighted above—protecting socioeconomic human rights alongside political-civil rights, protecting collective rights, implementing political restructuring, and reducing the influence of religion in politics, all four conducted within the canvas of civilian rule—comes in as step six in generating the human rights at home that Nigeria needs for a human rights foreign policy. Back to the Treaty of Westphalia (1648) setting up the nation-state system, governments have played a critical role in the life of every society.[181] The emphasis is on competent governments able and willing to serve the needs of their society,[182] which property Nigeria, for much of its post-independence history, unfortunately lacks. The country spent nearly 30 out of the 56 years of its independence under military rule. Since 1999, Nigeria has witnessed its longest period of civilian rule in its post-independence history with the relative freedom from repression such non-military rule affords. However, the quality of civilian rule so far has been poor, marked by numerous governmental malfeasances, including corruption (the use of public trust for private ends),[183] and little progress on poverty alleviation.[184]

One issue which points to the poverty of creative leadership under the Fourth Republic is the increased salience of religion highlighted in the preceding section. Although the Nigerian constitution forbids the adoption of a state religion, none of Nigeria's three presidents, all of them members of the People's Democratic Party (PDP),[185] which dominated the political system until it lost the presidential election in March of 2015 to the opposition All Progressives Congress (APC),[186] saw it fit to orchestrate a clarification by the Nigerian Supreme Court regarding the constitutionality of the twelve northern states' adoption of sharia law as criminal code, contrary to the Settlement of 1960. During his two terms in office as civilian president, Obasanjo unpersuasively took the position that the issue was the use of religion for political ends that will fizzle out on its own with time;[187] Yar'Adua, a Muslim, was too sick during the brief period he served as president to even broach the issue.

Neither did Jonathan, a Christian who spent five whole years in office before he left office in May 2015. There is little likelihood that the current leader, President Muhammadu Buhari, military Head of State from 1983 to 1985 and a Muslim noted for his past support of sharia law,[188] would be the one to put this matter to judicial test.

A second issue under the Fourth Republic pointing to poverty of creative leadership is the ability to reduce poverty among the population. A factor responsible for the fall of the Second Republic from 1979 to 1983 was the lack of any "serious effort to fight poverty[,]" creating a situation where "many losers in th[e] corrupt system welcomed military intervention."[189] The Fourth Republic risks a similar fate if it continues to make no progress in antipoverty programs. A third issue is the failure to "secure full residence rights for every citizen in all parts of the Federation" necessary for national integration.[190] Complicating the poverty of leadership skill is the continued influence of the military in Nigerian politics under the Fourth Republic, evident in the election of two retired generals—Obasanjo and Buhari. Each held office as military head of state and each spotted a governance style involving application of military ethos to non-military problems.[191] Along with the lack of movement on political restructuring, these leadership issues have combined to exert a negative tool on the country's foreign relations.[192] Economic development is a function of an attitude of hard work that creative leaders, such as Julius Nyerere, Tanzania's leader from 1960 until 1985, cultivate among their citizenry. More than half a century since independence, Nigeria lacks leaders able to build these attitudes.[193] Justifying Tanzania's recognition of Biafra in 1968, Nyerere blamed the troubles in Africa that Nigeria epitomized on weak governments rather than weak states.[194] Forty-six years after the war, the same weakness ineluctably still afflicts the rank of Nigerian leaders.[195]

In a democracy, ordinary people sometimes can work against their own common interests by electing unwise leaders, a propensity that the framers of the U.S. Constitution sought to curb by instituting the Electoral College.[196] A more immediate problem the Nigerian masses face, additional to this popular passion issue, is the scarcity of free and fair elections under the Fourth Republic. All the elections since 1999, including the one conducted by the departing military that brought General Obasanjo into office, lacked the free and fair quality.[197] The arguable exceptions were votes involving Goodluck Jonathan.[198] Given this occurrence, it is fair to conclude that, under the Fourth Republic, Nigeria's illiberal democracy holds elections barely free and fair that neither "reflect the reality of popular participation in politics" nor of "support for those elected."[199] Accordingly, Nigerian masses need free and fair votes in general elections now currently lacking, including presidential votes, to elect competent presidents.

External Support or Assistance

National action has priority in human rights protection and promotion, and external support is never a substitute for national action.[200] "[T]he long-term fate of human rights depends largely on the citizens whose rights are in question."[201] Donnelly recounts a number of reasons why this is the case. First, external actors lack the capacity for the intensive monitoring ultimately necessary to make human rights secure. Second, they lack the immediate incentives that, as a practical matter, are necessary to engage in the sustained efforts to force states to respect human rights. Third, ultimately external actors lack the power that ordinary citizens have to pressure their governments to respect and enforce their international human rights obligations.[202] In a word, ultimately "it is up to a free people to defend their own rights[,]" because "if they don't do that, international action almost certainly will come to nothing."[203] Individually and collectively, citizens must "demand that their governments respect" their human rights.[204] They must work to create "for themselves a society and a legal and political system where their human rights are respected, implemented, enforced, and enjoyed."[205]

Yet no gainsaying the primacy of national action, that primacy does not preclude the necessity for external support or assistance in building the human rights at home necessary for the conduct of a human rights policy. The entire United Nations system is built on "international cooperation";[206] in a non-autarkic international system, few countries can assist its people without help from abroad. For Nigeria as for any other United Nations member, international support is critical in the growth of human rights, as it can be for democracy.[207] This is a proposition many scholars share. Professors Harbeson and Rothchild advised that "major states and international organizations" can be "active partners of governments in making basic human rights part of the working foundations of contemporary states."[208] Similarly, Paul Redmond posited that human rights are "too important to be left to national governments exclusively but is a matter of joint, global responsibility."[209] International support is necessary, even decisive, both when violations are occurring[210] and when seemingly they are not occurring.[211]

SUMMATION

Nigeria is a state born in foreign affairs via British colonialism in Africa[212] that nearly sixty years since independence still derives most of its legitimacy as a state from the legal notions and trappings of international law, rather than the empirical ability to perform the functions of a state.[213] The country espouses a patina of ethical values abroad that it does not practice at home. For example, Nigeria keeps peace abroad that its longsuffering citizenry lacks at home. Under the Fourth Republic since 1999, it is a land that "grapple[s] with military predominance" where neither the legitimacy nor practice of constitutionalism is firmly entrenched.[214] For Nigeria, therefore, the road to a human rights foreign policy ineluctably lies in "remov[ing] the solecism of abuses at home, and a nominal commitment to international law abroad that currently marks its human rights policy."[215] Implementing human rights at home is a necessary step in the transition to a human rights–oriented foreign policy. This is because for political systems who identify themselves internally with the pursuit of human rights[,]" liberal democracies as we call them, "[c]arrying this pursuit over into their foreign policies thus seems 'natural.'"[216]

This chapter lays down seven steps to that journey that must be synchronized, rather than implemented sequentially—protecting economic rights along with political-civil rights, protecting collective rights, implementing political restructuring and reducing the influence of religion in politics, all within the predicates of civilian rule and a competent government, backed with the "auxiliary precaution"[217] of external support. On first appearance, international support seems out of place among these factors, but such assistance necessary to consolidate human rights at home does not in any way preclude national action. Implementing the seven steps will eliminate or ameliorate the problems of political corruption, with negative ramifications for the country's international image and for foreign direct investment, while generating the national cohesion that the country needs to formulate and execute foreign policy.[218] Without the implementation of increased human rights at home that resolves the paradox of "international influence and domestic paralysis,"[219] more colloquially, "beautiful abroad but ugly at home,"[220] Nigerian leaders realistically cannot seek an "active role in world affairs commensurate with their country's aspirations."[221] With this chapter at an end, focus turns to the pillars in the temple of Nigeria's human rights foreign policy, beginning with chapter 7 on redesigned peacekeeping.

NOTES

1. Constitution of the Fed. Republic of Nigeria, 1999 [hereinafter referred to as Nigerian Const. 1999], § 19(d).

2. See, e.g., Jacob Abiodun Dada, "Impediments to Human Rights Protection in Nigeria," *Annual Survey of Int'l & Comp. Law*, Vol. 18 (2012): 67 (identifying and discussing various factors, including absence of judicial independence, that constrain realization of human rights in the land as well as possible solutions, including steps like maintaining civilian rule covered in this chapter).

3. See Samantha Power & Graham Allison, eds., *Realizing Human Rights: Moving from Inspiration to Impact* (New York: St. Martin's Press, 2000): xiv (observing that "if a key challenge of the second half of the twentieth century was gaining universal acceptance of the idea that human rights existed or mattered, *the* key challenge for the decades ahead is to identify the policies and actions that most effectively realize human rights.") (emphasis in original).

4. "Who Said, 'Charity Begins at Home?'" *Bible or Not* (Apr. 24, 2010), http://bibleornot.org/who-said-charity-begins-at-home/. Variants of the idiom going back to the past include: "Charity begins at home, and justice begins next door" by Charles Dickens in 1844; "But how shall we expect charity towards others, when we are uncharitable to ourselves? Charity begins at home is the voice of the world" by Sir Thomas Browne in 1642; and "Charity should begin at himself" by John Wycliffe in 1380.

5. John Wycliffe, note 4.

6. Sir Thomas Browne, note 4.

7. S.O. Akinboye, "Beautiful Abroad but Ugly at Home: Issues and Contra[di] ctions in Nigerian Foreign Policy." University of Lagos Inaugural Lecture Series, 2013, www.unilag.edu.ng/opendocnew.php?.

8. Richard N. Haass, *Foreign Policy Begins at Home: The Case for Putting America's House in Order* (New York: Basic Books, 2014) (focusing on the United States; Haass is president of U.S. Council of Foreign Relations). For a similar theme, focused directly on Nigeria, see Reuben Abati, "What Is Obasanjo's Foreign Policy?," *Guardian Online* (Lagos) (Aug. 29, 1999) (on file with author) (maintaining that "[o]nly a people confident and a government strong at home can engage the rest of the world.").

9. Thomas E. Patterson, *The American Democracy, 8th Ed.* (New York: McGraw-Hill, 2008): 513–14 (discussing the economic dimension of national security policy, citing the warning of former U.S. president Dwight D. Eisenhower against "the unwarranted influence" and "misplaced power" of the military-industrial complex, the coalition of military establishment, industries that manufacture weapons, and members of Congress from constituencies that depend heavily on the arms industry that mutually benefit from a high level of defense spending). Eisenhower expressed the concern that sustained high levels of military spending and secrecy would only weaken America in the long run. Ibid., p. 514 (box), warning that it would be folly for Americans to weaken at home the very thing they are trying to strengthen abroad, given that excessive government secrecy, justified in the name of national security, threatened liberty. Ibid., pp. 514, 522.

10. Alison Brysk, *Global Good Samaritans: Human Rights as Foreign Policy* (New York: Oxford University Press, 2009): 19.

11. Ibid., p. 6.

12. See Andrew Lui, *Why Canada Cares: Human Rights and Foreign Policy in Theory and Practice* (Montreal, Canada: McGill-Queen's University Press, 2012): 75 (commenting on the statement of Lloyd Axworthy, then Canadian Foreign Affairs Minister).

13. Goodluck Jonathan, Address at the Retreat on the Review of Nigeria's Foreign Policy (Aug. 1, 2011), http://www.nigeriavillagesquare.com/index.php?option=com_content&allposts=1&catid=590&id=19313&view=arti cle&Itemid=1719, ¶¶ 16, 18.

14. A.J. Vincent, *Human Rights and International Relations* (New York: Cambridge Univ. Press, 1986): 130.

15. See Chinua Achebe, *There Was a Country: Personal History of Biafra* (New York: Penguin Press, 2012): 209–11, 228–39; Chimamanda N. Adiche, *Half of a Yellow Sun* (New York: Alfred A. Knopf, 2006), *passim* (work of fiction based on the Nigerian civil war from 1967 to 1970).

16. Akinboye, *supra* note 7.

17. For space reasons, the ensuing discussion does not, e.g., include the critical contributions of individuals and other non-state actors in protecting and promoting human rights. See, e.g., "The Role of Non-State Entities," Icelandic Human Rights Center, http://www.humanrights.is/en/human-rights-education-project/human-rights-concepts-ideas-and-fora/human-rights-actors/the-role-of-non-state-entities; and Declaration on the Right and Responsibility of Individuals, Groups[,] and Organs of Society to Promote and Protect Universally Recognized Human Rights and Fundamental Freedoms, U.N. Human Rights Office of the High Commissioner, Res. 53/144 adopted by the Gen. Assembly (Dec. 9, 1998), http://www.ohchr.org/EN/ProfessionalInterest/Pages/RightAndResponsibility.aspx.

18. See e.g., Dada, note 2, *passim*; and Toure Kazah-Toure, "Nigeria: Challenge to the State and Ways of Breaking through the Quagmire," *in* George Klay Kieh Jr., ed., *Beyond State Failure and Collapse: Making the State Relevant in Africa* (Lanham, MD: Lexington Books, 2007): 170–94 (citing a range of problems that includes lack of real democracy, no negotiated guarantees of collective rights, no adequate mechanism for tackling ethnic and religious conflicts, no true multiparty system, no genuinely democratic institutions, no agreement on ownership, control, and distribution of resources, no agreement on citizenship rights, etc.).

19. This is an issue that sometimes comes up in the literature. For example, should the appropriate minimal commitment to rights be toleration or more. See Amy Gutmann, "Introduction," *in* Michael Ignatieff, *Human Rights as Politics and Idolatry* (Princeton, N.J.: Princeton University Press, 2001): xxvi–xxvii (disagreeing that toleration is enough but, instead, arguing for a moral commitment anchored on toleration plus respect).

20. Jack Donnelly, "An Overview," *in* David P. Forsythe, ed., *Human Rights and Comparative Foreign Policy* (New York: United Nations University Press, 2000): 312.

21. Ibid. (Donnelly's emphasis).

22. "A Short Definition of Democracy," *Democracy Building*, http://www.democracy-building.info/definition-democracy.html.

23. Assuming, for the sake of argument, that we call Nigeria a democracy, it would be "illiberal democracy," rather than liberal democracy. *Illiberal democracies* are political systems that satisfy the procedural but not the substantive requirements of democracy. In these systems, leaders "routinely ignor[e] constitutional limits on their power," "depriv[e] their citizens of basic rights and freedoms[,]" and elections are held that "do not reflect the reality of popular participation in politics and support for those elected." Fareed Zakaria, "The Rise of Illiberal Democracy," *Foreign Affairs* (Nov./Dec. 1997), http://www.foreignaffairs.com/articles/53577/fareed-zakaria/the

-rise-of-illiberal-democracy. These regimes are contrasted from liberal democracies, such as in the United States and Europe, that are "marked not only by free and fair elections, but also by the rule of law, a separation of powers, and the protection of basic liberties," such as freedom of speech, assembly, religion, and property. Ibid.

24. Juan J. Linz & Alfred Stepan, *Problems of Democratic Transition and Consolidation: Southern Europe, South America, and Post-Communist Europe* (Baltimore, MD: Johns Hopkins University Press, 1996): 5.

25. Juan J. Linz & Alfred Stepan, "Toward Consolidated Democracies," *in* Larry Diamond et al. eds., *Consolidating the Third Wave Democracies: Themes and Perspectives* (Baltimore, MD: Johns Hopkins University Press, 1997): 16. See also Adam Przeworski, *Democracy and the Market* (New York: Cambridge University Press, 1991): 30, 31 (indicating that democracy works "when all the relevant political forces have some specific minimum probability of doing well," such that those who lose elections or fail to have their demands met "may stay with the democratic game if they believe that even losing repeatedly under democracy is better for them than a future under an alternative system.").

26. See Toyin Falola & Matthew M. Heaton, *A History of Nigeria* (New York: Cambridge University Press, 2008): 192–93 (portraying the evolution of the country's 36 states and their locations).

27. "Federal Capital Abuja," *Online Nigeria* (Dec. 2, 2003), http://www.onlinenigeria.com/links/abujaadv.asp?blurb=387 (providing background information on the logic behind the relocation to Abuja as well as the personalities that planned the movement).

28. See Larry Diamond, "Nigeria: Pluralism, Statism, and the Struggle for Democracy," *in* Larry Diamond et al., eds., *Democracy in Developing Countries: Africa*, Vol. 2 (Boulder, CO: Lynne Rienner Publishers, 1988): 45–49 (discussing the transition to the Second Republic from 1975 to 1979).

29. See Chinonye Obiagwu & Chidi Anselm Odinkalu, "Nigeria: Combating Legacies of Colonialism and Militarism," *in* Abdullahi Ahmed An-Na'im ed., *Human Rights under African Constitutions: Realizing the Promise for Ourselves* (Philadelphia, PA: University of Pennsylvania Press, 2003): 211–250 (including military rule among the factors responsible for human rights abuses in the country).

30. *Executive lawlessness*, marked by contempt for judicial rulings, and utter disrespect of judicial institutions, took root during the period of military rule in Nigeria. See, e.g., Mike A. A. Ozekhome, "The Nigerian Judiciary—15 Years of Democracy," *Pointblanknews.com,* http://pointblanknews.com/pbn/articles-opinions/the-nigerian-judiciary-15-years-of-democracy/ (last visited Nov. 24, 2014).

31. Naomi Chazan et al., *Politics and Society in Contemporary Africa, 3d Ed.* (Boulder, CO: Lynne Rienner Publishers, 1999): 187–88 (commenting on the downsides of patron-client relationships in Africa). See also Richard A. Joseph, *Democracy and Prebendal Politics in Nigeria: The Rise and Fall of the Second Republic* (New York: Cambridge University Press, 1987), *passim* (documenting and lamenting the massive corruption that led to the demise of Nigeria's Second Republic from 1979 to 1983; *prebendalism*, derived impertinently from the Roman Catholic prebend doctrine is the term Joseph coined for the Nigerian variety of patronage).

32. See James Rupert, "Corruption Flourished in Abacha's Regime," *Washington Post* (Jun. 9, 1998): A01, http://www.washingtonpost.com/wp-srv/inatl/longterm/nigeria/stories/corrupt060998.htm (reporting on the unmatched scale of corruption, broached in chapter 4, that marked the military government under General Sani Abacha from 1993 to 1998); David Imhonopi & Moses Urim Ugochukwu, "Leadership Crisis and Corruption in the Nigerian Public Sector: An Albatross of National Development," *African Symposium: An Online Journal of the African Educational Research Network*, Vol. 13 (Jun. 2013): 82, http://www.ncsu.edu/aern/TAS13.1/TAS13.1_Imhonopi.pdf (commenting on the Babaginda regime from 1985 to 1993); Chinua Achebe, *The Trouble with Nigeria* (Ibadan, Nigeria: Heinemann, 1983): 42 (noting that "[f]rom fairly timid manifestations in the 1960s," corruption in Nigeria grew "bold[ly] and ravenous[ly]," much of this during periods of military rule).

33. Philip C. Aka, "The Military, Globalization, and Human Rights in Africa," *Journal of Human Rights*, Vol. 18 (2002): 387. Scholars like the late Claude Ake questioned the hypothesis postulating positive relationship between authoritarianism and development. See Claude Ake, *Democracy and Development in Africa* (Washington, D.C.: Brookings Institution, 1996): 158 (maintaining essentially that "development is part of what democracy is about"; therefore that "[a] case for authoritarianism's being positively correlated to development does not really arise, because democracy is part of the very meaning of political development."). Ake contended that "[p]olitical authoritarianism has its own specificity, which markedly affects its consequences." Ibid., p. 128. Part of this specificity is that in East Asia, unlike in Africa, the political class "was able to realize some of the *economically functional values of democracy*, such as accountability, transparency, the rule of law, and negotiated consensus." Ibid., p. 158 (emphasis added). Similarly, see Barack Obama, "Speech in Ghana on African Development" (Jul. 12, 2009): 3, http://www.voanews.com/wm/live/special-events/english-obama-ghana-event/vb.asx (arguing that Africa "needs strong institutions," such as strong parliaments, honest police forces, independent judges, a free press, and a vibrant private sector and civil society, not "strongmen.").

34. See, e.g., Philip C. Aka, "Nigeria since May 1999: Understanding the Paradox of Civil Rule and Human Rights Violations under President Olusegun Obasanjo," *San Diego Int'l Law Journal*, Vol. 4 (2003): 209 (assessing the first four years of the Obasanjo government from 1999 to 2003); and Ignatius Akaayar Ayua & Dakas C.J. Dakas, "Federal Republic of Nigeria," in John Kincaid & George Alan Tarr, eds., *Constitutional Origins, Structure, and Change in Federal Countries* (Montreal, Canada: McGill-Queen's University Press, 2005): 267 (characterizing Nigeria under the Fourth Republic since 1999, as a land that "grapple[s] with military predominance" where neither the legitimacy nor practice of constitutionalism is firmly entrenched).

35. Clifford Ndujihe et al., "Power Sector: Senate Probes OBJ, Yar'Adua, Jonathan," *Vanguard* (Lagos) (Aug. 14, 2015 5:01 AM), http://www.vanguardngr.com/2015/08/power-sector-senate-probes-obj-yaradua-jonathan/.

36. Ibid.

37. According to news accounts, Colonel Sambo Dasuki, National Security Adviser to former president Jonathan, was accused of awarding "phantom contracts" to buy 12 helicopters, four fighter jets, and bombs and ammunitions worth $2 billion

that were never supplied. The result of the misappropriation, according to the stories, was that Nigerian soldiers mandated to combat the terrorism from the northeast ravaging the land went into battle ill prepared and inadequately fed. Dasuki was said to have usurped the role of the Ministry of Defense in procuring weapons. See "Nigeria Orders Arrest of Ex-Adviser Over $2 Billion Arms Deal," *Al Jazeera* (Nov. 18, 2015 08:03 GMT), http://www.aljazeera.com/news/2015/11/nigeria-orders-arrest-adviser-2bn-arms-deal-151118043340314.html; "Nigerian Ex-President Goodluck Jonathan Stole $2 billion via Fake Arms Deals, Current President Says," *Japan Times* (Nov. 18, 2015), http://www.japantimes.co.jp/news/2015/11/18/world/nigerian-ex-president-goodluck-jonathan-stole-2-billion-via-fake-arms-deals-current-president-says/#.Vszw_pwrK1s. For another perspective on the scandal, see Siobhan O'Grady, "In Nigeria, $2 Billion in Stolen Funds Is Just a Drop in the Corruption Bucket," *Foreign Policy* (Nov. 18, 2015 6:47 PM), http://foreignpolicy.com/2015/11/18/in-nigeria-2-billion-in-stolen-funds-is-just-a-drop-in-the-corruption-bucket/ (suggesting that there is more to the scandal than meets the eyes, drawing on the insights of the Africanist scholar J. Peter Pham, who commented on the "personal history between" Dasuki and Buhari that goes back to 1985, and who is concerned that Buhari's crackdown on corruption in this and other cases may be "a populist substitute for addressing some [structural] issues that may be much more unpopular," including the government's failure to diversify its revenue streams.).

38. Plato, "The Myth of the Cave," *in* Jonathan E. Adler & Catherine Z. Elgin, eds., *Philosophical Inquiry: Classic and Contemporary Readings* (Indianapolis, IN: Hackett Publishing Company, Inc., 2007): 26. Based on this premise, Plato advised that "it is those who are *not* lovers of ruling who must rule." *Id.* (emphasis added).

39. See Ben Nwabueze, "Corrupt Practices: Igbo Leaders' Position on Probe of Past Governments," *Vanguard* (Aug. 13, 2015 9.05 a.m.), http://www.vanguardngr.com/2015/08/corrupt-practices-igbo-leaders-position-on-probe-of-past-govts/ (detailing various sources of law dealing with corruption in Nigeria—common law, statutory law, and the Constitution—the last two of which include §172 of the 1999 Constitution (§209 in the case of States), the Code of Conduct Bureau and Tribunal Act, Cap. 56 of the Laws of the Federation 1990 ed., the Corrupt Practices and Related Offenses Act, 2000, and the Economic and Financial Crimes Commission Act); Patrick H. O'Neill et al., *Cases in Comparative Politics, 4th Ed.* (New York: W. W. Norton & Co., 2012): 719 (recounting other reform initiatives, including a bill to reform the oil industry that stalled in the National Assembly).

40. See Nwabueze, note 39.

41. Under General Obasanjo (president from 1999–2007), for two straight years (2002 and 2003), Transparency International ranked Nigeria the second most corrupt country in the world—despite the fact that Obasanjo was a co-founder of the organization. "Nigeria Angry at Being Rated Second Most Corrupt," *IRIN* (Oct. 9, 2003), http://www.irinnews.org/report/46630/nigeria-nigeria-angry-at-being-rated-second-most-corrupt. More recently, in 2013, Nigeria ranked 144th out of 177 nations surveyed in Transparency International's Corruption Perceptions Index (CPI) for that year, scoring 25 out of a possible 100 points. Uduma Kalu, "Nigeria Is 33rd Most Corrupt Country—Transparency Int'l," *Vanguard* (Lagos) (Dec. 4, 2013), http://

www.vanguardngr.com/2013/12/nigeria-33rd-corrupt-country-transparency-intl/. For 2014, Nigeria moved down just a bit to 136th most corrupt out of 175 countries surveyed, scoring 27 out of a possible 100 points. See Toluwani Eniola, "Nigeria Now 39th Most Corrupt Nation, Says TI," *Punch* (Lagos) (Dec. 4, 2014), http://www.punchng.com/news/nigeria-now-39th-most-corrupt-nation-says-ti/.

42. J. Peter Pham, Nigeria's Foreign Policy: An Inquiry into Sources and Prospects, Paper Prepared for Presentation at an Int'l Conference in Lisbon, Portugal (Nov. 8–9, 2007): 99, www.ipri.pt/eventos/pdf/JPeterPham_paper.pdf.

43. See Daniel Jordan Smith, *A Culture of Corruption: Everyday Deception and Popular Discontent in Nigeria* (Princeton, N.J.: Princeton University Press, 2008), *passim* (portraying the widespread nature of corruption in the daily lives of many Nigerians).

44. See Joseph, note 31 (which applied the concept of prebendalism to depict the scourge of corruption that took place under that civilian administration).

45. For example, in the presidential elections for 2003, "the leading contenders for the office of president were mostly retired military officers: Olusegun Obasanjo of the Peoples' Democratic Party (PDP), Muhammadu Buhari of the All Nigeria Peoples Party (ANPP), Odumegwu Ojukwu of the All Progressive Grand Alliance (APGA), and Ike Nwachukwu of the National Democratic Party (NDP)." Ayua & Dakas, note 34, p. 274, n.59. A redux occurred in 2007 where in the run up to the presidential election of that year, generals Ibrahim Babangida, Muhammadu Buhari, and Buba Marwa "[were] touted as leading contenders." Ibid. Finally, until he won in March of 2015, General Buhari was a candidate in all but the election in March of 1999 that inaugurated the Fourth Republic. See "Nigeria's Muhammadu Buhari in Profile," *BBC News* (Mar. 31, 2015), http://www.bbc.com/news/world-africa-12890807.

46. "Nigeria's Muhammadu Buhari in Profile," note 45.

47. See Ofeibea Quist-Arcton, "Nigeria Rejects Term-Limit Change in Constitution," *N[ational] P[ublic] R[adio]* (May 17, 2006 6:00 AM ET), http://www.npr.org/templates/story/story.php?storyID=5410583; Craig Timberg, "Bid to Allow Nigerian a Third Term Hits Snag," *Washington Post* (May 13, 2006), http://www.washingtonpost.com/wp-dyn/content/article/2006/05/12/AR2006051200518.html.

48. See Robyn Dixon, "Umaru Yar'Adua Dies at 58; Nigerian President," *L.A. Times* (May 7, 2010), http://articles.latimes.com/2010/may/07/local/la-me-umaru-yaradua-20100507; John Campbell, *Nigeria: Dancing on the Brink* (Lanham, MD: Rowman & Littlefield Publishers, 2013): 72; Christian Purefoy, "Goodluck Jonathan: By Name and Nature?," *CNN* (Apr. 17, 2011 10:36 pm EDT), http://www.cnn.com/2010/WORLD/africa/05/06/nigeria.jonathan/.

49. Larry Berman & Bruce Allen Murphy, *Approaching Democracy, 8th Ed.* (New York: Pearson, 2013): 15.

50. See ibid., p. 15.

51. See Aka, note 34, pp. 237–55 (analyzing General Obasanjo's record relating to a set of four crises: the trouble over resource control and environmental degradation in the Niger Delta, the trouble relating to the adoption of Sharia law as legal code by 12 northern states, the agitation for self-determination in the Southeast, and military reprisals at Odi and Benue State for security forces killed by warring groups in these communities).

52. See Reuters, "A Year on From Nigerian Election Victory, Buhari's Reforms Founder," *New York Times* (Feb. 25, 2016, 6:54 AM EST), http://www.nytimes.com/reuters/2016/02/25/world/africa/25reuters-nigeria-politics.html?_r=0. See also Alabi Williams, "It's Time to Review Nigeria," *Guardian* (Lagos) (Jun. 12, 2016 3:47 a.m.), http://guardian.ng/opinion/its-time-to-review-nigeria/ (noting that "[o]n many occasions, President Buhari has exhibited lack of interest in debates, just like it was under military regimes. He would rather deploy arms to deal with certain issues, while he feigns disinterest in others.").

53. See Amartya Sen, "Democracy as a Universal Value," *in* Mark Kesselman & Joel Krieger eds., *Readings in Comparative Politics: Political Challenges and Changing Agendas* (Boston, MA: Cengage Learning, 2006): 175–76 (commenting on three ways, direct, instrumental, and constructive, through which democracy "enriches the lives of the citizens."); Adam Michnik, "After the Revolution," *New Republic* (Jul. 2, 1990): 28 (depicting democracy as "freedom institutionalized.").

54. Obiagwu & Odinkalu, note 29, p. 232.

55. Immigration and Refugee Board of Canada, Nigeria: Information on the Civil Liberty Organization (CLO), Its Leadership, Its Activities, the Arrest of Its Members and Its Involvement in Demonstrations That Followed the Annulment of the 12 June 1993 Elections (Mar. 1, 1994), http://www.refworld.org/docid/3ae6ab3a24.html; Abdul Raufu Mustapha, "Civil Rights and Pro-Democracy Groups in and Outside Nigeria," *in* 'Kunle Amuwo et al., eds., *Nigeria during the Abacha Years (1993–1998)* (Lagos: IFRA Nigeria, 2001): 143–83.

56. Obiagwu & Odinkalu, note 29, p. 243.

57. Ibid.

58. *Winston Churchill, Churchill by Himself: The Definitive Collection of Quotations*, edited by Richard M. Langworth (New York: PublicAffairs, 2008): 574 (observing that "[n]o one pretends that democracy is perfect or all-wise[,]" but, to the contrary, "*democracy is the worst form of Government except for all those other forms that have been tried from time to time*.") (emphasis added).

59. See, e.g., Frank L. Wilson, *Concepts and Issues in Comparative Politics: An Introduction to Comparative Analysis* (Upper Saddle River, N.J.: Prentice Hall, 1996): 142–43 (pointing out that "[m]ilitary regimes are, after all, authoritarian regimes[,] [i]nherently illegitimate, . . . [and] abusive of basic human rights."); Paul Brooker, *Non-Democratic Regimes: Theory, Government, and Politics, 2d Ed.* (New York: Palgrave Macmillan, 2009): 2 (noting that "there are major behavioral differences between dictatorship by military and by a political party").

60. Diamond, note 28, p. 33 (observing that "the ethnic complexity of the country . . . represents an irrepressible social pluralism that cannot be effectively managed by authoritarian means."). This is one reason military rule in Nigeria is considered an aberrational episode justified on the grounds that soldiers are cleaning up the mess in the political system to clear the ground for a timely return to civilian rule. Philip C. Aka, "Nigeria: The Need for an Effective Policy of Ethnic Reconciliation in the New Century," *Temple Int'l & Comparative Law Journal* (2000): 352. All military administrations in the country, from Ironsi to Gowon to Muhammad/Obasanjo to Babangida to even Abacha, including those like Gowon and Babangida that ultimately failed to

keep their promise, embraced this formula—except for the Buhari regime from 1983 to 1985. "Political Transitions," *in* Helen Chapin Metz, ed., *Nigeria: A Country Study* (Washington, D.C.: GPO for the Library of Congress, 1991), http://countrystudies.us/nigeria/74.htm.

61. Constitution of the Fed. Republic of Ethiopia (Aug. 21, 1995) [hereinafter referred to as Ethiopian Const. 1995], http://www.refworld.org/docid/3ae6b5a84.html. See also Max Siollun, "Nigeria Is Coming Apart at the Seams," *Foreign Policy* (Feb. 8, 2016), https://foreignpolicy.com/2016/02/08/nigeria-is-coming-apart-at-the-seamsbiafra/ (observing that "[f]or three decades after the war, military dictatorships suppressed all secessionist" agitations that under the Fourth Republic since 1999 are now coming to the fore).

62. Christopher Clapham, "Democratization in Africa: Obstacles and Prospects," *Third World Quarterly*, Vol. 14 (1993): 437–38 (advising African governments to wrap themselves with popular legitimacy, given that if "the mighty Soviet Union breaks up into 15 different fragments, there is no way in which an artificial African state can hold together unless most of its people want it to.").

63. Garth le Pere, review of Adekeye Adebajo & Abdul Raufu Mustapha, eds., *Gulliver's Troubles: Nigeria's Foreign Policy after the Cold War* (Scottsville, South Africa: University of KwaZulu-Natal Press, 2008), *African Journal of Conflict Resolution*, Vol. 8 (2008), http://www.accord.org.za/publications/book-reviews/638-gullivers-troubles-nigerias-foreign-policy-after-the-cold-war.

64. See Goodluck E. Jonathan, Address at a Retreat on the Review of Nigeria's Foreign Policy (Aug. 1, 2011), http://www.nigeriavillagesquare.com/index.php?option-com_content&allposts-1&catid=590&id=19313&view=article&Itemid=1719 (stating that "[a]s a nation," Nigerians took the "right decision to embrace democracy," adding that democracy is the tool Nigerians need to "build a just, fair, and inclusive nation[,]" and that for him, "there is no greater indignity, no greater disrespect for the values that bind us together as a nation than to deprive citizens of a say in who would govern them."). Olalekan Adetayo, "Nigerians Won't Regret Electing Me, Says Buhari," *Punch* (Lagos) (Jun. 4, 2015), http://www.punchng.com/news/nigerians-wont-regret-electing-me-says-buhari-2/ (quoting Buhari, who participated in the coup that overthrew the Second Republic in 1983, to the effect that "[t]here is now a national consensus that our chosen route to national development is democracy[,]" and that "[t]o achieve our objectives, we must consciously work to improve the democratic system."); "Accept Democracy as Lifestyle, Not Government[al] System, Buhari Urges Nigerians," *TheWill* (Online) (Jun. 19, 2015), http://thewillnigeria.com/news/accept-democracy-as-lifestyle-not-government-system-buhari-urges-nigerians/ (reporting Buhari's advocacy for the adoption of democracy as "a lifestyle" for development).

65. In Federalist No. 51, James Madison stressed the "necessity of auxiliary precautions," "[i]n framing a government which is to be administered by men over men," as an antidote against the imperfectness of human beings. The Federalist No. 10 (James Madison) (Feb. 6, 1877). Madison observed, "It may be a reflection on human nature" that the elaborate separationist devices he recommended "should be necessary to control the abuses of government," adding rhetorically: "But what is government

itself but the greatest of all reflections on human nature?" Ibid. The same need for auxiliary precautions is advised here.

66. See, e.g., Peter R. Baehr, "Mobilization of the Conscience of Mankind: Conditions of Effectiveness of Human Rights NGOs" (Sept. 18, 1996): 9, http://www.gdrc.org/ngo/lecture14.html (commenting on the discrepancy between norm and practice, embedded in the fact that "most governments in the world at some time or other violate" human rights, a discrepancy that "creates the space in which human rights [N]on-[G]overnmental [O]rganizations can operate.").

67. See, e.g., Norimitsu Onishi, "Nigeria's Comics Pull Punch Lines from Deeper Social Ills," *New York Times* (Dec. 5, 2015), http://www.nytimes.com/2015/12/06/world/africa/nigerias-comics-pull-punch-lines-from-deeper-social-ills.html (associating the emergence of stand-up comedy as part of the entertainment industry in the country with the return to democratic rule since 1999).

68. John F. Kennedy, Inaugural Address of President John F. Kennedy (Jan. 20, 1961), John F. Kennedy Presidential Library & Museum, http://www.jfklibrary.org/Research/Research-Aids/Ready-Reference/JFK-Quotations/Inaugural-Address.aspx.

69. William J. Clinton, "Remarks to a Joint Session of the Nigerian National Assembly in Abuja, Aug. 26, 2000," *in Public Papers of the Presidents of the United States: William J. Clinton, 2000–2001* (Washington, D.C.: Best Books, 2000): 1706. See also President Clinton's Address to the Nigerian Joint Assembly, https://www.youtube.com/watch?v=Z0uzicpb1Is (YouTube video of the address published Apr. 19, 2012). Instructively, Clinton advised Nigerians to be patient and give democracy a chance because "[r]eal change demands perseverance and patience[,]" and because "after all, the road of freedom is the only road worth taking." Clinton, "Remarks to a Joint Session of the Nigerian National Assembly in Abuja." Op. cit., p. 1710.

70. Philip C. Aka, "The 'Dividend of Democracy': Analyzing U.S. Support for Nigerian Democratization," *Boston College Third World Law Journal*, Vol. 22 (2002): 225–79 (focusing on the external factor of U.S. support for Nigeria's democracy).

71. Int'l Crisis Group, *Nigeria: Want in the Midst of Plenty*, Africa Report No. 113 (Jul. 19, 2006): 1. A side-effect of this mass impoverishment is that under its Fourth Republic Nigeria has "produce[d] millions of migrants, essentially economic refugees, who live throughout Africa, Europe, and the U.S." Ibid.

72. See "Is Nigeria a Poor Country of Rich Men or a Rich Country of Poor Men?," *Leadership* (Abuja) (Apr. 7, 2014 2:39 AM), http://leadership.ng/columns/363727/nigeria-poor-country-rich-men-rich-country-poor-men; "Poverty in Nigeria: Rich Country, Poor People," *Poverties.org* (Mar. 2012 updated Apr. 2013), http://www.poverties.org/poverty-in-nigeria.html. "Protests in Biafra: Go Your Own Way," *Economist* (London) (Nov. 28, 2015), http://www.economist.com/news/middle-east-and-africa/21679210-half-century-after-war-angry-biafrans-are-agitating-again-go-your-own-way (pointing out that "[d]espite oil wealth, Nigerians were twice as likely to be poor in 2010 as they were in 1980.").

73. Adopted in 2001 by African leaders, NEPAD is a program designed to promote sustainable economic development and reduce poverty, among other goals. See Philip C. Aka, "NEPAD and the Movement for Popular Participation in Development

(MPPD) in Africa," *Human Rights & Globalization Law Review,* Vol. 3 (2009–2010): 79–148, *passim*.

74. "Reforming Nigeria: A Conversation with Ngozi Okonjo-Iweala," *Foreign Affairs* (Mar./Apr. 2014), http://www.foreignaffairs.com/discussions/interviews/-nigeria; see also Abba Mahmood, "Nigeria's Africa Policy in Perspective," *Leadership* (Dec. 26, 2013), leadership.ng/columns/Thursday-column/343/nigerias-africa-policy-in-perspective (pointing out that "[w]ith over 100 million people living below poverty line, Nigeria's population is not an asset but a burden.").

75. See Onishi, note 67.

76. Vienna Declaration and Program of Action, ¶ 14, U.N. Gen. Assembly, World Conference on Human Rights, Jul. 12, 1993, A/CONF.157/23, Endorsed by Gen. Ass. Res. 48/121, Dec. 20, 1993, http://www.ohchr.org/EN/ProfessionalInterest/Pages/Vienna.aspx.

77. Like many Africans, Nigerians are outcome-oriented in their support of democracy. See Philip C. Aka, "Education, Economic Development, and Return to Democratic Politics in Nigeria," *Journal of Third World Studies*, Vol. 18(1) (2001): 22 (disclosing that agitation in Nigeria for democratic rule "has something to do with the belief most Nigerians held that the only government [that is] . . . able to improve their lot is a democratically-elected one."); Robert J. Mundt & Oladimeji Aborisade, "Politics in Nigeria," *in* Gabriel A. Almond et al., eds., *Comparative Politics Today: A World View* (New York: Longman, 2000): 727 (conveying that the attraction of democracy for Nigerians is "its association with prosperity.").

78. Regarding public service, one galling topic that immediately comes to mind is the inability of the various governments under the Fourth Republic since 1999 to generate enough electricity to serve the needs of the Nigerian public. With a population of about 170 million people, Nigerian leaders generated only about 4,000 megawatts (MW) of electricity, compared, e.g., to South Africa with 53 million (less than one-third Nigeria's population) of 44,175 MW. See Adewale Maja-Pearce, "Nigeria Does Generate More Electricity Now Than It Did 15 Years Ago," *Africa Check* (Nov. 2014), https://africacheck.org/reports/nigeria-does-generate-more-electricity-now-than-it-did-15-years-ago/.

79. Nigerian Const. 1999, note 1, chapter II, Arts. 13–24 (setting forth the "Fundamental Objectives and Directive Principles of State Policy"), and chapter IV, Arts. 33–44 (dealing with "Fundamental Rights.").

80. For more on these rights, see chapter 2 which specified the conceptual framework of this study.

81. For more on this and other instruments, see chapter 1 containing the introduction of this study.

82. See, e.g., Aka, note 34, at 216. Little wonder that one non-governmental organization in Nigeria laments that the socioeconomic profile of Nigeria's 1999 constitution reduces it to little more than "a treatise on abdication of responsibilities." Ibid., quoting Committee for the Defense of Human Rights, Annual Report on the Human Rights Situation in Nigeria 1999 (Jul. 2000): 100.

83. Vienna Declaration and Program of Action, note 76, ¶ 13.

84. Ibid., ¶ 14.

85. Campbell, note 48, pp. 11–24 (grappling with the telling question, "If Nigeria Is So Rich, Why Are Nigerians So Poor?").

86. Philip C. Aka, "Human Rights as Conflict Resolution in Africa in the New Century," *Tulsa Journal of Comparative & Int'l Law*, Vol. 11 (Fall 2003): 201.

87. Vienna Declaration and Program of Action, note 76, ¶ 5.

88. Ibid., ¶ 13.

89. See Obinna Chima, "Nigeria's Unemployment Rate May Rise by 2%," *This-Day* (Lagos) (Jan. 7, 2014), http://www.thisdaylive.com/articles/nigeria-s-unemployment-rate-may-rise-by-2/168227. The actual numbers released by the country's National Bureau of Statistics are 23.9 percent in 2011 and 29.5 percent in 2013. Ibid.

90. Susan Lund & Arend van Wamelen, "Lions on the Move: 10 Things You Don't Know about Africa's Booming Economy," *in* J. Tyler Dickovick & Jonathan Eastwood, eds., *Current Debates in Comparative Politics* (New York: Oxford University Press, 2015): 44.

91. The logic behind this name, as the legal scholar Professor Umozurike conveys, is because these rights require "the solidarity of all peoples," including "the cooperation of the other members of the international community to carry into effect." U. Oji Umozurike, *The African Charter on Human and Peoples' Rights* (Leiden, Netherlands: Brill Publishers, 1997): 51.

92. See Vincent, note 14, p. 3 (pointing out that although "[t]he subject of a right, the right-holder, might be most obviously an individual[,]" "[b]ut it might also be a group—a family, a tribe, a company, a nation, a state, a region, a culture, even the globe itself."). Collective rights are credited to the new states which became members of the United Nations following decolonization in Africa and Asia in the post–World World II period. See Peter R. Baehr & Monique Castermans-Hollerman, *The Role of Human Rights in Foreign Policy, 3d Ed.* (New York: Palgrave Macmillan, 2004): 14. Arguably, even the Universal Declaration of Human Rights anticipated these group rights. After observing in its opening article that human beings are persons "endowed with reason and conscience" who "should act toward one another in a spirit of brotherhood[,]" the document stipulated that "[e]veryone has duties to the *community* in which alone the free and full development of his personality is possible." *Universal Declaration of Human Rights*, G.A. Res. 217 A (III), U.N. GAOR, 3d Sess., U.N. Doc. A/810 (1948), Art. 29 (emphasis added).

93. Vienna Declaration and Program of Action, note 76, ¶ 5.

94. Aka, note 86, p. 186.

95. Vienna Declaration & Program of Action, note 76, ¶ 5.

96. Aka, note 34, pp. 215–16, 274.

97. See Aka, note 34, at 237–55 (commenting on the handling of a set of four crises under General Obasanjo, including: the trouble over resource control and environmental degradation in the Niger Delta, the trouble relating to the adoption of sharia law as legal code by 12 northern states, and the agitation for self-determination in the Southeast).

98. One country that quickly comes to mind is Ethiopia. Like Nigeria, Ethiopia is sizable with numerous ethnic groups (over 93 million people in 2015 with over 80 eth-

nic groups vs. over 182 million people in the same period with over 250 ethnic groups for Nigeria). Like Nigeria too, Ethiopia is a federal state. And like Nigeria, Ethiopia fought a civil war where many people died (from 1974 to 1991, over 16 years in which 1.4 people died vs. a three year period where over three million people died in the case of Nigeria). For Ethiopia, from 1961, the country battled an insurgency from Eritrea following the (forcible) incorporation of the territory into Ethiopia in 1952. Yet the two countries drew different lessons from their experiences with violence and human rights abuses. For Nigeria, the lesson was to centralize power out of an "apprehension that a weak federal center [w]ould enable secession" and lead to disintegration. Ayua & Dakas, note 34, p. 251. For Ethiopia, on the other hand, the experience led to power devolution, including a constitutional provision permitting secession following the successful breakaway of Eritrea in 1991. Art 39(1) of the Ethiopia's 1995 Constitution stipulates, "Every Nation, Nationality[,] and People in Ethiopia has an unconditional right to self-determination, including the right to secession." Ethiopian Const. 1995, note 61, Art. 39(1). Ethiopia is especially instructive because it is the headquarters of the Organization of African Unity, since 2000 the African Union, noted for its insistence on maintenance of colonial boundaries in Africa to avoid "balkanization," which reason Ethiopia under Emperor Haile Selassie (1930–1974), opposed Biafra. See James Podesta, "Haile Selassie 1892–1975," *Contemporary Black Biography* (1994), http://www.encyclopedia.com/topic/Haile_Selassie.aspx.

99. See International Covenant on Civil and Political Rights, G.A. Res. 2200A (XXI), U.N. GAOR, Supp. No. 16, U.N. Doc. A/6316 (1966), Art. 1,§ 2; International Covenant on Economic, Social, and Cultural Rights, G.A. Res. 2200, U.N. GAOR, 21st Sess., Supp. No. 16 at 49–52, U.N. Doc. A16316, 993 U.N.T.S. 3, 6 I.L.M. 360 (1966). See also Aka, note 34, p. 274 (observing that "[p]romoting increased access to state power for all groups is a human rights issue in Nigeria," and advising that "[a]ccomplishing this purpose can also minimize opportunities for conflict that could result in human rights violations.").

100. Jack Donnelly, *International Human Rights, 4th Ed.* (Boulder, CO: Westview Press, 2013): xvii.

101. Ibid. See also Andrew Clapham, *Human Rights in the Private Sphere* (New York: Oxford University Press, 1993); Mary Robinson, "The Business Case for Human Rights," http://www.unhchr.ch/hurricane/huricane.nsf/0/e47d352dedc39697802566de0043b28e?OpenDocument.

102. See Achebe, note 32, p. 45 (positing that Nigeria has an "Igbo problem" rooted in the fact that one singular issue on which non-Igbo groups agree is "their common resentment of the Igbo.").

103. Philip C. Aka, "Prospects for Igbo Human Rights in Nigeria in the New Century," *Howard Law Journal*, Vol. 48 (Fall 2004): 168.

104. Ibid., p. 223, quoting quoting Oha-na-Eze Ndi-Igbo, "The Violations of Human and Civil Rights of Ndi Igbo in the Federation of Nigeria (1966–1999): A Call for Reparation and Appropriate Restitution (1999)": 39, http://www.westafricareview.com/war/vol2.2/ohaneze.pdf.

105. Aka, note 103, pp. 221–224 ("rebutting the claim that Igbos are no more victims of human rights atrocities than other Nigerians").

106. Ibid., pp. 224–28. See also Philip C. Aka, "Bridging the Gap Between Theory and Practice in Humanitarian Action: Seven Practical Steps to Humanitarian Integrity in Nigeria," *Critical Investigations into Humanitarism in Africa (CIHA) Blog* (Feb. 25, 2016), http://www.cihablog.com/bridging-the-gap-between-theory-and-practice-in-humanitarian-action-seven-practical-steps-to-humanitarian-integrity-in-nigeria/ (pointing out that "Nigeria has a poor history of reparations for past human rights abuses, with possible negative ramifications for humanitarian integrity.").

107. Aka, note 103, p. 226.

108. See Hakeem O. Yusuf, "Human Rights Violations Investigation Commission, the Oputa Panel (Nigeria)," *in* Lavinia Stan & Nadia Nedelsky, eds., *Encyclopedia of Transitional Justice* (New York: Cambridge University Press, 2013): 161–65.

109. See Charles Manga Fombad, "Transitional Justice in Africa: The Experience with Truth Commissions," Hauser Global Law Sch. Program (May/June 2008), http://www.nyulawglobal.org/globalex/Africa_Truth_Commissions.html (discussion focusing on Nigeria).

110. See notes 101–2 and corresponding text.

111. Int'l Crisis Group, note 71, p. 2.

112. Ayua & Dakas, note 34, p. 242.

113. Ibid.

114. Ibid., p. 249, citing a *Guardian* newspaper (Lagos) editorial of Dec. 6, 1999, p. 20.

115. Orchestrated killings of Igbo in Kano, a metropolitan city in northern Nigeria, along with large-scale destruction of Igbo property, convinced British colonial authorities that Nigeria, "if it was to be a nation, must be a federation, with as few subjects reserved for the Central Government as would preserve national unity." A.H.M. Kirk-Greene, *Crisis and Conflict in Nigeria: A Documentary Sourcebook, Vol. 1* (London: Oxford University Press, 1971): 10 (quoting the diary of the British Colonial Secretary). Consequently, the 1954 constitution, otherwise known as the Lyttleton Constitution, after Oliver Lyttleton, then governor-general of the country, formalized this arrangement.

116. One such critic notably was General Emeka Odumegwu Ojukwu, former Biafran leader, who in a 1994 lecture analogized the country's unity to Jonah in the belly of the Whale—the Whale being Hausa-Fulani and Jonah the rest of the country, notably the Igbo who have craved fruitlessly for inclusion into the mainstream of Nigerian politics since their forced re-annexation into the country in 1970.

> For a man to whom unity remains that of Jonah in the belly of the Whale, that man must question his situation. He is not comfortable in the Whale's belly. It is dark. It is soggy. He wants out lest he dies. The man owes himself to get out despite the fact that the Whale has felt no discomfort. To this man in extremis lies the obligation to quit.

Emeka Odumegwu Ojukwu, "Nigeria: The Truths Which Are Self-Evident," *Sunday Magazine* (Mar. 6, 1994): 17.

117. Ayua & Dakas, note 34, p. 250.

118. Nigerian Const. 1999, note 1, Art. 1(3).

119. The six are the South-East, South-West, South-South, North-East, North-West, and North Central. See Calista Ezeaku, "Should the Six Geopolitical Zones

Become Federating Units in Nigeria?" *Tide* (Lagos) (Feb. 11, 2013), http://www.thetidenewsonline.com/2013/02/11/should-the-six-geopolitical-zones-become-federating-units-in-nigeria/.

120. Nigerian Const. 1999, note 1, 2d schedule, Part I (enumerating the "exclusive legislative list").

121. Ibid., 2d schedule, Part II (enumerating the "concurrent legislative list").

122. See Nigerian Const. 1999, note 1, Art. 4(7) (a) (leaving to the States "any matter not included in the Exclusive Legislative List"). *Cf.* The Constitution of the United States (1789), 10th Amend. (providing that "[t]he powers not delegated to the United States by the Constitution, nor prohibited by it to the States, are reserved to the States respectively, or to the people.").

123. Nigerian Const. 1999, note 1, 4th schedule (specifying the "functions of a local council").

124. One such call notably came from the diplomat Emeka Anyaoku, Secretary General of the Commonwealth of Nations, 1990–2000. See Emeka Anyaoku, "Nigeria's Current Drift Towards Chaos," *Vanguard* (Lagos) (Nov. 12, 2013), http://www.vanguardngr.com/2013/11/nigerias-current-drift-towards-chaos-emeka-anyaoku/#sthas.3H7LjLA6.dpuf. Anyaoku re-presented his appeal for "true federalism" in Feb. of 2016. See "Anyaoku Proposes Reduction of Nigeria's 36 States into 6 Units," *Sun* (Lagos) (Feb. 3, 2016), http://sunnewsonline.com/new/anyaoku-proposes-reduction-of-nigerias-36-states-into-6-units/ (quoting Anyaoku's remarks during a conference at the University of Ibadan on Feb. 1, 2016, attributing Radio Nigeria as source for the news story).

125. See Festus Owete, "Between Jonathan's National Conference and Obasanjo's National Political Reform Conference: What You Need to Know," *Premium Times* (Abuja) (Feb. 16, 2014), http://www.premiumtimesng.com/news/155237-between-jonathans-national-conference-and-obasanjos-national-political-reform-conference.html. Obasanjo convened his conference in 2005, while Jonathan inaugurated his own conference in 2014. To restate, each of these conferences produced reports that were never implemented.

126. Obasanjo set up the committee because of recurring questions regarding the legitimacy of the charter imposed on Nigerians by the departing military regime. The Constitution proclaimed, "We the People" of Nigeria "having firmly and solemnly resolved [on various issues, including living "in unity and harmony as one indivisible and indissoluble sovereign nation under God"], do hereby make, enact, and give to ourselves the following Constitution." Nigerian Const. 1999, note 1 (preamble). Yet the document was adopted by military decree with no input from the public, and no opportunity to approve it in a national referendum. The template for this Constitution was the one of 1979, which was amended in several respects that separated it from its 1979 predecessor. The military chose this document over a 1989 constitution under Babangida (1985–1993) that was never fully implemented and a 1995 draft constitution by Abacha (1993–1998) that was abandoned in 1998 after his sudden death. See Ayua & Dakas, note 34, pp. 246–47.

127. Ayua & Dakas, note 34, p. 250, citing Report of the Presidential Committee on the Review of the 1999 Constitution: Vol.1: Main Report (Feb. 2001): 3.

128. Ibid., p. 250, citing Report of the Presidential Committee on the Review of the 1999 Constitution: Vol.1: Main Report (Feb. 2001): 37.

129. As Everett McKinley Dirksen, U.S. Senator from Illinois from 1951–1969, once famously stated, commenting on the U.S. federal budget, "A billion here, a billion there, and pretty soon you're talking about real money!" Cited in Michael E. Milakovich & George J. Gordon, *Public Administration in America, 11th Ed.* (Boston, MA: Wadsworth Cengage Learning, 2013): 327.

130. Ayua & Dakas, note 34, p. 265.

131. See "Nigeria," *in* M. Paul Lewis, ed., *Ethnologue: Languages of the World, 17th Ed.* (Dallas, TX: SIL Int'l, 2010).

132. See, e.g., J. Tyler Dickovick & Jonathan Eastwood, *Comparative Politics: Integrating Theories, Methods, and Cases* (New York: Oxford University Press, 2013): 179 (map of federal systems around the world). Based on the map, Nigeria is one of only four federal countries in Africa, the others being Comoros, Ethiopia, and South Africa. Ibid.

133. Dickovick & Eastwood, note 132, p. 179.

134. See notes 116 and 124.

135. Both a federal and con-federal systems are marked by division of powers between a central government and its constituent units. For a graphic explanation of the main elements of distinction between these two systems, vis-à-vis the unitary format, see Steffen W. Schmidt et al., *American Government and Politics Today 2005–2006 Edition* (Belmont, CA: Thomson Wadsworth, 2005): 83, Fig. 3–1 (in a confederal system, the non-center units are strong while the center is weak; in contrast, in a federal system, both the center and non-centers are strong in the issue areas assigned to them by the constitution. Additionally, in a federal system, both the center and the non-centers can act directly on the people, e.g., through taxation, whereas in a confederal system, the central government can only act on the people only through the non-centers).

136. Ojukwu, note 116, p. 22. Some commentators still consider Nigeria's numerous states as appropriate federating unit. See, e.g., Siddhartha Mitter, "To Find Progress in Nigeria, Think Local," *Foreign Policy* (May 26, 2016, 2.54 PM), http://foreignpolicy.com/2016/05/26/to-find-progress-in-nigeria-think local/ (arguing that as Nigeria's current government under General Buhari struggles to deliver reform during the president's first year in power, the time has come to look to the states as a potential source of change—that "[w]hat the federal government can't get done, perhaps the states can."). But as this very same source conceded, only a few of the 36 states are viable, measured by internally generated revenue. Ibid.

137. Ojukwu, note 116, p. 22. Elsewhere in the lecture, Ojukwu asserted that "[t]he oil, the gas, the mineral found under a man's property belongs to the man. This is a principle we must establish in this country." Ibid., p. 23. Ojukwu's proposition that "everybody owns all that is one's land or under it" appears to rhyme with the injunction in the international bill of human rights, regarding economic self-determination, that "[i]n no case may a people be deprived of its own means of subsistence." See note 99 (referring to the ICCPR and ICESCR).

138. The Aburi Accord is an agreement hammered out at a summit meeting on Jan. 4–5, 1967, between representatives of Nigerian federal government and the Eastern

Nigerian government at the initiation of the Ghanaian government in a last-ditch attempt, ultimately unsuccessful, to prevent a civil war. The agreement included a decision on the regionalization (decentralization) of the Nigerian army. The Aburi Accord envisaged a confederal system of government, explained in note 135. See Dapo Akinrefon, "Let's Return to Aburi Accord—Adeniyi," *Vanguard* (Lagos) (Jan. 30, 2012), http://stephendieseruvwe.com/2012/03/14/lets-return-to-aburi-accord-adeniyi/.

139. For the provision of the Ethiopian Constitution relating to right to self-determination, including secession, *see* note 98.

140. See Ojukwu, note 116, p. 22 (recommending every 15 years).

141. See note 115.

142. Note 120.

143. Ojukwu, note 116, p. 22.

144. Switzerland (population 8.3 million as of 2016) has a long tradition of republicanism. Its constitution adopted initially in 1848 following a civil war (but amended several times since then) provides for a (con)federation of one central government and 26 cantons with far-reaching autonomy. See "Switzerland's Political System and Government," *All About Switzerland*, http://swiss-government-politics.all-about-switzerland.info/. Under the constitution, the central government is charged with responsibility for foreign relations, national defense, customs examinations and tariffs, value-added taxes, railways, communications, and the like. Responsibility for all other matters, including police forces, education, health, and other social services belongs to the cantons. Ibid. The un-adopted Aburi Accord, referenced above, note 138, is the closest Nigeria has come to adopting a confederal system.

145. Professor Frank Emmert is one scholar who voiced this concern. Email on May 24, 2016, following the defense of the dissertation version of this book (opining that the restructuring proposal in the dissertation "set[s] the country up to dismembration . . .").

146. Atiku Abubakar, Restructuring for Nigeria's National Unity, Remarks during a Book Launching at the Yar'Adua Center, Abuja (May 31, 2016), http://opinion.premiumtimesng.com/2016/05/31/173089/.

147. Abubakar, note 146; Atiku Abubakar, Restructuring Nigeria for Greater National Integration and Democratic Stability, Paper Presented at the Umaru Musa Yar'Adua Memorial Hall, Kaduna (Jul. 30, 2016), http://www.elombah.com/index.php/special-reports/9123-how-to-restructure-nigeria-written-by-atiku-abubakar.

148. Reuben Abati, "Why We Need to Restructure Nigeria to Save It," *Info Square* (Online) (Jun. 3, 2016), http://infosquare.com.ng/tag/why-we-need-to-restructure-nigeria-to-save-it-by-reuben-abati/.

149. Williams, note 52.

150. Abubakar, note 146.

151. Ibid.

152. Abubakar, note 147.

153. Ibid.

154. Abubakar, note 146.

155. Ibid. This statement calls to mind the observation of Professor Achebe regarding the price Nigeria pays contending with "the legitimate grievance of a wrong

citizen" each time it perpetrates "social injustice and the cult of mediocrity" against a section of its own population. Achebe, note 32, p. 19.

156. Abubakar, note 146.

157. Abati, note 148.

158. Ibid.

159. Ibid.

160. Ibid.

161. Ibid.

162. Ibid.

163. Williams, note 52.

164. Ibid.

165. Ibid.

166. See Toyin Falola, *Violence in Nigeria: The Crisis of Religious Politics and Secular Ideologies* (Rochester, NY: University of Rochester Press, 1998), *passim*.

167. See Aka, note 60, p. 335.

168. See J. N. D. Anderson, *Law Reform in the Muslim World* (London: Athlone Press, 1976): 27–28 (depicting northern Nigeria as "the only place outside the Arabian peninsula in which the Islamic law, both substantive and procedural, was applied in criminal litigation—sometimes even in regard to capital offenses."). In the same vein, during the colonial period, British authorities limited the forms of punishment that could take place under sharia law, abolishing mutilation and torture and subjecting other harsh penalties to a repugnancy test, which test precluded application of a punishment form determined to be contrary to "natural law, equity, and good conscience." Ayua & Dakas, note 34, p. 248, n. 31.

169. Philip Ostien & Albert Dekker, "Sharia and National Law in Nigeria," *in* Jan Michiel Otto, ed., *Sharia Incorporated: A Comparative Overview of the Legal Systems of Twelve Muslim Countries in Past and Present* (Leiden, Netherlands: Leiden University Press, 2010): 567.

170. Ibid., pp. 566–67.

171. See Philip C. Aka, "Judicial Independence under Nigeria's Fourth Republic: Problems and Prospects," *California Western Int'l Law Journal*, Vol. 45 (Fall 2014): 38–39.

172. Ibid., p. 39.

173. The 12 sharia states are Bauchi, Borno, Gombe, Jigawa, Kaduna, Kano, Katsina, Kebbi, Niger, Sokoto, Yobe, and Zamfara. See "Analysis: Nigeria's Sharia Split," *BBC News* (Jan. 7, 2003), news.bbc.co.uk/2/hi/Africa/2632939.stm.

174. Ostien & Dekker, note 169, p. 576.

175. The group calls itself *Jama'atul Alhul Sunnah Lidda'wati wal jihad* in Arabic, meaning "people committed to the propagation of the prophet's teachings and jihad." Jeff Haynes, "Religion," *in* Peter Burnell et al., eds., *Politics in the Developing World, 4th Ed.* (New York: Oxford University Press, 2014): 123.

176. See Farouk Chothia, "Who Are Boko Haram Islamists?," *BBC News* (May 4, 2015), http://www.bbc.com/news/world-africa-13809501.

177. See "Boko Haram Fast Facts," *CNN Library* (Updated 3:03 PM ET, Feb. 19, 2016), http://www.cnn.com/2014/06/09/world/boko-haram-fast-facts/.

178. See Conor Gaffey, "Biafra Protests Prompt Separation Anxiety in Nigeria," *Newsweek* (Mar. 1, 2016 10:47 AM), http://www.newsweek.com/2016/03/11/nigeria-biafra-nnamdi-kanu-protests-432002.html (estimating the number of people killed as 20,000); Charlotte Alfred, "Boko Haram Actually Kills More People in Terror Attacks Than ISIS," *Huffington Post* (Nov. 18, 2015 04:55 PM ET), http://www.huffingtonpost.com/entry/boko-haram-isis_us_564cd890e4b00b7997f8c15d. (commenting on reports that found Boko Haram to have overtaken the Islamic State of Iraq and Syria (ISIS) as the "most deadly terror group in the world.").

179. See *Boko Haram Fast Facts,* note 177. See also Adam Nossiter, "In Town of Missing Girls, Sorrow, but Little Progress," *New York Times* (May 12, 2015), http://www.nytimes.com/2014/05/12/world/africa/in-town-of-missing-girls-sorrow-but-little-progress.html.

180. Leaders are distinguished from mere power holders. Instead, they are office holders capable of producing social change that will satisfy the authentic yearnings of their followers. See James MacGregor Burns, *Leadership* (New York: Harper Torchbooks, 1978): 4–5.

181. See "Good Governance and Human Rights," U.N. Human Rights Office of the High Commissioner, http://www.ohchr.org/EN/Issues/Development/GoodGovernance/Pages/GoodGovernanceIndex.aspx (tying governance to human rights).

182. Ibid.; see also Burns, note 180.

183. See notes 35–44 and corresponding text.

184. See notes 71–85 and corresponding text.

185. "People's Democratic Party (PDP)," *Encyclopedia Britannica*, http://www.britannica.com/topic/Peoples-Democratic-Party-political-party-Nigeria.

186. "About APC," *All Progressives Congress*, http://apc.com.ng/index.php/about-apc.

187. Benson Ohihon Igboin, "'The President of Nigeria Has No Final Say': Sharia Law Controversies and Implications for Nigeria," *Central & East European Online Library* (2014): 265–90, http://www.ceeol.com/search/article-detail?id=180187.

188. Buhari expressed support for strong implementation of sharia law, but walked back that position and defended freedom of religion for all when he ran for president in 2015. See Brenda Daldorph, "Muhammadu Buhari: 'The Converted Democrat?'" *France 24* (latest update Apr. 13, 2015), http://www.france24.com/en/20150401-nigeria-buhari-president-elections-coup-africa.

189. Ayua & Dakas, note 34, p. 246.

190. Nigerian Const. 1999, note 1, Art. 15(3)(b).

191. See notes 45–52 and corresponding text. To be sure, the jury is still out regarding Buhari's civilian regime inaugurated in May of 2015. But after one year in office, there is still little sign of any improvement on leadership style. See "Crude Tactics," *Economist* (London) (Jan. 30, 2016), http://www.economist.com/news/middle-east-and-africa/21689584-cheap-oil-causing-currency-crisis-nigeria-banning-imports-no (noting perceptible progress in the war against terrorism and political corruption, but also instructively observing that Buhari is using the same jaded approaches to issues, including economic management, that he applied when he seized power over 30 years ago—with poor results).

192. See Adebajo & Mustapha, eds., *Gulliver's Troubles,* note 63, p. 2 (lamenting the disconnect between the country's high-minded aspirations for a leadership role abroad juxtaposed with the petty ambitions, kleptomania, and small-mindedness of some Fourth Republic leaders).

193. Nyerere opined, "Clear water requires piping. That pond must be drained. Work! But it requires knowledge, technical know-how. Germany was virtually razed, and Japan, but they had the necessary attitudes and skills for reconstruction." For Nyerere, the role of an effective leader is "to build these attitudes." William Edgett Smith, *We Must Run While They Walk: A Portrait of Africa's Julius Nyerere* (New York: Random House, 1971): 5.

194. For Nyerere, uncritical adherence to colonial countries vis-à-vis self-determination on the ground that "every African state has its own Biafra" is "a stupid nonsense" that "confuses the weakness of African governments with the weakness of African states, which is a very different thing; governments have fallen, but the states have remained. There is a desire to be together." Quoted in Smith, note 193, p. 280.

195. In a statement that also lends testimony to the paucity of political restructuring in the land, former U.S. ambassador to Nigeria, John Campbell, noted that "Nigeria's top political personalities have largely remained the same since the end of the civil war—they have merely aged in place." Campbell, note 48, p. 141.

196. Under the U.S. political system, the Electoral College refers to the body of electors that chooses the president. Thomas E. Patterson, *The American Democracy, 11th Ed.* (New York: McGraw-Hill, 2013): 46. During the Constitutional Convention in Philadelphia in 1787, "[d]irect election of the president was twice proposed and twice rejected because it would link executive power directly to popular majorities." Ibid. The compromise became the Electoral College, under which "[e]ach state would have the same number of electoral votes as it had members in Congress and could select its electors by a method of its choosing." Ibid. See also Eric Black, "Why the Constitution's Framers Didn't Want Us to Directly Elect the President," *MinnPost* (Oct. 17, 2012), https://www.minnpost.com/eric-black-ink/2012/why-constitution-s-framers-didn-t-want-us-directly-elect-president. Over time, however, the U.S. Constitution was altered in a manner that gave more power to the people. Andrew Jackson, president from 1828 to 1837, is the chief executive credited with linking the people and the presidency. Patterson, *op. cit.*, p. 48 (explaining how Jackson created that linkage with the positive result that, today, except for few instances where a candidate wins the presidency after losing the popular vote, "[t]he candidate who gets the most popular votes nationally is also likely to finish first in enough states to win a majority of the electoral votes.").

197. See, e.g., Salahu Mohammed Lawal, "An Appraisal of Corruption in the Nigerian Electoral System," *European Scientific Journal*, Vol. 11 (2015): 256–73 (analysis ranging up to the 2011 elections wherein the author reached the verdict that "conduct of credible, free and fair election has been eluding [the] Nigerian nation."); J. Oshola Omotola, "Elections and Democratic Transition in Nigeria under the Fourth Republic," *African Affairs*, Vol. 109 (2010): 535–53 (covering the 1999, 2003, and 2007 general elections); and Victor Oguejiofor Okafor, ed., *Nigeria's Stumbling Democracy and Its Implications for Africa's Democratic Movement* (Westport, CT: Praeger, 2008) (focusing on the 2007 general elections).

198. See, e.g., Babatunde Oyekanmi, 2015 General Elections and the Role of INEC, Paper Presented at a Conference in Jul. 2015, http://www.inecnigeria.org/wp-content/uploads/2015/07/Conference-Paper-by-Tunde-Oyekanmi.pdf (observing that, vis-à-vis prior votes, the "2015 general elections were a huge success, but there is the need to continue to reform."). INEC is the acronym for Independent National Electoral Commission, the agency charged with responsibility for the conduct of elections in Nigeria.

199. Zakaria, note 23.

200. See Donnelly, note 100, pp. 162–63 (commenting on "[t]he priority of national action" in human rights struggles); Basil Davidson, *Modern Africa: A Social and Political History, 3rd Ed.* (New York: Longman, 1994): 265–68 (harping on the imperatives of self-development, including the lesson that people either develop themselves "or they do not develop at all.").

201. Donnelly, note 100, p. 163.

202. Ibid.

203. Ibid.

204. Ibid.

205. Ibid.

206. Charter of the United Nations (1945), 59 Stat. 1031, T.S. 993, 3 Bevans 1153, Art. 56 (stating that "[a]ll Members pledge themselves to take joint and separate action in cooperation with the Organization for the achievement of the purposes set forth in Article 55.").

207. See Michael J. Sodaro, *Comparative Politics: A Global Introduction* (Boston, MA: McGraw-Hill Higher Education, 2008): 233–34 (spotlighting a "favorable international environment" among ten conditions for democracy). Professor Sodaro defines these "external" or "outside influences" that can support democracy at home to include "[t]ransnational networks of nongovernmental organizations[,]" but instructively noted that "while external influences may be important," they do not preclude national action—given that, among other things, "[u]ltimately, the sources and nutrients of democracy must be homegrown if democracy is to germinate and blossom to its full potential." Ibid., p. 234. As is with democracy, so it is too with human rights.

208. John W. Harbeson & Donald Rothchild, "The African State and State System in Flux," *in* John W. Harbeson & Donald Rothchild, eds., *Africa in World Politics: The African State System in Flux, 3d Ed.* (Boulder, CO: Westview Press, 2000): 11.

209. Paul Redmond, "Transnational Enterprise and Human Rights: Options for Standard Setting and Compliance," *Int'l Law*, Vol. 37 (2003): 70.

210. See Donnelly, note 100, p. 163 (stating that where the environment is most repressive "external actors may have a decisive role in keeping the idea of human rights alive in national political discussions," but where the environment is "less repressive," they "may be able to provide vital support to isolated or fledgling local human rights advocates").

211. Ibid. (stating that "[i]n countries where the overall human rights situation ranges from not too bad to excellent, external actors can often achieve incremental changes in policies and may provide a useful, occasionally even vital, supplement to national actors.").

212. See Hanes Walton Jr. & Robert C. Smith, *American Politics and the African American Quest for Universal Freedom, 5th Ed.* (New York: Longman, 2010): 283 (depicting African Americans as a people "born in foreign affairs through African slavery and the slave trade.").

213. See Robert Jackson & Carl Rosberg, "Why Africa's Weak States Persist: The Empirical and the Juridical in Statehood," *World Politics* (1982): 1–24. Strong states control their boundaries and perform effectively the functions of security and provision of competent public services for their citizenry. In contrast, weak states base their statehood on non-empirical variables, including the legal notions and trappings of sovereignty and non-interference in the internal affairs of a country.

214. Ayua & Dakas, note 34, p. 270.

215. Philip C. Aka, "Human Rights in Nigeria's External Relations: Exigency, Methods, and Rebuttable Objections," *Buffalo Human Rights Law Review*, Vol. 21 (2014–2015): 25. *Cf.* Douglas C. Lovelace, Jr., "Foreword," *in* Clarence J. Bouchat, *The Causes of Instability in Nigeria and Implications for the United States* (Carlisle, PA: Strategic Studies Institute & U.S. Army War College Press, Aug. 2013): iii (dubbing the country "a swirling paradox of riches and poverty, growth and stagnation, *international influence and domestic paralysis*, cultural diversity, and ethnic and religious clashes.") (emphasis added).

216. Donnelly, note 100, p. 140.

217. Madison, note 65.

218. Pham, note 42, pp. 91–100 (discussing the historical and conceptual background related to the country).

219. Lovelace, Jr., note 215.

220. Akinboye, note 7.

221. Pham, note 42, p. 100.

Chapter Seven

Redesigning Peacekeeping to Make It More Human Rights Compliant

The chapter advances proposals on how to redesign or revamp Nigeria's peacekeeping initiatives to render this policy tool more human rights compliant. It is the third of six issues—after reconstruction of Nigerian national interest and increased human rights at home to impinge on Nigeria's external relations—and the first of four pillars in the temple of Nigeria's human rights foreign policy. Peacekeeping is the lifeblood of Nigerian foreign policy. More than any other, it is the tool, spanning the gamut of the three concentric circles of West Africa, Africa, and the globe (discussed in chapter 4), that personifies Nigeria's external relations. Peacekeeping was the issue with which, at independence in 1960, Nigeria used to cut its teeth in foreign affairs.[1]

Post-independence, the country has participated consistently in these missions—with the exception, notably, of a hiatus totaling 17 years, first for 12 years in between the Indian-Pakistan conflict of 1965–1966 and Lebanon from 1978–1983, and second for 5 years in between the conflict in Chad from 1982–1983 and the Iran-Iraq war from 1988–1991 (see table 7.1). More on these gaps later in the chapter. In the more than 50 years since its independence, Nigeria has contributed over 150,000 troops—made up of soldiers, police officers, and civilian experts—to United Nations and Organization of African Unity (OAU, later the African Union) peace operations,[2] 6 of which missions it commanded. These operations, whose Nigerian leaders we identify later in this discussion, are Angola, Congo, Liberia (two times), Sierra Leone, and South Sudan. In human and material terms, Nigeria has expended over $10 billion of its hard-earned money on peacekeeping missions and sacrificed over 2,000 of its nationals, who lost their lives while participating in these operations.[3] Key highlights of Nigeria's peacekeeping experience include the OAU mission in Chad which cost Nigeria $82 million,[4] as well as its participation in the conflicts in Liberia and Sierra Leone which cost about $8 billion and claimed the lives of about 1,500 peacekeepers.[5] "Although Nigeria's positions on various issues have changed over the years, its level of activity in international organizations has increased."[6] The sustained activism is due in no small part to peacekeeping.

It is for the foregoing reasons that this work, appropriately, gets its title from that activity. Specifically, the title of the book comes from an address that William J. Clinton, then-president of the United States, gave in August 2000 to a joint session of the Nigerian National Assembly.[7] Clinton praised Nigeria for the "extraordinary extent of [its] leadership for peace in West Africa and around the world," crystallized in "its commitment to peacekeeping."[8] He added instructively, for the punchline here,

> I hope our members of Congress who are here today will tell them to their colleagues back home. Over the past decade, with all its problems, Nigeria has spent $10 billion and sacrificed hundreds of its soldiers' lives for peace in West Africa. . . . *In these ways, you are building the record of a moral superpower.*[9]

President Clinton was accompanied on the visit by his daughter, Chelsea, and a delegation of 1,000 persons, including hundreds of U.S. business leaders hoping to strengthen trade ties with Nigeria.[10] Three questions which frame the discussion in this chapter are: (1) What is peacekeeping?, (2) What are the factors involved in the evolution of Nigerian peacekeeping since independence in 1960?, and (3) What steps should be implemented and designed to make Nigerian peacekeeping human rights compliant?

DEFINING *PEACEKEEPING*

Peacekeeping is "a technique designed to preserve the peace . . . where fighting has been halted, and to assist in implementing agreements achieved by the peacemakers."[11] It is a *third party intervention* designed to maintain peace with a set of guiding principles that include the consent of the parties to the conflict, impartiality (or neutrality), and the non-use of force, save in self-defense.[12] Peacekeepers are charged with several functions that, in addition to maintaining peace and security, include protecting civilians, assisting in the disarmament, demobilization, and integration of former combatants, supporting the organization of elections, as well as protecting and promoting human rights and assisting in restoring the rule of law.[13] In a word, as United Nations literature indicates, "[o]ver the years, peacekeeping has evolved from a primarily military model of observing cease-fires and the separation of forces after inter-state wars, to incorporate a complex model of many elements—military, police[,] and civilian—working together to help lay the foundations for sustainable peace."[14]

Peacekeeping is distinguished from three other concepts—peacebuilding, peacemaking, and peace enforcement—that it is closely related to. Newly won peace is a fragile commodity that could relapse into conflict if not preserved. *Peacebuilding* is designed to reduce the risk of such relapse by strengthening national capacities for conflict management, thereby laying the foundation for sustainable peace and development.[15] In contrast to peacebuilding, which is post conflict, *peacemaking* involves ongoing conflicts. Specifically, it generally involves measures designed to address ongoing conflicts, such as diplomatic action—by officials within or outside the United Nations system, unofficial and nongovernmental groups or even private individuals working independently—to help hostile parties understand their differences and bring them to a negotiated agreement.[16] Last but not least is *peace enforcement.* The term involves the application of a range of coercive measures, including the use of military force, requiring the explicit authorization of the Security Council,[17] consistent with the collective security imperatives of the United Nations.[18]

The connection of these terms to peacekeeping is borne out by the fact that today, "[p]eace operations are rarely limited to one type of activity."[19] Instead, the boundaries of the concepts blur, particularly the three that require no authorization from the United Nations Security Council. For example, "[w]hile U.N. *peacekeeping operations* are, in principle, deployed to support the implementation of a ceasefire or peace agreement, they are often required to play an active role in *peacemaking* efforts and may also be involved in early *peacebuilding* activities."[20]

As the reader would have gleaned from the discussion so far in this section, peacekeeping as we know it today is a United Nations invention.[21] Yet, although arguably the United Nations Charter anticipated the practice, it is a child of serendipity not mentioned in the United Nations Charter. Instead, peacekeeping evolved as an innovative attempt to deal with a number of regional conflicts needed to promote international security where, due to the Cold War from World War II in 1945 until 1991 with the breakup of the Soviet Union, great-power agreement was difficult or impossible. As the scholar and veteran observer of the United Nations system Inis L. Claude Jr. instructively and memorably observed, peacekeeping "repealed the proposition that the organization should undertake to promote order by bringing the great powers into troubled situations. . . . Henceforward, the task of the United Nations was to be defined as that of keeping the great powers out of such situations."[22]

EVOLUTION OF NIGERIAN PEACEKEEPING SINCE INDEPENDENCE IN 1960

Table 7.1 encapsulates Nigeria's peacekeeping operations since 1960 from least to most recent activity. The ensuing discussion highlights the features of the country's achievements in the field, together with inferences germane to those features. First is the lengthiness of the table speaking to a robustness that demonstrates a passion for these operations. Nigeria's engagements in peace operations span many regions of the world, including the Caribbean, Europe, and Asia. However, consistent with the avowed focus on Africa in its foreign relations, the country devotes much of its peacekeeping energies to African countries.[23] Second, based on the diagram, Nigerian peacekeeping operations evolved in three contexts—the United Nations, the OAU (subsequently AU), and bilaterally—encompassing ECOWAS (along with its monitoring outfit, ECOMOG) as a fourth context down the line following the formation of the community in 1975.[24] Third, many of Nigerian peacekeeping activities are military observation. Fourth, most of Nigeria's peacekeeping occurs in multilateral settings with rather few being bilateral. The occurrence speaks to the excessive emphasis on multilateralism in Nigerian foreign behavior which this study addresses in chapter 9. Fifth, a point adverted to already in the second paragraph of this chapter, three sectors of Nigerian society from which Nigeria draws its peacekeepers are the military, the police, and civilian experts. However, most peacekeepers are soldiers. Given their dominance in peacekeeping going back to the early days of the country's independence, the Nigerian military[25]—along with the police officers and civilian experts who assist them—is the most notable institution in the *implementation* of Nigerian foreign policy, second only to diplomats who also play a major role in *formulating* those policies.

Feature number six returns to the two gaps totaling 17 years in Nigeria's otherwise consistent engagement since independence in peace operations referred to in the second paragraph of this chapter. Those gaps—the first for 12 years from 1966 to 1978 and the second for 5 years from 1983 to 1988, coincided with the regimes of General Gowon (1966–1975) and General Buhari (1983–1985). One possible explanation for the absence of activity is national security challenges at home of a kind that foreclose mobilizing troops abroad. For Gowon that domestic issue was the civil war from 1967 to 1970. Additionally, the lack of activity might also have spelled antipathy for peacekeeping operations as a tool of foreign policy given that Gowon remained in office for five long years after the civil war during which period he helped form the Economic Community of West African States (ECOWAS).[26] This point bears noting, given that, with two other leaders who served as military Head of State—General Johnson Aguiyi-Ironsi in 1966 before him and General Olusegun Obasanjo after him—Gowon was part of the United Nations peacekeeping mission in the Congo.[27]

Even here too, the war arguably factored in: ECOWAS was an attempt to secure the West African sub-region, beginning with close-door neighbors, to avoid the type of interference in Nigeria's internal affairs by foreign actors, including Western powers, that led to the recognition of Biafra, by two states in the sub-region, Gabon and the Ivory Coast, who were, and still are, allies of France. Biafra was the former Eastern Region of the country that attempted unsuccessfully to break away from Nigeria. Next to Buhari, as military Head of State, he was an insular leader who focused exclusively on the economic troubles that his junta presented as the basis for the overthrow of the Shagari administration (1979–1983) that he succeeded.[28]

In 2004, after participating in peacekeeping for many years, Nigeria established a training center, Peacekeeper Wing (PKW), to facilitate its peacekeeping activities. Initially part of the Nigerian Army Infantry Corps Center, the institution was upgraded to a freestanding center in 2009, on which date it also took its current name Nigeria Army Peacekeeping Center (NAPKC).[29] Based in Kaduna, a metropolitan city in northern Nigeria,[30] the Center is headed by a commandant, currently Major-General Imomotimi Birigeni.[31] The government indicated it upgraded the Center because of "the overriding need to ensure that [Nigerian] peacekeepers are placed on the same pedestal of professional competence" supposedly with their counterparts elsewhere, "in accordance with U.N. requirements."[32] The Center provides training to Nigerian troops before they are shipped for peacekeeping duties abroad. According to information taken from its website, as of 2014, the Center has delivered "over 230 courses and trained over 53,000 peacekeepers."[33]

Training activities at the Center include courses in: pre-deployment training; command-and-staff operations skill; train-the-trainers; driver's training; combat life savers; junior leadership; military observation; peace operations planning; disarmament, demobilization, and reintegration; civil-military cooperation; negotiation skills; effective methods of instruction; basic peace support operations for defense correspondents; and protection of civilians.[34] To increase the training exposure of its peacekeepers, the Center collaborates with external agencies, including the United Nations Institute for Training and Research (UNITAR), the Africa Contingency Operations Training and Assistance (ACOSTA), France's Reinforcement of African Capacity to Maintain Peace (RECAMP in its French acronym), and Canada's Military Training Assistance Program (MTAP). Established in 1963 by General Assembly Resolution 1934 (XVIII) of Dec. 11, 1963, UNITAR is the training arm of the United Nations system.[35] The mission of the organization "is to

Table 7.1. Nigerian Peacekeeping Operations since 1960 (from Least to Most Recent)

Serial No.	*Peacekeeping Site*	*Period*	*Under whose auspice?*	*Description of Mission*
1.	Congo	1960–1964	UN (ONUC)	Mission in response to the Congo crisis to which Nigeria sent a military battalion,[a] along with police officers
2.	New Guinea	1962–1963	UN (UNSF)	Security force to which Nigeria sent military observers
3.	Tanzania	1964	Bilateral agreement	Mission in which Nigeria sent a military battalion
4.	India-Pakistan conflict	1965–1966	UN (UNIPOM)	Military observation mission
5.	Lebanon	1978–1983	UN (UNIFIL)	An interim force to which Nigeria sent a military battalion and staff officers
6.	Chad	1981–1982	Bilateral agreement	Mission, codenamed "Operation Harmony I," to which Nigeria sent a military battalion and staff officers
7.	Chad	1982–1983	OAU	Mission, codenamed "Operation Harmony II," to which Nigeria sent a military brigade[b]
8.	Iran-Iraq conflict	1988–1991	UN	Military observation mission
9.	Angola	1989–91	UN (AVEM I)	Verification mission
10.	Angola	1991–92	UN (AVEM II)	Verification mission
11.	Angola	1992–95	UN (UNAVEM III)	Verification mission
12.	Namibia	1989–90	UN (UNTAG)	Transition assistance mission
13.	Western Sahara[c]	1991–	UN (MINURSO)[d]	Military observation mission
14.	Iraq-Kuwait	1991	UN (UNIKOM)	Military observation mission
15.	Kosovo	1991	UN (UNMIK)	Interim mission
16.	Cambodia	1992–1993	UN (UNTAC)	Transitional authority mission
17.	Somalia	1992–95	UN (UNOSOM I)	Mission to monitor and observe a ceasefire

Serial No.	Peacekeeping Site	Period	Under whose auspice?	Description of Mission
18.	Somalia	1992–95	UN (UNOSOM II)	Nation-building mission (disarm armed factions, restore law and order, etc.)
19.	Former Yugoslavia	1992–93	UN (UNPROFOR)	Protection force to which Nigeria contributed military battalion and staff officers
20.	Mozambique	1992–95	UN (UNOSOZ)	Mission to monitor and verify ceasefire
21.	Sierra Leone	1992–	UN (UNOMSIL)	Peace observation mission
22.	Rwanda	1992–93	OAU	Peace monitoring mission to which Nigeria sent a military battalion
23.	Bosnia and Herzegovina	1993	UN (UNMIBH)	Nation-building mission involving a range of functions, including law enforcement and police reform
24.	Rwanda	1993–95	UN (UNAMIR)	Assistance mission
25.	Croatia	1993–95	UN (UNCRO)	Confidence restoration mission
26.	Aouzo Strip[e]	1994	UN (UNASOG)	Military observation mission
27.	Tajikistan	1994–2000	UN (UNMOT)	Military observation mission
28.	Macedonia	1995–2000	UN (UNPREDEP)	Prevention deployment mission
29.	Eastern Slovenia	1996–98	UN (UNTAES)[f]	Transition administration mission
30.	Prevlaka[g]	1996–2000	UN (UNMOP)	Military observation mission
31.	Angola	1997	UN (MONUA)[h]	Military observation mission
32.	Liberia	1990–97	ECOWAS (ECOMOG)[i]	Ceasefire monitoring mission codenamed "Operation Harmony" to which Nigeria sent a military division[j]
33.	Sierra Leone	1997–2000	ECOWAS (ECOMOG)	Ceasefire monitoring mission codenamed "Operation Sandstorm"
34.	Dambe Region, Croatia	1998	UN	Civilian police support mission

(*continued*)

Table 7.1. *Continued*

Serial No.	*Peacekeeping Site*	*Period*	*Under whose auspice?*	*Description of Mission*
35.	Sierra Leone	1995–2005	UN (UNAMSIL)	Mission to implement a peace agreement as well as to disarm, demobilize, and reintegrate armed factions
36.	Democratic Republic of Congo	2000–	UN (MONUC)[k]	Mission to enforce a ceasefire agreement
37.	East Timor	2000	UN (UNTAET)	Transition authority mission
38.	Liberia	2003	ECOWAS (ECOMIL)	Nigeria deployed 1,500 troops along with 120 police officers
39.	Côte d'Ivoire	2003	ECOWAS (ECOMICI)	Nigeria sent a medical and signals team
40.	Côte d'Ivoire	2004–	UN (UNOCI)	Mission designed to facilitate peace agreement to end the Ivorian civil war (2002–7).
41.	Sudan	2004	AU (AMIS)	Nigeria deployed 1,500 troops in Darfur
42.	Haiti	2004	UN (MINUSTAH)[l]	Stabilization mission
43.	Darfur, Sudan	2007–	AU and UN (UNAMID)	Hybrid operation
44.	Somalia	2007–	AU (AMISOM)	Nigeria sent 200 police officers
45.	Democratic Republic of Congo	2010–	UN (MONUSCO)[m]	Stabilization mission
46.	Abyei (South Sudan)	2011–	UN (UNISFA)	Interim security mission
47.	South Sudan	2011–	UN	
48.	Guinea Bissau	2012	ECOWAS (ECOMOG)	Ceasefire monitoring mission where Nigeria contributed 186 troops
49.	Mali	2013–	AU (AFISMA) and UN (UNMISMM)[n]	AU-UN hybrid multidimensional integrated stabilization mission to which Nigeria contributed 1,200 troops
50.	Central African Republic	2014–	UN (UNMISM)	Multidimensional integrated stabilization mission

[a]A quick primer on military terms. A battalion is a combat unit of 500–800 soldiers. Three to five battalions, anywhere from 1,500 to 4,000 soldiers, make up a brigade. A division is the basic fighting unit of many armies. The size of a division varies from about 10,000 to 18,000 soldiers. Most divisions have three or more brigades of roughly equal size. A corps has anywhere from 50,000 to 100,000 soldiers and can comprise two or more divisions and support troops. Valerie Turner, "How Many Troops Make Up a Brigade, Battalion, Company, Etc.?," *Orlando Sentinel* (Mar. 29, 2003), http://articles.orlandosentinel.com/2003-03-29/news/0303290257_1_support-troops-battalion-divisions.

[b]See note a for the meaning of this term.

[c]This is a disputed territory on the northwest coast of Africa, bordered by Morocco, Mauritania, and Algeria, that Morocco still claims ownership of. See "Western Sahara," CIA World Factbook, https://www.cia.gov/library/publications/the-world-factbook/geos/wi.html; "Western Sahara Profile," *BBC News Africa* (Jan. 7, 2014), http://www.bbc.com/news/world-africa-14115273; Jenn Abelson, "Western Sahara: Why Africa's Last Colony Can't Break Free," *Boston Globe* (Jun. 16, 2013), https://www.bostonglobe.com/ideas/2013/06/15/western-sahara-why-africa-last-colony-can-break-free/87jACxXfU5bVUtqEe6uyrM/story.html.

[d]This is the acronym in French of Mission des Nations Unites pour l'Organisation d'un Référendum au Sahara Occidental or, in English, the United Nations Mission for the Referendum in Western Sahara.

[e]The name stands for a strip of land in northern Chad, which lies along the border with Libya. See "Aozou Strip," *Encyclopedia Britannica*, http://www.britannica.com/place/Aozou-Strip. Chad and Libya quarreled over ownership of the territory. Frank Jacobs, "The World's Largest Sandbox," *N. Y. Times* (Nov. 7, 2011 9.30 p.m.), http://opinionator.blogs.nytimes.com/2011/11/07/the-worlds-largest-sandbox/; United Nations Aouzou Strip Observer Group (UNASOG) (May/June 1994), http://www.un.org/en/peacekeeping/missions/past/unasog.htm; Gino J. Naldi, "The Aouzou Strip Dispute—A Legal Analysis," *Journal of African Law*, Vol. 33 (Sp. 1998): 72–77.

[f]The full name of this mission, not borne out in the acronym or else it will be too long, is the United Nations Transitional Administration for Eastern Slovenia, Baranja, Western Sirmium in Croatia. See "Croatia: United Nations Transitional Administration for Eastern Slovenia, Baranja, Western Sirmium," UNTAES (Jan. 1996–Jan. 1998), http://www.un.org/en/peacekeeping/missions/past/untaes.htm.

[g]Prevlaka is a peninsula in the southern border between Croatia and Yugoslavia. Croatia and former Yugoslavia disagreed over ownership of this territory, now part of Croatia, following the breakup of Yugoslavia into several independent states. See Gerald Henry Blake et al., *The Maritime Boundaries of the Adriatic Sea* (Durham, U.K.: IBRU, 1996): 42.

[h]Though Angola is Portuguese speaking, the acronym is French for Mission d'Observation des Nations Unies à l'Angola or, in English, the United Nations Observer Mission in Angola.

[i]ECOWAS refers to the Economic Community of West African States, the subject of chapter 10. The acronym ECOMOG stands for the Economic Community of West African States Monitoring Group, an alliance of peacekeepers contributed by Nigeria and other ECOWAS member-states. The ceasefire monitoring group was created in 1990 in the wake of the first Liberian civil war from 1989 to 1996. See "Profile: ECOMOG," *BBC News* (Jun. 17, 2004 15:15 GMT 16:15 UK), http://news.bbc.co.uk/2/hi/africa/country_profiles/2364029.stm. The conflict in Liberia took place in two stages, the first from 1989–1996, and the second from 1999–2003. See "Liberia: Conflict," Peace Direct, http://www.insightonconflict.org/conflicts/liberia/conflict-profile/; UNMIL Background, U.N., http://www.un.org/en/peacekeeping/missions/unmil/background.shtml.

[j]See note a for the meaning of this term.

[k]The acronym is French for Mission de l'Organization des Nations Unies en Républic démocratique du Congo or, in English, the United Nations Mission in the Democratic Republic of Congo.

[l]The acronym is French for Mission des Nations Unies pour la stabilization en Haiti or, in English, the United Nations Stabilization Mission in Haiti.

[m]The acronym is French for Mission de l'Organisation des Nations Unies pour la stabilization en République démocratique du Congo or, in English, the United Nations Organization Stabilization Mission in the Democratic Republic of Congo.

[n]This operation is two missions in one: the International Support Mission in Mali (AFISMA), led by Africans, and the United Nations Security Council–approved Multidimensional Integrated Stabilization Mission in Mali (MINUSMA). See Andrew Clark, "Mali," Encyclopedia Britannica, http://www.britannica.com/place/Mali/Government-and-society#ref1180547. Nigeria made its contribution to AFISMA. Adeniyi, note 6.

Sources: Table created by author drawing on multiple sources, including: Adeniyi, note 6; Chilaka Francis Chigozie & Odoh Samuel Ituma, "Nigerian Peacekeeping Operations Revisited," *Singaporean Journal of Business Economics & Management Studies*, Vol. 4 (2015); Suleiman Hamman et al., "The Role of Nigeria in Peacekeeping Operations from 1960 to 2013," *Int'l Affairs & Global Strategy*, Vol. 21 (2014): 42–45; and Maryam Ahmadu-Suka, "Nigeria: 186 Soldiers for Guinea Bissau Peacekeeping Mission," *Daily Trust* (Abuja) (Nov. 22, 2012).

develop capacities of individuals, organizations, and institutions to enhance global decision making and to support country-level action for shaping a better future."[36] It is an autonomous body within the U.N. system, governed by a Board of Trustees and headed by an executive director. The organization is supported solely by voluntary contributions from governments, intergovernmental organizations, foundations, and other non-government sources.[37] Managed and funded by the U.S. Department of State, ACOTA is an American initiative designed to improve the ability of African countries to respond quickly to crises by providing militaries who are beneficiaries of the program with the training and equipment they need to implement peace support or humanitarian operations. The organization replaced the African Crisis Response Initiative (ACRI) in 2004.[38] Operating under the aegis of the U.N. and in agreement with the African Union, RECAMP aims to help African states to acquire military capabilities that will enable them to conduct peace operations in Africa.[39] Last but not least, MTAP supports and reinforces the international mission of the Canadian military by training the military forces of other countries, particularly states in the developing world, in peace operations, including developing the capability of these militaries to operate effectively in joint forces with the Canadian military. The program originated in agreements Canada made in the early 1960s to provide military training assistance to certain newly independent Commonwealth countries.[40]

Nigeria engages in peacekeeping for various economic and non-pecuniary reasons.[41] Starting with the economic reason, Nigeria receives reimbursements in some cases running into hundreds of thousands in U.S. dollars for its participation in United Nations peacekeeping, to the financial benefits of the country and the peacekeepers.[42] For instance, for its participation in the United Nations Mission in Sierra Leone (UNAMSIL), Nigeria received a reimbursement of a little over US $798,000 for use of major equipment and provision for "self-sustainment" for the initial two battalions deployed in the mission from Dec. 27, 1999 to Jan. 26, 2000.[43] However, the country spends its own money rather than gets reimbursed when it participates in peace operations mandated by ECOWAS or the AU. It is estimated that Nigeria spent over $10 billion on ECOMOG missions in Liberia and Sierra Leone (the amount then U.S. president Clinton referred to during the course of his address to the Nigerian National Assembly referred to in the opening sentences of this chapter) during the civil wars in those two countries.[44] In short, because Nigeria is reimbursed for costs incurred in United Nations peacekeeping missions, the financial challenge for the country in peacekeeping occurs with respect to regional and sub-regional peace operations.[45] "[D]espite the importance and centrality of Africa to Nigeria's foreign policy[,]" the economic attraction of United Nations operations vis-à-vis AU and ECOWAS engagements has made the former more appealing for the country.[46] For the soldiers as a group that form the face of Nigerian peace operations, participation in these activities has become "part of the military's internal rewards system" for promotion.

For this reason, given also the generous allowances in hard currency that soldiers receive when they participate in United Nations–sponsored peace operations[47] and the opportunity for training in modern peace techniques that these rounds of duty afford, the Nigerian Armed Forces strongly support United Nations peacekeeping.[48] Next to the non-pecuniary reasons, Nigeria embraced peacekeeping initially out of a desire to play a leadership role in Africa—a goal that expanded over time to include others, such as exposure of soldiers and police personnel to the techniques of modern peace operations that United Nations peacekeeping affords; and a desire to build up credentials for a seat in a modified United Nations Security Council.[49]

As indicated in the opening paragraphs of this chapter, Nigeria has commanded some of the peace missions it has featured in. Six soldiers who have served as United Nations force commanders are: Major-General Johnson Aguiyi-Ironsi (Congo) who rose to become the country's first military Head of State, Major-General Chris Garuba (Angola), Lt. General Isaac Obiakor (Liberia), Major-General Joseph Owonibi (Liberia), Gen. Martin Luther Agwai (Darfur), and Major-General Moses Obi (South Sudan). Obiakor and Agwai also served as Chief Military Adviser and Deputy Military Adviser, respectively, at United Nations Headquarters.[50] Some Nigerian civilians have similarly occupied important positions in United Nations peacekeeping as Special Representative of the United Nations Secretary General. These include: Ibrahim Gambari, Joint AU-UN Special Representative and Head of the United Nations Mission in Darfur; Olu Adeniji, Central African Republic and Sierra Leone; and Margaret Vogt, Central African Republic.[51]

To end this discussion on the evolution of Nigerian peacekeeping since independence, two points need to be kept in mind. First not directly related to Nigerian foreign policy yet germane to it, which a careful reading of the table reveals, is the rifeness of conflicts in Africa.[52] Given the high level of conflicts in the region that continues even with the end of the Cold War, in choosing peacekeeping as an anchor of its foreign policy, Nigeria presciently selected an area of particular need for Africa. Secondly, peacekeeping demonstrates one of the contradictions of the Nigerian state, speaking to the paradox of "beautiful abroad and ugly at home"[53] that the adoption of a human rights foreign policy could resolve for the country. "Physician, heal thyself!" is a popular saying whose lesson Nigerian leaders pay no heed to, given that at home Nigeria is often burdened by the very same conflicts it strives to solve for other people abroad. Reading from the diagram above, in 1964–1966,

Nigeria was involved in peacekeeping activities in the India-Pakistan conflict, the latter of which period (1966) overlapped the pogrom of about 100,000 Igbos and other Easterners in northern Nigeria.[54] Under Babangida, Nigeria performed peacekeeping in various parts of the world—Bosnia and Herzegovina, Croatia, and Rwanda, where in one instance it deployed one military battalion, the same year the administration annulled a presidential election that created so much fracas, especially within Lagos and other areas in the Southwest that is home of Moshood Abiola, the presumed winner of the cancelled election.[55] Finally, in 1998, a crisis-ridden military regime under the Abacha dictatorship undertook peacekeeping initiatives to restore a civilian regime in Sierra Leone.[56] In short, it is fair to say that, save for a war or the idiosyncratic disposition of an insular leader who chooses to focus his attention on domestic issues, Nigeria engaged in peacekeeping abroad even when there were crises at home that could use peace measures.

To put the issue of crisis at home and peacekeeping abroad into some more perspective, since 2009, Nigeria has battled terrorist violence by the Boko Haram group that has fought to turn the country into an Islamic state in a bloody campaign that has killed over 20,000 citizens, displaced millions from their homes, and done untold damage to government and private property.[57] This is in addition to the longstanding militancy in the Niger Delta over environmental degradation from oil exploration and demands for more revenue allocation by impoverished communities in that region.[58] Due to these security issues, the Nigerian government has, as the security analyst Adesoji Adeniji points out, reprioritized its troop deployments such that "[a]n increasing number of troops are being recalled from peace operations, including Mali, and redeployed to restive regions within the country."[59]

MAKING NIGERIAN PEACE OPERATIONS HUMAN RIGHTS-COMPLAINT

By itself, peacekeeping even under the more structured setting of the United Nations (given the world body's longer experience with this scheme) is *not* a human rights tool, if it is not human rights complaint. To use the United Nations Mission in Sierra Leone (UNAMSIL) as an example, as one study poignantly observed, "[t]he initial success of the peacekeepers helped obscure some of the troubling aspects of the intervention[,]" some inconsistent with human rights, that included "the lack of an international mandate, the use of mercenary in peacekeeping operations[,] and the very undemocratic nature of the Nigerian regime."[60] Given this reality, the conceivable way for Nigeria to make its peacekeeping enterprise human rights complaint is to embrace international standards embedded in human rights, humanitarian law, appreciation of the intersection between the two, and human rights education.

A brief statement is necessary here on the relationship between human rights and humanitarian law. The two concepts are complementary in the sense that "[b]oth strive to protect the lives, health[,] and dignity of individuals, albeit from a different angle."[61] Another point of similarity is that "[t]he duty to implement [humanitarian law] and human rights lies first and foremost with States."[62] Next to the distinction between the two, humanitarian law (HL) applies in situations of armed conflict and aims to protect people who are not fighters (noncombatants) or are no longer taking part in hostilities (i.e., they are wounded or have surrendered or are taken as prisoners of war). The rules embodied in HL impose duties on all parties to a conflict, compared to human rights, which apply to everyone.[63] In contrast, human rights protect the individual at all times, both in war and peace alike. However, some human rights treaties permit governments to derogate from certain rights in situations of public emergency, whereas no such derogations are permitted under HL because that law was conceived for emergency situations, specifically armed conflicts. The legal anchor of human rights consists of the United Nations Charter, along with the international bill of human rights, made up of the Universal Declaration of Human Rights (1948) and the two human rights instruments, the International Covenant on Civil and Political Rights as well as the International Covenant on Economic, Social, and Cultural Rights (both of which came into force in 1976), among other core global human rights instruments. The legal anchor of HL consists of the Geneva Conventions, a set of international treaties dating back to 1864 and amplified by numerous changes, some as recent as 1978, dealing with a multiplicity of topics, including the treatment of civilians during wars, humane treatment of prisoners of wars, and treatment rules regarding care of the wounded and sick.[64] The legal foundation of HL also includes the Convention on the Prevention and Punishment of the Crime of Genocide (1948), known for short as the Genocide Convention.

In a Nigerian society riven with regional, ethnic, religious, and class divisions,[65] the military and police perceive themselves to be among the only "national institutions."[66] It is probably this feature that pushed these two groups to the forefront as the face of the country in peacekeeping missions abroad.[67] But, historically, none of the two has a reputation for respecting human rights and humanitarian laws at home.[68] The Nigerian army participated in the pogrom against the Igbo in northern Nigeria in 1966.[69] Similarly, during the Nigerian civil war from 1967 to 1970, Nigerian federal troops perpetrated human rights abuses against the Igbo and other Easterners for breaking away from Nigeria for which until today they have not been held accountable.

Dispensing with provisions of the Geneva Conventions for the "humane" conduct of war, these "troops incessantly and wantonly bombed unarmed civilian targets, including open busy markets, and deliberately used economic blockades and starvation as a weapon of war[]" of a manner that leaves open the interpretation of the war as genocide.[70]

Most recently, in responding to the wave of terrorist activities in northeastern Nigeria since 2009 that has spread out into some other parts of the country, Nigerian security forces have abused the human rights of suspects to the extent that the U.S. government and some human rights groups have voiced concerns regarding the human rights of terrorism suspects.[71] The Nigeria police have a similar dubious reputation for cruelty in its dealings with citizens at home.[72] This is particularly true with the Nigerian Mobile Police (MOPOL), nicknamed "kill and go" by the masses of the Nigerian people because of its tendency to perpetrate extrajudicial murder with impunity.[73] Between them, Nigerian soldiers and the police share a history of corruption, the (ab)use of public office—and trust—for private ends. One shameful monument of the symbiosis are police so-called roadside checkpoints which Daniel J. Smith pinpointed as "the most notorious and popularly recognized symbol of everyday corruption" in Nigeria.[74] This is a practice of illegal extortion wherein the police and soldiers set up makeshift roadblocks, where they repeatedly stop and besiege the drivers of countless private and public vehicles who drive on Nigerian roads as well as hassle the passengers of these vehicles.[75] Smith averred that during the period he lived in Nigeria from 1989–1997, "hardly a month passed without media reports or oral testimony from my friends and acquaintances about people who had been harassed, beaten, or shot in confrontations at checkpoints with the police or military."[76]

There is evidence that the attitude of general disrespect of human rights at home by Nigerian security forces did not stop there but instead extended abroad into peacekeeping missions. A report released in 1993 by Human Rights Watch found that the ECOMOG forces in Liberia that Nigeria led failed to integrate human rights into its peace campaigns largely because for the Nigerian commanders, observing human rights during the operation was a mission left for "[o]ther organizations" that the military should not be bothered with.[77] Ten years later, the problem remained not only in Liberia but also as well in Sierra Leone. Like in Liberia, Nigeria troops also form the bulk of ECOWAS peacekeepers in Sierra Leone. In July 2003, Human Rights Watch wrote an open letter to President John Kufuor of Ghana in his capacity as ECOWAS president, as the organization was poised to send soldiers into Liberia to end the conflict in the country.[78]

The letter urged Kufuor to ensure that the peacekeepers deployed in Liberia "act[] in full accordance with international human rights and humanitarian law, and with a clear mandate to protect civilians."[79] On the one hand, Human Rights Watch gave ECOMOG credit for helping to "restore security, which resulted in an improvement in the human rights situation."[80] On the other hand, the organization called the troops out for a litany of abuses, with impunity, that included responsibility "for extensive looting, harassment and arbitrary detention of civilians," as well as violation of "international humanitarian law by conducting indiscriminate air strikes against civilians and civilian objects, including violations of medical neutrality."[81] In Sierra Leone, the violations were no less egregious and included "summary executions of suspected rebels or collaborators," in some of which senior officers were present or took part; "use of child soldiers, and indiscriminate bombings against civilians"; violation of medical neutrality during a January 11, 1999, operation during which ECOMOG troops "stormed a hospital, proceeded to drag wounded rebels from their beds, and executed them on hospital groups"; and sexual exploitation of women and solicitation of child prostitutes.[82] In the light of the abuses that it recounted, Human Rights Watch made a number of recommendations aimed at minimizing abuses of human rights, including providing the peacekeepers about to be sent to Liberia with appropriate training in international human rights and humanitarian law before they ship.[83]

It took until 2004 for Nigeria to set up separate training programs for its peacekeepers. This is an unduly long period for a country with a long history of engaging in these missions as a pathway to a leadership role in Africa and the world. Yet when a center was created, none of the various courses it offered for peacekeepers on its face included human rights and humanitarian law. This is despite the fact that United Nations peacekeeping materials specified human rights among the duties assigned to peacekeepers,[84] and despite the fact, further, that the Nigerian Army said its purpose of upgrading the Center in 2009 was to place Nigerian peacekeepers on the same pedestal of professional competence with their counterparts elsewhere, consistent with the United Nations' requirements.[85] Old habits die hard. Assuming, for the sake of argument, that some of the courses essentially contained human rights and humanitarian law, based on the accounts of their stewardship in Liberia and Sierra Leone by Human Rights Watch reviewed in the preceding paragraph, there is no evidence that Nigerian peacekeepers internalized these values. Armed forces which violate the rights of their citizens at home will have difficulty respecting those of proverbial strangers abroad.

Having commented on the necessity for an international standard embedded in human rights and humanitarian laws, both of which Nigerian peacekeeping still lacks, one more element necessary to complete this discussion on a redesigned peacekeeping for Nigeria is human rights education.[86] Beginning with the Universal Declaration of Human Rights (UDHR) in 1948, *education*, broadly defined, has been an important tool for promoting the "strengthening of respect for human rights and fundamental freedoms."[87] Among other acts of enlightenment, education in human rights should inform citizens of their rights; "lead to an understanding of, and sympathy for, the concepts of democracy, justice, equality, freedom, solidarity, peace, dignity, and rights and responsibilities; and build their awareness that oppressive laws and inappropriate traditions may be reformed."[88] While there is no uniform or universal content to that education, the common core should include "familiarity with the main international documents on human rights; people, movements, and key events in the historical struggle for human rights, the main categories of human rights, along with duties or obligations, and incidents of discrimination, including racism and sexism."[89] As the United Nations Commission on Human Rights advised, the key is that "knowledge of human rights, both in its theoretical dimension and in its practical application . . . be established as a priority in educational policies."[90]

As Eleanor Roosevelt, first chair of the United Nations Commission on Human Rights that oversaw the drafting of the UDHR and other core human rights instruments, taught in 1958, "the destiny of human rights is in the hands of all our citizens in all our communities."[91] Education on human rights is the "small places close to home," "the world of the individual person," where human rights begin."[92] Part of this education for Nigerian soldiers is that they must subordinate themselves to civilian control, rather than seize the reins of government as they did time and again before 1999.[93]

Adopting international standards embedded in human rights, humanitarian law, as well as the intersection between the two, and human rights education, facilitates the peacekeeping role of Nigerian peacekeepers. It fits the needs of the victims of conflicts that Nigerian peacekeepers minister to, while facilitating better cooperation with external agencies, such as UNITAR, ACOTA, RECAMP, and MTAP[94]—already following these standards—with whom NAPKC, the Nigerian training agency, collaborates.

SUMMATION

More than 55 years after Nigerian founding fathers discovered it as a gateway to a leadership role in Africa,[95] peacekeeping still dominates the face of Nigerian foreign policy. From 2000 to 2010, under the Fourth Republic since 1999, Nigeria ranked among the top seven contributors to United Nations peacekeeping.[96] Long military rule in the land guaranteed continued support for peace missions, but so also were the idiosyncratic imprints of three military leaders, Babangida, Abacha, and Obasanjo, particularly the last who also served two terms until 2007 as civilian president under the Fourth Republic.[97] Over the period the goals sought for these missions have expanded to include practical training not available domestically for the soldiers that form the bulk of these missions. Given their expensiveness and questions by a growing number of Nigerians regarding returns from the investment on these missions, some Nigerian leaders under the Fourth Republic, such as General Obasanjo, have pushed for greater burden sharing to reduce the weight of these missions on Nigerian taxpayers.[98] It is doubtful though that these readjustments will lead to complete phase-out of these missions for reasons of inertia but also because, on a practical note, there are few arrows in the quiver of Nigerian foreign policy to replace peacekeeping.

By themselves peace missions are not human rights compliant, unless a state makes them so. Although it has established a training center for its peacekeepers since 2004, Nigeria has yet to integrate human rights into its training programs or to help inculcate these values into the minds of its peacekeepers. Achieving that sensitivity mandates embracement of international standards rooted in human rights, humanitarian law, the intersection between the two, and human rights education. In analyzing Nigerian peacekeeping experiences, commentators point up a range of lingering impediments that includes a litany of issues down to advice to learn French, Portuguese, Spanish, and Arabic to minimize some of the communication problems Nigerian peacemakers confront when dealing with non-English-speaking countries,[99] but little to nothing about human rights. More properly, respect of human rights and humanitarian law should top these recommendations.

The changing nature of peacekeeping coupled with the domination of the decision making concerning this matter by the military raises a question regarding the apparatus of Nigerian foreign policy, which question chapter 8 following this one deals with. Compared to their military counterparts, Nigerian civilian leaders appear to be more wary about peace missions. For example, under the Second Republic from 1979 to 1983, President Shehu Shagari recalled Nigerian peacekeepers from Lebanon, following the Israeli invasion of the country.[100] The issue raises a question regarding popular input into decisions on peacekeeping, among the issues addressed in chapter 8 on reshaping the Nigerian foreign policy apparatus in a human-rights direction.

NOTES

1. See Festus Ugboaja Ohaegbulam, *Nigeria and the United Nations' Mission to the Democratic Republic of the Congo: A Case Study of the Formative Stages of Nigeria's Foreign Policy* (Gainesville, FL: University Press of Florida, 1982), *passim.* In actuality, because the United Nations Operation in the Congo (ONUC) spans the

period July 1960–June 1964, see "Republic of the Congo: United Nations Operation in the Congo," ONUC (July 1960–June 1964), U.N., http://www.un.org/en/peace keeping/missions/past/onuc.htm, Nigeria's participation in peace operations predated the country's independence on Oct. 1, 1960, by more than two months. ONUC is the acronym in French of Organisation des Nations Unies au Congo or, in English, the United Nations Organization in the Congo. The Congo is a French-speaking country.

2. Adekeye Adebajo, "Nigeria," *in* Alex J. Bellamy & Paul D. Williams, eds., *Providing Peacekeepers: The Politics, Challenges, and Future of United Nations Peacekeeping Contributions* (New York: Oxford University Press, 2010): 245. Founded in May 1963, the OAU metamorphosed into the African Union in 2000. See Constitutive Act of the African Union (2000), OAU Doc. CAB/LEG/23.15 (Jul. 11, 2000), http://www.africa-union.org; Rachael L. Swarns, "African Leaders Drop Old Group for One That Has Power," *New York Times* (Jul. 9, 2002), http://www .nytimes.com/2002/07/09/international/africa/09AFRI.html (reporting that African leaders replaced the OAU with the AU because, although the OAU "championed the continent's long and successful struggle against white oppressors," the organization "stood mostly silent when black autocrats emerged in their wake.").

3. Henry Umoru, "Nigeria Lost 2,000 Soldiers, $10 bn. in Peacekeeping Operations," *Vanguard* (Lagos) (Oct. 25, 2010 1:21 AM) (quoting a lecture on Nigerian foreign policy by a Nigerian-born scholar). Different commentators quote different figures for the amount that Nigeria has spent on peacekeeping and over what time frame. See, e.g., "The Perils of Liberian Peacekeeping," *BBC News* (Aug. 4, 2003, 15:35 GMT 16:35 UK), http://news.bbc.co.uk/2/hi/africa/3113009.stm (quoting General Olusegun Obasanjo, civilian president of the country at the time this story appeared, to the effect that "Nigeria had spent some $12 bn during two years without any help from the [W]est.").

4. Umoru, note 3.

5. Adebajo, note 2, p. 245.

6. "Foreign Relations," *in* Helen Chapin Metz, ed., *Nigeria: A Country Study* (Washington, D.C.: GPO for the Library of Congress, 1991), http://countrystudies .us/nigeria/80.htm; Adesoji Adeniyi, "Peacekeeping Contributor Profile: Nigeria," *Providing for Peacekeeping* (Apr. 24, 2015), http://www.providingforpeacekeeping .org/2015/04/24/peacekeeping-contributor-profile-nigeria/ (stating that "[p]eacekeeping is one of the activities through which Nigeria has assumed the position of a key player in international conflict management.").

7. The Nigerian National Assembly is a bicameral legislature made up of a *House of Representatives* (lower house, based on population) and a *Senate* (upper house, symbolizing the equality of the Senate with three members from each of the 36 states plus one senator from the Federal Capital Territory at Abuja). Constitution of the Fed. Republic of Nigeria, 1999, Art. 48.

8. William J. Clinton, "Remarks to a Joint Session of the Nigerian National Assembly in Abuja, Aug. 26, 2000," *in Public Papers of the Presidents of the United States: William J. Clinton, 2000–2001* (Washington, D.C.: Best Books, 2000): 1710; President Clinton's Address to the Nigerian Joint Assembly (Aug. 26, 2000),

https://www.youtube.com/watch?v=Z0uzicpb1Is (YouTube video of the speech published Apr. 19, 2012).

9. Clinton, "Remarks to a Joint Session of the Nigerian National Assembly," note 8, p. 1705 (emphasis added).

10. "Clinton Praises 'New Nigeria,'" *BBC News* (Aug. 26, 2000, 18:01 GMT 19:01), http://news.bbc.co.uk/2/hi/africa/897423.stm.

11. United Nations, *United Nations Peacekeeping Operations: Principles and Guidelines* (New York: Dept. of Peacekeeping Operations, 2008): 18.

12. "What Is Peacekeeping," U.N., http://www.un.org/en/peacekeeping/operations/peacekeeping.shtml.

13. Ibid.

14. United Nations, note 11, p. 18.

15. "Peace and Security," U.N., http://www.un.org/en/peacekeeping/.

16. Ibid.

17. Ibid.

18. *Collective security* is a collective defense arrangement guaranteeing "security for individual nations by collective means" in an attempt to maintain international peace. Roland N. Stromberg, "Collective Security," *Encyclopedia of the New American Nation,* http://www.americanforeignrelations.com/A-D/Collective-Security.html. Under this arrangement, which predated the formation of the United Nations, "an aggressor against any one state is considered an aggressor against all other states, which act together to repel the aggressor." "Collective Security," *Encyclopedia Britannica*, http://www.britannica.com/topic/collective-security.

19. "Peace and Security," note 15.

20. Ibid.

21. See generally Ronald Hatto, "From Peacekeeping to Peacebuilding: The Evolution of the Role of the United Nations in Peace Operations," *Int'l Review of the Red Cross*, Vol. 95 (2013): 495–515 (appropriately depicting the U.N. as the main player in setting up peace operations).

22. Inis L. Claude Jr., *The Changing United Nations* (New York: Random House, 1965): 32.

23. Of the 49 peace operations on table 7.1, 33, making up 67 percent (two-thirds) of the entire operations, were on Africa.

24. Discussion on ECOWAS and ECOMOG is saved for chapter 10.

25. The Nigerian military consists of three branches: the army and navy, established in 1958, and the air force, founded in 1964. "Nigeria—Ministry of Defense," *Global Security*, http://www.globalsecurity.org/military/world/nigeria/mod.htm.

26. More discussion on this community, including its use as tool in the application of Nigerian foreign policy is saved for chapter 10.

27. Adebajo, note 2, at 247.

28. See "Nigeria's Muhammadu Buhari in Profile," *BBC News* (Mar. 31, 2015), http://www.bbc.com/news/world-africa-12890807 (observing that in addition to a "war against indiscipline," as military leader, Buhari opened another war front involving about 500 politicians, officials, and businessmen, whom he sent to jail as part of his campaign against corruption).

29. Adeniyi, note 6.

30. "Kaduna, Nigeria," *Encyclopedia Britannica*, http://www.britannica.com/place/Kaduna-Nigeria.

31. "Welcome," Nigeria Army Peacekeeping Center, http://www.napkc.org/index.php.

32. "About Us," Nigeria Army Peacekeeping Center, http://www.napkc.org/training.php.

33. Ibid. Elsewhere in its website, the Center claims that it "has taught over 230 courses in diverse aspects of peacekeeping operations to over 44,000 individuals and organizations." "Welcome," note 31. It is not clear which, between 53,000 and 44,000, is the correct number trained.

34. "Highlight," Nigeria Army Peacekeeping Center, http://www.napkc.org/training.php.

35. *About Us: The Institute*, UNITAR, http://www.unitar.org/the-institute.

36. Ibid.

37. Ibid.

38. "Fact Sheet on Africa Contingency Operations Training and Assistance (ACOTA)," *Council on Foreign Relations* (Jun. 15, 2008), http://www.cfr.org/africa-sub-saharan/fact-sheet-africa-contingency-operations-training-assistance-acota/p22318.

39. See Ruth Nabakwe, "France Continues Peacekeeping Initiatives for Africa," *Pan African News Agency* (Jan. 23, 2002), https://www.globalpolicy.org/component/content/article/199/41018.html.

40. Andrew P. Rasiulis, "The Military Training Assistance Program (MTAP): An Instrument of Diplomacy," *Canadian Military Journal* (Autumn 2001): 63–64, http://www.journal.forces.gc.ca/vo2/no3/doc/63-64-eng.pdf.

41. See Adeniyi, note 6 (dividing those reasons into political, normative, security, economic, and international).

42. See ibid.

43. Ibid.

44. The civil war in Sierra Leone took place from 1991–2002. See "Sierra Leone," *Global Security*, http://www.globalsecurity.org/military/world/war/sierra_leone.htm; and Se Young Jang, "The Causes of the Sierra Leone Civil War," *E-Int'l Relations Students* (Oct. 25, 2012), http://www.e-ir.info/2012/10/25/the-causes-of-the-sierra-leone-civil-war-underlying-grievances-and-the-role-of-the-revolutionary-united-front/. The conflict in Liberia took place in two stages, the first from 1989–1996, and the second from 1999–2003. Part of the reason the amount was hefty was that Nigeria had to provide support to keep participating countries in West Africa aboard who threatened to pull out due to lack of funds. Adeniji, note 6. Finally on the estimate of $10 billion quoted as the amount expended on the peacekeeping missions, see the comment about differential figures in note 3.

45. Adeniji, note 6.

46. Ibid.

47. By 1993, the United Nations paid its peacekeeping soldiers almost $1,000 per month, compared to about $5–$10 per day, averaging anywhere from $150–$300 per

month, that ECOMOG paid its soldiers. Human Rights Watch, *Waging War to Keep the Peace: The ECOMOG Intervention and Human Rights, Vol. 5* (Jun. 1993): 17, https://www.hrw.org/legacy/reports/1993/liberia/.

48. See Adeniji, note 6.

49. Ibid.; Adebajo, note 2, p. 247. With respect to the opportunity it affords for practical training, there are some within the armed forces who view peacekeeping missions as "police work" that erodes rather than builds their battle readiness. Ibid.

50. Adeniji, note 6.

51. Ibid.

52. Philip C. Aka, "Human Rights as Conflict Resolution in Africa in the New Century," *Tulsa Journal of Comparative & Int'l Law*, Vol. 11 (Fall 2003): 179–80 (pointing out that "[o]f forty-two peacekeeping missions in the world organized by the United Nations as of 2000, thirteen, or little less than one-third of the overall number, took place in Africa.").

53. S. O. Akinboye, "Beautiful Abroad but Ugly at Home: Issues and Contra-[di]ctions in Nigerian Foreign Policy." University of Lagos Inaugural Lecture Series, 2013, www.unilag.edu.ng/opendocnew.php?.

54. See Herbert Ekwe-Ekwe, *Biafra Revisited* (Dakar, Senegal: African Renaissance, 2006): 77.

55. See, e.g., Aderemi Suleiman Ajala, "Yoruba Nationalism: Culture, Politics[,] and Violence in South-Western Nigeria (1900–2009)," Institut für Ethnologie und Afrikastudien, Johannes Gutenberg-Universität, Mainz, Germany, Working Paper No. 107 (2009), http://www.ifeas.uni-mainz.de/Dateien/AP107.pdf (commenting on agitations within and outside the country, including the establishment of a radio station in the United States in the wake of the annulment); "Rioting in Nigeria Kills at Least 11," *New York Times* (Jul. 7, 1993), http://www.nytimes.com/1993/07/07/world/rioting-in-nigeria-kills-at-least-11.html.

56. See Suleiman Hamman et al., "The Role of Nigeria in Peacekeeping Operations from 1960 to 2013," *Int'l Affairs & Global Strategy*, Vol. 21 (2014): 43; Norimitsu Onishi, "What War Has Wrought: Sierra Leone's Sad State," *N. Y. Times* (Jan. 31, 1999), http://www.nytimes.com/1999/01/31/world/what-war-has-wrought-sierra-leone-s-sad-state.html?pagewanted=all.

57. For two among the numerous commentaries in academic and popular media on the group, see John Ford, "The Origins of Boko Haram," *Nat'l Interest* (Jun. 6, 2014), http://nationalinterest.org/print/feature/the-origins-boko-haram-10609; Farouk Chothia, "Who Are Nigeria's Boko Haram Islamists?," *BBC News* (May 4, 2015), http://www.bbc.com/news/world-africa-13809501.

58. See, e.g., Int'l Crisis Group, *Nigeria: Want in the Midst of Plenty*, Africa Report No. 113 (Jul. 19, 2006); Larry Diamond, "Foreword," *in* Rotimi T. Suberu, *Federalism and Ethnic Conflict in Nigeria* (United States Institute of Peace, 2001): x; Jedrzej F. Frynas, *Oil in Nigeria: Conflict and Litigation Between Oil Companies and Village Communities* (Hamburg & London: Lit Verlag, 2000); and Ken Saro-Wiwa, *A Month and a Day: A Detention Diary* (London: Penguin Books, 1996). This issue was earlier covered in chapter 1 in the portion on the exigency for increased infusion of human rights in Nigeria's external relations.

59. Adeniji, note 6.

60. Hamman et al., note 56, p. 43.

61. "What Is the Difference between Humanitarian Law and Human Rights Law?" Int'l Committee of the Red Cross, https://www.icrc.org/eng/resources/documents/misc/5kzmuy.htm.

62. Ibid.

63. Ibid.

64. See, e.g., Emily Crawford & Alison Pert, *International Humanitarian Law* (New York: Cambridge University Press, 2015): 1–27 (discussing the historical development of international humanitarian law).

65. See Gerald McLoughlin & Clarence J. Bouchat, *Nigerian Unity: In the Balance* (Carlisle, PA: Strategic Studies Institute & U.S. Army War College Press, Jun. 2013), http://www.strategicstudiesinstitute.army.mil/pdffiles/PUB1159.pdf (commenting on why Nigeria's continuation as a cohesive functioning state is important to the United States, but why the existence of the country as a unified state is in jeopardy).

66. See "Nigeria—Ministry of Defense," note 25 (stating that Nigerian military leaders "revel in and brag about" their role "as the bulwark against Nigerian anarchy[,]" and the country's "one indispensable institution, committed to Nigerian unity and sovereign survival") *cf.* with Max Siollun, *Oil, Politics[,] and Violence: Nigeria's Military Coup Culture (1966–1976)* (New York: Algora Publishing, 2009): 172 (commenting on how, before the Second Republic in 1979–83, some within the army justified continued military rule on the ground that the military was "the only truly national institution" that could, ironically, guarantee political stability).

67. During the period of military rule in Nigeria that spanned nearly three decades, some military regimes ruled in partnership with the police. The two that particularly come to mind are the Gowon Administration (1966–1975) and Muhammadu Buhari's (1983–1985). Both governments included senior police officers as governors and members of the highest policymaking bodies. See Tekena N. Tamuno, "The Nigeria Police Force and Public Security and Safety: Major Challenges and Opportunities since 1930," *in* Laurent Fourchard & Isaac Olawale Albert, eds., *Security, Crime and Segregation in West African Cities since the 19th Century* (Paris, France: Karthala Editions, 2003): 127.

68. For works on the history of the Nigerian Army, see Nigerian Army Education Corps & School, *History of the Nigerian Army 1863–1992* (Abuja: Nigerian Army Headquarters, 1992); and Norman J. Miners, *The Nigerian Army, 1956–1966* (London: Methuen, 1971) (covering the period 1956 to 1966). On the police, see Cheta Nwanze, "A Short History of the Nigerian Police Force," *The Trent Online*, http://www.thetrentonline.com/cheta-nwanze-short-history-nigeria-police-force/.

69. See Mark Curtis, "Nigeria's War Over Biafra, 1967–70," edited extract from Mark Curtis, *Unpeople: Britain's Secret Human Rights Abuses* (New York: Vintage Books, 2004): 2, https://markcurtis.wordpress.com/2007/02/13/nigeria biafra-1967-70/ (stating that "[r]eports circulated that troops from the northern region had participated in the massacres" of Igbo in Sept. of 1966).

70. Aka, note 52, p. 180, n.7; Toyin Falola & Adebayo Oyebade, *Hot Spot: Sub-Saharan Africa* (Santa Barbara, CA: ABC-CLIO, 2010): 74–76 (wondering whether

the untold killings, infliction of human suffering, and destruction of property that took place in the four years from 1966 until 1970 were in the legitimate pursuit of a "war of unity" or amounted to genocide as Biafrans alleged). More details on the Geneva Conventions are provided in note 64 and corresponding text.

71. See, e.g., Michael Martinez, "Kerry: Nigeria Acknowledged Human Rights Abuses in Terror Fight," *CNN* (May 25, 2013, updated 1:49 PM ET), www.cnn/com/2013/05/25/world/africa/nigeria-kerry-human-rights (U.S. Secretary of State John Kerry defending the Nigerian government's right to defend itself against terror groups, but simultaneously taking exception to its human rights record responding to terrorist attacks); Amnesty Int'l, *Stars on Their Shoulders[,] Blood on Their Hands: War Crimes Committed by the Nigerian Military* (Jun. 3, 2015), http://www.amnestyusa.org/research/reports/stars-on-their-shoulders-blood-on-their-hands-war-crimes-committed-by-the-nigerian-military (finding that since March 2011, more than 7,000 persons died in military detention and more than 1,200 were unlawfully killed since Feb. 2012).

72. See Human Rights Watch, *"Rest in Pieces": Police Torture and Deaths in Custody in Nigeria* (Jul. 2005), https://www.hrw.org/reports/2005/nigeria0705/ (report documenting the frequent use of torture by the Nigerian police); Adewale Maja-Pearce, "Changing Nigeria's Cruel Police Culture," *New York Times* (Oct. 7, 2014), http://www.nytimes.com/2014/10/08/opinion/adewale-maja-pearce-changing-nigerias-cruel-police-culture.html (commenting on sensitivity of the need to respect human rights, against the background of a culture of lawlessness and cruelty, marked aplenty by extra-judicial executions of suspected armed robbers, detentions without trial, use of torture to extract confessions, and unrelieved assault and battery of suspects).

73. Sam Olukoya, "Nigeria's Trigger Happy Police," *BBC News* (May 11, 2001, 15:33 GMT 16:53 UK), http://news.bbc.co.uk/2/hi/africa/1322017.stm.

74. Daniel Jordan Smith, *A Culture of Corruption: Everyday Deception and Popular Discontent in Nigeria* (Princeton, N.J.: Princeton University Press, 2008): 61.

75. Ibid.

76. Ibid.

77. Human Rights Watch, note 47, p. 3 n.8, quoting an interview in Monrovia, Liberia, on Mar. 9, 1993, with ECOMOG Chief of Staff, Brigadier S.V.L. Malu.

78. Janet Fleischman, Human Rights Watch, ECOWAS: Troops to Liberia Must Respect Human Rights, Letter to President John Kufuor, then Chairman of ECOWAS (Jul. 18, 2003), https://www.hrw.org/news/2003/07/18/ecowas-troops-liberia-must-respect-human-rights. At the time she issued this letter, Fleischman was Human Rights Watch's Washington Director for Africa. The letter was copied to a number of dignitaries, including President Joaquim Chissano, Chair of the African Union; Mohammad Ibn Chambas, Executive Secretary of ECOWAS; Olusegun Obasanjo, then President of Nigeria; Jacques Paul Klein, Special Representative of the Secretary-General and Coordinator of U.N. Operations in Liberia; Walter H. Kansteiner III, U.S. Assistant Secretary of State for African Affairs; and Dr. Jendayi Frazier, Senior Director for Africa, U.S. National Security Council.

79. Fleischman, note 78. Leading up to this appeal, Human Rights Watch (HRW) made a number of important observations. These include the point that HRW "has

documented human rights abuses by all sides to the conflicts in Liberia and Sierra Leone, including abuses by . . . ECOMOG," and that the "important successes" made in ECOMOG operations "have been offset by serious human rights abuses and a lack of accountability." Ibid. Among other things, HRW advised ECOWAS to "commit itself to ensuring its troops are adequately trained and able to meet their obligations under human rights and humanitarian law and to investigate and prosecute any officers or soldiers implicated in abuses." Ibid.

80. Fleischman, note 78.

81. Ibid.

82. Ibid.

83. Fleischman, note 78. Other pertinent recommendations include: integrating advisors with expertise in humanitarian law, establishing a disciplinary unit within the various ECOWAS contingent to secure accountability for human rights abuses by troops, and demobilizing and disarming all child soldiers. Ibid.

84. See note 13 and corresponding text.

85. See note 32 and corresponding text.

86. As the U.S. diplomat David Scheffer once observed in a lecture on war crimes, "[c]ombatants are as likely to know as much about the laws of war as they do about quantum mechanics." David Scheffer, The Clear and Present Danger of War Crimes, Address, University of Oklahoma College of Law (Feb. 24, 1998), quoted in David P. Forsythe, *Human Rights in International Relations, 3d Ed.* (New York: Cambridge University Press, 2013): 317. Many peacekeepers need education on human rights precisely because, as Scheffer observed, they are not well versed in humanitarian law.

87. Universal Declaration of Human Rights, G.A. Res. 217 A (III), U.N. GAOR, 3d Sess., at art. 26, U.N. Doc. A/810 (1948).

88. Philip C. Aka, "The Military, Globalization, and Human Rights in Africa," *Journal of Human Rights*, Vol. 18 (2002): 435.

89. Ibid.

90. Ibid.

91. Eleanor Roosevelt, "In Your Hands: A Guide for Community Action for the Tenth Anniversary of the Universal Declaration of Human Rights" (Mar. 27, 1958), quoted in Jo Anne Wilson-Keenan, *From Small Places: Toward the Realization of Literacy as a Human Right* (Springer, 2015): 28.

92. Ibid. For studies on Mrs. Roosevelt's contributions to human rights, particularly her role in the drafting and adoption of the UDHR, see Mary Ann Glendon, *A World Made New: Eleanor Roosevelt and the Universal Declaration of Human Rights* (New York: Random House, 2001); Carol Anderson, *Eyes on the Prize: The United Nations and the African American Struggle for Human Rights, 1944–1955* (New York: Cambridge University Press, 2003) (a less hagiographic chronicle which documented how Eleanor Roosevelt worked against any enforcement powers for United Nations human rights bodies, thereby assuring Southern Democrats that racial segregation had nothing to fear from human rights).

93. See Aka, note 88, pp. 435–36. In an address to a graduating class of the National War College, Abuja, on Jul. 24, 1999, President Olusegun Obasanjo broke down

the elements of the doctrine of military subordination to civil authority as involving acceptance of five principles thus: elected civilian president as Commander-in-Chief of the Armed forces; civilian headship of the Ministry of Defense and other strategic establishments; decisions regarding the goals and conduct of military operations must serve the political and strategic goals established by the civil authority; application of civilized principles to all military investigations and trials; and right of civil authority, meaning the highest court of the land, to review any actions or decisions taken by military judicial officers. Cited in John Simpkins, *The Role of Constitution-Building Processes in Democratization: Case Study Nigeria* (Sweden: Institute for Democracy & Electoral Assistance, 2004): 17–18, n.53.

94. Regarding these agencies, see notes 35–40.

95. Adebajo, note 2, p. 247.

96. See table of contents of contents, pp. vii–viii, of Bellamy & Williams, eds., *Providing Peacekeepers*, note 2. As of Feb. 2012, Nigeria deployed 5,726 peacekeepers in U.N. missions in Sudan's Darfur region, Liberia, Côte d'Ivoire, the Democratic Republic of Congo, South Sudan, Western Sahara, Haiti, Lebanon, and East Timor. This placed the country as the fifth largest contributor after Bangladesh, Pakistan, India, and Ethiopia. Adebajo, note 2, p. 245.

97. Ibid., p. 246.

98. Ibid.

99. For a sample, see Hamman et al. note 56, pp. 43–45 (fingering rationalization of manpower, training and doctrine, logistics, funding, and administrative issues as areas of concern); Ahmed Musa Sule, "Nigeria's Participation in Peacekeeping Operations," Thesis, Certificate-in-Training in U.N. Peace Support Operations (2013), cdn.peaceopstraining.org/thesis/sule.pdf (identifying manpower rationalization given the security challenges of terrorism at home, training and doctrine, logistics, and clear mandate for operations, and language barriers as areas of major concern); William M. Wando, "Challenges, Benefits, and Recommendations for Continued Nigerian Peacekeeping," Paper for the Naval War College, Newport, R.I. (Nov. 2, 2012), http://www.dtic.mil/dtic/tr/fulltext/u2/a569419.pdf. (identifying high rate of infection for sexually transmitted diseases, including HIV/AIDs, among returning peacekeepers; and perceived corruption indicated by underpayment of peacekeepers' allowances as concerns); and Adekeye Adebajo, "Sad Deterioration of Nigeria's Foreign Policy," *B[usiness] D[ay] L[ive]* (Johannesburg) (May 6, 2013), http://za.news.yahoo.com/sad-deterioration-nigeria-foreign-policy-051439591.html (commenting on the "deterioration of Nigeria's foreign policy" in the Fourth Republic, during the presidency of Goodluck Jonathan (2010–2015), including the performance of Nigerian peacekeepers which he assessed as falling below U.N. standards).

100. Adebajo, note 2, p. 247.

Chapter Eight

Reshaping Nigeria's Foreign Policy Machinery in a More Human Rights–Sensitive Direction

A reshaped foreign policy machinery is the pillar, next after redesigned peacekeeping (chapter 7), on the temple of Nigerian human rights foreign policy unveiled in chapter 1. This chapter canvasses and presents ideas on how to reshape Nigeria's foreign policy apparatus in a more human rights direction. Every state which conducts relations with other countries has institutions involved in the formulation and implementation of its foreign policies. Nigeria is no different. Given their classified nature, the intricacies of foreign policy decision making is a topic where relatively little information exists.[1] This is especially so for a developing country like Nigeria.[2]

A noted approach in problem solving is to move from the known to the unknown, to begin the search for answers from an area with the most light, rather than from a point of darkness.[3] Consistent with this conventional wisdom, this chapter developed a template of the U.S. foreign policy machinery, a source in the literature with proverbial more light, which it then applies to Nigeria. The approach is consistent with the Most-Similar-Systems (MSS) design in Comparative Politics. Under this research technique, the researcher compares cases that are similar with respect to a number of factors but with distinct outcomes, the logic being that the more similar the cases being compared, the more possible it should be to isolate the factors responsible for the dissimilarities observed between the two cases.[4] Along with Within-Case Comparison (WCC), MSS design forms the methodology of this work laid out in chapter 2. Unlike MSS design, WCC involves the study of one country at different points in time and space. It is the approach that informed the preceding chapters, specifically chapters 1, 4, 5, and 6. Although flashes of WCC appear in this chapter, unlike those chapters, much of the ensuing discussion is guided by the MSS design.

To rationalize the use of the U.S. foreign policy machinery as a template for the study of Nigeria, we have to justify singling out the country as a state whose system is most similar to Nigeria. The United States shares several similarities with Nigeria: both countries have large populations, both are federal systems, both operate the presidential system of government, and both are longstanding trading partners. Nigeria became a federation of three regions in 1954 while still a dependent country,[5] and restructured that federation in 1963 with the addition of a fourth region.[6] Under its First Republic from 1960 to 1966, Nigeria married its federal system with a parliamentary form of government modeled after the United Kingdom—a classically unitary, rather than federal, state—wherein executive powers were shared between two officials: a president whose powers were ceremonial, even though he was also commander-in-chief of the Armed Forces, and a prime minister lodged with real powers.[7] Following the failure of the First Republic from 1960 to 1966, a civil war, and the experience of military rule for 13 years including 3 years of war, in 1979, Nigeria replaced its parliamentary system with a presidential system of government patterned on the United States. It has since then operated a United States–style presidential system.[8]

A major reason given for jettisoning the parliamentary system is its separation of the head of state from head of government. According to the Committee which drafted Nigeria's 1979 constitution, the separation amounted to a division between real authority and formal authority, not only meaningless in the light of African political experience and history but also difficult to maintain in practice.[9] As the Committee elaborates, "No African Head of State has been known to be content with the position of a mere figurehead," something the experiences of countries which have used this system, including Nigeria, lend testimony to.[10] For "[i]n these countries, the system has resulted in a clash of personalities and of interests, a conflict of authority and an unnecessary complexity and uncertainty in governmental relations."[11] The separation also "fails to provide a clear focal point of loyalty, which is indispensable to national integration."[12] In contrast, under a presidential system of government, "[t]he single executive has the merit of unity, energy[,] and dispatch."[13] The Committee took due cognizance of the potential "danger of dictatorship" embedded in a presidential system of government, but posited that "the ultimate sanction against usurpations of power is a politically conscious society jealous of its constitutional rights to choose those who direct its affairs."[14] For Nigeria, the adoption of a presidential system removed the seeming anomaly of superimposing a parliamentary government on a federal system that pre-1979 the country endured.

TEMPLATE OF THE U.S. FOREIGN POLICY MACHINERY

The U.S. foreign policy machinery comprises five separate yet interconnected components: the Constitution; Congress; the president; an executive branch made up of foreign affairs, defense, the intelligence community, and the economic agencies; and public opinion.[15]

The Constitution of 1789 both grants and limits the powers of Congress (particularly the Senate) and the president relating to foreign affairs. The powers of Congress include the authority to regulate commerce within and outside the United States, to declare war, to raise and support armies, and to provide and maintain a navy, among others.[16] The powers of the president include the role of commander-in-chief of the armed forces and of state militias when called into national service, to make treaties with the advice and consent of two-thirds of the Senate, to nominate and appoint ambassadors and other public ministers again with the advice and consent of two-thirds of the Senate, and the power to execute the laws, including an obligation to take care that those laws are faithfully executed.[17] Constitutional scholars, such as Edward S. Corwin, view the provisions in the U.S. Constitution relating to foreign affairs as an "invitation to struggle" between Congress and the president "for the privilege of directing American foreign policy."[18] This is because, as the Foreign Policy Association explains, "[s]afeguards built into the [document] prevent tyranny, yet they frequently pit Congress against the executive branch, make it difficult to develop and implement a cohesive foreign policy, create uncertainty as to what that policy is, and give foreign governments and special interests an opportunity to apply pressure at many points, not just one."[19]

The next component of American foreign policy machinery is the U.S. Congress. Suspicious of executive power, those who wrote the American Constitution singled out Congress as the most democratic of the three branches of government.[20] For this reason, the framers of that Constitution assigned Congress the "power of the purse," that is, the power to tax and control government spending.[21] This means that, save for certain emergencies, the president usually cannot spend money that was not appropriated by Congress.[22] Furthermore, the Constitution assigns the Senate a special role in the foreign policy process, signified in the power "to advise the President in negotiating agreements, to consent to them once they have been signed, and to approve presidential appointments, including the Secretary of State, other high officials of the State Department, ambassadors and career foreign service officers."[23] In a nutshell, under the U.S. system, six basic ways through which Congress makes foreign policy are: resolution and policy statements; legislative directives; legislative pressure; legislative restrictions, evident, for example, in denial of funding; informal advice; and congressional oversight.[24]

The third element of the U.S. foreign policy bureaucracy is the president.[25] The president combines the ceremonial role of *head of state* with the executive powers of *head of government* held by two persons in a parliamentary system.[26] As head of government, the president "formulates foreign policy, supervises its implementation and attempts to obtain the resources to support it[,]" as well as "organizes and directs the departments and agencies that play a part in the foreign policy process."[27] In addition to the powers already mentioned before, U.S. presidents have other powers, both those expressed and implied by the Constitution germane to the discussion here, including the power to receive foreign ambassadors and effectively recognize foreign governments; the ability to shape the national agenda and public opinion related to that agenda by bringing issues to the forefront of public attention; and the power to commit the nation to a particular diplomatic course of action that, once he does so, can be difficult for his opponents to alter.[28] Part of the reason for this advantage is the evolution of practices, such as executive agreements, in the case of treaty making, that permit the president to get around some of the cumbersome constitutional processes in dealing with foreign governments.[29] In sum, under the U.S. system, the president or the executive branch can make foreign policy through six basic means as follows: responses to foreign events, proposals for legislation, negotiation of international agreements, policy statements, policy implementation, and independent action.[30]

The fourth element of the U.S. foreign policy bureaucracy is the executive branch of the U.S. government made up of foreign affairs, defense, the intelligence community, and the economic agencies. Beginning with *foreign affairs*, the agency that immediately comes to mind is the Department of State, under the Secretary of State who reports directly to the president. Along with the Foreign Service, its professional diplomatic corps, the department is charged with responsibility for negotiating with foreign governments and intergovernmental organizations; marshalling and defending the United States' position in the world; monitoring, analyzing, and reporting conditions in foreign countries and intergovernmental organizations that bear on the United States' interests; representing the American people and U.S. policies to the world; promoting U.S. trade and investment; and looking after the well-being of U.S. nationals overseas.[31] Other key agencies associated with the foreign affairs unit are: the Agency for International Development; the Arms Control and Disarmament Agency; and the United States Information Agency, including Radio Free Europe, Voice of America, and Radio Liberty.[32]

Next under the executive branch is *defense*. The lead agency under this unit is the Department of Defense, headed by the Secretary of Defense, a civilian who is a member of the president's cabinet. Other agencies associated with this unit are: the Joint Chiefs of Staff, and the National Security Council (NSC). The Joint Chiefs of Staff is a strategy board made up of the senior officers from the four branches of the U.S. military: the Army, Air Force, Marine Corps, and Navy.[33] The chairman of the Joint Chiefs of Staff, a military person, is the principal military adviser to the president.[34] The NSC is made up of the president, the vice president, the secretaries of State, the Secretary of Defense, and the chairman of the Joint Chiefs of Staff.[35] Created under the National Security Act,[36] the NSC helps the president manage and coordinate foreign policy.[37] Headed by the president's national security adviser, the NSA staff comprises specialists in geographic areas and function issues, such as arms control.[38] Another agency subsumable under this unit is the Department of Energy in matters relating to nuclear energy.[39]

Following defense is the intelligence community. The term *intelligence community* (IC) refers to a collection of 16 agencies, including the Central Intelligence Agency (CIA), National Security Agency (NSA), and the Federal Bureau of Investigation (FBI).[40] The IC is headed by the director of National Intelligence, who is the principal advisor to the president.[41] Broadly speaking, this community does two things. First it collects information on whatever issue forms the object of their intelligence (e.g., how many nuclear weapons China possesses), assesses the accuracy and reliability of that information, and disseminates it to decision makers. Secondly, with the president's approval, the intelligence community, most notably the CIA, undertakes clandestine operations.[42] In the wake of the terrorist attacks of September 2001, the U.S. government created the Department of Homeland Security, combining 22 separate agencies dealing with a range of issues, including antiterrorism, border security, cybersecurity, disaster relief, immigration, and trade, to centralize intelligence analysis collected by these various agencies.[43] Last but not least under the executive branch are the *economic agencies*, notably the departments of Agriculture, Commerce, Treasury, and the U.S. Trade Representative.[44]

The fifth and final component of the U.S. foreign machinery is public opinion. Societal sources, including public opinion, play an important role in American foreign relations.[45] Specifically, along with the media, public opinion ranks among key "democratic checks on" U.S. foreign policy.[46] The public has a duty to assess the country's interests in world affairs, among other obligations.[47] Issues for public consideration relating to foreign policy include the proper relationship between the United States and the United Nations, the proper role of peacekeeping operations and foreign aid programs, and the balance of economic and political interests against humanitarian and environmental concerns.[48] Decision makers respond to these questions within the context of the American people's never-ending "experiment in self-government and the democratic limits established in the Constitution."[49] The fact of the matter is that in the United States, "[t]he voice of public opinion occasionally penetrates the carefully encrypted speech and muffled secrecy of foreign policy making to have an impact."[50] While there is no clarity regarding the precise impact of public opinion in U.S. foreign policy, at the very least, that opinion "plac[es] new items on the political agenda."[51]

An important distinction is made between foreign policy *formulation* and *implementation*. Under the scheme set up by the U.S. Constitution, foreign policy *formulation* requires the participation of the president, Congress, the executive branch, and the public. Conversely, implementation of foreign policy is the exclusive responsibility of the president and his subordinates in the executive branch. The distinction between the two sometimes can be a fine line difficult to maintain in practice, but as the Foreign Policy Association explains, using the Persian Gulf as example, formulation of policy occurs when, say, a decision is made to protect the security of the Gulf, whereas implementation of policy occurs when the government sends, say, the U.S. Navy to achieve that security.[52]

NIGERIA AND THE UNITED STATES: TWO SIMILAR CONSTITUTIONAL SYSTEMS, VASTLY DIFFERENT OUTCOMES WITH RAMIFICATIONS FOR PRINCIPLED FOREIGN POLICY

Which of the five components identified for the United States in the preceding discussion does Nigeria have, and which one, if any, is missing? Before delving into these elements, some comments are necessary on various ways federalism in Nigeria is different from federalism in the United States. The same seeds planted on different soils bear different fruits, partly because their nutrients are different. This is the same with political institutions. One way in which federalism in Nigeria differs from federalism in the United States is that, unlike in the latter where two levels of government—national and state—share powers,[53] in Nigeria, powers are divided among three levels of government: national, state, and local governments.[54] Put differently, whereas in the United States, local governments are creatures of the states,[55] in Nigeria the constitution recognizes all three levels of government and vests them with powers. A second major difference is that, vis-à-vis the United States, in Nigeria many powers are centralized in the hands of the national government at Abuja, at the expense of the other two levels of government.[56] For example, the constitution enumerates 68 items under the "exclusive legislative list" that, as a matter of law, the other two levels of government may not interfere with.[57] This is compared to 30 powers under the "concurrent legislative list" of shared authority between the national and state governments,[58] a list where, consistent with a supremacy clause, national authority preempts state powers whenever a conflict occurs between the two;[59] and only two "functions" for the local governments.[60] While states under the Nigerian system have "residual powers," the equivalent of "reserved powers" of the states under the U.S. Constitution,[61] this does not reduce the seeming lopsidedness in power in favor of the center, at the expense of sub-national governments. What makes this lopsidedness troubling is that the Nigerian constitution includes what in the United States may be called a "necessary and proper clause" which gives the national government implied powers germane to any expressed power. That clause is No. 68 on the exclusive list granting to the national government power over "[a]ny matter incidental or supplemental to any matter mentioned elsewhere in this list."[62] Additionally, the Nigerian Constitution permits the president to "issue a Proclamation of a state of emergency in the Federation or any part thereof."[63]

Exactly what type of federation lodges all of these powers in one central government? Military rule in Nigeria created an authoritarian order[64] that de-vitalized Nigerian federalism. In contrast, the United States has approached democracy uninterruptedly without the handicap of such dictatorial rule.[65] Nigeria's Fourth Republic leaders have had the opportunity to reverse the centralization of the political system that they have not seized, partly because of the domination of the Fourth Republic by retired military generals. Be that as it may, the 1999 constitution vests responsibility for foreign affairs on the national government, to the exclusion of the other levels of government.[66] Like its 1979 predecessor, it also enumerated the foreign policy objectives of the country.[67]

Like with the United States, the first element in Nigeria's foreign policy machinery would be the country's charter document, the Fourth Republic Constitution adopted in 1999.[68] Because the preceding paragraph on Nigerian federalism covered that document with which, in the ordinary scheme of things, it is inextricably linked, the following discussion will be limited to the legitimacy of the charter document. Like the 1979 Constitution, Nigeria's 1999 Constitution was brought into force via a decree promulgated by the departing military.[69] But unlike its predecessor, the 1999 Constitution received little popular input from the masses of the Nigerian people before its passage into law. This was despite the fact that, like its predecessor, the document included a statement in its preamble to the effect that the generality of the Nigerian people ordained it.[70] Therein springs the source of the question regarding the legitimacy of the document. Some commentators believe that the document passed this legitimacy test,[71] while others disagree.[72] This debate goes to the heart of political restructuring, part of the discussion on increased human rights at home, covered in chapter 6, on the road to a human rights foreign policy for Nigeria. In sum, though of questionable paternity, like the United States, Nigeria has a constitution that grounds its foreign policy machinery.

Like the United States too, Nigeria has an elected legislature known in the vernacular of Nigerian politics as the National Assembly as part of its foreign policy machinery. Nigeria's National Assembly comprises two chambers: a Senate (or upper house), representing the equality of the states, and a House of Representatives (lower house), based on population. The Senate has 109 members, three each from the thirty-six states, and one member representing the capital territory of Abuja. The House of Representatives comprises 360 members elected based on proportional representation.[73] Like legislatures in other democratic systems, the Nigerian National Assembly has a major role in foreign policy. In addition to the "power of the purse,"[74] both the Senate and the House of Representatives have committees that provide oversight on the president and the executive branch relating to foreign affairs.[75] For the Senate, that committee is the standing Committee on Foreign Relations, while for the House of Representatives, it is the Committee on Inter-Parliamentary Relations.[76] To use the Senate as example, the Committee on Foreign Relations performs oversight duties on the Ministry of Foreign Affairs and is charged with functions such as protecting Nigerian citizens abroad and approving technical assistance to foreign countries.[77]

Also like the United States, Nigeria boasts an executive president as part of its foreign policy machinery.[78] The president's power extends to executing and maintaining the Constitution, federal laws, and other matters on which the National Assembly has power to make laws.[79] He also has law-making authority that, in addition to the power to veto a bill, includes the power to modify an existing law to bring it into conformity with the Constitution.[80] The president can exercise these powers either directly or indirectly through his vice president, ministers, or officers in the national public service.[81] These powers loom large, viewed in the light of the broad and expansive nature of the exclusive legislative list.[82] However, his authority is not limitless. In addition to being limited to two-terms in office, the president is also subject to checks by other branches of the government that include possible impeachment for "gross misconduct,"[83] and judicial review of his executive actions.[84]

As the Constitutional Drafting Committee put it in 1977, the president "would have to depend on the legislature for legislation to implement his policies and for funds to execute his measures[,]" an occurrence that mandates that he cooperate with the legislature to facilitate his governance, to the benefit of the political system.[85]

A fourth element that, like the United States Nigeria has in its foreign policy toolbox, is an executive branch outside the office and person of the president, yet under his authority, broken up into subunits for foreign affairs, defense, the intelligence community, and economic agencies. Under foreign affairs, the most notable agency is the Ministry of Foreign Affairs.[86] It is one of 25 national agencies under the rearrangement by General Muhammadu Buhari who took office in May of 2015.[87] This domain also includes think tanks like the Nigerian Institute of International Affairs (NIIA) referenced in the discussion in chapter 5 on reconstructing Nigeria's national interest. Another sub-element is defense, notably the Ministry of Defense.[88] Just like in the United States and depending on the issue involved, other agencies may participate in decisions relating to foreign policy.

Yet another sub-element is the intelligence community, in Nigerian parlance, National Intelligence Agency, charged with responsibility for foreign intelligence and counterintelligence operations.[89] The community comprises three entities: the Office of the National Security Adviser (ONSA); the Department of State Services (DSS), otherwise known as the State Security Service (SSS); and the Defense Intelligence Agency (DIA).[90] The DSS is the primary domestic intelligence agency of the country.[91] Headed by the National Security Adviser, it operates as a department within the office of the president.[92] The DIA is responsible for military intelligence. Created in June 1986 under Decree No. 19, now Cap. 278 of the Laws of the Federation, the DIA replaced the National Security Organization, dissolved by Decree No. 19.[93] Sometimes included in the intelligence community is the Criminal Investigation Department (CID) of the Nigeria police, charged with responsibility for domestic crime detection and prevention.[94]

Based on the template from the United States, the fifth and final element in Nigeria's foreign policy apparatus is public opinion. But even keeping in mind the distinction between foreign policy formulation and implementation, referenced in the discussion on the United States, which necessarily also applies to Nigeria, this element is lacking. Studies relating to decision making in Nigerian external relations reveal that the country's foreign policy "has never been directly related to the needs of the masses of the people";[95] and that, save for a few high-profile issues, such as the Congo Civil War, during the First Republic (1960–1966), "[t]he government hardly bothers to seek endorsements of its policies from the general public."[96] This lacuna raises the question, as one former Nigerian foreign minister aptly put it, "[w]hose foreign policy are we talking about anyway?"[97] Yet just like in the United States, public opinion can be a democratic check on Nigerian foreign policy. And no less than the American public, Nigerian masses have legitimate obligations within their seemingly democratic system that include a duty to assess their country's interests in world affairs. Finally, just like their counterparts in the United States, what prevents the public in Nigeria from contributing ideas that can place new items on the political agenda—such as a calibration of their country's Africa-centered foreign policy in the aftermath of the decolonization struggle in Africa hallmarked by the achievement of majority rule in South Africa in 1994? Table 8.1 presents a recap of Nigeria's foreign policy machinery.

RESHAPING NIGERIA'S FOREIGN POLICY MACHINERY IN A HUMAN RIGHTS–SENSITIVE DIRECTION

Shaping Nigeria's foreign policy machinery in a human rights–sensitive direction requires that we first articulate the problems that confront that apparatus. There are three such problems that are more or less interrelated: a lack of public input, cohesiveness, and intergovernmental consultation. The first, already broached in the preceding section, is a lack of popular input. Nigerian foreign policy "reflect[s] the needs and aspirations of a national super elite of business, bureaucratic, military, and traditional ruling groups."[98] As a corollary, at any point in time, only "a tiny segment" of the Nigerian population is involved in foreign policy[99]—and that does *not* include the masses of the people whose well-being should form the basis for the conduct of any foreign policy. Instead, much of the time, foreign policy in the country is "personality-influenced"[100] as well as "formulated, articulated, and implemented in highly elitist circles"[101] without the benefit of any input from the masses and often unreflective of their needs.[102]

To give an example with the Ministry of Foreign Affairs, an agency closely associated with the formulation and implementation of Nigerian foreign policy, the foreign policymaking team consists of the minister and his or her immediate staff, plus "a small foreign policy elite comprising other top government officials, interest group leaders, academicians, top military officers, religious leaders, and journalists"—who exert influence on policy through direct pressure on the government or indirectly through communiqués and press releases.[103] Because this elite-driven approach to foreign policy making leaves matters too much "in the hands of the minister and his officials, foreign policy positions could change *radically* from one

Table 8.1. Recap of Nigeria's Foreign Policy Machinery

	Foreign Policy Machinery							
				Executive Branch				
Period	*Constitution*	*National Assembly*	*Chief Executive*	*Foreign Affairs*	*Defense*	*Intel. Comm.*	*Econ. Agencies*	*Public Opinion*
First Republic	Yes	Yes	Prime Minister	Yes	Yes	Yes	Yes	Little to none
First round of military rule	None	None	Military dictator	Yes	Yes	Yes	Yes	None
Second Republic	Yes	Yes	President	Yes	Yes	Yes	Yes	None
Second round of military rule	None	None	Military dictator	Yes	Yes	Yes	Yes	None
Fourth Republic	Yes	Yes	President	Yes	Yes	Yes	Yes	Little to none

Source: Table created by author.

minister to another, depending on the minister's orientation."[104] To get a sense of that radicalness, in the period since the country's independence in 1960, Nigeria has had 27 foreign ministers (see table 8.2), translated into about one minister every two years.

The same lack of popular input is observable in peacekeeping, one of the most visible faces of Nigerian foreign policy. As one comment on Nigeria's peacekeeping profile indicated, domestic public opinion plays little, if any, role in the decision to recruit and deploy peacekeepers.[105] The legislature which consists of the people's elected representatives should play a check-mating role that unfortunately it does not. This is because, as the analyst elaborates, "[o]n this matter, there seem[s] to be very good understanding between the executive and legislative arms of government[,]" with virtually no need for popular input.[106]

This is not to suggest that public opinion should perfectly reflect majority preferences, for it does not, not even in the United States.[107] Government policy in the United States "does not always reflect popular desires."[108] Instead, the country experiences "difficulty in translating public will into public policy within a complex framework of divided powers," a situation compounded by the fact that the "common will" of the people does not always coincide with the "common good" of society.[109] This is more so in areas of less salience for many citizens like foreign relations.[110] However, although "a perfect reflection of popular desires is surely beyond the capability of any government[,]" on many issues in the U.S. government policies come "reasonably close to the general directions of public opinion."[111] These include certain foreign policy matters. As indicated before, along with an independent media, public opinion plays a critical checking role in U.S. foreign policy.[112] The fact of the matter is that there is a better appreciation and sensitivity by officialdom, almost completely lacking in Nigeria, that public input should be a natural part of the foreign policymaking machinery.

The small public input into foreign policy in Nigeria may be expected during military era, not that it justifies it, given the non-representative nature of military regimes. But there is little justification for this state of affairs during civilian administrations. From every indication, this has not changed under the Fourth Republic since 1999. In allaying apprehension that an executive presidency could lead to a dictatorship, the committee which drafted Nigeria's 1979 Constitution opined that "the ultimate sanction against usurpations of power is a politically conscious society jealous of its constitutional rights to choose those who direct its affairs."[113] Yet under the Fourth Republic, Nigeria leaders exclude public opinion from foreign policy. The lack of popular input into Nigerian foreign policy is interfaced with a lack of cohesiveness in the design and implementation of that policy. Ac-

Table 8.2. Nigeria's Foreign Ministers since 1960

Serial No.	*Name of Minister*	*Period*	*Administration*	*Years in Office*
1.	Abubakar T. Balewa	First Republic, 1960–66	Abubakar T. Balewa	1960–61
2.	Jaja A. Wachuku	First Republic, 1960–66	Abubakar T. Balewa	1961–65
3.	Nuhu Bamali	First Republic, 1960–66	Abubakar T. Balewa	1965–66
4.	Okoi Arikpo	First round of military rule, 1966–79	Yakubu Gowon	1967–75
5.	Joseph Garba	First round of military rule, 1966–79	Murtala Mohammed-Olusegun Obasanjo	1975–78
6.	Henry Adefope	First round of military rule, 1966–79	Olusegun Obasanjo	1978–79
7.	Ishaya Audu	Second Republic	Shehu Shagari	1979–83
8.	Emeka Anyaoku	Second round of military rule, 1983–99	Muhammadu Buhari	1983
9.	Ibrahim Gambari	Second round of military rule, 1983–99	Muhammadu Buhari	1984–85
10.	Bolaji Akinyemi	Second round of military rule, 1983–99	Ibrahim Babangida	1985–87
11.	Ike Nwachukwu	Second round of military rule, 1983–99	Ibrahim Babangida	1987–89
12.	Rilwanu Lukman	Second round of military rule, 1983–99	Ibrahim Babangida	1989–90
13.	Ike Nwachukwu	Second round of military rule, 1983–99	Ibrahim Babangida	1990–93
14.	Matthew Mbu	Second round of military rule, 1983–99	Ibrahim Babangida and Ernest Shonekan	1993
15.	Babagana Kingibe	Second round of military rule, 1983–99	Sani Abacha	1993–95
16.	Tom Ikimi	Second round of military rule, 1983–99	Sani Abacha	1995–98

(continued)

Table 8.2. *Continued*

Serial No.	*Name of Minister*	*Period*	*Administration*	*Years in Office*
17.	Ignatius Olisemeka	Second round of military rule, 1983–99	Abdulsalami Abubakar	1998–99
18.	Sule Lamido	Fourth Republic since 1999	Olusegun Obasanjo	1999–2003
19.	Oluyemi Adeniju	Fourth Republic since 1999	Olusegun Obasanjo	2003–6
20.	Ngozi Okonjo-Iweala	Fourth Republic since 1999	Olusegun Obasanjo	2006
21.	U. Joy Ogwu	Fourth Republic since 1999	Olusegun Obasanjo	2006–7
22.	Ojo Maduekwe	Fourth Republic since 1999	Goodluck Jonathan	2007–10
23.	Henry O. Ajumogobia	Fourth Republic since 1999	Goodluck Jonathan	2010–11
24.	Olugbenga Ashiru	Fourth Republic since 1999	Goodluck Jonathan	2011–13
25.	Viola Onwuliri	Fourth Republic since 1999	Goodluck Jonathan	2013–14
26.	Aminu B. Wali	Fourth Republic since 1999	Goodluck Jonathan	2014–15
27.	Geoffrey Onyeama	Fourth Republic since 1999	Muhammadu Buhari	2015–

Source: Table created by author

cording to Professor Ibrahim Gambari, former foreign minister of Nigeria, the country's foreign policy is controlled by a super-elite, not known for its selflessness,[114] that is "deeply divided along ethnic, regional, religious, and ideological lines[.]"[115] This is an assessment other scholars share. These include the Africanist Peter Pham who posits that under the Fourth Republic, as in the past, foreign policymaking and implementation in the land remain un-institutionalized;[116] as well as professors Ayua and Dakas who jointly observed that Nigeria's Constitution lacks provision for intergovernmental consultation in foreign affairs and defense,[117] among others.[118]

From a human rights standpoint, the solutions here track the problems. First, foreign policy decision making in Nigeria somehow needs to integrate public opinion than is presently the case now. The opportunity for the public to have a say in their own government is both an issue of democracy as well as a human rights concern.[119] Second, Nigeria should create more sense of nationhood necessary for effective conduct of human rights by implementing the various strategies for increased human rights at home discussed in chapter 6. Third, it may be necessary for Nigeria to integrate intergovernmental consultation in the document additional to the informal channels that now exist. Nigeria may also consider the possibility of assigning its embassies some human rights role the way the United States has done since the presidency of Jimmy Carter from 1976 to 1980. U.S. embassies today play a critical role in the preparation and production of the *Country Reports on Human Rights Practices* released by the State Department in the spring of every year.[120] On his narrative regarding the United States' road to a human rights policy, Carter asserted that soon after he took office, he declared his "intention to regard every American ambassador as my personal human rights rapporteur: I asked them to take personal responsibility for writing and submitting their Country Reports on human rights."[121]

Similarly, Nigerian Fourth Republic leaders should use the language of human rights in formulating domestic and foreign policy;[122] they need their own "personal human rights rapporteur." Although there is no suggestion for anything on the scale of the *Country Reports*, Nigerian foreign desks could develop a niche in human rights, additional to their present roles. Part of the reforms that need to be implemented should include proper funding of its Foreign Ministry—"foreign policy cannot be run on a shoe string"[123]—as well as pruning down the number of its diplomatic missions abroad to a more manageable number.[124]

SUMMATION

Little literature exists on decision making in Nigerian foreign policy. To get around the obstacle, this chapter developed a template from the United States that it then applied to Nigeria. Like the United States, Nigeria also operates a federal system of government which it first adopted in 1979, under its Second Republic, in place of the parliamentary system of government that it inherited from the United Kingdom. Using a template developed from the U.S. system rhymes with the Most-Similar-Systems (MSS) design that is part of the methodology of this work (see chapter 2). The application demonstrates that Nigeria's foreign policy machinery is similar to the United States in many respects, except public opinion. The chapter identifies and discusses various steps which Nigeria can take to reshape its foreign policy in a human rights direction. The first is to inject popular influence into the formulation of foreign policy both as a matter of democracy and human rights. The second is to create more cohesiveness necessary for the conduct of foreign policy by implementing the measures enumerated in chapter 6 on increased human rights in Nigerian domestic life. The country could also make its embassies abroad a center for human rights than it has done so far. Finally, it could next reinforce these measures by injecting more bilateralism in its foreign policy, the topic of chapter 9 next after this discussion.

NOTES

1. For a pioneering work dissecting the nature of these decisions and the models that can be applied to understand them, see Graham Allison, *Essence of Decision: Explaining the Cuban Missile Crisis* (Boston, MA: Little Brown, 1971) (study on the decision making relating to the dispute between the United States and the Soviet Union regarding the unimplemented attempt of the Soviet Union to place nuclear weapons in Cuba supposedly to insulate it from possible U.S. invasion).

2. One of the few studies on decision making in Nigerian foreign policy that turned up in the course of my research is Ufot Bassey Inamete, *Foreign Policy Decision-Making in Nigeria* (Selinsgrove, PA: Susquehanna University Press, 2001). The study is dated and, except for the first two years up to its appearance in 2001, does not cover the period of the Fourth Republic since 1999.

3. See Scott Greer, *The Logic of Social Inquiry* (Chicago: Aldine Publishing Company, 1969): 128–29 (recounting the allegory regarding the proverbial drunk who looked for his keys under a lighted lamp post where he could see "clearly," rather than in the darkness where he lost them).

4. See J. Tyler Dickovick & Jonathan Eastwood, *Comparative Politics: Integrating Theories, Methods, and Cases* (New York: Oxford University Press, 2013): 14–16 (Oxford University Press, 2013) (including the illustration with Ghana and Togo).

5. See Bonaventure I. Ozoigbo, "Federal Balancing in Nigeria: A Paradigm for Democracy," *African Journals Online*, Vol. 66 (2008): 71–72.

6. "Politics in the Crisis Years," *in* Helen Chapin Metz, ed., *Nigeria: A Country Study* (Washington, D.C.: GPO for the Library of Congress, 1991), http://countrystudies.us/nigeria/22.htm.

7. See Constitution of the Federation of Nigeria, 1960, http://www.worldstatesmen.org/nigeria_const1960.pdf, *esp*. Art. 81(1) (lodging the executive powers of the country on a prime minister appointed by the governor-general); and Constitution of the Fed. Republic of Nigeria, 1963, https://www.dawodu.com/const63.pdf, *esp*. Arts. 84(1) and 87(1) (vesting the executive authority of the Federation on the president, but, in practice, to be exercised on his behalf by a prime minister appointed by the president).

8. See Constitution of the Fed. Republic of Nigeria, 1979, http://www.constitutionnet.org/files/nig_const_79.pdf [hereinafter referred to as Nigerian Const., 1979], *esp*. Art. 122(1) (vesting the executive powers of the country on a directly-elected president of the Federation); Constitution of the Fed. Republic of Nigeria, 1999 [hereinafter referred to as Nigerian Const., 1999], *esp*. Art. 130(1)–(2) (vesting the executive powers of the country on a directly-elected president, who is the Head of State, Chief Executive, and Commander-in-Chief of the Armed Forces of the Federation).

9. Federal Republic of Nigeria, *Report of the Constitution Drafting Committee Containing the Draft Constitution, Vol. 1* (Enugu, Nigeria: Ministry of Education & Information, Printing Division, 1977): xxx [hereinafter referred to as *Const. Drafting Committee Rept.*].

10. Ibid.

11. Ibid.

12. Ibid.

13. Ibid.

14. Ibid.

15. Larry Berman & Bruce Allen Murphy, *Approaching Democracy, 8th Ed.* (New York: Pearson Education Inc., 2013): 529; Glenn P. Hastedt, *American Foreign Policy: Past, Present, Future, 6th Ed.* (Upper Saddle River, N.J.: Pearson Prentice Hall, 2006): 219–43; "How U.S. Foreign Policy Is Made," Foreign Policy Association, http://www.fpa.org/features/index.cfm?act=feature&announcement_id=45&show_sidebar=0.

16. The Constitution of the United States (1789), Art. 1 (enumerating the powers of Congress) [hereinafter referred to as U.S. Const.].

17. U.S. Const., note 16, Art II (enumerating the powers of the president).

18. See Harold J. Krent, *Presidential Powers* (New York: New York University Press, 2005), *passim*.

19. "How U.S. Foreign Policy Is Made," note 15.

20. "How U.S. Foreign Policy Is Made," note 15.

21. Ibid.

22. Ibid.

23. Ibid. The Foreign Policy Association notes poignantly that in the wake of the Vietnam War (1954–1975), "Congress became more involved in foreign affairs," but that over time, its effectiveness waned as presidents "found ways to circumvent requirements for Congress' approval." Ibid.

24. Richard F. Grimmett, Cong. Research Serv., Foreign Policy Roles of the President and Congress (1999), http://fpc.state.gov/6172.htm.

25. Given the democratic thrust of the U.S. system and the central role of the chief executive in that system, the president of the United States is intriguingly indirectly elected via an electoral college, rather than directly by the American people. For an explanation of this seeming anomaly, see Eric Black, "Why the Constitution's Framers Didn't Want Us to Directly Elect the President," *MinnPost* (Minneapolis) (Oct. 17, 2012), https://www.minnpost.com/eric-black-ink/2012/10/why-constitution-s-framers-didn-t-want-us-directly-elect-president. Reasons for mediating the people's choice with an electoral college of wise men impervious to popular passion included that the framers of the U.S. Constitution "were a fairly aristocratic bunch, many of whom had mixed feelings about 'democracy,' which they sometimes regarded as mob rule[,]" and because state constitutions at the time provided insufficient checks against democracy. Ibid. What makes the indirect election of the president even stranger is that one of those framers, Alexander Hamilton, canvassed for "energy" in a chief executive. See The Federalist No. 70 (Alexander Hamilton) (Mar. 15, 1788) (contending that "[e]nergy in the executive is a leading

character of good government[,]" necessary for protecting the "community against foreign attacks[,]" "steady administration of the laws[,]" and protection of property, among other benefits, compared to a "feeble executive," which can spell "feeble execution" and ultimately "bad government"). Could it be that Madison's notion of an energetic president was an administrative juggernaut, for bureaucratic efficiency reason, insulated from substantive popular control?

26. See Berman & Murphy, note 15, pp. 160 and 162 (discussing the roles of the president as Chief of State and Chief Executive).

27. "How U.S. Foreign Policy Is Made," note 15.

28. Ibid.

29. Ibid.

30. Grimmett, note 24.

31. "How U.S. Foreign Policy Is Made," note 15.

32. Berman & Murphy, note 15, p. 529.

33. "How U.S. Foreign Policy Is Made," note 15.

34. Ibid.

35. Ibid.

36. Pub. L. 80–253, 61 Stat. 495 (1947).

37. "How U.S. Foreign Policy Is Made," note 15; "Truman Signs the National Security Act," *This Day in History* (Jul. 26, 1947), http://www.history.com/this-day-in-history/truman-signs-the-national-security-act.

38. "How U.S. Foreign Policy Is Made," note 15.

39. Ibid.

40. "Members of the IC," Office of the Director of Nat'l Intelligence, http://www.dni.gov/index.php/intelligence-community/members-of-the-ic. The 13 others are: Air Force Intelligence, Army Intelligence, Coast Guard Intelligence, Defense Intelligence Agency, Dept. of Energy, Dept. of Homeland Security, Dept. of State, Dept. of the Treasury, Drug Enforcement Administration, Marine Corps Intelligence, National Geospatial-Intelligence Agency, National Reconnaissance Office, and Navy Intelligence. Ibid.

41. "Organization," Office of the Director of Nat'l Intelligence, http://www.dni.gov/index.php/about/organization. The office was created under the Intelligence Reform and Terrorism Prevention Act, Pub. L. 108–458, 118 Stat. 3638, of Dec. 17, 2004.

42. "How U.S. Foreign Policy Is Made," note 15.

43. "Department of Homeland Security," *USA.org*, https://www.usa.gov/federal-agencies/department-of-homeland-security. The department was created under the Homeland Security Act, Pub. L. 107–209, 116 Stat. 2135 of Nov. 25, 2002.

44. Berman & Murphy, note 15, p. 529.

45. See Eugene R. Wittkopf et al., *American Foreign Policy: Pattern and Process, 7th Ed.* (Belmont, CA: Thomson Wadsworth, 2008): 239–323 (commenting on the influence of societal sources, comprising public opinion, interest groups, and the mass media, on American foreign policy).

46. See Berman & Murphy, note 15, pp. 534–45.

47. See Berman & Murphy, note 15, p. 535.

48. Ibid.

49. Ibid.

50. Berman & Murphy, note 15, p. 535. An example that professors Berman and Murphy cited here was the Vietnam War (1955–1975) wherein popular discontent made the U.S. government to retrace its steps and reverse a longstanding policy. Ibid.

51. Hastedt, note 15, pp. 138–39.

52. "How U.S. Foreign Policy Is Made," note 15.

53. See U.S. Const., note 16, Art. IV (on interstate relations, particularly § 4 mandating the national government to "guarantee to every State in this Union a Republican Form of Government," and protect them from invasion), Art. V (amendment powers involving the national government and states); Art. VI (the supremacy clause involving the national government and states), Art. VII (ratification mentioning only the states), and 10th Amend. (indicating two levels of government, national and states). See also Martha A. Field, "The Differing Federalisms of Canada and the United States," *Law & Contemporary Problems*, Vol. 55 (1992): 107 (comparing the role of the states in the U.S. federal system vis-à-vis the provinces in the Canadian federal system).

54. See Nigerian Const., 1999, note 8, Art. 7(1) (guaranteeing "a system of local government by democratically elected local government councils.").

55. "State and Local Governments," *Am. Gov't*, http://www.ushistory.org/gov/12.asp (indicating that "[s]tate constitutions determine the structure, role, and financing of state and local levels of government.").

56. See Reuben Abati, "Restructure Nigeria to Save It," *Info Square* (Online) (Jun. 3, 2016), http://infosquare.com.ng/why-we-need-to-restructure-nigeria-to-save-it-by-reuben-abati/ (observing that in the guise of a federal system, Nigeria actually operates a "unitary federalism" "where nothing constructive happens in government except it is sanctioned by Abuja, and by one man, the president of Nigeria. The Federal Government of Nigeria and the president are so constitutionally powerful that other tiers of government are at best appendages.").

57. Nigerian Const., 1999, note 8, 2d schedule, Part I.

58. Nigerian Const., 1999, note 8, 2d schedule, Part II.

59. See Nigerian Const., 1999, note 8, Art. 4(5) (stipulating that "[i]f any Law enacted by the House of Assembly of a State is inconsistent with any law validly made by the National Assembly, the law made by the National Assembly shall prevail, and that other Law shall, to the extent of the inconsistency, be void.").

60. Nigerian Const., 1999, note 8, 4th schedule (listing non-onerous functions like naming roads and numbering houses, licensing bicycles and trucks, regulating laundries, regulating movement and keeping of pets, among other local issues).

61. See Nigerian Const., 1999, note 8, Art. 4(7) (a) (leaving to the States "any matter not included in the Exclusive Legislative List."). For the U.S., see U.S. Const., note 16, 10th Amend. (providing that "powers not delegated to the United States by the Constitution, nor prohibited by it to the States, are reserved to the States respectively, or to the people.").

62. Nigerian Const., 1999, note 8, 2d. Schedule, Part I. Part III(2) of the document interprets this provision to include "offenses," matters relating to the "jurisdiction, powers, practice and procedure of" courts, and land acquisition and tenure.

See Charles Kumolu, "Constitution[al] Amendment: National Assembly Moves to Restructure Nigeria," *Vanguard* (Lagos) (Jan. 13, 2013, 12:40 AM), http://www.vanguardngr.com/2013/01/constitution-amendment-nassembly-moves-to-restructure-nigeria/ (quoting Mohammed Lawal Uwais, former Chief Justice of Nigeria, to the effect that "[s]ince 1979, the powers of the central government have increased to the detriment of the states."). Justice Uwais elaborated that "[b]y 1960, 44 items were on the exclusive list, while 28 were on the concurrent list. In the Republican [1963] constitution, 45 items were on the exclusive list, while 29 were on the concurrent list. In the 1979 constitution, 67 items were on the exclusive list, while 12 were on the concurrent list. In the 1999 constitution, 68 items were on the exclusive list, while 12 items were on the concurrent list." Ibid.

63. Nigerian Const., 1999, note 8, Art. 305(1).

64. Ignatius Akaayar Ayua & Dakas C.J. Dakas, "Federal Republic of Nigeria," *in* John Kincaid & George Alan Tarr, eds., *Constitutional Origins, Structure, and Change in Federal Countries* (Montreal, Canada: McGill-Queen's University Press, 2005): 244.

65. Berman & Murphy, note 15, p. 2 (comparing the U.S. and former communist Czechoslovakia).

66. Nigerian Const., 1999, note 8, 2d. Schedule, Part I (listing "external affairs" as No. 26 on the list).

67. To speak to the similarity of the two documents, both enumerated the country's foreign policy objectives under Art. 19 of each document. Compared to its earlier counterpart, however, the 1999 constitution is more elaborate. In addition to stipulating promotion of African integration and unity, international cooperation for consolidating universal peace and combating all forms of racial discrimination, the 1999 document also has language on the national interest, respect for international law and treaty, and promotion of a just world economic order. *Cf.* Nigerian Const., 1979, note 8, Art. 19 *with* Nigerian Const., 1999, note 8, Art. 19.

68. Unlike the U.S. Constitution noted for brevity, these two presidential constitutions are overly long. Using the latter as example, the document includes a preamble, eight chapters divided into 320 articles, and seven schedules, and runs into nearly 130 pages, vis-à-vis the U.S.'s eight pages without the Amendments. Reasons for the lengthiness include that the Nigerian Constitution in one document covered all three levels of government, and because it delves into matters that in other countries are left to ordinary statutes. Ayua & Dakas, note 64, p. 248.

69. Constitution of the Federal Republic of Nigeria (Promulgation) Decree No. 24 (May 5, 1999).

70. Nigerian Const., 1999, note 8 (preamble) (stating "[w]e the people of the Federal Republic of Nigeria, having firmly and solemnly resolved [on various ideals, including "to live in unity and harmony as one indivisible and indissoluble sovereign nation under God"] do hereby make, enact and give to ourselves the following Constitution.").

71. This appears to be the position of some Nigerian constitutional scholars. See Ayua and Dakas, note 64, pp. 246–48. The Constitution Debating Coordinating Committee the departing military set up to look into the matter and advise it took the position that Nigerians "were near unanimous that the 1979 Constitution had been

tried and tested and, therefore, provides a better point of departure in the quest for constitutionalism in Nigeria." Quoted in Ayua & Daka, note 64, p. 247. Ayua and Dakas appeared to share this position.

72. For one example of this view, see John Simpkins, *The Role of Constitution-Building Processes in Democratization* (Sweden: Int'l Institute for Democracy & Electoral Assistance, 2004): 8, 13 (positing that, vis-à-vis its 1979 predecessor, "there was little genuine public dialog and consultation in the drafting of the 1999 Constitution[;]" to the contrary, "[t]he drafting and consultation process that resulted in the 1999 Constitution is noteworthy for the lack of involvement of non-governmental stakeholders.").

73. "Africa: Nigeria," *in CIA World Factbook* (2014), https://www.cia.gov/library/publications/the-world-factbook/geos/ni.html. Kano and Lagos States have the most representation, each with twenty-four members, while the Federal Capital Territory has the least representation in the chamber with two members. *Id.*

74. See The Federalist No. 78 (Alexander Hamilton) (May 28, 1788) (stating that the Executive holds "the sword of the community," and the legislature "the purse," whereas the judiciary, having neither "force nor will," is left with "merely judgment.").

75. See Atah Pine, "Parliamentary Diplomacy and Foreign Policy in Nigeria's Fourth Republic," *Blogger* (Jul. 1, 2009), http://atahpine.blogspot.com/2009/07/parliamentary-diplomacy-and-foreign.html.

76. Ibid.

77. Ibid.

78. Unlike the U.S. president, the president in Nigeria is directly elected without the need for the mediated influence of an electoral college. See note 25.

79. Ayua & Dakas, note 64, p. 259.

80. Ibid.

81. Nigerian Const., 1999, note 8, Art. 148(1).

82. Ayua & Dakas, note 64, p. 259.

83. Nigerian Const., 1999, note 8, Art. 143(2)(b).

84. See ibid., Art. 235 (providing that, except for pardons, "no appeal shall lie to any other body or person from any determination of the Supreme Court.").

85. Const. Drafting Committee Rept., note 9, p. xxx.

86. Starting in 1957 as the External Division of the Office of the Prime Minister, the name of this agency has changed several times over the years. In 1960, it was called the Ministry of Foreign Affairs and Commonwealth Relations, then Ministry of External Affairs in 1963 before arriving at its current name of Ministry of Foreign Affairs in 1991. See "Ministry of Foreign Affairs," *ConnectNigeria.com*, www.connectnigeria.com/businesses/ministry-of-foreign-affairs-14273.html.

87. See "Ministries of Nigeria," *Ngex!*, http://www.ngex.com/nigeria/govt/officials/ministers.htm.ministers.htm. The twenty-four others are: agriculture; aviation; budget and national planning; communication; defense; education; environment; federal capital territory; finance; health; industry, trade, and investment; information; internal affairs; justice; labor and employment; Niger Delta; petroleum resources; power, works, and housing; science and technology; solid minerals; transportation; water resources; women affairs; and youth and sports. Ibid.

88. See Celestine Oyom Bassey & Charles Quarker Dokubo, *Defense Policy of Nigeria: Capability and Context: A Reader* (Bloomington, IN: AuthorHouse, 2011): 395–408 (commenting on "intelligence gathering in a crisis state."); Joseph Babatunde Fagoyinbo, *The Armed Forces: Instrument of Peace, Strength, Development[,] and Prosperity* (Bloomington, IN: AuthorHouse, 2013) (hagiographic chronicle of the Nigerian armed forces). The Nigerian military consists of three branches: the army and navy, established in 1958, and the air force, founded in 1964. "Nigeria—Ministry of Defense," *Global Security*, http://www.globalsecurity.org/military/world/nigeria/mod.htm.

89. "Nigeria: The National Intelligence Agency (NIA) at Twenty—A Tribute," *Daily Trust* (Abuja), http://allafrica.com/stories/200607200663.html.

90. Ibid.

91. Ibid.

92. Ibid.

93. Ibid.

94. "Nigeria," *in* Dilip K. Das & Michael Palmiotto, eds., *World Police Encyclopedia, Vol. 2* (New York: Routledge, 2006): 622.

95. Ibrahim A. Gambari, *Theory and Reality in Foreign Policy Making: Nigeria after the Second Republic* (Atlantic Highlands, N.J.: Humanities Press Int'l, Inc., 1989): 5.

96. Ibrahim A. Gambari, *Party Politics and Foreign Policy: Nigeria under the First Republic* (Zaria, Nigeria: Ahmadu Bello University Press, 1980): 151. On the Congo Civil War from 1960 to 1964, see, e.g., Ryan Hurst, "Congo Civil War (1960–1964)," *Black Past*, http://www.blackpast.org/gah/congo-civil-war-1960-1964.

97. Gambari, note 95, p. 5. Professor Gambari was Nigeria's foreign minister from 1984 until 1985 (see table 8.2).

98. Gambari, note 95, p. 5.

99. Ibid.

100. J. Peter Pham, Nigeria's Foreign Policy: An Inquiry into Sources and Prospects, Presentation for Int'l Conference, Lisbon, Portugal (Nov. 8–9, 2007): 95–6, www.ipri.pt/eventos/pdf/JPeterPham_paper.pdf.

101. Gambari, note 95, p. 5.

102. See notes 95–97.

103. "Foreign Relations," *in* Metz, ed., note 6.

104. Ibid. (emphasis added).

105. Adesoji Adeniyi, "Peacekeeping Contributor Profile: Nigeria," *Providing for Peacekeeping* (Apr. 24, 2015), http://www.providingforpeacekeeping.org/2015/04/24/peacekeeping-contributor-profile-nigeria/.

106. Ibid.

107. See Berman & Murphy, note 15, pp. 266–67 (reflecting on the extent to which public policy in the U.S. mirrors public opinion).

108. Ibid., p. 267.

109. Ibid.

110. Berman & Murphy, note 15, pp. 264–65 (commenting on various factors accounting for stability and change in public opinion, including salience, "the extent to which people see an issue as having a clear impact on their own lives.").

111. Ibid., p. 267.

112. See notes 45–51 and corresponding text.

113. Const. Drafting Committee Rept., note 9, p. xxx.

114. Gambari, note 95, p. x.

115. Ibid., p. 5.

116. Pham, note 100, pp. 95–96.

117. Ayua & Dakas, note 64, p. 266.

118. Adekeye Adebajo, "Sad Deterioration of Nigeria's Foreign Policy," *B[usiness] D[ay] L[ive]* (Johannesburg) (May 6, 2013), http://za.news.yahoo.com/sad-deterioration-nigeria-foreign-policy-051439591.html (contending that Nigeria's foreign policy under Goodluck Jonathan, president from 2010–2015, "lack[ed] strategic vision.").

119. For example, the Universal Declaration of Human Rights provides that "[t]he will of the people" "expressed in periodic and genuine elections" "shall be the basis of the authority of government." See Universal Declaration of Human Rights, Art. 21(3), G.A. Res. 217 A (III), U.N. GAOR, 3d Sess., U.N. Doc. A/810 (1948).

120. For more on this important human rights tool, see Philip C. Aka, "The *Country Reports on Human Rights Practices* and U.S. Human Rights Policy in a Changing World," *Perspectives on Global Development & Technology*, Vol. 14 (2015): 238.

121. Jimmy Carter, "The American Road to a Human Rights Policy," *in* Samantha Power & Graham Allison, eds., *Realizing Human Rights: Moving from Inspiration to Impact* (New York: St. Martin's Press, 2000): 54.

122. This insight comes from South Africa where, under Nelson Mandela from 1994 to 1999, an exchange ensued regarding application of human rights in the country's foreign policy. See Tiyanjana Maluwa, "Human Rights and Foreign Policy in Post-Apartheid South Africa," *in* David P. Forsythe, ed., *Human Rights and Comparative Foreign Policy* (New York: United Nations University Press, 2000): 250.

123. Dapo Fafowora, "Review of Nigeria's Foreign Policy," *Nation* (Jun. 4, 2015), http://thenationonlineng.net/review_of_nigerias-foreign-policy.

124. Nigeria has 105 embassies abroad. See "Directory of Nigerian Missions Abroad," Nigerian Foreign Service, http://www.fsc-nigeria.org/dir_nigmissions.html. Fafowora advised that the number be cut down "immediately to 100, and thereafter to not more than 80." Fafowora, note 123.

Chapter Nine

The Need for More Symmetry Between Multilateral and Bilateral Activities in Nigeria's External Relations

This chapter is the third of four pillars in the temple of Nigeria's human rights foreign policy. The two pillars preceding this one are redesigned peacekeeping, covered in chapter 7, and reshaped foreign policy machinery, addressed in chapter 8. As its title betrays, the concern that drives this chapter is the need for more symmetry between multilateral and bilateral activities in Nigeria's external relations. Stated differently, successful application of human rights in external affairs requires a proper mixture between multilateral and bilateral activities in external relations. However, Nigeria's foreign policy is too heavily anchored on multilateral engagements and less on bilateral activities. To engage in principled foreign policy of the type associated with global Good Samaritans, the hallowed rank of political communities who consistently apply human rights in their external relations,[1] Nigeria has to include more bilateral activities in its foreign policy toolbox.

The task of this chapter is to marshal measures that Nigeria can use to achieve the proper balancing of multilateral and bilateral activities in its external relations. Achieving that symmetry does not dictate that Nigeria be a great or even middle power.[2] What the symmetry mandates is that Nigeria punch within its capability weight, rather than below, as it now does. Supposedly small powers like Costa Rica, which distinctively punch above their weight in international human rights, "did not require wealth or power to afford the luxury of pursuing a principled foreign policy."[3] Chapter 12 devoted to possible objections to the argument for Nigeria to adopt a human rights–oriented foreign policy elaborates this point. This chapter is, in some sense, a follow up to the discussion in chapter 8 on the need to reshape the Nigerian foreign policy apparatus in a more human rights–sensitive direction. However, for reasons that will become obvious later in the ensuing discussion, it is important enough to stand by itself, in its own right, among the pillars in the temple of Nigerian human rights policy.

Multilateral policies are important in a globalized world where sometimes states tackle human rights challenges by stitching together a "coalition of the willing," rather than go it alone.[4] At the same time, Nigerian external relations are overly hued in the multilateral angle, inconsistent with the requirements of a human rights–based foreign policy, hence this analysis. Three questions that frame the ensuing discussion are: (1) What are the major means through which Nigeria implements its foreign relations?, (2) Which of those tools are bilateral?, and (3) What should Nigeria do to achieve more symmetry between multilateral and bilateral activities in its foreign policy toolbox?

THREE MAJOR MEANS THROUGH WHICH NIGERIA IMPLEMENTS ITS FOREIGN RELATIONS

Table 2.1 in chapter 2 dealing with the conceptual framework for this study enumerated eight conceivable (or illustrative) tools that states use to apply human rights in their relations with other countries. The tools, together with their foreign relation content, defined in terms of multilateral or bilateral properties, are:

- indicators of commitment to international human rights, such as the number of human rights multilateral treaties that a state in question ratified (more *multilateral* than bilateral);
- peacekeeping and related engagements (more *multilateral* than bilateral);
- economic, military, and diplomatic assistance to other states or foreign aid (more *bilateral* than multilateral);
- activities related to the sheltering of refugees or humanitarian assistance (more *bilateral* than multilateral);
- publishing human rights reports (more *multilateral* than bilateral);
- promoting democracy in another country (more *bilateral* than multilateral);
- loss of economic or other forms of assistance arising from the state's commitment to human rights (more *bilateral* than multilateral); and
- miscellaneous exchanges and contacts related to human rights, such as private and public diplomacy (more *bilateral* than multilateral).

Among this lot, two that emerge as major means through which Nigeria implements its foreign relations are peacekeeping operations, and foreign aid, plus ECOWAS, not featured in the table as a third means. The first and last items are covered elsewhere in this study—as indicated before, peacekeeping in chapter 8 and ECOWAS in chapter 10—leaving foreign aid as the only item needing to be addressed in this section.

The vehicle that Nigeria uses to promote its foreign assistance is the Technical Aid Corp (TAC) scheme. TAC was born in 1987 during the regime of General Ibrahim Babangida, Head of State from 1985 to 1993. It is a volunteer outfit, something in the mold of the United States' Peace Corps program,[5] through which Nigeria sends experts in diverse fields, such as medical doctors, pharmacists, nurses, lecturers, lawyers, architects, accountants, and engineers to other countries to assist these foreign countries with their developmental needs under mutually agreed conditions.[6] Initially limited to countries in Africa and the Caribbean, the program has since been expanded to include Pacific countries.[7] TAC provides "an alternative to direct financial (cash) assistance to African, Caribbean and the Pacific Countries," demonstrates Nigeria's commitment to cooperation with developing countries, forms "a practical transfer of knowledge and expertise from Nigerian professionals" to beneficiary countries "in a well-structured and more coordinated manner," helps "cement[] existing relations between Nigeria and the recipient countries," and expands Nigeria's diplomatic presence in the world by "[e]stablishing presence in countries [where] for economic reasons, Nigeria has no resident diplomatic Missions."[8] It also systematized previous technical assistance initiatives going back to the 1960s wherein Nigeria seconds (i.e., posts a worker for a limited duration) technical experts to various African counties.[9]

African, Caribbean, and Pacific countries which have benefited from the TAC program include Belize, Benin Republic, Brazil, Burkina Faso, Burundi, Cape Verde, Central African Republic, Democratic Republic of the Congo, Djibouti, Dominican, Equatorial Guinea, Ethiopia, Fiji, Gambia, Guinea Bissau, Guyana, Jamaica, Kenya, Lesotho, Liberia, Mozambique, Namibia, Niger Republic, Rwanda, São Tomé and Principe, Senegal, Seychelles, Sierra-Leone, Swaziland, Uganda, Venezuela, Vietnam, and Zambia.[10] Under the TAC program, as of 2011, over 4,000 volunteers have been deployed to 38 countries.[11] Praised by some commentators as a "pearl of South-South cooperation,"[12] TAC represents a departure from the conventional North-South pattern of aid.[13] Meles Zenawi, prime minister of Ethiopia from 1995 to 2012, once praised the program as "the only volunteer service of its kind currently operated by an African country," that also "challenges the commonly held perception that Africa is only a recipient of aid."[14] TAC is run by the Directorate of Technical Aid Corps, an agency under the Ministry of Foreign Affairs.[15]

PEERING THROUGH THE THREE MEANS FOR BILATERAL CONTENT

Of the three means for implementing Nigeria's foreign relations spotlighted above, on the surface, only the TAC is bilateral, while the other two—peacekeeping and ECOWAS—are multilateral, or to use the language of table 2.1, more multilateral than bilateral. But just asserting the lack of bilateralism is not enough; it is necessary that the researcher dig deeper by gauging the extent of the lack of bilateralism of each tool. The scrutiny begins with peacekeeping. Although by its very nature multilateral, *not* all peacekeeping missions are multilateral. Rather, some peacekeeping initiatives are bilateral. One such example was the conflict in Tanzania from January 12 to September 26, 1964, triggered by an army mutiny.[16] Five hundred Nigerian peacekeepers were deployed in the land on March 31, 1964, to replace some withdrawn British forces.[17] The troops kept peace in Tanzania for six months before they left on September 26, 1964.[18] But instances of bilateral peacekeeping by Nigeria are rare and did not change the essentially multilateral nature of the country's peacekeeping endeavors.

Looking past Nigeria, a rare example of a bilateral peacekeeping program is the Canadian Military Training Assistance Program (MTAP). One of the purposes of the scheme is the promotion of "Canadian bilateral defense relations," subject to the condition that the assistance "must promote democratic principles, the rule of law, protection of human rights and international stability."[19] As the head of the program elaborates, the "MTAP assists other nations' forces in developing the capability to operate effectively in joint missions with the CF, thereby making burden sharing more effective and efficient."[20]

In contrast, Nigeria has no such bilateral training program. In 2004, decades after its entrance into peacekeeping missions, Nigeria established a training program for its own peacekeepers that it does not use to train non-Nigerian peacekeepers. The Center could be developed to offer courses that at the least include peacekeepers from West African countries under a sharing arrangement of the kind Canada uses in its MTAP program. Until that moment, Nigerian peacekeeping remains largely multilateral.

The next object of attention is ECOWAS. Like with peacekeeping missions, Nigeria's activities in ECOWAS are also more multilateral than bilateral. This is still so, even though as the discussion in chapter 10 makes clear, Nigeria constitutes more than 50 percent of the population of the economic community and contributes more than one-third of its budget. Like Canada's MTAP program,[21] ECOWAS affords an opportunity for burden sharing in peacekeeping. However, unlike the Canada program, ECOWAS originated as an economic integration tool that developed a military outfit along the way in an attempt to promote its initial goal as a custom union. As chapter 10 also shows, in addition to the opportunity it affords for burden sharing in peacekeeping, over the years and for Nigeria as well as for other members of the community, ECOWAS has in and of itself metamorphosed into a forum for the application of human rights in external affairs. However, these desirable features cannot and did not change the community's basic character as a multilateral tool in the implementation of Nigeria's foreign policy.

The last but not least object of attention is the TAC, the vehicle of Nigeria's foreign aid program. Compared to peacekeeping missions and ECOWAS, the TAC is by its nature bilateral. However, as the discussion in the last section makes clear, the program is still fledgling and lacking in robustness. Information on the program is sketchy, but there is little evidence that the scheme is properly funded. The United Nations recommends a minimum target of .7 percent of a sponsoring country's gross domestic product (GDP) as allocation to foreign aid[22] that, given the falling prices of oil, the mainstay of Nigeria's economy, it is doubtful that the program meets, especially in the light of the domestic needs of the country.

It is necessary to pursue this discussion to its logical conclusion by examining the remaining bilateral instruments from table 2.1 to gauge how Nigeria did on those tools. The three that apply here are: activities relating to sheltering refugees (humanitarian assistance); promoting democracy in other countries; and miscellaneous exchanges and contacts related to human rights, such as private and public diplomacy. Starting with contributions in refugee work, Nigeria has no distinctive record of achievement in this field, apart from its important contributions to the liberation movement in southern Africa that ended in 1994 with the achievement of majority rule in South Africa. As opposed to providing help in this area, Nigeria is itself a recipient of humanitarian assistance, arising from tens of millions of internally displaced persons (IDPs) that the numerous conflicts within its boundaries, time and again since its independence in 1960, have generated.[23]

Next is promotion of democracy abroad. The only such achievement that comes to mind is the absurdity in 1998 when the brutal dictator General Sani Abacha (1993–1998) undertook peacekeeping designed to restore a civilian regime in Sierra Leone while firmly maintaining Nigeria under repressive military rule.[24] This brings us finally to miscellaneous exchanges and contacts related to human rights, including diplomacy. These are the reasons countries maintain diplomatic missions abroad. On the surface, Nigeria seems to do this well with its 105-odd diplomatic mission overseas. Looking at the matter more closely, however, there are notable downsides. First, the country's foreign services are poorly funded;[25] and second, because of its use of ambassadorial postings as a form of political patronage,

Nigeria maintains embassies in countries where it has "no real economic or strategic interests."[26] The lesson on this last tool is that, in and of itself, creating embassies, especially ones that are not properly funded, is not bilateral relations in the sense the term is used here.

Compounding the lack of bilateral content in Nigeria's external relations is the fact that there is room for more energy in the multilateral tasks that occupy the space of the country's external relations. Because this study has commented extensively on peacekeeping and ECOWAS on which topics it devoted one whole chapter each, the only topic that could use some more discussion here would be indicators of commitment to international human rights. As shown in chapter 1, Nigeria is a party to numerous regional and global human rights treaties, including core instruments. However, the country's 1999 constitution forbids the enforcement of treaties that have not been enacted into law by the National Assembly, the country's supreme lawmaking body, a process that is fraught with long delays. Secondly, the country sometimes ratifies multilateral treaties, such as the Geneva Conventions, that it makes little effort to comply with.[27] To be sure, this is not an attribute limited to Nigeria, given that many other countries in the world also pay a lip service to international human rights.[28] But a country that aspires to a major role in world politics or seeks to engage in principled foreign policy can do more to its glory and the benefit of the international human rights regime.

Still on indicators of commitment to international human rights, there is no indication on the record of appreciable Nigerian support for global institutions, such as voluntary donations to the United Nations Office of High Commissioner for Human Rights or diplomatic support for the International Criminal Court. The paucity is a marked contrast, for example, to Costa Rica, which at the United Nations alone, "has played a part in virtually every major human rights initiative and institution—vastly disproportionate to its size, wealth, and power";[29] and South Africa which, in the period since its achievement of majority rule, has "hosted an unprecedented series of global and regional conferences."[30] For Costa Rica, major highlights of the multilateral commitments include the country's instrumental role leading to the establishment in 1993 of the Office of the United Nations High Commissioner for Human Rights,[31] its campaign for the Optional Protocol to the Convention against Torture, adopted by the U.N. in December of 2002,[32] and its sponsorship of the First World Conference on Human Rights in 1982.[33] For South Africa, major highlights of those multilateral energies include the United Nations' Conference on Racism in 2001 that it hosted.[34] Similarly, the country's support for multilateralism includes its willingness to endure reprisals for its principled promotion of international law. For example, in 2003, Pretoria chose a reduction in U.S. aid rather than sign an impunity agreement with the United States to exempt it from the International Criminal Court.[35]

WHAT NEEDS TO BE DONE

The thing that needs to be done tracks the problem identified in the previous section. Of the three major implements Nigeria uses to conduct its foreign relations, only one, lacking in robustness, is bilateral. The way therefore to achieve symmetry between bilateral and multilateral tools in Nigerian foreign relations is to put more bilateral content into its foreign policy toolbox. There is no suggestion that Nigeria give up the multilateral instruments—peacekeeping and ECOWAS—that it now depends upon largely to implement its foreign relations. To the contrary, it should streamline those tools along the lines of the international human rights standard suggested in the respective chapters on these topics while increasing the bilateral contents of its overall relations with other countries.

Nigeria could possibly do these things within its present economic means if it rationalizes its resources better. That rationalization must include diversification of its now oil-based economy as well as the maintenance of a proper balance between fertility rate and economic growth to provide the means for principled foreign policy work. This may necessitate forging new relations outside Africa over and above its policy thrust for too long centered on Africa. As one commentator perceptively advised, Nigeria's "search for a new role . . . in world affairs should involve a region-by-region review of its foreign policy with a view to redefining its national interests and foreign policy objectives,"[36] and it should specifically focus on "bilateral relations with certain regional economic and military powers that have emerged" recently: China and India in Asia, the United States and the European Union, specifically Germany and France; Argentina, Brazil, and Mexico in Latin America; and mutually beneficial relationships with the World Bank and the International Monetary Fund while expanding ties with the African Development Bank.[37]

Nigeria currently has 105 diplomatic missions in the world.[38] Putting more bilateral content into its foreign relations does not mandate that the country create more embassies abroad that are not properly funded. To the contrary, the country may have to immediately reduce its missions abroad to a number consistent with economic realities,[39] paying careful attention to a variety of factors, including the "economic or strategic interests" of each embassy and eschewing the use of foreign postings as a form of political patronage.[40]

SUMMATION

Belief in the usefulness of the United Nations as an instrument for safeguarding the independence of small states ranked among the objectives of Nigerian foreign policy during the early years of Nigeria's independence.[41] The thinking is testimony to a foreign policy hued toward multilateralism that should no longer dictate policy nearly 60 years after the country's independence within which period petroleum products have replaced agricultural exports as mainstay of Nigeria's economy. To achieve the status of a principled foreign policy state, Nigeria must accumulate more bilateral activities. While multilateral engagements are important, many tools of a principled foreign policy are bilateral. Five out of the illustrative eight tools on table 2.1, or over 62 percent, are bilateral. Similarly, many countries who consistently apply human rights in their external affairs have a variety of implements for the job that is not limited to multilateral initiatives.

Activities weighted excessively in multilateralism, at the expense of bilateral tools, betray a lack of readiness for principled foreign policy. One of the lessons distilled from studies of countries who consistently apply human rights in their external relations is that even smallish states can punch above their weight when "that weight is well developed and *well distributed*."[42] Nigeria's recognition as a budding "moral superpower" is tied to peacekeeping, a multilateral instrument, which many decades after independence remains the sole anchor of its foreign policy kit. To consolidate its fledgling democracy and contribute to the international human regimes, Nigeria needs more bilateral activities in its foreign policy toolbox. Central to the discussion in this chapter is the distinction between human rights in international relations and human rights in foreign relations.[43] The first calls to mind multilateral activities while the second is more associated with bilateral activities. While both are important in the sense that without the first, the second probably would not exist, vis-à-vis the first, the second ties into the concept of principled foreign policy at the heart of this study. With this chapter and pillar concluded, there is just one element left in the temple of Nigeria's human rights foreign policy analyzed in this book. That topic, focus of chapter 10, is ECOWAS as a tool of human rights.

NOTES

1. Alison Brysk, *Global Good Samaritans: Human Rights as Foreign Policy* (New York: Oxford University Press, 1998), *passim* (case study of six states and a coalition of six groups, some of them states).

2. For one position on the small, middle, and great-power doctrine in international relations, see Gareth Evans, "Middle Power Diplomacy," lecture delivered in Santiago, Chile (Jun. 29, 2011), http://www.gevans.org/speeches/speech441.html (positing that while *middle power diplomacy* is a useful concept in international relations, identifying the countries which form these *middle powers* with any precision "is an exercise fraught with peril.").

3. Brysk, note 1, p. 118. Judging by population size alone, Costa Rica had 3 million people, compared to Nigeria's 135 million people as of 2009 when the Brysk study was published. See ibid., pp. 8–17.

4. See, e.g., Steve Schifferes, "U.S. Names 'Coalition of the Willing,'" *BBC News* (Mar. 18, 2003, 21:38 GMT), http://news.bbc.co.uk/2/hi/americas/2862343.stm; Lionel Beehner, "The 'Coalition of the Willing,'" Council on Foreign Relations (Updated Feb. 22, 2007), http://www.cfr.org/iraq/coalition-willing/p9340; "Operation Iraqi Freedom," White House (Mar. 27, 2003), http://georgewbush-whitehouse.archives.gov/news/releases/2003/03/20030327-10.html.

5. "Peace Corps," John F. Kennedy Presidential Library & Museum (Boston, MA), http://www.jfklibrary.org/JFK/JFK-in-History/Peace-Corps.aspx. During a speech on Nov. 2, 1960, in San Francisco, President John J. Kennedy proposed "a peace corps of talented men and women" who would dedicate themselves to the progress and peace of developing countries. Ibid. The proposal became reality when on Mar. 1, 1961, Kennedy signed an executive order creating the organization. The ideological rivalry between the United States and the Soviet Union, embedded in the Cold War, had a hand in the creation of the Peace Corps. Kennedy observed that the Soviet Union "had hundreds of men and women, scientists, physicists, teachers, engineers, doctors, and nurses . . . prepared to spend their lives abroad in the service of world communism," whereas the United States had none. Ibid. Therefore, through the Peace Corps, he would involve Americans more actively in the cause of democracy, peace, development, and freedom. Tanganyika (merged into Tanzania in 1964) and Ghana were the first countries to participate in the program. On Sept. 22, 1961, Kennedy signed into law a bill passed by Congress that made the Peace Corps a permanent federal agency within the State Department. It remained part of the State Department until 1981 when it became an independent agency. Ibid.

6. See Salami B. Olawale, "The Prelude to Babangida Regime's Foreign Policy Initiatives," *Mediterranean Journal of Social Sciences*, Vol. 5 (2014): 83, www.mcser.org/journal/index.php/mjss/article/view/2120; "The Transformation of Technical Aid Corps Scheme," *Sun* (Lagos) (Aug. 20, 2014), http://sunnewsonline.com/new/the-transformation-of-technical-aid-corps-scheme/.

7. "Nigeria's Technical Aid Corps for ACP Countries to Expand to Brazil, Venezuela, Vietnam," *ACP* (Sept. 10, 2014), http://www.acp.int/content/news-nigerias-technical-aid-corps-acp-countries-expand-brazil-venezuela-vietnam.

8. "Welcome to the Directorate of Technical Aid Corps," Directorate of Technical Aid Corps, http://www.dtac.gov.ng/DTAC/dtac/aboutDTAC#.

9. Olawale, note 6. According to Olawale, compared to these past programs, TAC "place[s] less financial burden on the recipient countries." Ibid., p. 83.

10. "Welcome to the Directorate of Technical Aid Corps," note 8; "Nigeria's Technical Aid Corps for ACP Countries to Expand to Brazil, Venezuela, Vietnam," note 7.

11. Samiu Babalola, "Nigeria's Technical Aid Corps: Pearl of South-South Cooperation," *Africa Platform for Development Effectiveness* (Dec. 21, 2011), http://www.africa-platform.org/resources/nigerias-technical-aid-corps-pearl-south-south-cooperation.

12. Babalola, note 11.

13. The literature on development makes a distinction between a Global North and Global South. It is a distinction based on level of economic development, rather than strictly on geography as the name would suggest. The Global North includes the economically developed societies of Europe, North America, Australia, Israel, and others. In contrast, the Global South includes the developing societies of Africa, India, China, Brazil, Mexico, and others. Lemuel Ekedegwa Odeh, "A Comparative Analysis of Global North and Global South Economies," *Journal of Sustainable Development in Africa*, Vol. 12 (2010): 338, http://www.jsd-africa.com/Jsda/V12No3_Summer2010_A/PDF/A%20Comparative%20Analysis%20of%20Global%20North%20and%20Global%20South%20Economies%20(Odeh).pdf. Based on this distinction, "South-South cooperation" is another way of saying cooperation among developing countries that have yet to attain the high level of economic development found in the Global North.

14. Quoted in "Welcome to the Directorate of Technical Aid Corps," note 10.

15. Ibid.

16. See "Tanzania (1961–Present)," University of Central Arkansas, http://uca.edu/politicalscience/dadm-project/sub-saharan-africa-region/tanzania-1961-present/.

17. Ibid.

18. Ibid.

19. Andrew P. Rasiulis, "The Military Training Assistance Program (MTAP): An Instrument of Military Diplomacy," *Canadian Military Journal* (Autumn 2001): 63, http://www.journal.forces.gc.ca/vo2/no3/doc/63-64-eng.pdf.

20. Rasiulis, note 19.

21. See notes 19–20 and corresponding text.

22. See "What is the 0.7% Target?, 2002–2006," Millennium Project, http://www.unmillenniumproject.org/press/07.htm.

23. See Philip C. Aka, "Bridging the Gap Between Theory and Practice: Seven Practical Steps to Humanitarian Integrity in Nigeria, *CIHA Blog* (Feb. 25, 2016), http://www.cihablog.com/bridging-the-gap-between-theory-and-practice-in-humanitarian-action-seven-practical-steps-to-humanitarian-integrity-in-nigeria/.

24. See Norimitsu Onishi, "What War Has Wrought: Sierra Leone's Sad State," *New York Times* (Jan. 31, 2999), http://www.nytimes.com/1999/01/31/world/what-war-has-wrought-sierra-leone-s-sad-state.html?pagewanted=all (stating, *inter alia*, that Abacha attempted to "draw attention away from his record of abuse at home by promoting democracy abroad").

25. Dapo Fafowora, "Review of Nigeria's Foreign Policy," *Nation* (Jun. 4, 2015), http://thenationonlineng.net/review-of-nigerias-foreign-policy/. Fafowora advised instructively that "[f]oreign policy cannot be run on a shoe string." Ibid.

26. Ibid. These countries include Thailand and North Korea. Ibid.

27. See note 25 in chapter 1 of this book.

28. See David P. *Forsythe, Human Rights in International Relations, 3d Ed.* (New York: Cambridge University Press, 2012): vii (pointing out that "states continue to profess their commitment to at least some [human rights] standards, even as their record of compliance is often far short of what it should be"); and Peter R. Baehr, "Foreign Policy," *in Encyclopedia of Human Rights, Vol. 5* (New York: Oxford University Press, 2009): 237 (observing that "[m]uch lip service is paid to the notion of human rights" even as these rights remained abused all across the world).

29. Brysk, note 1, p. 96.

30. Brysk, note 1, p. 173.

31. Brysk, note 1, p. 97.

32. Ibid., p. 98.

33. Ibid., p.106.

34. Ibid., p. 173.

35. Ibid.

36. Fafowora, note 25.

37. Ibid. Nigeria's ties to the global monetary institution is circumspect in the sense that, as Fafowora advised, the country "should maintain good relations with [them] while rejecting advice from them that is not in [Nigeria's] long-term economic interests." Ibid.

38. See "Directory of Nigerian Missions Abroad," Nigerian Foreign Service, http://www.fsc-nigeria.org/dir_nigmissions.html.

39. Instructively, Fafowora advised that "[t]he number of [Nigeria's] diplomatic missions should be reduced immediately to 100, and thereafter to not more than 80." Fafowora, note 25.

40. Fafowora, note 25.

41. See Ibrahim A. Gambari, *Party Politics and Foreign Policy: Nigeria under the First Republic* (Zaria, Nigeria: Ahmadu Bello University Press, 1980): 55–6.

42. Brysk, note 1, p. 223 (emphasis added).

43. Example of these categories, drawing on the literature related to this topic, would be Forsythe, note 28, *esp.* his notion of "[t]he politics of liberalism in a realist world," *liberalism* here denoting human rights, ibid., pp. 317–45, vis-à-vis Brysk, note 1, *passim*, and David P. Forsythe, ed., *Human Rights and Comparative Foreign Policy* (New York: United Nations University Press, 2000), *passim*. Forsythe, note 28, expresses the general notion of human rights in international relations, institutionalized via the United Nations system that multilateral human rights policies call to mind, compared to the last two sources connecting human rights with mostly bilateral foreign policies—for a hint, the word *foreign policy* is in both texts.

Chapter Ten

The Economic Community of West African States (ECOWAS) and Human Rights in Nigeria's External Relations

This chapter is the fourth and final pillar—after redesigned peacekeeping, reshaped foreign policy machinery, and increased bilateralism in foreign relations—in the temple of Nigeria's human rights foreign policy set forth in chapter 1 of this study. Two complementary elements of the temple, denominated "steps," each of which has also been addressed in earlier chapters, are reconstructed national interest and increased human rights at home. Except perhaps for peacekeeping, no tool features in Nigeria's external relations or forms the face of those relations like ECOWAS. Like peacekeeping, this tool is multilateral though more capacious than peacekeeping if only because it is also the *context* for expression of external relations in instances when Nigeria conducted peacekeeping under the auspices of ECOWAS.

PRIMER ON ECOWAS

The Economic Community of West African States (ECOWAS) came into being on May 28, 1975, when 15 out of the 19 countries in West Africa,[1] spanning three received languages reflecting the colonial heritages of the member-states,[2] signed in Lagos, then the Nigerian capital city, the treaty setting up the organization.[3] The fifteen countries were: Benin, Burkina Faso (then Upper Volta), Côte d'Ivoire (then Ivory Coast), the Gambia, Ghana, Guinea, Guinea-Bissau, Liberia, Mali, Mauritania, Niger, Nigeria, Senegal, Sierra Leone, and Togo.[4] In 1977, Cape Verde joined, bringing the number of member-states to 16,[5] but the number fell back to 15, its current number, when Mauritania left the organization in 2000 over issues that include a disagreement relating to ECOWAS's decision to establish a common currency by 2004, which would have displaced Mauritania's currency, the Quguiya.[6] (See table 10.1 showing the current membership of the organization.) ECOWAS is not coterminous with West Africa. Put differently, based on the geographical definition of *West Africa* in the first sentence under this section, four West African countries which could have been part of but do not belong in ECOWAS are Cameroon, Chad, Equatorial Guinea, and Mauritania. Although 1975 is recognized as the date of the community's formation, ECOWAS did not become operational until November 1976, on which date the five protocols annexed to the treaty received the minimum number of ratification to bring them into force,[7] and, in a real sense, not until 1990 when the trade liberalization scheme of the organization, slated for 1977, took off 13 years behind target.[8] Until 1990, "the community was preoccupied with the establishment of institutions deemed important for its success, and the ratifications of protocols and conventions to clarify issues relating to the community."[9] On a larger note, following the signature of the ECOWAS treaty in 1975, "[s]everal objections, reservations, obstacles, and foot-draggings involving member states prevented a smooth delivery of ECOWAS."[10]

As initially designed, ECOWAS was an economic cooperation arrangement meant to ultimately lead to the achievement of a custom union (i.e., free trade zone) in West Africa,[11] through a range of gradual steps that include: raising the standard of living of the people in the member-states, promoting economic stability, and fostering good relations among member-states, all the while contributing to the economic development of Africa.[12] Premised on the conviction that "forms of bilateral and multilateral economic cooperation existing in the sub-region give hope for wider cooperation,"[13] ECOWAS is "an integrated union" "governed in accordance with the principles of democracy, rule of law, and good governance" "where the population enjoys free movement, have access to efficient education and health systems and engage in economic and commercial activities while living in dignity in an atmosphere of peace and security."[14]

To realize these ambitious goals, the organization sought to pursue, in stages, a set of objectives that includes: eliminating custom duties; abolishing quantitative and administrative restrictions on trade; abolishing the obstacles to the free movements of persons, services, and capital among member-states; harmonizing and coordinating national policies; establishing joint venture enterprises; establishing a common market; creating a single monetary zone; and promoting the flow of information among the various populations, organizations, media, and workers within the community.[15] ECOWAS is one of eight regional economic communities in Africa recognized by the African Union (AU).[16] Along with ECOWAS, five of the eight regional economic communities have been designated as "pillars," or building blocks, of the African Economic Community (AEC), an Africa-

Table 10.1. ECOWAS Member-States with Distinctive Characteristics as of 2015

Serial No.	*Country*	*Population (in millions)*	*Land Area (in sq. km)*	*GDP (Billions in U.S. $)*	*Former Colonizer*
French-speaking					
1.	Benin	10.6	112,620	10	France
2.	Burkina Faso (formerly Upper Volta)	17.4	274,200	15	France
3.	Côte d'Ivoire (formerly Ivory Coast)	21.1	322,463	38	France
4.	Guinea	12.6	245,860	7 (2014 estimate)	France
5.	Mali	16	1,240,000	13	France
6.	Niger	19.1	1,267,000	9	France
7.	Senegal	15.1	196,190	17	France
8.	Togo	7.2	56,785	5	Germany and France
English-speaking					
9.	Liberia	4.6	111,370	2	None, but close ties with the U.S.
10.	Gambia	approx. 2	11,300	1	U.K.
11.	Ghana	approx. 28	238,540	33	U.K.
12.	Nigeria	approx. 179	923,768	657 (for 2017)	U.K.
13.	Sierra-Leone	6.4	71,740	6	U.K.
Portuguese-speaking					
14.	Cape Verde	.52	4,033	2	Portugal
15.	Guinea-Bissau	1.79	36,120	1	Portugal

All of the amounts (in the column for GDP) are estimates. Note that the available estimates for Guinea and Nigeria, respectively, are for 2014 and 2017. The figures are taken from *Global Finance*, a monthly magazine published in the United States and headquartered in New York. See "About Us," *Global Finance*, www.gfmag.com/about-us/.

Source: Table created by the author.

wide economic union of 54 member-states.[17] The other four are COMESA, ECCAS, the IGAD, and SADC.[18] The headquarters of the community is located in Abuja, Nigeria's federal capital. ECOWAS covers a landmass of about 5.1 million square kilometers with a population estimated at over 334 million people in 2015 (see table 10.1). Based on the diagram, Nigeria made up 53 percent of the community's population and 76 percent of its total GDP of $652 billion in 2015. These features plus the fact that Nigeria contributes nearly one-third of the community's annual budget make the country the undisputed linchpin of the community.[19]

Several unsuccessful events predating and leading up to the formation of ECOWAS in 1975 include: the creation in 1945 of the CFA franc that brought the French-speaking portion of West Africa into a single currency union; a proposal in 1964 by Liberian president William Tubman for an economic union for West Africa; signature of an agreement for an economic union in 1965 by Côte d'Ivoire, Guinea, Liberia, and Sierra Leone;[20] tour of 12 West African countries from July to August of 1972 by the leaders of Nigeria and Togo, General Yakubu Gowon and General Gnassingbe Eyadema, drumming up support for economic integration;[21] and the declaration in 1973 by the Organization of African Unity regarding cooperation, development, and economic independence in Africa.[22]

ECOWAS is a product of various influences at work at the time, including pan-Africanism,[23] lobby energies by non-government organizations, and the encouragement of the Economic Commission for Africa (ECA),[24] a United Nations agency. Additionally for Nigeria, there were some unique factors at play revolved around a crystallization of several lessons learned from the civil war of 1967 to 1970. The first is to pay more attention to its West African neighbors to minimize the possibility of these neighbors providing "staging grounds for extra-regional powers" who may want to "destabilize or dismember Nigeria."[25] Gabon and Côte d'Ivoire, two of the four African countries that recognized Biafra, are in West Africa.[26] Additionally, following the war, the Biafran leader, Chukwuemeka Odumegwu Ojukwu (1933–2011) lived in Côte d'Ivoire until his pardon and return to Nigeria in 1982.[27] In place of France (or any other extra-regional power), ECOWAS offered itself "as an alternative source of funds, ideas, and economic and trade relations" for West African countries, thereby minimizing the potential influence of these extra-regional powers on these neighboring countries.[28] A related lesson is that it pays to keep the focus of its foreign policy on Africa since many African countries, under the OAU, determined to maintain colonial boundaries, were persuaded by the argument of the Nigerian leadership that the civil war was Nigeria's "internal affairs." A third lesson was that Nigeria found value in expanding its relationship to the socialist world since the Soviet Union filled its request for arms when the Western powers initially rejected that request. Finally, ECOWAS also afforded a more structured tool, formerly non-existent, for channeling assistance to these and other African countries. Before ECOWAS, "except for contributions to the African Development Bank, what passed for Nigeria's foreign aid in the region tended to be haphazard and dependent on the whims of the former head of state, General Yakubu Gowon."[29]

Several key multilateral instruments govern the operations of ECOWAS. The first is the treaty signed in Lagos in 1975 setting up the organization.[30] Due to inadequate commitment to the objectives of economic integration, progress on a number of targets lagged behind by many years.[31] The situation is compounded by the existence of competing economic integration arrangements in West Africa, in addition to UMA referenced earlier,[32] that includes Communauté Economique de l'Afrique de l'Quest (CEAO),[33] and the Mano River Union (MRU). CEAO was founded in 1973 to replace a predecessor, the Union Douaniere de l'Afrique de l'Quest (UDEAO) or West African Customs Union, established in June 1966. Like its predecessor, CEAO comprised six countries: Burkina Faso, Côte d'Ivoire, Mali, Mauritania, Niger, and Senegal, plus Benin and Togo as observer-members.[34] Founded in 1973, the MRU comprises four countries: Côte d'Ivoire, Guinea, Liberia, and Sierra Leone.[35] Back to the founding ECOWAS treaty of 1975, the instrument was revised in 1993 in an attempt to accelerate the pace of integration while taking into account changed circumstances in the previous two decades.[36] The revised treaty embodied several new economic and political targets, including the achievement of a common market and a single currency, creation of a Community Parliament, and the creation of a Community Court of Justice (discussed below) to replace the Tribunal in the 1975 treaty.[37]

An eye-catching expression in the document is the conviction expressed by the governmental leaders who adopted the agreement to the effect that "the integration of the Member States into a viable regional Community may demand the partial and gradual pooling of national sovereignties to the Community within the context of a collective political will."[38] The statement raises eyebrows given the tendency of many African states to guard their sovereignties jealously.[39] Some of the fundamental principles the document recites reflect the changing times: in addition to typical provisions, such as non-aggression between and among member-states, regional peace through good neighborliness, and peaceful settlement of disputes among member-states, there are also statements about promoting and protecting human rights, "accountability, economic and social justice and popular participation in development," and promoting and consolidating democracy in member-states.[40]

Via its language, as recounted in the preceding paragraph, the revised treaty also appeared to codify or update several protocols that were adopted before 1993. These include the Protocol Relating to Non-Aggression of 1978, which enjoined member-states to "refrain from the threat and use of force or aggression" against one another; the Protocol Relating to Mutual Assistance on Defense, effective from 1986, which committed ECOWAS member states to a collective defense agreement; the Declaration of Political Principles of

1991, which set forth member-states' commitment to uphold human rights, democracy, and the rule of law; and the Protocol on Democracy and Good Governance, designed to address problems, such as corruption and instability, that are root causes of conflicts.[41]

ECOWAS INSTITUTIONS AND HUMAN RIGHTS

To facilitate its work of economic integration, ECOWAS created a set of several institutions, key of which include the Authority of Heads of State and Government (AHSG), a Council of Ministers (CM), a Secretariat, a Community Parliament, a Community Court of Justice (CCJ), and the Economic Community of West African States Monitoring Group (ECOMOG). The AHSG is the supreme decision-making body of ECOWAS,[42] and the entity vested with responsibility for the general direction and control of the community.[43] As its very name implies, the AHSG comprises Heads of State and Government of member-states,[44] meets at least once a year in ordinary session,[45] and is headed by a chairman, elected by the authority from its own ranks.[46] Next after in importance to the AHGS, the CM[47] is tasked with a range of responsibilities that includes reviewing the functionality of the organization consistent with the treaty, making recommendations to the AHSG, giving directions to all subordinate institutions of ECOWAS, and overseeing the operations of the organization.[48] It comprises the minister in charge of ECOWAS affairs of every member-state or any other minister an affected member-state may choose to represent it in the Council,[49] meets at least twice a year in ordinary session,[50] and is headed by a Chairman of Council elected from its own ranks.[51]

ECOWAS's Secretariat is located in Abuja, Nigeria.[52] It is headed by an Executive Secretary,[53] who is charged with the day-to-day administration, and is accountable to the Council of Ministers and the AHGS.[54] The Executive Secretary is elected for a four-year term,[55] and assisted by four deputies,[56] each in four areas critical to the work of the community.[57] In 2006, the Secretariat was converted into a Commission, comprised of a president, a vice president, and 15 commissioners.[58] Like the Secretariat, the Community Parliament is located in Abuja.[59] It is a consultative and advisory body, not a legislative assembly in the real sense of the word, charged with a range of responsibilities, including the power to create institutions, modify strategies to accelerate economic integration, define basic principles for accounting and financial management, and promote cooperative links. It is not directly elected; instead, its membership is constituted from the membership of the legislatures of each member-state. Comments on the Community Court of Justice are saved for later in this section.

This leaves out ECOMOG as the remaining institution to be discussed here. ECOMOG is the non-standing, military outfit of ECOWAS vested with responsibility for monitoring ceasefires. Formed in 1990 on the eve of Liberia's first civil war (1989–1997), ECOMOG has since then featured in several peacekeeping missions: Liberia in 1990 until 1997 when the troops left following the elections that year in that country; Sierra Leone in 1997 until 1998 when ECOMOG troops helped reinstate a president dislodged from power by rebels; Guinea-Bissau in 1999 to keep peace after an armed conflict between the president and a rebel military chief; Sierra Leone in 1999, whose capital Freetown ECOMOG troops recaptured after a guerrilla offensive; and Guinea-Liberia borders where ECOMOG troops were stationed to stop guerrilla infiltration.[60] In addition to these institutions, ECOWAS has technical commissions in numerous subject areas,[61] and a money house, the ECOWAS Bank for Investment and Development (EBID).[62]

Under the revised treaty, together with protocols leading to the adoption of the treaty in 1993 and protocols adopted after it, ECOWAS activities have been underlain with concepts of democracy, human rights, and the rule of law.[63] However, no singular institution of the community is directly connected with human rights like the Community Court of Justice. To draw out the connection to human rights that this section makes, the rest of the material will focus on the Court. Like the Secretariat and Community Parliament, the CCJ is located in Abuja.[64] The Court was established in 1991 as a permanent institution, rather than an *ad hoc* tribunal,[65] an incarnation of the Tribunal of the Community under the 1975 Treaty, with a mandate "to ensure the observance of law and of the principles of equity [as well as] the interpretation and application of the provisions of the Revised Treaty" and related instruments of the community.[66] It has *contentious* jurisdiction on a range of issues that includes: failure by member-states to honor their obligations under Community law; competence to adjudicate any dispute relating to interpretation and application of Community acts; disputes between institutions of the Community and their officials; cases dealing with liability for or against the Community; and of particular importance in this section, cases regarding violation of human rights that occur in any member state.[67] Equally, the Court has *advisory* jurisdiction authorizing it to provide "legal advisory opinion on any matter that requires interpretation of the Community text."[68] The revised treaty of 1993 created an Arbitration Tribunal of the Community.[69] Pending the establishment of the Arbitration Tribunal, the Court also has competence in matters of arbitration.[70]

The CCJ has seven judges "appointed by the Authority of Heads of State of Government, from nationals of Member States, for a four-year term of office, upon recommendation of the Community Judicial [C]ouncil."[71] Its judgments "are binding on the Member States, the institutions of the Community and on individuals and corporate bodies."[72] In 2005, the jurisdiction of the Court was broadened to include determination of cases of human rights violations "that occur in any member state."[73] Ever since, the CCJ has assumed a level of activity in the adjudication of human rights issues second to none in Africa that legal scholars have praised.[74]

ECOWAS's peacekeeping initiatives, designed to minimize the regional impacts of the crises in Liberia and Sierra Leone during the 1990s, led to human rights abuses by peacekeeping forces, such as looting, expropriation, theft, and sexual exploitation of women and children.[75] These violations highlighted the need in ECOWAS member-states, including Nigeria, for conflict resolution procedures, and the necessity for human rights as a guarantor of regional security.[76] Human rights non-governmental organizations (NGOs) were a major factor in the securement of approval in 2005 to broaden the CCJ's jurisdiction to include human rights within the ECOWAS region; the advocacy of these NGOs led to the broadened role for the Court.[77] Part of the argument of the NGOs in supporting an enlarged role for the CCJ in human rights was that the Court's work is precisely necessary in a sub-region like West Africa "where the judiciary is an arm of the executive."[78]

What sets this Court apart from other sub-regional judicial tribunals, such as the East African Court of Justice, the Tribunal of the South African Development Community, and the continent-based African Court of Human and Peoples' Rights, are its three distinctive features of direct access for private parties, an unrestricted human rights jurisdiction, and no requirement for a litigant to first exhaust domestic remedies.[79] Nigerian Fourth Republic leaders helped to instigate the grant of increased authority for the Court[80] and they have shown no indication so far that they disapprove its active human rights jurisprudence.[81] Nigerian leaders probably calculated that it was in the country's national interest to support a permanent court (rather than an *ad hoc* tribunal) that adjudicates the trade and related disputes of economic integration, while simultaneously dealing with human rights issues within national borders with potential to militate against regional security, if left unaddressed.[82] As indicated elsewhere, the activism of the CCJ in human rights since 2005 is a positive story for judicial independence in Nigeria.[83] "A sub-regional outfit yet located right inside Nigeria, the Community Court of Justice provides an alternative adjudicative point for litigants, especially on human rights issues, while putting pressure on Nigerian domestic courts in a manner that represents a boon to judicial independence."[84]

ECOWAS AND THE APPLICATION OF HUMAN RIGHTS IN NIGERIA'S EXTERNAL RELATIONS

ECOWAS serves two major roles regarding the application of human rights in Nigeria's external relations: as a tool and as a context. Beginning with the *tool* role, properly utilized, ECOWAS could be a vehicle for burden sharing that lifts some of the financial weight in peacekeeping operations off Nigeria at a time of declining government revenue from oil for its still undiversified economy. This was the point that then U.S. president William J. Clinton made in his address in August of 2000 to a joint session of the Nigerian National Assembly. After praising Nigeria and its leaders for "building the record of a moral superpower,"[85] Clinton told Nigerian lawmakers "I know that many of you have often felt the burden of your peacekeeping was heavier than the benefit. I know you have felt that."[86] However, he said, "there's no one else in West Africa with the size, the standing, the strength of military forces to do it. If you don't do it, who will do it?"[87] He then added, soothingly and most instructively, for our purpose here: "But you should not have to do it alone. . . . [D]espite your size, you cannot lead alone, and you shouldn't have to pay the enormous price."[88] The challenge for Nigerian leaders is how to achieve the proper utilization that will make ECOWAS an efficient tool of burden sharing in peacekeeping. Given the scale of Nigeria's problem with corruption, some of the estimated $10 billion in peacekeeping that Clinton cited during his address[89] may have gone into the private pockets of corrupt Nigerian officials rather than invested in peacekeeping.

Therefore, such streamlining must deal with the corruption in peacekeeping while eliminating the human rights abuses associated with Nigerian peacekeeping missions, both with respect to operations conducted under ECOWAS as well as those undertaken outside it. In addition to the benefit embedded in peacekeeping that ECOWAS provides for Nigerian policy, the community equally offers itself as a context that Nigeria could use in the pursuit of a human rights foreign policy. As described elsewhere,

> ECOWAS holds great potential as an efficient tool for human rights–based foreign policy—not just for Nigeria, but also for the other members of the organization. In the pursuit of its foreign policy, Nigeria has shown a decided preference for multilateral forms (as opposed to bilateral dealings), consistent with its status as a developing nation. A revamped ECOWAS helps the country maintain that preference with the added benefit as an organization within its zone of influence that Nigeria leads—compared to broader forums, such as African regional and U[nited] N[ations] global institutions.[90]

This second role comes with a downside, however; namely, the excessive weight of multilateral activities vis-à-vis bilateralism in Nigeria's external relations commented upon in chapter 9 of this work. But as that chapter suggests, Nigeria can get around this problem by including more bilateral arrows in its foreign policy quiver.

SUMMATION

ECOWAS is a major factor in the formulation and execution of Nigerian foreign policy second only to, if not comparable, to peacekeeping—with which technique it is also coterminous in those instances where, via its military arm ECOMOG, the community provides the context for peacekeeping. What makes ECOWAS remarkable is that, compared to peacekeeping there at the moment of Nigeria's independence in 1960, ECOWAS evolved as an instrument of Nigerian foreign policy only beginning in 1975 in the aftermath of the "trauma" of the country's civil war in 1970.[91]

While the promises of economic benefits envisaged by its founders have yet to materialize, ECOWAS's non-economic payoffs have been enormous, if not spectacular. Created to resolve disputes over the rules of economic integration,[92] the organization's Community of Justice soon turned itself into a scene of activity in human rights adjudication, to the benefit of judicial independence and the rule of law in Nigeria. Additionally, as the preceding section explains, the organization serves important roles as both tool and context for Nigerian foreign policy that Nigeria could work to improve, keeping in mind the drawback for bilateral relations, with negative ramifications for human rights foreign policy, that excessive dependence on multilateral activities spells for the country's external relations. The next two chapters tie together the themes of the work. The last of the two, chapter 12, is devoted to rebutting possible objections to the argument in this study for a human-rights-based foreign policy for Nigeria.

NOTES

1. West Africa encompasses 19 of the 54 countries in Africa: Benin, Burkina Faso,Cameroon, Cape Verde, Chad, Côte d'Ivoire, Equatorial Guinea, Ghana, Guinea, Guinea-Bissau, Liberia, Mali, Mauritania, Niger, Nigeria, São Tomé and Principe, Senegal, Sierra Leone, and Togo. The sub-region has a landmass of 7,924,592 sq. km and a population estimated at 375,477,000 as of 2014. See T.C. McCaskie, "Western Africa," *Encyclopedia Britannica*, http://www.britannica.com/place/western-Africa.

2. Paralleling the colonial heritages of the member-states, the official languages of ECOWAS are English, French, and Portuguese. See Revised Treaty of the Economic Community of West African States (ECOWAS) (Jul. 24, 1993), Art. 87, http://www.refworld.org/docid/492182d92.html [hereinafter referred to as ECOWAS Revised Treaty]. Compare Art. (1) (stipulating that "official languages of the Community shall be all West African languages so designated" alongside English, French, and Portuguese) with Art. 87(2) (stipulating that the working languages of the Community shall be English, French[,] and Portuguese.").

3. See Treaty of the Economic Community of West African States (ECOWAS) (May 28, 1975) (preamble) [hereinafter referred to as ECOWAS 1975 Treaty].

4. See Economic Community of West African States (ECOWAS), http://www.ecowas.int/.

5. See José Luís Rocha, "Cape Verde and ECOWAS: The Challenge of Regional Integration," *Portuguese Journal of Int'l Affairs* (Autumn/Winter, 2010): 1.

6. See David Oladipupo Kuranga, *The Power of Interdependence: Lessons from Africa* (New York: Palgrave Macmillan, 2012): 112 (commenting on some of the disagreements leading to Mauritania's withdrawal of its membership). Mauritania concentrated its economic integration energies after it left on the Arab Maghreb Union (UMA), note 16, of which it was a founding member.

7. Charles D. Jebuni et al., "A Case-Study of the Economic Community of West African States (ECOWAS)," *in* Ademola Oyejide et al., eds., *Regional Integration and Trade Liberalization in SubSaharan Africa: Regional Case-Studies, Vol. 3* (London: Macmillan Press Ltd., 1999): 24. The protocols, not relevant to the discussion here, are enumerated along with 24 others, in an appendix to the Jebuni et al. article. See ibid., pp. 56–9 (Table 2A.1, Summary of the Protocols Annexed to the ECOWAS Treaty).

8. Debuni et al., note 7, p. 24.

9. Ibid.

10. Ibrahim A. Gambari, *Theory and Reality in Foreign Policy Making: Nigeria after the Second Republic* (Atlantic Highlands, N.J.: Humanities Press Int'l, Inc., 1980): 62. Additionally, as Professor Gambari pointed out, citing Ghana and Nigeria at various points as examples, "during [economic] downturns, ECOWAS members tended to adopt restrictive national policies, which frustrated movement and retarded the momentum toward integration in" ECOWAS. Ibid., p. 63.

11. See ECOWAS 1975 Treaty, note 3, Art. 13. See also ibid., Art. 27 (providing for gradual removal of obstacles to free movement of people and goods).

12. Jebuni et al., note 7, p. 29. The overall goal, as ECOWAS literature subsequently put it, was the creation of "a borderless, peaceful, prosperous[,] and cohesive region, built on good governance." See "Vision 2020," ECOWAS, www.ecowas.int/about_ecowas/vision-2020/; ECOWAS Vision 2020: Toward a Democratic and Prosperous Community (Jun. 2010), www.ecowas.int/wp-content/uploads/2015/01/ECOWAS-VISION-2020.

13. ECOWAS 1975 Treaty, note 3 (preamble).

14. "Basic Information," ECOWAS, www.ecowas.int/about-ecowas/basic-information/. See also Jerry Ukaigwe, *ECOWAS Law* (Springer, 2016): 3.

15. ECOWAS 1975 Treaty, note 3, Art. 2(a)-(j).

16. The AU is the association of independent states in Africa that, in 2000, replaced the Organization of African Unity (OAU) established in May of 1963. See Constitutive Act of the African Union, OAU Doc. CAB/LEG/23.15 (Jul. 11, 2000), http://www.africa-union.org; Rachael L. Swarns, "African Leaders Drop Old Group for One That Has Power," *N.Y. Times* (Jul. 9, 2002), http://www.nytimes.com/2002/07/09/international/africa/09AFR.html. The other seven communities recognized by the AU are the Arab Maghreb Union (UMA), Common Market for Eastern and Southern Africa (COMESA), Community of Sahel-Saharan States (CEN-SAD), East African Community (EAC), Economic Community of Central African States (ECCAS), the Intergovernmental Authority on Development (IGAD), and the Southern African Development Community (SADC). UMA is French for L'Union du Maghreb arabe. Formed in Feb. of 1989, the organization comprises five member-states: Algeria, Libya, Mauritania, Morocco, and Tunisia. See UMA, http://www.maghrebarabe.org/en/. COMESA was formed in Dec. of 1994 and has 20 member-states: Burundi, Comoros, Democratic Republic of the Congo, Djibouti, Egypt, Eritrea, Ethiopia, Kenya, Libya, Madagascar, Malawi, Mauritius, Rwanda, Seychelles, South Sudan, Sudan, Swaziland, Uganda, Zambia, and Zimbabwe. See Common Market for Eastern and South Africa, http://www.comesa.int/. CEN-SAD is French for Communauté des Etats Sahélo-Sahariens. The organization was formed in Feb. of 1993 and has 28 member-states: Benin, Burkina Faso, Central African Republic, Chad, Comoros, Côte d'Ivoire, Djibouti, Egypt, Equatorial Guinea, Eritrea, Gambia, Ghana, Guinea, Guinea-Bissau, Kenya, Libya, Liberia, Mali, Morocco, Niger, Nigeria, São Tomé and Principe, Senegal, Sierra Leone, Somalia, Sudan, Togo, and Tunisia. See "CEN-SAD Celebrates 13th Anniversary," *PanaPress*, http://www.panapress.com/CEN-SAD-celebrates-13th-anniversary---12-756752-29-lang2-index.html. The EAC was originally founded in 1967, collapsed in 1977, and was revived in July of 2000. The organization comprises five states: Burundi, Kenya, Rwanda, Tanzania, and Uganda. See East African Community: One People, One Destiny, http://www.eac.int/. The ECCAS was founded in Oct. of 1983 and comprised 10 member-states: Angola, Burundi, Cameroon, Central African Republic, Chad, Democratic Republic of the Congo, Equatorial Guinea, Gabon, Republic of the Congo, and São Tomé and Principe. See Economic Community of Central African States, http://www.ceeac-eccas.org/index.php/fr/. The IGAD was founded in Jan. of 1986 and has eight member-states: Djibouti, Eritrea, Ethiopia, Kenya, Somali, South Sudan, Sudan, and Uganda. See IGAD, http://www.igad.org/. The SADC was founded in April 1980 (as South African Development Coordinating Conference, SADCC) and comprises 15 member-states: Angola, Botswana, Democratic Republic of the Congo, Lesotho, Madagascar, Malawi, Mauritius, Mozambique, Namibia, Seychelles, South Africa, Swaziland, Tanzania, Zambia, and Zimbabwe. See Southern African Development Community: Toward a Common Future, http://www.sadc.int/.

17. "Basic Information," ECOWAS, note 14.

18. See "Profile: Economic Community of West African States (ECOWAS)," Institute for Security Studies, https://www.issafrica.org/AF/RegOrg/unity_to_union/ecowasprof.htm; "African Union (AU) and Regional Economic Communities (RECs)

in Africa," U.N. Econ. Commission for Africa, http://www.uneca.org/oria/pages/african-union-au-regional-economic-communities-recs-africa. In Feb. of 1998, these five "pillars" signed the Protocol on Relations between the AEC and Regional Economic Communities (RECs). "Profile: Economic Community of West African States (ECOWAS)," *op. cit.*

19. Femi Aribisala, "ECOWAS Imperative for Nigeria," *Nigeria Development & Finance Forum*, http://www.nigeriadevelopmentandfinanceforum.org/PolicyDialogue/Dialogue.aspx?Edition=63 (last visited Feb. 28, 2015).

20. In an address commemorating the 40th anniversary of ECOWAS, the political scientist and former Nigerian foreign minister Bolaji Akinyemi gave an artful interpretational spin on the failed attempt by these four countries to promote economic cooperation. His conclusion was that an existentialist security threat "drove that initiative but that threat was not sufficiently grave to bring the initiative to fruition." Akinyemi, address on May 25, 2015, *in* "ECOWAS at 40: The Driving Philosophy of Multinationalism," *Guardian* (Lagos) (Jun. 3, 2015 3:44 AM), http://www.ngrguardiannews.com/2015/06/ecowas-40-the-driving-philosophy-of-multinationalism/. The premise leading to that conclusion was: "The fact that the first West African coup d'état happened in Togo, a coup allegedly promoted by Ghana, which also was having a difficult relationship with Côte d'Ivoire, might have spurred Liberia to reach out to Sierra Leone, Côte d'Ivoire, Guinea for a security alliance. Liberia and Sierra Leone were and still are small states which were never nervous of a supposedly expansionist Ghana. Guinea was having a nervous relationship with France." Ibid.

21. "Profile: Economic Community of West African States (ECOWAS)," note 18; "History," ECOWAS, www.ecowas.int/about-ecowas/history/. One event that may be included among the milestones leading up to ECOWAS in 1975 is a blueprint on future economic association the Biafran government released on Aug. 29, 1967. Upon their breakaway in May of 1967 as an independent country, the Biafrans (formerly Eastern Nigerians) released a Biafran Memorandum on Proposed Future Association with the rest of Nigeria. The text of the memorandum is *reprinted* in A.H.M. Kirk-Greene, *Crisis and Conflict in Nigeria: A Documentary Sourcebook 1966–1969, Vol. 2* (London: Oxford University Press, 1971): 163–65.

22. ECOWAS 1975 Treaty, note 3 (preamble).

23. Jebuni, note 7, p. 24; see also Akinyemi's statement in his address referred to in note 20 where, among other things, he depicted ECOWAS as "a product of those institutions that started as far back as 1900 when the first pan-African congress was held, through the West African Students Union founded in 1925, through the West African National Congress formed in 1946 and through the Organization of African Unity established in 1963"; as a "consciousness that grew in a putative form on those trans-Atlantic slave ships, through its pan African stage, now to a West African stage."

24. Jebuni, note 7, p. 24.

25. Ibrahim A. Gambari, *Political and Comparative Dimensions of Regional Integration: The Case of ECOWAS* (Atlantic Highlands, N.J.: Humanities Press International, 1991): 19.

26. Ibid.

27. Robert D. McFadden, "Odumegwu Ojukwu, Breakaway Biafra Leader, Dies at 78," *N.Y. Times* (Nov. 26, 2011), http://www.nytimes.com/2011/11/27/world/africa/odumegwu-ojukwu-leader-of-breakaway-republic-of-biafra-dies-at-78.html?_r=0; see also Akinyemi's address, note 20 (calling Ojukwu's "taking up residence in exile in Côte d'Ivoire" "a leftover issue from the civil war" that was a factor in the creation of ECOWAS).

28. See Gambari, note 25, p. 19.

29. Ibid., pp. 18–19.

30. ECOWAS 1975 Treaty, note 3.

31. See notes 8–10 and corresponding text. As one news magazine pointed out, the treaty of 1975 was little more than "a detailed declaration of interest," forming the basis for more work, rather than "a record of negotiated agreement." Gambari, note 25, p. 30, quoting *West Africa* (May 19, 1995): 558.

32. See note 16.

33. See Allechi M'Bet, *The CEAO and UEMOA within ECOWAS: The Road Ahead towards West African Economic Integration, in* Ademola Oyejide et al. eds., *Regional Integration and Trade Liberalization in SubSaharan Africa: Synthesis and Review, Vol. 4* (London: Macmillan Press Ltd., 1999): 66–85.

34. Ibid., pp. 66–67.

35. "About Us," Mano River Union, http://manoriverunion.int/About_Us.html.

36. ECOWAS Revised Treaty, note 2. Some of these intervening events include the coming into force of the African human rights instrument, the African Charter on Human and Peoples' Rights in 1986, and the formation in 1991 of the African Economic Community. Ibid. (preamble). Under the revised scheme of things, the organization "shall ultimately be the sole economic community in the region for the purpose of economic integration and the realization of the objectives of the African Economic Community." Ibid., Art. 2.

37. ECOWAS Revised Treaty, note 2.

38. Ibid. (preamble).

39. During the period of the Cold War until about 1991, the Organization of African Unity (OAU) tolerated human rights atrocities under the guise of doctrines such as respect for the territorial integrity of African states and non-interference in the domestic affairs of other countries. Philip C. Aka, "Human Rights as Conflict Resolution in Africa in the New Century," *Tulsa Journal of Comparative & Int'l Law*, Vol. 11 (Fall 2003): 187–90 (commenting on human rights in Africa up to the end of the Cold War); Rhoda E. Howard, *Human Rights in Commonwealth Africa* (Lanham, MD: Rowman & Littlefield, 1986): 5 (observing that during this period, "[t]he rights of black Africans inside the borders of independent African states appear[ed] to be of little real concern to the OAU.").

40. ECOWAS Revised Treaty, note 2, Art. 4.

41. "Profile: Economic Community of West African States (ECOWAS)," note 18.

42. ECOWAS Revised Treaty, note 2, Art. 7(1) (creating the AHSG as "the supreme institution of the Community.").

43. Ibid., Art. 7(2).

44. Ibid.

45. Ibid., Art. 8(1). The Authority could meet in extraordinary session if the Chairman convenes that session or a member-state requests it, provided the request is supported by a simple majority of the member-states. Ibid.

46. Ibid., Art. 8(2).

47. Ibid., Art. 10(1) (establishing the Council).

48. Ibid., Art. 10(3) (a)–(i).

49. Ibid., Art. 10(2).

50. Ibid., Art. 11(1). The Council is also authorized to meet in extraordinary session convened by the Chairman of the Council at the request of a member-state, supported by a simple majority of the council. Ibid.

51. Ibid., Art. 11(2).

52. Ibid., Art. 17(1) (establishing the Secretariat of the organization).

53. Ibid., Art. 17(2).

54. See ibid., Art. 19(1)(2)(3)(a)–(i).

55. Ibid., Art. 18(1).

56. Ibid., Art. 17(2) (providing that the Executive Secretary shall be "assisted by Deputy Executive Secretaries and such other staff as may be required for the smooth functioning of the Community.").

57. "Profile: Economic Community of West African States (ECOWAS)," note 18. The four such areas now are political affairs, defense, and security; integration (involving agriculture and environment, trade and industry, human development, and the Community Computer Center); policies harmonization (involving economic policy and trade as well as customs policy); and administration and finance. Ibid.

58. See "Basic Information," ECOWAS, note 14.

59. See ECOWAS Revised Treaty, note 2, Art. 13(1) (creating the parliament).

60. See "Profile: Ecomog," *BBC News* (Jun. 17, 2004, 15:15 GMT 16:15 UK), http://news.bbc.co.uk/2/hi/africa/country_profiles/2364029.stm; "ECOMOG: Peacekeeping or Participant?" *BBC News* (Feb. 11, 1998, 18:00 GMT), news.bbc.co.uk/2/hi/Africa/55719.stm.

61. The 1975 treaty enumerates four such committees: trade, customs, immigration, monetary, and payments commission; industry, agriculture, and natural resources commission; transport, telecommunications, and energy commission; and social and cultural affairs commission. See ECOWAS 1975 Treaty, note 3, Art. 4.1(a)-(e).

62. See "Economic Community of West African States (ECOWAS)," *ECOWAS in Brief*, http://www.comm.ecowas.int/sec/index.php?id=about_a&; Terry M. May, *Historical Dictionary of International Organizations and the Middle East* (Lanham, MD: Rowman& Littlefield, 2015): 165.

63. See note 40.

64. See ECOWAS Revised Treaty, note 2, Art. 15(1) (establishing the Court).

65. "About Us," Community Court of Justice—ECOWAS, http://www.courtecowas.org/site2012/index.php?option=com_content&view=article&id=2&Itemid=5.

66. "About Us," Community Court of Justice—ECOWAS, note 65.

67. Ibid. A *contentious* jurisdiction is the authority to decide a case that is limited to matters in controversy between the parties. It is the flipside to advisory opinion explained in the next footnote.

68. "About Us," Community Court of Justice—ECOWAS, note 65. An advisory jurisdiction is one regarding an opinion "rendered by a court at the request of the government or an interested party indicating how the court would rule on a matter should adversary litigation develop." *Black's Law Dictionary, 6th Ed.* (Eagan, MN: West Publishing, 1991): 35 (defining *advisory opinion*). Stated differently, vis-à-vis a contentious jurisdiction, note 67, an advisory opinion is "an interpretation of the law without binding effect." Ibid.

69. ECOWAS Revised Treaty, note 2, Art. 16 (1).

70. "About Us," Community Court of Justice—ECOWAS, note 65.

71. Ibid.

72. ECOWAS Revised Treaty, note 2, Art. 15(4). Its decisions "are not subject to appeal," but parties can apply for revision of a judgment by the Court. "About Us," Community Court of Justice—ECOWAS, note 63.

73. Karen J. Alter et al., "A New International Human Rights Court for West Africa: The ECOWAS Community Court of Justice," *American Journal of Int'l Law*, 107 (2013): 737–79.

74. Ibid.

75. Ibid., p. 772.

76. Ibid.

77. See ibid., pp. 750–53.

78. Ibid., p. 763.

79. Ibid., pp. 753–56.

80. Ibid., p. 747.

81. Ibid., pp. 758–61.

82. Ibid., pp. 772–73.

83. See Philip C. Aka, "Judicial Independence under Nigeria's Fourth Republic: Problems and Prospects," *California Western Int'l Law Journal*, Vol. 45 (Fall 2014): 37–45 (commenting on two factors of Nigerian politics with potential implications for judicial independence, "the invigoration of the ECOWAS Community Court of Justice" being the "potentially positive" force).

84. Ibid., p. 45.

85. William J. Clinton, "Remarks to a Joint Session of the Nigerian National Assembly in Abuja, Aug. 26, 2000," *in Public Papers of the Presidents of the United States: William J. Clinton, 2000–2001* (Washington, D.C.: Best Books, 2000): 1710.

86. Ibid., p. 1710.

87. Ibid.

88. Ibid.

89. Ibid., p. 1705 (observing that "[o]ver the past decade, with all its problems, Nigeria has spent $10 billion and sacrificed hundreds of its soldiers' lives for peace in West Africa.").

90. Philip C. Aka, "Human Rights in Nigeria's External Relations: Exigency, Methods, and Rebuttable Objections," *Buffalo Human Rights Law Review*, Vol. 21 (2014–2015): 22.

91. General Ibrahim B. Babangida, Nigeria's military dictator from 1985 to 1993, once assessed the civil war as "the most painful national trauma . . . whose

emotional scars will continue to haunt us for years to come." Alison Sussman, "Babangida, Ibrahim 1941–," *Encyclopedia.com*, http://www.encyclopedia.com/doc/1G2-2870600010.html.

92. One of those seemingly economic disputes with strong bearing in human rights was the "tit for tat" involving the expulsion of supposedly illegal aliens from member states that Nigeria conducted during a period of economic difficulties under its Second Republic from 1979 to 1983, in seeming retaliation of Ghana's own expulsion of Nigerian workers earlier on. See Jean-Marie Henckaerts, *Mass Expulsion in Modern International Law and Practice* (Leiden, Netherlands: Martinus Nijhoff Publishers, 1995): 66–71 (study of the problems of mass expulsion of aliens, migrant workers, and stateless persons in international law, including several case studies, one of them Nigeria's mass expulsion of migrant workers). Ironically, this was the type of arbitrary expulsion that Art. 27 of ECOWAS's 1975 treaty (providing for elimination of obstacles militating against the free movement of people and goods), was designed to prevent.

Part III

CONCLUSIONS

Chapter Eleven

Enacting Serious Reforms at Home and Abroad

CONSOLIDATING DEMOCRACY AT HOME BY DOING GOOD ABROAD

The rank of global Good Samaritans who apply human rights consistently in their foreign affairs is wide open.[1] These states produce important international human rights goods,[2] as well as "build global governance[,]" ultimately "reshap[ing] the meaning of sovereignty" in a manner that includes human rights as a norm of legitimacy.[3] Nigeria can join the rank of these global Good Samaritans and contribute to the international human rights regime. But, although important, that is not the main import of this work. Application of human rights in external relations is also important because of what it does for Nigeria in its own right at home. This study is an account on human rights in Nigerian foreign policies that necessarily includes a narrative of the domestic forces that drive those foreign policies.

Human rights abroad can bolster Nigeria's democracy at home the same way it has done for Costa Rica and Canada, especially Canada which, like Nigeria, has a federal system of government. In addition to contributing to the international human rights regime, Canada uses application of human rights in external relations in a targeted attempt to cement individual rights as the cornerstone of its federalism as well as to mitigate friction between the country's diverse social groups, including communities in French-speaking Quebec.[4] Under the Fourth Republic as before it, Nigeria is a state held down by its Lilliputian leaders.[5] The country needs to close the gap between the aspirations of its citizens and the performance of its leaders. As former President Clinton said during a state visit to Nigeria, at home and abroad, Nigeria must be a state "worthy of its people's dreams."[6] Human rights can build Nigeria;[7] embracement of international standards embedded in human rights is the key to attaining that mark. This researcher flirted with the term *political system* before settling for *democracy* in the title above. The choice of *democracy*, throughout this work denominated *civilian rule*, is deliberate because of the low content of non-military rule in the country. Still, vis-à-vis the institutionalized repression of military dictatorship, experiment in democratic rule is the foundation for any political and socioeconomic progress in the country. Given its unceasing history of instability, including numerous coups, countercoups, and a vicious civil war, Nigeria is a country noted for its dubious mastery of "the art of dancing on the precipice without falling over."[8] But such flirt with disaster is not sustainable. And should Nigeria disintegrate due to unrelieved human rights abuses, successor states to the parent state will still grapple with the same problem of human rights challenges without the benefit of a large republic that an incoherent Nigeria now affords, hence the significance of this work—even though the concept of a large republic can stand some qualification here.[9]

Nigeria needs a human rights policy with more breadth and depth to match its aspirations for a credible leadership role in Africa and the world. Nearly six decades since its independence in 1960, the tool that mainly drives Nigeria's external relations is an unreformed peacekeeping. This is inadequate for a country of gargantuan human and natural resource endowments that aspires for a leadership role in West Africa, Africa, and the globe. Although human rights policy is an integral component of general foreign policy, the application of human rights in foreign policy is a more demanding task that Nigeria needs to embrace. To be sure, applying human rights is not costless. Instead, it could bring discomforts, such as disruption in normal diplomatic relations, limited commercial opportunities, infliction of domestic economic hardship, alliance structures that may be strained, or retaliation by a target state.[10]

In brief, an enhanced and more systematic application of human rights in Nigeria's foreign relations will:

- remove the solecism of abuses at home, and a nominal commitment to international law abroad that currently marks its human rights policy,[11]
- bring increased harmonization to domestic and foreign policies, and
- inject a more credible accent to its foreign policy initiatives and aspirations for a leadership role in Africa and beyond that will turn it into a giant with real, rather than clay, feet.[12]

When was the last time that a Nigerian leader used the language of human rights in formulating domestic or foreign policy?[13] Nigerian governments at all levels, civil society (non-governmental sector), and the general public must get into the habit of using human rights in their debates on domestic and international issues.[14] Nigeria needs to embrace the type of serious reforms at home and abroad that only the international human rights approach makes possible. Nigeria is a microcosm of Africa and mirrors some of the problems the region faces.[15] For this reason, talk about any "renaissance" in the continent in this century will remain just talk until the country implements serious domestic and foreign reforms.[16]

The foreign affairs analyst Fareed Zakaria took a position several years ago in the debate regarding the seeming decline of U.S. global power.[17] Zakaria decried the "kind of unreflective ancestor worship" that appears to have taken hold of the American mind.[18] Those who wrote the United States' Constitution, he said, were individuals who "constantly adapt[ed] their views"; they were versed in the favorite American pastime of "contemplating decay" and thinking "a great deal about decline" when things are still going well.[19] In a nutshell, the framers of the U.S. Constitution were individuals who advised "bold, persistent experimentation," always aware that America "was a work in progress, an unfinished enterprise that would constantly be in need of change, adjustment, and repair."[20] To thrive as a state in the twenty-first century, Nigeria needs to enact reforms in several areas of its national life all the way to external relations with the same spirit of bold and persistent experimentation.

REVISITING THE FOUR RESEARCH QUESTIONS THAT FRAMED THIS STUDY

Influence of Human Rights in External Relations

The first of the four question, drawing insight from the work of Professor Brysk,[21] is, *precisely* what influence do human rights have in Nigeria's external relations? Stated differently, *how far* does the country have to go to join the club of global Good Samaritans who consistently apply human rights in their external affairs? Human rights has an influence in Nigeria's external affairs. But it is an inchoate influence with no force at home to ground and sustain it. Instead, for example, Nigeria keeps peace abroad that it does not have at home. This condition of beautiful abroad but ugly at home creates an unsatisfactory spottiness of "now you see it, now you don't,"[22] begging for resolution if the country is to assume its proper role in Africa and the larger world.

Exigency for Increased Infusion of Human Rights in Nigeria's External Relations

The question here, as stated in chapter 1, was: What factors at this time make increased application of human rights in external affairs exigent for Nigeria?

These reasons were recounted in chapter 1 but could bear recapitulation here. For one thing, broadly speaking, Nigeria is a state invented by human rights. To whom much is given, much is expected. Secondly, Nigeria can punch more within its weight, rather than below it, by contributing more through its word and action, especially the latter, to international human rights. Thirdly, for Nigeria, application of human rights in external affairs may be the only practical opportunity to contribute to the international human rights regime. Fourthly, injecting more human rights into Nigeria's external relations could harmonize the country's domestic and foreign policies, to the benefit of democracy at home. It is about time Nigeria quit stretching its luck of dancing on the precipice without falling over. Fifthly, relating to the last factor, infusing more human rights into Nigeria's foreign relations will help to build a culture of the rule of law, necessary to consolidate democracy in the land. Finally, Nigeria has the infrastructure to conduct a human rights–based foreign policy, if it rationalizes its resources well.

Methods That Can Be Used to Facilitate the Application of More Human Rights in Nigeria's External Relations

The question here, as stated in chapter 1, was: What possible *methods* can Nigeria use to facilitate the application of more human rights in its external relations? This work unearthed and discussed various methods, based on Nigeria's strength and activities related to the field, encapsulated in a temple of two steps and four pillars comprising: reconstructed national interest, increased human rights at home, a redesigned peacekeeping, reshaped foreign policy machine, increased bilateralism in foreign relations, and the handy use of the Economic Community of West African States (ECOWAS) as a human rights tool. Because each contributes to the overall integrity of the temple, as a category neither the steps nor pillars are superior or inferior to the other. In the discussion on increased human rights at home, this researcher stressed the necessity to synchronize, rather than implement, the seven measures sequentially. The advice applies similarly with the steps and pillars that make up the temple. Although all of the steps require attention, two are particularly critical. These are increased human rights at home and the need for more symmetry between multilateral and bilateral elements in Nigeria's foreign policy.

Possible Objections to the Argument of This Work and Their Rebuttals

The question here, as framed in chapter 1, was: What are the possible objections that could be raised to the case for more human rights in external relations this study makes, and what are the conceivable rebuttals to those objections? More discussion on this prong is saved for chapter 12 dealing with the topic.

REVISITING THE THEORETICAL CONTRIBUTIONS OF THIS STUDY

Broadly speaking, this work contributes to the campaign to treat human rights as genuine national interest, rather than a sporadic appendage to general foreign policy,[23] using Nigeria as window into the world. More narrowly, it ties Nigeria, a key state in Africa, into the literature on human rights in comparative foreign policy.[24] Consistent with the comparative accent, the methodology of choice was within-case comparison (WCC) involving the study of Nigeria at different points in time and space, in some cases, when the occasion called for it, beyond the period from 1960 to the present that forms the timeline of this book. There were times too when the WCC was combined with the most-similar-systems (MSS) design, involving a comparison of some aspects of the Nigerian system to the United States', whose presidential system of government the country used to replace the parliamentary system that it inherited from the United Kingdom. The comparison reached its highest and most obvious point in chapter 8 on reshaping Nigeria's foreign policy machinery. Mixing the two techniques in analyzing Nigeria guards against possible errors of interpretation and provides "a set of comparisons against additional cases or evidence," in the best tradition of comparative checking.[25]

Next to theory, the framework singled out for this study was constructivism. Compared to the rival theories juxtaposed with it in chapter 3, the approach boasts "a wider remit of how interests are defined,"[26] including allowances that anarchy (the lack of a world government) is what states make of it, foreign policy is what states make of it, and the national interest may be what the state and its citizens are interested in, not always state security. Because, compared to its rivals, constructivism perceives the contexts in which states interact in external relations to range from cooperative to competitive, in a manner that permit them to respond in many different ways, the approach affords the most scope for application of human rights in external relations. Little wonder that a growing number of works dealing with the application of human rights in external affairs, some of which studies received extensive treatment in chapter 3, utilize this framework. This study on Nigeria now importantly joins this list of studies.

In his work on Canada, among the studies surveyed in chapter 3, Andrew Lui maintained that "constructivism has difficulty explaining the rhetoric-reality gap in Canadian human rights politics," elaborating that, while the theory "offers a useful explanation of the underlying motivations behind human rights pursuits, it falls short of addressing the inherent trade-offs and competing priorities of statecraft."[27] This researcher is unable to corroborate such finding with respect to Nigeria. For one thing, there is insufficient evidence. Unlike their counterparts in Canada and elsewhere, Nigerian leaders hardly use the language of human rights in their formulation and execution of domestic and foreign policies. More than realism or idealism, Nigerian foreign policy behavior faulted by many of its citizens as "doing too much in the African continent without corresponding positive outcome"[28] fits with constructivism. Still, given the trailblazing character of this work, firm conclusions on the extent to which constructivism helps us understand Nigeria's foreign policy behaviors are premature at this point and must await future studies. Social science research views the world as it *is*, but also as it *should* be in instances when agreed-upon criteria exist among social scientists for the ideals of what should be. This research combines the best of what is and what should be, *describing* the application of human rights in Nigerian foreign policy the way it is now while *prescriptively* incorporating suggestions on the way forward.

NOTES

1. See Alison Brysk, *Global Good Samaritans: Human Rights as Foreign Policy* (New York: Oxford University Press, 2009), *passim*.

2. As Professor Brysk explains, the influence of these states "can be critical for framing and ratifying treaties, creating and staffing multilateral institutions, monitoring and sanctioning offenders, assisting victims, directing resources, implementing peace processes, catalyzing transnational initiatives or emerging issues, and introducing new understandings of rights to the global agenda." Ibid., p. 3.

3. Ibid., p. 4.

4. See Andrew Lui, *Why Canada Cares: Human Rights and Foreign Policy in Theory and Practice* (Montreal, Canada: McGill-Queen's University Press, 2012): 7, 32.

5. See Adekeye Adebajo & Abdul Raufu Mustapha, eds., *Gulliver's Troubles: Nigeria's Foreign Policy after the Cold War* (Scottsville, South Africa: University of KwaZulu-Natal Press, 2008): 2 (lamenting the disconnect between the country's high-minded aspirations for a leadership role abroad juxtaposed with the petty ambitions, kleptomania, and small-mindedness of some Fourth Republic leaders).

6. William J. Clinton, "Remarks Following Discussions with President Olusegun Obasanjo of Nigeria and an Exchange with Reporters in Abuja, Nigeria, Aug. 26, 2000," *in Public Papers of the Presidents of the United States: William J. Clinton, 2000–2001* (Washington, D.C.: Best Books, 2000): 1701.

7. See Fran Quigley, *How Human Rights Can Build Haiti: Activists, Lawyers, and the Grassroots Campaign* (Nashville, TN: Vanderbilt University Press, 2014), *passim* (focusing on Haiti).

8. John Campbell, *Nigeria: Dancing on the Brink* (Lanham, MD: Rowman & Littlefield Publishers, 2013): xxiv.

9. For Nigeria, this notion of a "large republic" can be easily overstretched. This is because, as the U.S. senator Eugene McCarthy (1916–2005) indicated in 1969, urging the intervention of the U.S. government in the Nigerian civil war on the side of breakaway Biafra, Nigeria is populous enough to allow for more than one viable state. See his May 16, 1969, speech, *reprinted* in A.H.M. Kirk-Greene, *Crisis and Conflict in Nigeria: A Documentary Sourcebook 1966–1969, Vol. 2* (London: Oxford University Press, 1971): 401–3. McCarthy believed that Nigeria has resource advantages that make it "viable without the eastern region." Ibid., p. 404. For the seceding eastern region, he said, "[e]ven without some minority tribes, Biafra would be a populous country by African standards, larger than three-fourths of the African countries. Only [ten] of some [forty] African countries would be larger." Ibid. Given the large population of each of the three major ethnic groups, numbering into the tens of millions, the statement is no less true today than it was 47 years ago.

10. David Gillies, *Between Principle and Practice: Human Rights in North-South Relations* (Montreal, Canada: McGill-Queen's University Press, 1996): 50.

11. Philip C. Aka, "Human Rights in Nigeria's External Relations: Exigency, Methods, and Rebuttable Objections," *Buffalo Human Rights Law Review, Vol. 21* (2014–2015): 25; S.O. Akinboye, "Beautiful Abroad but Ugly at Home: Issues and Contra[di]ctions in Nigerian Foreign Policy," University of Lagos Inaugural Lecture Series, 2013, www.unilag.edu.ng/opendocnew.php? (pooh-poohing Nigeria's tendency to "exhibit acts of benevolence abroad" while spotting a domestic environment "marked by ugliness[,] including a sheer lack of direction on how to achieve development"); and Douglas C. Lovelace, Jr., "Foreword," *in* Clarence J. Bouchat, *The Causes of Instability in Nigeria and Implications for the United States* (Carlisle, PA: Strategic Studies Institute & U.S. Army War College, Aug. 2013): iii (characterizing Nigeria's portraiture as "international influence and domestic paralysis").

12. See, e.g., Eghosa E. Osaghae, *Crippled Giant: Nigeria since Independence* (Bloomington, IN: Indiana University Press, 1998), *passim* (commenting on structural impediments predating the country's independence that turned it into a "crippled giant.").

13. The insight that inspires this question is South Africa where, under Nelson Mandela, an exchange ensued regarding application of human rights in the country's foreign policy. See Tiyanjana Maluwa, "Human Rights and Foreign Policy in Post-Apartheid South Africa," *in* David P. Forsythe, ed., *Human Rights and Comparative Foreign Policy* (New York: United Nations University Press, 2000): 250–75.

14. Chidi A. Odinkalu, "Why More Africans Don't Use Human Rights Language," *Human Rights Dialog*, Vol. 2 (Dec. 1999), www.carnegiecouncil.org/publications/archive/dialogue/2_01/articles/602.html.

15. See Oladimeji Aborisade & Robert J. Mundt, *Politics in Nigeria, 2d Ed.* (New York: Longman, 2002): xi–xii (stating that "[n]either Nigeria nor any other country can stand for all of Africa, for Africa is marked by great diversity. Still, if to know Nigeria is not necessarily to know Africa, it is a good place to begin, for there will

be little that is surprising in politics elsewhere on the continent to one who is well acquainted with the Nigerian experience.").

16. The notion of *renaissance* is one anchored in Africa's pan-Africanist past, back to the very beginning of the last century, that some African intellectuals, most prominently Thabo Mbeki, former South African president, have resurrected. In a speech, "I Am African," marking this recent movement, that he gave in Cape Town, South Africa, on May 8, 1996, Mbeki stated that to make the twenty-first century the century for Africa the continent must, first, "capture the intellectual space to define its future and therefore the imperative to develop its intellectual capital." *Quoted in* Lazarus Sauti, "Thabo Mbeki's Legacy to Africa," *Herald* (Zimbabwe) (Sept. 16, 2013), http://www.herald.co.zw/thabo-mbekis-legacy-to-africa/. Next, it must "rebuild and sustain [its] universities and other centers of learning, attract back to Africa the intelligentsia that has migrated to the developed North, build strong links with the intelligentsia in the African Diaspora and give" these individuals "the time and space they need to help" shape the future of Africa. Ibid.

17. See Fareed Zakaria, "Are America's Best Days Behind Us?" *Time* (Mar. 3, 2011), http://content.time.com/time/magazine/article/0,9171,2056723,00.html (last visited Mar. 14, 2016).

18. Ibid.

19. Ibid. Zakaria posited, not inaccurately, that it is this state of mind that stimulated the type of innovative reforms that had kept the United States globally competitive. Ibid.

20. Ibid.

21. See Brysk, note 1, *passim*.

22. Robert Charles Smith, *Racism in the Post-Civil Rights Era: Now You See It, Now You Don't* (New York: SUNY Press, 1995), *passim* (commenting on racism in the United States in the post–civil rights era).

23. Jack Donnelly, *International Human Rights, 4th Ed.* (Boulder, CO: Westview Press, 2013): 139–47.

24. See David P. Forsythe, "Introduction," *in* David P. Forsythe, ed., *Human Rights and Comparative Foreign Policy* (New York: United Nations University Press, 2000): 17 (stating that "[w]ith an unlimited budget and a multi-volume project, we could have added numerous states that merit study: France, Norway, Germany, *Nigeria*, Kenya, Mexico, Brazil, Pakistan, Israel, the Philippines, etc.") (emphasis added).

25. J. Tyler Dickovick & Jonathan Eastwood, *Comparative Politics: Integrating Theories, Methods, and Cases* (New York: Oxford University Press, 2013): 17–19, 609 (glossary).

26. Lui, note 4, p. 116.

27. Ibid., p. 163. Based on the observation, Lui reached the conclusion that "a conceptual framework that centers on identities and international norms cannot explain those instances in which behavior differs markedly from the underlying narrative." Ibid.

28. Hadi Y. Al-Hassa, "Evaluating Nigerian Foreign Policy at 50," *Gamji.com* [no date included, but probably published in 2010], http://www.gamji.com/article/9000/news9139.htm.

Chapter Twelve

But So What?

Two Possible Objections to the Argument in This Work and Two Rebuttals to Those Objections

There are two main and interconnected objections to the argument for increased application of human rights in Nigeria's external affairs made in this study. These objections are that Nigeria needs to meet domestic needs first before it can worry about applying human rights abroad, and that the application of human rights in external affairs is an issue of an unclosed gap between words and action that even major states like the United States still have a problem with. However, as the ensuing discussion elaborates, each of these objections lacks merit and is unavailing.

OBJECTION POINTING TO UNMET DOMESTIC NEEDS

The first objection is "so what": isn't it premature to talk about human rights in foreign affairs for a country where, to use but one indicator, an estimated two-thirds of the population lives below the poverty line?[1] Put differently, wouldn't the elevated requirements of human rights[2] in foreign affairs amount to an overkill for fledgling legal and political communities like Nigeria, whose hands are already full, struggling to secure these super-rights at the domestic level—given that, as many ordinary Nigerians would say it in Pidgin English,[3] *person go drink tea first before him drink over-tea* (corruption of Ovaltin, a delicious cocoa brew). This objection tracks the concern in some part of the literature that a certain threshold of development and security necessary for state survival and welfare needs may have to be sufficiently satisfied to permit the pursuit of a human rights–oriented foreign policy.[4]

The answer is that Nigeria, a state born in international relations via British colonialism in Africa, has the capability to pull through a human rights foreign policy, if it reduces wastes and rationalizes its human and material resources better than it does now. Infusing more human rights into Nigeria's foreign affairs will facilitate the work of democracy at home—just as it does for countries like Costa Rica[5] and Canada[6]—while enriching, adding color, and providing a higher shooting target for Nigerian leaders and foreign policy officialdom in conducting foreign policy.[7] As indicated in chapter 6 on the need for increased human rights at home to drive foreign policy, what the many years of the Fourth Republic has demonstrated is that civilian rule does not automatically result in high-quality rule. Because a human rights foreign policy is arguably more onerous than one *not* anchored on those values, application of human rights in external relations adds more quality to governance at home and puts to rest the paradox of "ugly at home and beautiful abroad" that now passes for Nigerian human rights policy. Political communities who visit ill on "strangers" abroad will have no difficulty finding maleficent strangers at home.[8] In short, the demarcation between tea and over-tea is a false dichotomy for a Nigerian public which, under the Fourth Republic since 1999, has been treated to neither tea nor over-tea.

Moreover, stipulating universal threshold of development and security to be met before pursuit of a human rights foreign policy may impose preconditions that for some countries should productively be synchronized with the implementation of such policy. Studies on the behaviors of states who consistently apply human rights in their foreign policies have shown that "good citizens are made, not born"[9] in the sense that "although some national values and experiences harmonize readily with human rights, foreign policy projection of those norms must be learned and mobilized."[10] Also, there is no requirement that the mobilization of those norms be perfect,[11] given that every state has its "blind spots and insufficiencies" in human rights.[12] Instead, principled foreign policy states need only to be "good-enough Good Samaritans,"[13] who, for example, "foster bridges between areas of strength and lagging sectors."[14]

There is no requirement that Nigeria punch above its weight in applying human rights in external affairs the way global Good Samaritans like Costa Rica have impressively done. However, given its human and material endowments, Nigeria punches below its weight. At the very least, at this point in its national history, Nigeria should be ranking among the regional "tigers" from the global South that Brysk indicated are aspiring to take their place in the conduct of human rights–based foreign policies.[15] For Nigeria, the requisite national value harmonizing with human rights that can form the basis for principled foreign policy learning would include its experience in peacekeeping and its habit of eschewing the use of force in disputes with neighbors. It could also include resources anchored on the rule of law, such as "persuasion by ideas, openness to civil society," and "dedicated diplomats," among others.[16]

The aspect of this objection regarding a certain threshold of development and security supposedly necessary to ground a human rights foreign policy brings up a power-status distinction (whether great, middle, or small) that is inapplicable here, even inappropriate, particularly with respect to Nigeria. This is because a country might be a great power and not apply human rights in its external affairs. An example here would be Japan that Brysk included in her case study. Japan applies human rights weakly in its external affairs.[17] And its records caution against the undue expectation that "as countries develop or democratize or Westernize[,] they will automatically reach out to help strangers and build global governance[.]"[18] In contrast, there are comparatively small powers—of which Costa Rica and South Africa come to mind—which more robustly apply human rights in their external affairs. Costa Rica does not even have an army,[19] the symbol of great-power status for many countries in our still realist-dominated international community.[20] Professor Donnelly delved into this matter in his book on international human rights, commenting on differences in human rights policies.[21] He took issue with the claim by the Norwegian writer and politician Jan Egeland to the effect that "small and big nations are differently disposed to undertaking coherent rights-oriented foreign policies."[22] Following thoughtful examination of the matter, Donnelly concluded:

> Differences between the United States and the like-minded countries are largely matters of choice. Norway and the Netherlands place a relatively high value on international human rights not because they are small and weak but because of how their citizens understand themselves, their place in the world, and the obligations associated with their identity.[23]

Similarly, power status has little relevance in whether or not Nigeria adopts a human rights–oriented foreign policy. In sum, the proposition regarding a threshold of development and security necessary for the implementation of a human rights foreign policy, assuming that threshold exists, creates sequences that should be usefully synchronized. It also mistakes capability to apply human rights in external relations with power status—when in actuality some materially poor states like Costa Rica maintain a respectable human rights foreign policy while supposedly rich ones like Japan lack or maintain that policy nominally.

Finally, applying human rights in external relations resonates with the indivisibility of these rights, one of the byproducts of the World Conference on Human Rights in Vienna in June 1993.[24] The declaration and program of action adopted at the end of that conference indicated that "[a]ll human rights are universal, indivisible and interdependent and interrelated."[25] While making room for variations between and within regions, the declaration stated that "it is the duty of States, regardless of their political, economic and cultural systems to promote and protect all human rights and fundamental freedoms."[26]

In the aftermath of the World Conference on Human Rights in Vienna in 1993, "all states, regardless of national history and mythology" have become "compelled to confront the international law and diplomacy of human rights."[27] These states include the likes of China which in 1993 opposed the concept of universal rights and viewed such rights as intervention into the domestic affairs of other nations.[28] Just as the spread of human rights forbids demarcation between political-civil rights and socioeconomic rights, today countries must infuse their relations with other countries with human rights, rather than limit themselves to enforcement of human rights domestically. Such extension of human rights into external relations, continuation of domestic policy by other means,[29] rhymes with the injunction of the Vienna declaration for the international community to "treat human rights globally in a fair and equal manner, on the same footing, and with the same emphasis."[30] For a time now the talk has been about how to move from inspiration to impact in realizing human rights.[31] Application of these rights in foreign policy is one practical way to effect that transition.

OBJECTION AS TO UNCLOSED GAP

Another possible objection to the argument in this book for a human rights–oriented foreign policy for Nigeria relates to the complaint about unclosed gap between domestic and foreign policies. The objector will argue that even democratic heavyweights like the United States have such gaps. There is some merit to that argument; no one can minimize the setback to international human rights posed by the abdication of United States' leadership in the field before the terrorist attacks of September 11, 2001,[32] that has lingered into the period of the Obama presidency even with the changed tone in American human rights policy since Barack Obama took office in 2009.[33] Conceivably, it is this occurrence that necessitated the scout for "global good Samaritans" to fill some of the gap in the United States' leadership.[34] But such comparison of Nigeria to the United States can be overstretched. The U.S. is a nation "in search of itself" in an ongoing attempt to realize its founding principles,[35] and a state that played an instrumental role in the evolution of the modern human rights movement,[36] drawing on a natural rights doctrine in its Declaration of Independence that goes back to the British philosopher John Locke.[37] These include the propositions that all humans are created equal and "endowed by their Creator with certain unalienable Rights," including "Life, Liberty and the Pursuit of Happiness" (i.e., property); and that "Governments are instituted among Men" and charged precisely with the obligation to secure, rather than destroy, these rights.[38] In contrast, for all its enormous potentials, Nigeria still has a long way to go in these efforts, a shortfall that necessitates academic and policy-oriented attention of the type this work fosters.

Nigeria perceives itself as "giant of Africa" and potential leader of the Black world. In the words of one foreign minister of the country, there is no black story, "unless it is a Nigerian *success* story."[39] This is a role that Nigerian leaders accepted in the first decade of the country's independence before oil displaced agriculture as mainstay of the country's economy. It is a role that Nigerian leaders in the Fourth Republic have not shown any indication to abandon even with blasting criticisms from the media and the public of the country's Africa-centered foreign policy as insufficiently driven by self-interest.[40] Adopting a human rights–based foreign policy will put more meaning into Nigeria's self-image as giant of Africa than it does now. The country boasts norms and experiences harmonizing with human rights that it now needs to mobilize in its external relations. On a final note regarding the "so what" question that drives this chapter, an objector may legitimately argue that Nigeria may be building the record of a moral superpower at the time when Clinton made this observation in 2000, but not so today into the second decade of its Fourth Republic. The rebuttal would be that maintaining democracy for this length of time, for a nation notorious for its instability given the context democracy provides for resolution of any problem, whether domestic or in foreign policy, is good progress. Given a choice between half empty or half full, the latter narrative is preferable.

NOTES

1. See, e.g., "Nigerians Living in Poverty Rise to Nearly 61%," *BBC News* (Feb. 13, 2012), http://www.bbc.com/news/world-africa-17015873.

2. *Human rights* and other key terms in this study are defined in chapter 2 unveiling the conceptual framework of the book. The elevation part comes in because, as one human rights scholar after another has observed, these rights are super-rights. See, e.g., Louis Henkin, "Human Rights: Ideology and Aspiration, Reality and Prospect," in Samantha Power & Graham Allison eds., *Realizing Human Rights: Moving from Inspiration to Impact* (New York: St. Martin's Press, 2000): 5 (praising these rights as "claims as of right," "limitations on democracy" that, although not absolute, can "trump even a public interest duly determined in a democratic society."); Jack Donnelly, *International Human Rights, 4th Ed.* (Boulder, CO: Westview Press, 2013): 20 (contending that "[t]o assert one's human rights is to attempt to change political practices . . . so that it will no longer be necessary to claim those rights as human rights.").

3. Pidgin English is a "broken" form of English, often used by non-literate or semi-literate persons as a convenient medium of communication in place of the pure English form in Nigeria's multiethnic communities spanning about 500 languages or dialects. For a text on the "language," see Nick Faraclas, *Nigerian Pidgin* (New York: Routledge, 2013).

4. Alison Brysk, *Global Good Samaritans: Human Rights as Foreign Policy* (New York: Oxford University Press, 2009): 7.

5. This is one of the six countries that Professor Brysk profiled in her work. See Brysk, note 3, pp. 95–118, *esp.* 116–117. In a parody of a children's story, Brysk called Costa Rica "The Little Country That Could." Ibid., p. 95. Costa Rica is instructive because with a population of only 3 million people (vis-à-vis Nigeria's 135 million denizens as of 2009 when the Brysk study was published), ibid., pp. 8–17, and with an economy based mainly on tourism, agriculture, and export of electronic products, the country lacks the size and resource endowments of Nigeria.

6. See Andrew Lui, *Why Canada Cares: Human Rights and Foreign Policy in Theory and Practice* (Montreal, Canada: McGill-Queen's University Press, 2012): 173 (disclosing that besides contributing to the international human rights regime, Canada has a "more selfish, inward-looking reasons for [its] international behavior on human rights" embedded in an attempt to improve its federal system).

7. We live in a world where the Responsibility to Protect (referred to colloquially as "R2P") has emerged as a norm. David P. Forsythe, *Human Rights in International Relations, 3d Ed.* (New York: Cambridge University Press, 2012): 4–5. Under this shaping rule, "while sovereign states ha[ve] the primary responsibility for protecting human rights in their jurisdictions, if [these] states prove[] unwilling or unable to prevent gross violations, outside parties ha[ve] the responsibility to become involved." Ibid. Countries which make serious efforts to incorporate human rights into their foreign affairs stand a better chance of shouldering this added burden compared to states which do not.

8. See Mae C. King, *Basic Currents of Nigerian Foreign Policy* (Washington, D.C.: Howard University Press, 1996): 3–31, 237–41 (commenting on "relations with strangers," externally as well as internally, including that "Nigerian nationalism constantly seeks to reconcile differences that are a source of estrangement among citizens.").

9. Brysk, note 4, p. 221.

10. Ibid.

11. Ibid., pp. 221–22 (discussing the lesson of "Good-Enough Good Samaritans").

12. Ibid., p. 222.

13. Ibid., pp. 221–22.

14. Ibid., p. 222.

15. Brysk, note 4, p. 230. The tigers, four of them altogether, are Argentina, Brazil, Chile, and South Korea. Ibid.

16. Ibid., p. 118 (commenting on "latent resources" Costa Rica possesses, other countries can adapt, all of which factors "can be assisted externally," and can "help to strengthen democracy at home as well as abroad.").

17. During a special-topics course in political science, International Human Rights Law and Politics, this writer taught at Chicago State University in spring of 2014, where the Brysk book featured among the required texts, the class questioned the status of Japan as global Good Samaritan, given several statements on the "limitations of Japan's global citizenship." Grounds for that uncertainty included the very title of the Japan chapter, "Peace without Justice," Brysk, note 4, p. 148; the revelation that "Japan has been a leading aid provider and multilateralist, but a slow and even reluctant human rights advocate[,]" ibid., p. 149; and the finding that "Japan is a consumer rather than a generator of international law, and international law has been imported by civil society groups rather than systematically adopted by government as a constitutive feature of national identity[,]" ibid., p. 162. See also Yozo Yokota & Chiyuki Aoi, "Japan's Foreign Policy towards Human Rights: Uncertain Changes," *in* David P. Forsythe, ed., *Human Rights and Comparative Foreign Policy* (New York: United Nations University Press, 2000): 115–45 (characterizing the country's human rights policy as "uncertain.")

18. Brysk, note 4, p. 221.

19. The country abolished its army in 1948. See Tanisha Ellis Hayles, "Costa Rica—A Country without an Army and Proud of It," *Jamaica Observer* (Kingston) (Mar. 2, 2014), http://www.jamaicaobserver.com/columns/Costa-Rica---a-country-without-an-army-and-proud-of-it_16147133; David P. Barash, "Costa Rica's Peace Dividend: How Abolishing the Military Paid Off," *L. A. Times* (Dec. 15, 2013), http://articles.latimes.com/2013/dec/15/opinion/la-oe-barash-costa-rica-demilitarization-20131208. The result is that "[t]o this day, Costa Rica has no army, navy or air force, no heavy weapons of any kind. *There are local police forces but no national defense force*." Barash, *op. cit.* (emphasis added).

20. See Forsythe, note 7, pp. 317–43 (commenting on "the politics of liberalism in a realist world."). Professor Forsythe posits that "[t]he international law of human rights is based on liberalism, but the practice of human rights all too often reflects a realist world." Ibid., p. 317.

21. Donnelly, note 2, pp. 130–33.

22. Quoted in ibid., p. 130. Specifically, Egeland posited that the measured human rights accomplishments of the United States are "because of, rather than in spite, of her superpower status." Donnelly, note 2, p. 130, quoting Jan Egeland, *Impotent Superpower-Potent Small State: Potentialities and Limitations of Human Rights Objectives in the Foreign Policies of the United States and Norway* (Oslo: Norwegian University Press, 1988): 3, 5.

23. Donnelly, note 2, p. 133.

24. See "World Conference on Human Rights, 14–25 June 1993, Vienna, Austria," United Nations Human Rights Office of the High Commissioner, http://www.ohchr.org/EN/ABOUTUS/Pages/ViennaWC.aspx; "World Conference and the Vienna Declaration," *BBC World Service*, http://www.bbc.co.uk/worldservice/people/features/ihavearightto/four_b/treaties_vienna.shtml.

25. Vienna Declaration and Program of Action (Jun. 25, 1993), United Nations Human Rights Office of the High Commissioner, http://www.ohchr.org/EN/ProfessionalInterest/Pages/Vienna.aspx, ¶ 5.

26. Ibid.

27. David P. Forsythe, "Introduction," *in* Forsythe, ed., *Human Rights and Comparative Foreign Policy*, note 17, pp. 3–4.

28. Ibid. In 1998, China ratified the International Covenant on Economic, Social, and Cultural Rights, the same year it *signed* the International Covenant on Political and Civil Rights, but has yet to ratify. See "China: Ratify Key International Human Rights Treaty," Human Rights Watch (Oct. 3, 2013), https://www.hrw.org/news/2013/10/08/china-ratify-key-international-human-rights-treaty.

29. See Peter Calvert, *The Foreign Policy of New States* (New York: St. Martin's Press, 1986): viii (maintaining that foreign policy is "ancillary to domestic policy and serves its needs.").

30. "Vienna Declaration and Program of Action," note 25, ¶ 5.

31. See Power & Allison, eds., *Realizing Human Rights*, note 2, *passim*.

32. Henkin, note 2, p. 38, n.61.

33. Philip C. Aka, "The *Country Reports on Human Rights Practices* and U.S. Human Rights Policy in a Changing World," *Perspectives on Global Development & Technology*, Vol. 14 (2015): 241.

34. See Brysk, note 4, *passim*.

35. Theodore H. White, *America in Search of Itself: The Making of the President 1956–1980* (New York: Harper & Row, 1982), *passim*. President Barack Obama made this same point in an address at the 66th session of the United Nations General Assembly on September 14, 2014, in New York, where he advised U.S. enemies not to exploit the troubles in Ferguson, Missouri, to deflect attention from their own human rights abuses. See White House, Office of the Press Secretary, "Remarks by President Obama in Address to the United Nations General Assembly" (Sept. 28, 2014), www.whitehouse.gov/the-press-office/2014/09/24/remarks-president-obama-address-united-nations-general-assembly [hereinafter referred to as Obama's U.N. address]. Ferguson gained notorious international attention when on Aug. 9, 2014, a white police officer shot an unarmed black teenager to death, sparking widespread protests and civil unrest that went on for months. See, e.g., Dara Lind et al., "An Uneasy Peace in Ferguson," *Vox* (Aug. 21, 2014), www.vox.com/2014/8/11/5988925/mike-brown-killing-shooting-case-ferguson-police-riots-st-louis. Obama conceded with critics that the United States occasionally "have failed to live up to [its] ideals," but nevertheless maintained that unlike many countries in the world, within "the open space of democracy," "America is a country that has steadily worked to address [its] problems, to make [its] union more perfect, [and] to bridge the divides that existed at the founding of this nation." Obama's U.N. Address.

36. Mary Ann Glendon, *A World Made New: Eleanor Roosevelt and the Universal Declaration of Human Rights* (New York: Random House 2001), *passim*.

37. See Philip C. Aka, Review of Lutz Oette, ed., *Criminal Law Reform and Transitional Justice: Human Rights Perspectives for Sudan* (Burlington, VT: Ashgate Publishing, 2011), *Africa Today*, Vol. 59 (Summer 2013): 135–36, n.1.

38. *Declaration of Independence* (Jul. 4, 1776), http://www.archives.gov/exhibits/charters/declaration_transcript.html.

39. Ojo Maduekwe, foreign minister from 2007–10, cited in Monday Dickson, "Citizen Diplomacy in President Umaru Musa Yar'Adua's Nigeria, 2007–2009: An Assessment," *Int'l Journal of Politics & Good Governance*, Vol. 1 (2010): 5, http://onlineresearchjournals.com/ijopagg/art/59.pdf.

40. See Reuben Abati, "The Gains of Jonathan's Diplomacy," *Premium Times* (Lagos) (Sept. 9, 2012), http://www.premiumtimesng.com/news/99498-the-gains-of-jonathans-diplomacy-by-reuben-abati.html (arguing that "[t]he world had changed a lot since Nigeria distributed its oil wealth to other countries and asked for nothing in return" and that "[t]he new strategy[,]" which he said Goodluck Jonathan, president from 2010 to 2015 favors, "called for partnership, mutual respect, enhanced and innovative diplomacy, and constructive exchange.").

Appendix

Biblical Passages Related to Human Rights

Note: All statements come from the New International Version of the Bible.

Isaiah 1:17	"Learn to do right; seek justice. Defend the oppressed. Take up the cause of the fatherless; plead the case of the widow."
Matthew 6:2	"So when you give to the needy, do not announce it with trumpets, as the hypocrites do in the synagogues and on the streets, to be honored by others. Truly I tell you, they have received their reward in full."
Matthew 25: 35–36	"For I was hungry, and you gave me something to eat, I was thirsty and you gave me something to drink, I was a stranger and you invited me in, I needed clothes and you clothed me, I was sick and you looked after me, I was in prison and you came to visit me."
Matthew 25: 44–45	"They also will answer, 'Lord, when did we see you hungry or thirsty or a stranger or needing clothes or sick or in prison, and did not help you?'" "He will reply, 'Truly I tell you, whatever you did not do for one of the least of these, you did not do for me.'"
Acts 20:35	"In everything I showed you that by working hard in this manner you must help the weak . . ."
James 1:27	"Religion that God our Father accepts as pure and faultless is this: to look after orphans and widows in their distress and to help oneself from being polluted by the world.

References

Abati, Reuben. 2016. "Why We Need to Restructure Nigeria to Save It." *Info Square* (Online) (Jun. 3), http://infosquare.com.ng/why-we-need-to-restructure-nigeria-to-save-it-by-reuben-abati/.

Abati, Reuben. 2016. "The President as Chief Diplomat." *YNaija.Com* (Lagos) (Apr. 17).

Abati, Reuben. 2012. "The Gains of Jonathan's Diplomacy." *Premium Times* (Lagos) (Sept. 9), http://www.premiumtimesng.com/news/99498-the-gains-of-jonathans-diplomacy-by-reuben-abati.html.

Abati, Reuben. 1999. "What Is Obasanjo's Foreign Policy?" *Guardian Online* (Lagos) (Aug. 29) (copy on file).

"Abdulsalam Abubakar." *Online Nigeria*, http://www.onlinenigeria.com/abubakar.asp.

Abegunrin, Olayiwola. 2009. *Africa in Global Politics in the Twenty-First Century: A Pan-African Perspective*. New York: Palgrave Macmillan.

Abegunrin, Olayiwola. 2003. *Nigerian Foreign Policy under Military Rule, 1966–1999*. Westport, CT: Praeger.

Abelson, Jenn. 2013. "Western Sahara: Why Africa's Last Colony Can't Break Free." *Boston Globe* (Jun. 16), https://www.bostonglobe.com/ideas/2013/06/15/western-sahara-why-africa-last-colony-can-break-free/87jACxXfU5bVUtqEe6uyrM/story.html.

Aborisade, Oladimeji & Robert J. Mundt. 2002. *Politics in Nigeria, 2d Ed.* New York: Longman.

"About APC." All Progressive Congress, http://apc.com.ng/index.php/about-apc.

"About Us." Community Court of Justice—ECOWAS, http://www.courtecowas.org/site2012/index.php?option=com_content&view=article&id=2&Itemid=5.

Abubakar, Atiku. 2016. Restructuring Nigeria for Greater National Integration and Democratic Stability. Paper Presented at the Umaru Musa Yar'Adua Memorial Hall, Kaduna. (Jul. 30), http://www.elombah.com/index.php/special-reports/9123-how-to-restructure-nigeria-written-by-atiku-abubakar.

Abubakar, Atiku. 2016. Restructuring for Nigeria's National Unity, Remarks during a Book Launching at the Yar'Adua Center, Abuja. (May 31), http://opinion.premiumtimesng.com/2016/05/31/173089/.

"Accept Democracy as Lifestyle, Not Government[al] System, Buhari Urges Nigerians." 2015. *TheWill* (Jun. 19), http://thewillnigeria.com/news/accept-democracy-as-lifestyle-not-government-system-buhari-urges-nigerians/.

Achebe, Chinua. 2012. *There Was a Country: A Personal History of Biafra*. New York: Penguin Press.

Achebe, Chinua. 1983. *The Trouble with Nigeria*. Ibadan, Nigeria: Heinemann.

Adebajo, Adekeye. 2013. "Sad Deterioration of Nigeria's Foreign Policy." *B[usiness] D[ay] Live* (Johannesburg) (May 6), http://za.news.yahoo.com/sad-deterioration-nigeria-foreign-policy-051439591.html.

Adebajo, Adekeye. 2010. "Nigeria." Pp. 245–68. In Alex J. Bellamy & Paul D. Williams, eds., *Providing Peacekeepers: The Politics, Challenges, and Future of United Nations Peacekeeping Contributions*. New York: Oxford University Press.

Adebajo, Adekeye. 2002. *Liberia's Civil War: Nigeria, ECOMOG, and Regional Security in West Africa*. Boulder, CO: Lynne Rienner Publishers.

Adebajo, Adekeye. 2002. *Building Peace in West Africa: Liberia, Sierra Leone, and Guinea-Bissau*. Boulder, CO: Lynne Rienner Publishers.

Adebajo, Adekeye & Abdul R. Mustapha, eds. 2008. *Gulliver's Troubles: Nigeria's Foreign Policy after the Cold War*. Scottsville, South Africa: University of KwaZulu Press.

Adedeji, Adebayo. 1976. Report of the Committee on the Review of Nigerian Foreign Policy, Including the Economic and Technical Cooperation. Lagos: Government Printer.

Adedeji, Lanre. "Telecommunications and the Nigerian Economy." *Lawyers Chronicle*, http://thelawyerschronicle.com/telecommunications-and-the-nigerian-economy/ (last visited Mar. 23, 2015).

Adeleye, Adisa. 2013. "The Old and the New: Which Way Forward?" *Vanguard* (Lagos) (Nov. 15), http://www.vanguardngr.com/2013/11/old-new-way-forward/.

Ademoyega, Adewale. 1981. *Why We Struck: The Story of the First Nigerian Coup*. Ibadan, Nigeria: Evans Brothers Ltd.

Adeniyi, Adesoji. 2015. "Peacekeeping Contributor Profile: Nigeria." *Providing for Peacekeeping* (Apr. 24), http://www.providingforpeacekeeping.org/2015/04/24/peacekeeping-contributor-profile-nigeria.

Adetayo, Olalekan. 2015. "Nigerians Won't Regret Electing Me, Says Buhari." *Punch* (Lagos) (Jun. 4), http://www.punchng.com/news/nigerians-wont-regret-electing-me-says-buhari-2/.

Adetula, Victor A.O. 2010. "Between National Security Considerations and Good Neighborliness: Nigeria and the Challenge of Cross-Border Crime in West Africa." Pp. 295–308. In Celestine Oyom Bassey & Oshita D. Oshita, eds., *Governance and Border Security in Africa*. Lagos: Malthouse Press.

Adichie, Chimamanda N. 2006. *Half of a Yellow Sun*. New York: Alfred A. Knopf.

Adler, Emanuel. 1997. "Seizing the Middle Ground: Constructivism in World Politics." *European Journal of International Relations*, Vol. 3(3): 319–63.

Adler, Jonathan E. & Catherine Z. Elgin, eds. 2007. *Philosophical Inquiry: Classic and Contemporary Readings*. Indianapolis, IN: Hackett Publishing Co., Inc.

"Advancing American Energy," *White House*, https://www.whitehouse.gov/energy/securing-american-energy.

"African Union (AU) and Regional Economic Communities (RECs) in Africa." United Nations Economic Commission for Africa, http://www.uneca.org/oria/pages/african-union-au-regional-economic-communities-recs-africa.

Ahmadu-Suka, Maryam. 2012. "Nigeria: 186 Soldiers for Guinea Bissau Peacekeeping Mission." *Daily Trust* (Abuja) (Nov. 22), http://allafrica.com/stories/201211220936.html.

Ajaebili, C.N. 2011. "The Option of Economic Diplomacy in Nigeria's Foreign Policy." *International Journal of Humanities & Social Science*, Vol. 1: 277–80, http://www.ijhssnet.com/journals/Vol_1_No_17_Special_Issue_November_2011/30.pdf.

Ajala, Aderemi Suleiman. 2009. Yoruba Nationalism: Culture, Politics[,] and Violence in South-Western Nigeria (1900–2009), Institut für Ethnologie und Afrikastudien, Johannes Gutenberg-Universität, Mainz, Germany, Working Paper No. 107, http://www.ifeas.uni-mainz.de/Dateien/AP107.pdf.

Ajere, Jonathan. 2012. "Regional Voluntarism: The Sustainability of Nigerian Afrocentrism." *E-International Relations* (Jul. 19), http://www.e-ir.info/2012/07/19/regional-voluntarism-the-sustainability-of-nigerian-afrocentrism/.

Aka, Philip C. 2016. "Bridging the Gap Between Theory and Practice: Seven Practical Steps to Humanitarian Integrity in Nigeria." *CIHA Blog* (Feb. 25), http://www.cihablog.com/bridging-the-gap-between-theory-and-practice-in-humanitarian-action-seven-practical-steps-to-humanitarian-integrity-in-nigeria/.

Aka, Philip C. 2015. "The *Country Reports on Human Rights Practices* and U.S. Human Rights Policy in a Changing World." *Perspectives on Global Development & Technology*, Vol. 14: 238–60.

Aka, Philip C. 2014–2015. "Human Rights in Nigeria's External Relations: Exigency, Methods, and Rebuttable Objections." *Buffalo Human Rights Law Review*, Vol. 21: 1–26.

Aka, Philip C. 2014. "Judicial Independence under Nigeria's Fourth Republic: Problems and Prospects." *California Western International Law Journal*, Vol. 45(1): 1–78.

Aka, Philip C. 2013. Review of Lutz Oette, ed., *Criminal Law Reform and Transitional Justice: Human Rights Perspectives for Sudan* (Burlington, VT: Ashgate, 2011), *Africa Today*, Vol. 59(4) (Summer): 131–37.

Aka, Philip C. 2009–2010. "NEPAD and the Movement for Popular Participation in Development (MPPD) in Africa." *Human Rights & Globalization Law Review*, Vol. 3: 79–148.

Aka, Philip C. 2009. "Introductory Note to the Human Rights Action Plan for China (2009–2010)." *Int'l Legal Material*, Vol. 48: 841–45.

Aka, Philip C. 2006. "Analyzing U.S. Commitment to Socioeconomic Human Rights." *Akron Law Review*, Vol. 39 (2): 417–63.

Aka, Philip C. 2004. "Prospects for Igbo Human Rights in Nigeria in the New Century." *Howard Law Journal*, Vol. 48(1) (Fall): 165–266.

Aka, Philip C. 2003. "Human Rights as Conflict Resolution in Africa in the New Century." *Tulsa Journal of Comparative & International Law*, Vol. 11 (Fall 2003): 179–209.

Aka, Philip C. 2003. "Nigeria since May 1999: Understanding the Paradox of Civil Rule and Human Rights Violations under President Olusegun Obasanjo." *San Diego International Law Journal*, Vol. 4: 209–76.

Aka, Philip C. 2002. "The Military, Globalization, and Human Rights in Africa." *Journal of Human Rights*, Vol. 18 (Summer): 361–438.

Aka, Philip C. 2002. "The 'Dividend of Democracy': Analyzing U.S. Support for Nigerian Democratization." *Boston College Third World Law Journal*, Vol. 22(2) (Spring): 225–79.

Aka, Philip C. 2001. "Education, Economic Development, and Return to Democratic Politics in Nigeria." *Journal of Third World Studies*, Vol. 18(1): 21–38.

Aka, Philip C. 2000. "Nigeria: The Need for an Effective Policy of Ethnic Reconciliation in the New Century." *Temple International & Comparative Law Journal*, Vol. 14(2): 327–61.

Ake, Claude. 1996. *Democracy and Development in Africa*. Washington, D.C.: Brookings Institution.

Akinboye, S.O. 2013. "Beautiful Abroad but Ugly at Home: Issues and Contra[di] ctions in Nigerian Foreign Policy." University of Lagos Inaugural Lecture Series, 2013, www.unilag.edu.ng/opendocnew.php?.

Akindele, Richard A. & Bassey Ate, eds. 2000. *Selected Readings on Nigeria's Foreign Policy and International Relations*. Lagos: Nigerian Institute of International Affairs and Vantage Publishers.

Akinrefon, Dapo. 2012. "Let's Return to Aburi Accord—Adeniyi." *Vanguard* (Lagos) (Jan. 30), http://stephendieseruvwe.com/2012/03/14/lets-return-to-aburi-accord-adeniyi/.

Alabi, Mojeed Olujinmi A. 2006. "Law Making in Pre-Colonial Yorubaland." Pp. 112–24. In Toyin Falola & Ann Genova, eds., *The Yoruba in Transition: History, Values, and Modernity*. Durham, N.C.: Carolina Academic Press.

Alfred, Charlotte. 2015. "Boko Haram Actually Kills More People in Terror Attacks than ISIS." *Huffington Post* (Nov. 18, 04:55 PM ET), http://www.huffingtonpost.com/entry/boko-haram-isis_us_564cd890e4b00b7997f8c15d.

Al-Hassa, Hadi Y. Circa 2010. "Evaluating Nigerian Foreign Policy at 50." *Gamji.com*, http://www.gamji.com/article9000/news9139.htm.

Allison, Graham. 1971. *Essence of Decision: Explaining the Cuban Missile Crisis*. Boston, MA: Little Brown.

Alter, Karen J., et al. 2013. "A New International Human Rights Court for West Africa: The ECOWAS Community Court of Justice." *American Journal of International Law*, Vol. 107: 737–79.

Amnesty International. 2015. *Stars on Their Shoulders[,] Blood on their Hands: War Crimes Committed by the Nigerian Military* (Jun. 3), http://www.amnestyusa.org/research/reports/stars-on-their-shoulders-blood-on-their-hands-war-crimes-committed-by-the-nigerian-military.

Amstutz, Mark R. 1999. *International Ethics: Concepts, Theories, and Cases in Global Politics*. Lanham, MD: Rowland & Littlefield Publishers.

Amuwo, 'Kunle. 2001. "Introduction: Transition as Democratic Regression." Pp. 1–56. In 'Kunle Amuwo et al., eds., *Nigeria during the Abacha Years (1993–1998)*. Lagos: IFRA-Nigeria.

"Analysis: Nigeria's Sharia Split." 2003. *BBC News* (Jan. 7), news.bbc.co.uk/2/hi/Africa/2632939.stm.

Anderson, Carol. 2003. *Eyes on the Prize: The United Nations and the African American Struggle for Human Rights, 1944–1955*. New York: Cambridge University Press.

Anderson, J.N.D. 1976. *Law Reform in the Muslim World*. London: Athlone Press.

An-Naim, Abdullahi. 1993. "The National Question, Secession and Constitutionalism: The Mediation of Competing Claims to Self-Determination." Pp. 105–125. In Douglas Greenberg et al., eds., *Constitutionalism and Democracy: Transition in the Contemporary World*. New York: Oxford University Press.

Anya, Anya O. 2010. "Nigeria: The Human Capital Challenge." *African Journal of Physics*, Vol. 3: 5–30, http://sirius-b.ncat.edu.ncat.edu/asn/afps/ajp/ajp-ISOTPAND10/Proc%20ISPD%20book5–30.pdf.

Anyaoku, Emeka. 2013. "Nigeria's Current Drift Towards Chaos." *Vanguard* (Lagos) (Nov. 12), http://www.vanguardngr.com/2013/11/nigerias-current-drift-towards-chaos-emeka-anyaoku/#sthas.3H7LjLA6.dpuf.

"Anyaoku Proposes Reduction of Nigeria's 36 States into 6 Units." 2016. *Sun* (Lagos) (Feb. 3), http://sunnewsonline.com/new/anyaoku-proposes-reduction-of-nigerias-36-states-into-6-units/.

Aozou Strip. *Encyclopedia Britannica*, http://www.britannica.com/place/Aozou-Strip.

Aribisala, Femi. "ECOWAS Imperative for Nigeria." *Nigeria Development & Finance Forum*, http://www.nigeriadevelopmentandfinanceforum.org/PolicyDialogue/Dialogue.aspx?Edition=63 (last visited Feb. 28, 2015).

Ashiru, Olugbenga. 2011. Seminar to Review Nigeria's Foreign Policy (Jul. 28), http://www.mfa.gov.ng/news_one.php?article=41.

Associated Press. 1985. "Expelled Foreigners Pouring Out of Nigeria." *N.Y. Times* (May 4), http://www.nytimes.com/1985/05/05/world/expelled-foreigners-pouring out-of-nigeriaby-the-associated-press.html?pagewanted=print.

"Atlantic Charter." 1941. (Aug. 14), http://avalon.law.yale.edu/wwii/atlantic.asp.

Ayoade, J.A.A. (2010). "Nigeria: Positive Pessimism and Negative Optimism: A Valedictory Lecture," Nigerian Voice, Vol. 2 (Sept. 17), http://www.thenigerianvoice.com/print/34992/1/nigeria-positive-pessimism-and-negative-optimism-a.html.

Ayua, Ignatius Akaayar & Dakas C.J. Dakas. 2005. "Federal Republic of Nigeria." Pp. 239–75. In John Kincaid & George Alan Tarr, eds., *Constitutional Origins, Structure, and Change in Federal Countries*. Montreal, Canada: McGill-Queen's University Press.

Azikiwe, Ifeoma. 2013. *Nigeria: Echoes of a Century: 1914–1999, Vol. 1*. Bloomington, IN: AuthorHouse.

Babalola, Samiu. 2011. "Nigeria's Technical Aid Corps: Pearl of South-South Cooperation." *Africa Platform for Development Effectiveness* (Dec. 21), http://www.africa-platform.org/resources/nigerias-technical-aid-corps-pearl-south-south-cooperation.

Babarinde, Olufemi A. 1999. "Regionalism and African Foreign Policies." Pp. 215–36. In Stephen Wright, ed., *African Foreign Policies*. Boulder, CO: Westview Press.

Babatunde, Oyediji O. 2014. "Hausa/Fulani Pre-Colonial Political System in Nigeria." *Wordpress* (Mar. 30), http://www.profseunoyediji.wordpress.com/2014/03/30/hausafulani-pre-colonial-political-system-in-nigeria.

Baehr, Peter R. 2009. "Foreign Policy." Pp. 237–47. In *Encyclopedia of Human Rights*, Vol. 5. New York: Oxford University Press.

Baehr, Peter R. 2000. "Trials and Errors: The Netherlands and Human Rights." Pp. 49–86. In David P. Forsythe, ed., *Human Rights and Comparative Foreign Policy*. New York: United Nations University Press.

Baehr, Peter R. 1996. "Mobilization of the Conscience of Mankind: Conditions of Effectiveness of Human Rights NGOs." (Sept. 18), http://www.gdrc.org/ngo/lecture14.html.

Baehr, Peter R. & Monique Castermans-Holleman. 2004. *The Role of Human Rights in Foreign Policy, 3d Ed.* New York: Palgrave Macmillan.

Ball, Terence, et al. 2014. *Political Ideologies and the Democratic Ideal, 9th Ed.* Boston, MA: Pearson.

Barash, David P. 2013. "Costa Rica's Peace Dividend: How Abolishing the Military Paid Off." *L.A. Times* (Dec. 15), http://articles.latimes.com/2013/dec/15/opinion/la-oe-barash-costa-rica-demilitarization-20131208.

"Basic Information." ECOWAS, www.ecowas.int/about-ecowas/basic-information/.

Basic Writings of John Stuart Mill: On Liberty, the Subjection of Women, and Unilateralism. 2002. New York: Modern Library.

Bassey, Celestine Oyom & Charles Quarker Dokubo. 2011. *Defense Policy of Nigeria: Capability and Context: A Reader.* Bloomington, IN: AuthorHouse.

Beard, Charles A. 1934. *The Idea of National Interest: An Analytical Study in American Foreign Policy*. New York: Macmillan.

Beehner, Lionel. 2007. "The 'Coalition of the Willing.'" Council on Foreign Relations (Updated Feb. 22), http://www.cfr.org/iraq/coalition-willing/p9340.

Bellamy, Alex J. & Paul D. Williams, eds., *Providing Peacekeepers: The Politics, Challenges, and Future of United Nations Peacekeeping Contributions*. New York: Oxford University Press.

Bello, Ademola. 2010. "Umaru Yar'Adua: A Mediocre Administrator, the Least Prepared Nigerian President since Shehu Shagari." *Huffington Post* (May 13; 2:11 pm. EDT, updated May 25, 2011 4:30 pm EDT), http://www.huffingtonpost.com/ademola-bellow/umaru-musa-yaradua-a-medi_b_575125.html.

Bennett, John C. 1966. *Foreign Policy in Christian Perspective*. New York: Scribner's, 1966.

Berman, Larry & Bruce Allen Murphy. 2013. *Approaching Democracy, 8th Ed.* New York: Pearson Education, Inc.

Bhattacherjee, Anol. 2012. *Social Science Research: Principles, Methods, and Practices*. Scholar Commons Textbooks Collection.

"Biography of Alhaji Shehu Usman Aliu Shagari." *Biography*, http://thebiography.us/en/shagari-alhaji-shehu-usman-aliu.

Black, Eric. 2012. "Why the Constitution's Framers Didn't Want Us to Directly Elect the President." *MinnPost* (Oct. 17), https://www.minnpost.com/eric-black-ink/2012/10/why-constitution-s-framers-didn-t-want-us-directly-elect-president.

Black's Law Dictionary, Abridged 6th Ed. 1991. Eagan, MN: West Publishing.

Blake, Gerald Henry, et al. 1996. *The Maritime Boundaries of the Adriatic Sea*. Durham, UK: International Boundaries Research Unit (IBRU) Press.

Blas, Javier. 2014. "Victim of Shale Revolution, Nigeria Stops Exporting Oil to U.S." *Blogger* (Oct. 2; 10:12), http://blogs.ft.com/beyond-brics/2014/10/02/victim-of-shale-revolution-nigeria-stops-exporting-oil-to-us/.

"Boko Haram Fast Facts." 2016. *CNN Library* (Updated 3:03 PM ET, Feb. 19), http://www.cnn.com/2014/06/09/world/boko-haram-fast-facts/.

Bova, Russell. 2010. *How the World Works: A Brief Survey of International Relations*. New York: Longman.

"Brief Notes on Nigeria." *Online Nigeria*, http://www.onlinenigeria.com/history.asp.

Brooker, Paul. 2009. *Non-Democratic Regimes: Theory, Government, and Politics, 2d Ed.* New York: Palgrave Macmillan.

Brown, Ryan Lenora. 2015. "A Top Nigerian Export: Fervent Christianity." *Christian Science Monitor*. (Sept. 28), http://news.yahoo.com/top-nigerian-export-fervent-christianity-135101567.html.

Brysk, Alison. 2009. *Global Good Samaritans: Human Rights as Foreign Policy*. New York: New York: Oxford University Press.

Bukola, Akintola. 2007. "Nigeria and the World: A Review of Nigeria's Foreign Policy (1960–2007)." *Nigerian Army Quarterly Journal*, Vol. 3 (Dec.): 438–71.

Bump, Micah. 2006. "Ghana: Searching for Opportunities at Home and Abroad." *Migration Information Source* (Mar. 1), http://www.migrationpolicy.org/article/ghana-searching-opportunities-home-and-abroad.

Burns, James MacGregor. 1978. *Leadership*. New York: Harper Torchbooks.

Calvert, Peter. 1986. *The Foreign Policy of New States*. New York: St. Martin's Press.

Campbell, John. 2013. *Nigeria: Dancing on the Brink*. Lanham, MD: Rowman & Littlefield Publishers.

Campbell, Keith. 1978. Nigerian Foreign Policy and the Economic Community of West African States (ECOWAS), Occasional Paper, South African Institute of Int'l Affairs (Sept.).

Cárdenas, Emilio J. & María Fernanda Cañás. 2001. "The Limits of Self-Determination." Pp. 101–18. In Wolfgang Danspeckgruber, ed., *The Self-Determination of Peoples: Community, Nation, and State in an Interdependent World*. Boulder, CO: Lynne Rienner.

Carter, Jimmy. 2000. "The American Road to a Human Rights Policy." Pp. 49–61. In Samantha Power & Graham Alison, eds., *Realizing Human Rights: Moving from Inspiration to Impact*. New York: St. Martin's Press.

Cassel, Douglass. 1998. "The Universal Declaration at 50: Changing the World?" *Christian Century* (Dec. 23–30): 1249–51.

Charter of the United Nations. 1945. 59 Stat. 1031, T.S. 993, 3 Bevans 1153.

Chazan, Naomi, et al. 1999. *Politics and Society in Contemporary Africa, 3d Ed.* Boulder, CO: Lynne Rienner Publishers.

"Census History." 1993. In Helen Chapin Metz, ed., *Nigeria: A Country Study*. Washington D.C.: GPO for the Library of Congress.

Center for Energy Economics. *Gas Monetization in Nigeria.* http://www.beg.utexas.edu/energyecon/new-era/case_studies/Gas_Monetization_in_Nigeria.pdf.

Chigozie, Chilaka Francis & Odoh Samuel Ituma. 2015. "Nigerian Peacekeeping Operations Revisited." *Singaporean Journal of Business Economics & Management Studies*, Vol. 4. www.singaporeanjbem.com/pdfs/SG_vol_4_(2)/1.pdf.

Chima, Obinna. 2014. "Nigeria's Unemployment Rate May Rise by 2%." *This Day* (Lagos) (Jan. 7), http://www.thisdaylive.com/articles/nigeria-s-unemployment-rate-may-rise-by-2/168227.

"China: Ratify Key International Human Rights Treaty." 2013. *Human Rights Watch* (Oct. 3), https://www.hrw.org/news/2013/10/08/china-ratify-key-international-human-rights-treaty.

Chothia, Farouk. 2015. "Who Are Nigeria's Boko Haram Islamists," *BBC News Africa* (May 4), http://www.bbc.com/news/world-africa-13809501.

Chuku, Gloria. 2013. "Olaudah Equiano and the Foundation of Igbo Intellectual Tradition." Pp. 33–65. In Gloria Chuku, ed., *The Igbo Intellectual Tradition: Creative Conflict in African and African Diasporic Thought*. New York: Palgrave Macmillan.

Churchill, Winston. 2008. *Churchill by Himself: The Definitive Collection of Quotations*. Edited by Richard M. Langworth. New York: PublicAffairs.

Clapham, Andrew. 1993. *Human Rights in the Private Sphere*. New York: Oxford University Press.

Clapham, Christopher. 1993. "Democratization in Africa: Obstacles and Prospects." *Third World Quarterly*, Vol. 14(3): 423–38.

Clark, Andrew. "Mali." *Encyclopedia Britannica*, http://www.britannica.com/place/Mali/Government-and-society#ref1180547.

Claude Jr., Inis L. 1965. *The Changing United Nations*. New York: Random House.

Clinton, William J. 2000. "Remarks Following Discussions with President Olusegun Obasanjo of Nigeria and an Exchange with Reporters in Abuja, Nigeria, Aug. 26, 2000." Pp. 1701–5. In *Public Papers of the Presidents of the United States: William J. Clinton, 2000–2001.* Washington, D.C.: Best Books.

Clinton, William J. 2000. "Remarks to a Joint Session of the Nigerian National Assembly in Abuja, Aug. 26, 2000." Pp. 1705–10. In *Public Papers of the Presidents of the United States: William J. Clinton, 2000–2001*. Washington, D.C.: Best Books.

Clinton, William J. 2000. "Remarks at a State Dinner Hosted by President Olusegun Obasanjo of Nigeria in Abuja, Aug. 26, 2000." Pp. 1711–12. In *Public Papers of the Presidents of the United States: William J. Clinton, 2000–2001.* Washington, D.C.: Best Books.

"Clinton Praises 'New Nigeria.'" 2000. *BBC News* (Aug. 26; 18:01 GMT 19:01), http://news.bbc.co.uk/2/hi/africa/897423.stm.

"Collective Security." *Encyclopedia Britannica*, http://www.britannica.com/topic/collective-security.

Constitution of the Federal Republic of Ethiopia. 1995.

Constitution of the Federal Republic of Nigeria (Promulgation) Decree No. 24 (May 5, 1999).

Constitution of the Federal Republic of Nigeria. 1960.

Constitution of the Federal Republic of Nigeria. 1963.

Constitution of the Federal Republic of Nigeria. 1979.

Constitution of the Federal Republic of Nigeria. 1999.

Constitution of the United States of America. 1789.

Constitutive Act of the African Union. 2000. OAU Doc. CAB/LEG/23.15 (Jul. 11).

Cotton, Deborah H. & Godfrey O. Odongo. 2007. "The Magnificent Seven: Africa's Response to U.S. Article 98," *African Human Rights Law Journal*, Vol. 7: 1–34, http://www.ahrlj.up.ac.za/cotton-d-h-odongo-g-o.

Crabb Jr., Cecil V. 1972. *American Foreign Policy in the Nuclear Age, 3d Ed.* New York: Harper & Row.

Craven, Matthew. 2015. "Between Law and History: The Berlin Conference of 1884–1885 and the Logic of Free Trade." *London Review of International Law*, Vol. 3: 31–59.

Crawford, Neta C. 2002. *Argument and Change in World Politics: Ethics, Decolonization, and Humanitarian Intervention*. New York: Cambridge University Press.

Croatia: United Nations Transitional Administration for Eastern Slovenia, Baranja, Western Sirmium, UNTAES (Jan. 1996–Jan. 1998), http://www.un.org/en/peace keeping/missions/past/untaes.htm.

"Crude Tactics." 2016. *Economist* (London) (Jan. 30), http://www.economist.com/news/middle-east-and-africa/21689584-cheap-oil-causing-currency-crisis-nigeria-banning-imports-no.

Curtis, Mark. 2004. *Unpeople: Britain's Secret Human Rights Abuses*. New York: Vintage Books.

Dada, Jacob Abiodun. 2012. "Impediments to Human Rights Protection in Nigeria." *Annual Survey of International & Comparative Law*, Vol. 18: 67–92.

Daldorph, Brenda. 2015. "Muhammadu Buhari: 'The Converted Democrat?'" *France 24* (latest update Apr. 13), http://www.france24.com/en/20150401-nigeria-buhari-president-elections-coup-africa.

Danfulani, John. 2014. "The End of Apartheid: A Redefinition of Nigerian Foreign Policy." *IQSRJ Journal of Humanities & Social Science*, Vol. 19: 53–7, http://iosr journals.org/iosr-jhss/papers/Vol19-issue11/Version-3/I0191135357.pdf.

Danziger, James N. 2013. *Understanding the Political World: A Comparative Introduction to Political Science, 11th Ed.* New York: Pearson.

Davidson, Basil. 1994. *Modern Africa: A Social and Political History, 3d Ed.* New York: Longman.

"Declaration on the Right and Responsibility of Individuals, Groups[,] and Organs of Society to Promote and Protect Universally Recognized Human Rights and Fundamental Freedoms." 1998. U.N. Human Rights Office of the High Commissioner, Res. 53/144 adopted by the Gen. Assembly (Dec. 9), http://www.ohchr.org/EN/ProfessionalInterest/Pages/RightAndResponsibility.aspx.

Department of Homeland Security, USA.org, https://www.usa.gov/federal-agencies/department-of-homeland-security.

DeYoung, Karen. 2010. "Obama Redefines National Security Strategy, Looks Beyond Military Might." *Washington Post* (May 27; 4:46 PM), http://www.washingtonpost.com/wp-dyn/content/article/2010/05/27/AR2010052701044.html.

Diamond, Larry. 2001. "Foreword." Pp. x–xv. In Rotimi T. Suberu, *Federalism and Ethnic Conflict in Nigeria*. Washington, D.C.: United States Institute of Peace.

Diamond, Larry, et al., eds. 1997. *Transition without End: Nigerian Politics and Civil Society under Babangida*. Boulder, CO: Lynne Rienner Publishers.

Diamond, Larry. 1995. "Nigeria: The Uncivic Society and the Descent into Praetorianism." Pp. 417–91. In Larry Diamond et al., eds., *Politics in Developing Countries: Comparing Experiences with Democracy, 2d Ed*. Boulder, CO: Lynne Rienner.

Diamond, Larry. 1988. "Nigeria: Pluralism, Statism, and the Struggle for Democracy." Pp. 33–91. In Larry Diamond et al., eds., *Democracy in Developing Countries: Africa, Vol. 2*. Boulder, CO: Lynne Rienner Publishers & London: Adamantine Press, 1988.

Dickovick, J. Tyler & Jonathan Eastwood. 2013. *Comparative Politics: Integrating Theories, Methods, and Cases*. New York: Oxford University Press.

Dickson, Monday. 2010. "Citizen Diplomacy in President Umaru Musa Yar'Adua's Nigeria, 2007–2009: An Assessment." *International Journal of Politics & Good Governance*, Vol. 1, http://onlineresearchjournals.com/ijopagg/art/59.pdf.

"Directory of Nigerian Missions Abroad." Nigerian Foreign Service, http://www.fsc-nigeria.org/dir_nigmissions.html.

Dixon, Robyn. 2010. "Umaru Yar'Adua Dies at 58; Nigerian President." *L.A. Times* (May 7), http://articles.latimes.com/2010/may/07/local/la-me-umaru-yaradua-20100507.

Donnelly, Jack. 2013. *International Human Rights, 4th Ed*. Boulder, CO: Westview Press.

Donnelly, Jack & Debra Liang-Fenton. 2004. "Introduction." Pp. 3–25. In Debra Liang-Fenton ed., *Implementing U.S. Human Rights Policy*. Washington, D.C.: United States Institute of Peace Press.

Donnelly, Jack. 2000. "An Overview." Pp. 310–34. In David P. Forsythe, ed., *Human Rights and Comparative Foreign Policy*. New York: United Nations University Press.

Donnelly, Jack. 1998. *International Human Rights, 2d Ed*. Boulder, CO: Westview Press.

Dougherty, James E. & Robert L. Pfaltzgraff. 1990. *Contending Theories of International Relations: A Comprehensive Survey, 3d Ed*. New York: Harper & Row.

Dreams of Our Founding Fathers, Independence Day Speech by Tafawa Balewa, https://www.facebook.com/notes/fela-durotoye/dreams-of-our-founding-fathers-independence-day-speech-by-tafawa-balewa-october-/10150259870812185.

Economic Community of West African States (ECOWAS), http://www.ecowas.int/.

Economic Community of West African States Revised Treaty. 1993. http://www.internationaldemocracywatch.org/attachments/273_Ecowas%20Treaty.pdf.

"ECOWAS at 40: The Driving Philosophy of Multinationalism." 2015. *Guardian* (Lagos) (Jun. 3, 3:44 AM), http://www.ngrguardiannews.com/2015/06/ecowas-40-the-driving-philosophy-of-multinationalism/.

"ECOWAS Vision 2020: Toward a Democratic and Prosperous Community." 2010. (Jun.), www.ecowas.int/wp-content/uploads/2015/01/ECOWAS-VISION-2020.

Effiong, Joseph. 2012. "Reflections on Nigeria's Foreign Policy." *Journal of Social & Psychological Sciences*, Vol. 5, www.questia.com/read/1G1–314443206/reflections-on-nigeria-s-foreign-policy.

Egbo, Steve. 2003. *Nigeria and the World: A Treatise on Foreign Policy*. Enugu, Nigeria: John Jacobs Classic Publishers.

Ekwe-Ekwe, Herbert. 2006. *Biafra Revisited*. Dakar, Senegal: African Renaissance.

Embassy of the Federal Republic of Nigeria, Washington, D.C. n.d. Nigeria: Past, Present[,] and Future. http://www.nigeriaembassyusa.org/index.php?page=nigeria-past-present-and-future.

Emmert, Frank. 2016. Email Relating to Dissertation Defense. May 24 (copy with author).

Eniola, Toluwani. 2014. "Nigeria Now 39th Most Corrupt Nation, Says TI." *Punch* (Lagos) (Dec. 4), http://www.punchng.com/news/nigeria-now-39th-most-corrupt-nation-says-ti/.

Equiano, Olaudah. 1995 [originally published 1789]. *The Interesting Narrative of the Life of Olaudah Equiano: Written By Himself*. Edited with an intro. by Robert J. Allison. New York: Bedford/St. Martin's Press.

"Ernest Shonekan, Nigeria's Most Fugacious Leader." *Nairaland Forum*, http://www.nairaland.com/1336063/ernest-shonekan-nigerias-most-fugacious.

Esedebe, P. Olisanwuche. 1994. *Pan-Africanism: The Idea and Movement 1776–1991, 2d Ed.* Washington, D.C.: Howard University Press.

"Ethnicity and Race by Countries." *Infoplease*, http://www.infoplease.com/ipa/A0855617.html.

Eze, Osita C. 1984. *Human Rights in Africa: Some Selected Problems*. Lagos: Nigerian Institute of International Affairs and Macmillan Nigeria.

Eze, Osita C. & Peter A. Egom, eds. 2009. *Foreign Policy and Nigeria's Economic Development*. Lagos: Nigerian Institute of International Affairs.

Ezeaku, Calista. 2013. "Should the Six Geopolitical Zones Become Federating Units in Nigeria?" *Tide* (Lagos) (Feb. 11), http://www.thetidenewsonline.com/2013/02/11/should-the-six-geopolitical-zones-become-federating-units-in-nigeria/.

Ezirim, Gerald E. 2011. "Fifty Years of Nigeria's Foreign Policy: A Critical Review." *Sacha International Academic Journal*, http://www.academia.edu/345652/Fifty_Years_of_Nigeria_s_Foreign_Policy_A_Critical_Review.

Faal, Courtney. "Balewa, Sir Abubakar Tafawa (1912–1966)." *Blackpast.org*, http://www.blackpast.org/gah/balewa-sir-abubakar-tafawa-1912–1966.

"Fact Sheet on Africa Contingency Operations Training and Assistance (ACOTA)." 2008. Council on Foreign Relations (Jun. 15), http://www.cfr.org/africa-sub-saharan/fact-sheet-africa-contingency-operations-training-assistance-acota/p22318.

Fafowora, Dapo. 2015. "Review of Nigeria's Foreign Policy." *Nation* (Jun. 14), http://thenationonlineng.net/review-of-nigerias-foreign-policy/.

Fafowora, Dapo. 2013. "Lord Lugard and the 1914 Amalgamation of Nigeria." *Nation* (Feb. 28), http://thenationonlineng.net/lord-lugard-and-the-1914-amalgamation-of-nigeria-2/.

Fagoyinbo, Joseph Babatunde. 2013. *The Armed Forces: Instrument of Peace, Strength, Development[,] and Prosperity*. Bloomington, IN: AuthorHouse.

Falola, Toyin & Adebayo Oyebade. 2010. *Hot Spot: Sub-Saharan Africa*. Santa Barbara, CA: ABC-CLIO.

Falola, Toyin & Matthew M. Heaton. 2008. *A History of Nigeria*. New York: Cambridge University Press.

Falola, Toyin. 1998. *Violence in Nigeria: The Crisis of Religious Politics and Secular Ideologies*. Rochester, NY: University of Rochester Press.

Falola, Toyin, et al. 1994. *The Military Factor in Nigeria, 1966–1985*. Lewiston, N.Y.: Edwin Mellen.

Faraclas, Nick. 2013. *Nigerian Pidgin*. New York: Routledge.

Fatton, Jr., Robert. 1990. "Liberal Democracy in Africa." *Political Science Quarterly*, Vol. 105(3) (Autumn): 455–73.

Faul, Michell. 2014. "Nigeria: Economy $510B, Biggest in Africa." *USA Today* (Apr. 6), http://www.usatoday.com/story/money/business/2014/04/06/nigeria-economy-510-billion-biggest-in-africa/7389395/.

Fawole, Alade W. 2003. *Nigeria's External Relations and Foreign Policy under Military Rule, 1966–1999.* Ile-Ife, Nigeria: Obafemi Awolowo University Press.

Fearson, James D. 2003. "Ethnic and Cultural Diversity by Country." *Journal of Economic Growth*, Vol. 8 (Jun.): 195–212, https://web.stanford.edu/group/fearon-research/cgi-bin/wordpress/wp-content/uploads/2013/10/Ethnic-and-Cultural-Diversity-by-Country.pdf.

The Federalist No. 10 (James Madison) (Nov. 22, 1787).

The Federalist No. 70 (Alexander Hamilton) (Mar. 15, 1788).

The Federalist No. 78 (Alexander Hamilton) (May 28, 1788).

"Federal Capital Abuja." 2003. *Online Nigeria* (Dec. 2; 10:21:46 AM), http://www.onlinenigeria.com/links/abujaadv.asp?blurb=387.

Federal Republic of Nigeria. 1977. *Report of the Constitution Drafting Committee Containing the Draft Constitution, Vol. 1*. Enugu, Nigeria: Ministry of Education & Information, Printing Division.

Field, Martha A. 1992. "The Differing Federalisms of Canada and the United States." *Law & Contemporary Problems*, Vol. 55: 107–20.

"The First Republic." 1991. In Helen Chapin Metz, ed., *Nigeria: A Country Study*. Washington, D.C: GPO for the Library of Congress.

Fisher, Max. 2013. "A Revealing Map of the World's Most and Least Ethnically Diverse Countries." *Washington Post* (May 16), https://www.washingtonpost.com/news/worldviews/wp/2013/05/16/a-revealing-map-of-the-worlds-most-and-least-ethnically-diverse-countries/.

Fleischman, Janet (Human Rights Watch). 2003. "ECOWAS: Troops to Liberia Must Respect Human Rights." Letter to President John Kufuor, then Chairman of ECOWAS (Jul. 18), https://www.hrw.org/news/2003/07/18/ecowas-troops-liberia-must-respect-human-rights.

Fombad, Charles Manga. 2008. "Transitional Justice in Africa: The Experience with Truth Commissions." Hauser Global Law School Program. (May/Jun.), http://www.nyulawglobal.org/globalex/Africa_Truth_Commissions.html.

Ford, John. 2014. "The Origins of Boko Haram." *National Interest* (Jun. 6), http://nationalinterest.org/print/feature/the-origins-boko-haram-10609.

"Foreign Relations." 1991. In Helen Chapin Metz, ed., *Nigeria: A Country Study*. Washington D.C.: GPO for the Library of Congress.

Forsythe, David P. 2012. *Human Rights in International Relations, 3d Ed.* New York: Cambridge University Press.

Forsythe, David P. ed. 2000. *Human Rights and Comparative Foreign Policy*. New York: United Nations University Press.

Forsythe, David P. 2000. "Introduction." Pp. 1–18. In David P. Forsythe, ed., *Human Rights and Comparative Foreign Policy*. New York: United Nations University Press.

Forsythe, David P. 1998. "Human Rights Fifty Years after the Universal Declaration." *PS: Political Science & Politics*, Vol. 31 (Sept.): 507–11.

French, Howard W. 1995. "Nigeria Executes Critic of Regime; Nations Protest." *N.Y. Times* (Nov. 11), http://www.nytimes.com/1995/11/11/world/nigeria-executes-critic-of-regime-nations-protest.html?pagewanted=all.

Frynas, Jedrzej G. 2000. *Oil in Nigeria: Conflict and Litigation between Oil Companies and Village Communities.* Hamburg & London: Lit Verlag.

Gaadi, Donald Terfa. 2013. "Ethnic Groups and Geo-Political Regions in Nigeria." *Eagle Reporters* (Abuja) (Dec. 28; 1:49 PM), http://eaglereporters.com/2013/12/28/ethnic-group-and-geo-political-region-in-nigeria-by-donald-terfa/.

Gaffey, Conor. 2016. "Biafra Protests Prompt Separation Anxiety in Nigeria." *Newsweek* (Mar. 1, 10:47 AM), http://www.newsweek.com/2016/03/11/nigeria-biafra-nnamdi-kanu-protests-432002.html.

Gambari, Ibrahim. 2008. "From Balewa to Obasanjo: The Theory and Practice of Nigeria's Foreign Policy." Pp. 58–80. In Adekeye Adebajo & Abdul Raufu Mustapha, eds., *Gulliver's Troubles: Nigeria's Foreign Policy after the Cold War*. Scottsville, South Africa: University of Kwazulu-Natal Press.

Gambari, Ibrahim A. 1991. *Political and Comparative Dimensions of Regional Integration: The Case of ECOWAS.* Atlantic Highlands, N.J.: Humanities Press.

Gambari, Ibrahim A. 1989. *Theory and Reality in Foreign Policy Making: Nigeria after the Second Republic*. Atlantic Highlands, N.J.: Humanities Press, Inc.

Gambari, Ibrahim A. 1980. *Party Politics and Foreign Policy: Nigeria under the First Republic*. Zaria, Nigeria: Ahmadu Bello University Press.

Garba, Joe. 1991. *Diplomatic Soldiering: The Conduct of Nigerian Foreign Policy, 1975–1979*. Ibadan: Spectrum Books.

Gauchet, Marcel. 1997. "Right and Left." Pp. 242–45. In Pierre Nora & Lawrence D. Kritzman, eds., *Realms of Memory: Conflicts and Divisions*. New York: Columbia University.

Gbulie, Ben. 1981. *Nigeria's Five Majors: Coup d'état of 15th January 1966, First Inside Account*. Lagos: Africana Educational Publishers.

Geertz, Clifford, ed. 1963. *Old Societies and New States: The Quest for Modernity in Asia and Africa*. New York: Free Press of Glencoe.

George, Alexander L. & Andrew Bennett. 2005. *Case Studies and Theory Development in the Social Sciences*. Cambridge, MA: MIT Press.

Gesinde, Seyi. 2015. "Nigeria's Foreign Policy in the Eye of Global Challenge." *Tribune Online* (Lagos) (May 28), http://tribuneonlineng.com/content/nigeria%E2%80%99s-foreign-policy-eye-global-challenge.

Gettleman, Jeffrey. 2011. *After Years of Struggle, South Sudan Becomes a New Nation*, *N. Y. Times* (Jul. 9), www.nytimes.com/2011/07/10/world/africa/10sudan.html?pagewanted=1&r=2&hp&adxnnlx=1310234502–5nvX4GUBg0fK28Wp4F.

Gilles, David. 1996. *Between Principles and Practice: Human Rights in North-South Relations*. Montreal, Canada: McGill-Queen's University Press.

Glahn, Gerhard von & James Larry Taulbee. 2012. *Law among Nations: An Introduction to Public International Law, 10th Ed.* New York: Routledge.

Glendon, Mary Ann. 2001. *A World Made New: Eleanor Roosevelt and the Universal Declaration of Human Rights*. New York: Random House.

"Good Governance and Human Rights." U.N. Human Rights Office of the High Commissioner, http://www.ohchr.org/EN/Issues/Development/GoodGovernance/Pages/GoodGovernanceIndex.aspx.

"The Gowon Regime." In Helen Chapin Metz, ed., *Nigeria: A Country Study*. Washington, D.C: GPO for the Library of Congress.

Greer, Scott. 1969. *The Logic of Social Inquiry*. Chicago: Aldine Publishing Company.

Grigsby, Ellen. 2012. *Analyzing Politics: An Introduction to Political Science, 5th Ed.* Belmont, CA: Wadsworth Cengage Learning.

Grimmett, Richard F. 1999. Cong. Research Serv., *Foreign Policy Roles of the President and Congress*, http://fpc.state.gov/6172.htm.

Gutmann, Amy. 2001. "Introduction." Pp. vii–xxviii. In Michael Ignatieff, *Human Rights as Politics and Idolatry.* Princeton, N.J.: Princeton University Press.

Haass, Richard. 2014. *Foreign Policy Begins at Home: The Case for Putting America's House in Order*. New York: Basic Books.

"Haile Selassie 1892–1975, Former Ethiopian Emperor." *Encyclopedia.com*, http://www.encyclopedia.com/topic/Haile_Selassie.aspx.

Hamilton, Lee H. 1998. "Defining National Interest." *Christian Science Monitor* (Mar. 30), http://www.csmonitor.com/1998/0330/033098.opin.opin.2.html.

Hamman, Suleiman, et al. 2014. "The Role of Nigeria in Peacekeeping Operations from 1960 to 2013." *International Affairs & Global Strategy*, Vol. 21: 42–45.

Hanhimäki, Jussi & Odd Arne Westad, eds. 2004. *The Cold War: A History in Documents and Eyewitness Accounts*. New York: Oxford University Press.

Hannum, Hurst, et al. 2011. *International Human Rights: Problems of Law, Policy, and Practice, 5th Ed.* Alphen aan den Rijn, Netherlands: Wolters Kluwer,.

Harbeson, John W. & Donald Rothchild. 2000. "The African State and State System in Flux." Pp. 3–21. In John W. Harbeson & Donald Rothchild eds., *Africa in World Politics: The African State System in Flux, 3d Ed.* Boulder, CO: Westview Press.

Hastedt, Glenn P. 2006. *American Foreign Policy: Past, Present, Future, 6th Ed.* Upper Saddle River, N.J.: Pearson Prentice Hall.

Hatto, Ronald. 2013. "From Peacekeeping to Peacebuilding: The Evolution of the Role of the United Nations in Peace Operations." *International Review of the Red Cross*, Vol. 95: 495–515.

Hayles, Tanisha Ellis. 2014. "Costa Rica—A Country without an Army and Proud of It." *Jamaica Observer* (Kingston) (Mar. 2), http://www.jamaicaobserver.com/columns/Costa-Rica---a-country-without-an-army-and-proud-of-it_16147133.

Haynes, Jeff. 2014. "Religion." Pp. 119–31. In Peter Burnell et al., eds., *Politics in the Developing World, 4th Ed.* New York: Oxford University Press.

Healey, Joseph G. "African Proverb of the Month Nov. 2001." *Afriprov.org*, http://www.afriprov.org/african-proverb-of-the-month/27–2001proverbs/172-nov2001.html.

Henckaerts, Jean-Marie. 1995. *Mass Expulsion in Modern International Law and Practice*. Leiden, Netherland: Martinus Nijhoff Publishers.

Henkin, Louis. 2000. "Human Rights: Ideology and Aspiration, Reality and Prospect." Pp. 3–38. In Samantha Power & Graham Alison, eds., *Realizing Human Rights: Moving from Inspiration to Impact*. New York: St. Martin's Press.

Henkin, Louis. 1998. "The Universal Declaration and the U.S. Constitution." *PS: Political Science & Politics*, Vol. 31(3), (Sept.): 512–15.

Homeland Security Act, Pub. L. 107–209, 116 Stat. 2135 of Nov. 25, 2002.

"How Nigeria Won Its First Democratic Power Transfer," *Economist* (London) (Apr. 6, 2015, 23: 50), http://www.economist.com/blogs/economist-explains/2015/04/economist-explains-2.

"How U.S. Foreign Policy Is Made." Foreign Policy Association, http://www.fpa.org/features/index.cfm?act=feature&announcement_id=45&show_sidebar=0.

Howard, Rhoda E. 1986. *Human Rights in Commonwealth Africa*. Lanham, MD: Rowman & Littlefield.

Human Rights Watch. 2005. *"Rest in Pieces": Police Torture and Deaths in Custody in Nigeria* (Jul.), https://www.hrw.org/reports/2005/nigeria0705/.

Human Rights Watch. 2003. Bilateral Immunity Agreements (Jun. 25), http://www.hrw.org/legacy/campaigns/icc/docs/bilateralagreements.pdf.

Human Rights Watch. 1993. *Waging War to Keep the Peace: The ECOMOG Intervention and Human Rights*. (Jun.), https://www.hrw.org/legacy/reports/1993/liberia/.

Hurst, Ryan. "Congo Civil War (1960–1964)." *Black Past*, http://www.blackpast.org/gah/congo-civil-war-1960–1964.

Igboin, Benson Ohihon. 2014. Pp. 265–90. "'The President of Nigeria Has No Final Say': Sharia Law Controversies and Implications for Nigeria." *Central & East European Online Library*, http://www.ceeol.com/search/article-detail?id=180187.

Ignatieff, Michael. 2002. *Is the Human Rights Era Ending?* Pp. 103–6. In Allan J. Cigler ed., *Perspectives on Terrorism: How 9/11 Changed U.S. Politics*. Boston, MA: Houghton Mifflin Co.

Imhonopi, David & Moses Urim Ugochukwu. 2013. "Leadership Crisis and Corruption in the Nigerian Public Sector: An Albatross of National Development." *African Symposium: An Online Journal of the African Education Research Network*, Vol. 13 (Jun.): 78, http://www.ncsu.edu/aern/TAS13.1/TAS13.1_Imhonopi.pdf.

Immigration and Refugee Board of Canada. 1994. Nigeria: Information on the Civil Liberty Organization (CLO), Its Leadership, Its Activities, the Arrest of Its Members and Its Involvement in Demonstrations that Followed the Annulment of the 12 June 1993 Elections (Mar. 1), http://www.refworld.org/docid/3ae6ab3a24.html.

Inamete, Ufot Bassey. 2001. *Foreign Policy Decision-Making in Nigeria*. Selinsgrove, PA: Susquehanna University Press.

Intelligence Reform and Terrorism Prevention Act, Pub. L. 108–458, 118 Stat. 3638, of Dec. 17, 2004.

International Covenant on Civil and Political Rights. 1966 (Dec. 16), S. Treaty Doc. No. 95–20, 6 I.L.M. 368 (1967), 999 U.N.T.S. 171.

International Covenant on Economic, Social and Cultural Rights. 1966 (Dec. 16), S. Treaty Doc. No. 95–19, I.L.M. 360 (1967), 993 U.N.T.S. 3.

International Crisis Group. 2006. Nigeria: Want in the Midst of Plenty, Africa Report No. 113 (Jul. 19), http://www.crisisgroup.org/~/media/Files/africa/west-africa/nigeria/Nigeria%20Want%20in%20the%20Midst%20of%20Plenty.

International Committee of the Red Cross. 2004. (Jan. 1), https://www.icrc.org/eng/resources/documents/misc/5kzmuy.htm.

Isichei, Elizabeth. 1995. *A History of Christianity in Africa: From Antiquity to the Present*. Grand Rapids, MI: Wm. B. Eerdmans Publishing, 1995).

Isichei, Elizabeth. 1976. *A History of the Igbo People*. New York: Palgrave Macmillan.

Isichei, Elizabeth. 1973. *The Ibo People and the Europeans: The Genesis of a Relationship—to 1906*. New York: St. Martin's Press.

Jackson, Robert & Carl Rosberg. 1982. "Why Africa's Weak States Persist: The Empirical and the Juridical in Statehood." *World Politics*, Vol. 35: 1–24.

Jacobs, Frank. 2011. "The World's Largest Sandbox." *N. Y. Times* (Nov. 7; 9.30 p.m.), http://opinionator.blogs.nytimes.com/2011/11/07/the-worlds-largest-sandbox.

Jang, Se Young. 2012. "The Causes of the Sierra Leone Civil War." *E-International Relations Students* (Oct. 25), http://www.e-ir.info/2012/10/25/the-causes-of-the-sierra-leone-civil-war-underlying-grievances-and-the-role-of-the-revolutionary-united-front.

Jebuni, Charles D., et al. 1999. "A Case-Study of the Economic Community of West African States (ECOWAS)." Pp. 24–65. In Ademola Oyejide, eds., *Regional Integration and Trade Liberalization in SubSaharan Africa: Regional Case Studies, Vol. 3*. London: Macmillan Press Ltd.

Jervis, Robert. 1999. "Realism in the Study of World Politics." Pp. 331–52. In Peter J. Katzenstein et al., eds., *Explorations and Contestation in the Study of World Politics*. Cambridge, MA: MIT Press, 1999.

Jonathan, Goodluck. 2011. Address at the Retreat on the Review of Nigeria's Foreign Policy (Aug. 1), http://www.nigeriavillagesquare.com/index.php?option=com_content&allposts=1&catid=590&id=19313&view=arti cle&Itemid=1719.

Joseph, Richard. 1999. "Nigeria and the Challenge of Leadership." *Tell* (Lagos) (Jul. 5).

Joseph, Richard A. 1987. *Democracy and Prebendal Politics in Nigeria: The Rise and Fall of the Second Republic*. New York. Cambridge University Press.

Judge, Edward H. & John W. Langdon. 2010. *The Cold War: A Global History with Documents, 2d Ed.* Upper Saddle River, N.J.: Prentice Hall.

Kalu, Uduma. 2013. "Nigeria is 33rd Most Corrupt Country—Transparency Int'l." *Vanguard* (Lagos) (Dec. 4), http://www.vanguardngr.com/2013/12/nigeria-33rd-corrupt-country-transparency-intl/.

"Kaduna, Nigeria." *Encyclopedia Britannica*, http://www.britannica.com/place/Kaduna-Nigeria.

Karl, Terry Lynn. 1997. *The Paradox of Plenty: Oil Books and Petro-States*. Berkeley, CA: University of California Press.

Kazah-Toure, Toure. 2007. "Nigeria: Challenge to the State and Ways of Breaking through the Quagmire." Pp. 170–94. In George Klay Kieh Jr., ed., *Beyond*

State Failure and Collapse: Making the State Relevant in Africa. Lanham, MD: Lexington Books.

Kennedy, Anthony. 2006. *Justice Kennedy Address*, CSPAN (Aug. 5), www.c-span .org/video/?193757–1/justice-kennedy-address (Keynote Address by Justice Anthony M. Kennedy at the Meeting of the American Bar Association, Honolulu, HI).

Kennedy, John F. 1961. Inaugural Address of President John F. Kennedy (Jan. 20), John F. Kennedy Presidential Library & Museum, http://www.jfklibrary.org/Research/Research-Aids/Ready-Reference/JFK-Quotations/Inaugural-Address.aspx.

Kerstein, Mark. 2011. "The U.S. and the ICC: Towards a Closer Relationship?" *Justice in Conflict* (Apr. 10), http://justiceinconflict.org/2011/04/10/the-us-and-the-icc-towards-a-closer-relationship/.

Kew, Darren & Peter Lewis. 2013. "Nigeria." Pp. 188–241. In Mark Kesselman, ed. *Introduction to Politics of the Developing World, 6th Ed*. Boston, MA: Cengage Learning.

King, Mae C. 1996. *Basic Currents of Nigerian Foreign Policy*. Washington, D.C.: Howard University Press.

Kirk-Greene, A.H.M. 1971. *Crisis and Conflict in Nigeria: A Documentary Sourcebook, Vol. 1*. London: Oxford University Press.

Kirk-Greene, A.H.M. 1971. *Crisis and Conflict in Nigeria: A Documentary Sourcebook 1966–1969, Vol. 2*. London: Oxford University Press.

Kirk-Greene, Anthony. 1997. "The Remedial Imperatives of the Nigerian Constitution, 1922–1992." Pp. 31–53. In Larry Diamond et al., eds., *Transition without End: Nigerian Politics and Civil Society under Babangida*. Boulder, CO: Lynne Rienner Publishers.

Krasner, Stephen D. 1982. "Structural Causes and Regime Consequences: Regimes as Intervening Variable," *International Organization*, Vol. 36, (Spring): 185–205.

Krent, Harold J. 2005. *Presidential Powers*. New York: New York University Press.

Kuhn, Thomas. 1996. *The Structure of Scientific Revolutions, 3d Ed*. Chicago: University of Chicago.

Kumolu, Charles. 2013. "Constitution[al] Amendment: National Assembly Moves to Restructure Nigeria." *Vanguard* (Lagos) (Jan. 13, 12:40 AM), http://www.vanguardngr.com/2013/01/constitution-amendment-nassembly-moves-to-restructure-nigeria/.

Kuranga, David Oladipupo. 2012. *The Power of Interdependence: Lessons from Africa*. New York: Palgrave Macmillan.

"Kwame Nkrumah's Vision." 2000. *BBC World Service* (Sept. 14), www.bbc.co.uk/worldservice/people/highlights/000914_nkrumah.shtml.

Kwarteng, Kwasi. 2012. "Nigeria's Current Troubles and Its British Colonial Roots." *Globalist* (Mar. 9), http://www.theglobalist.com/nigerias-current-troubles-and-its-british-colonial-roots/.

Land and Maritime Boundary between Cameroon and Nigeria (Cameroon v. Nigeria: Equatorial Guinea Intervening), Int'l Court of Justice (Oct. 10, 2002), http://www.icj-cij.org/docket/index.php?p1=3&p2=3&k=74&case=94&code=cn&p3=4.

Lauren, Paul Gordon. 2011. *The Evolution of International Human Rights: Visions Seen*. Philadelphia, PA: University of Pennsylvania Press.

Law, Robin. 1991. *The Slave Coast of West Africa 1550–1750: The Impact of the Atlantic Slave Trade on an African Society*. Oxford, U.K.: Clarendon Press.

Lawal, Salahu Mohammed. 2015. "An Appraisal of Corruption in the Nigerian Electoral System." *European Scientific Journal*, Vol. 11: 256–73.

The Legacy of the Frontline States, Building Security in Southern Africa, Monograph No. 43 (Nov. 1999), https://www.issafrica.org/pubs/Monographs/No43/TheLegacy.html.

Legge, James. 1971. *Confucian Analects, the Great Learning, and the Doctrine of the Mean*. Mineola, N.Y.: Dover Publications.

LeVan, A. Carl & Oladimeji Aborisade. 2014. "Politics in Nigeria." Pp. 631–74. In G. Bingham Powell, Jr. et al., eds., *Comparative Politics Today: A World View, 11th Ed*. New York: Pearson.

Liang-Fenton, Debra. 2004. "Conclusion: What Works?" Pp. 435–61. In Debra Liang-Fenton ed., *Implementing U.S. Human Rights Policy*. Washington, D.C.: United States Institute of Peace Press.

"Liberia: Conflict." *Peace Direct*, http://www.insightonconflict.org/conflicts/liberia/conflict-profile/.

Lillich, Richard B., et al. 2006. *International Human Rights: Problems of Law, Policy, and Practice, 4th Ed*. New York: Aspen Publishers.

Lind, Dara, et al. 2014. "An Uneasy Peace in Ferguson." *Vox* (Aug. 21), www.vox.com/2014/8/11/5988925/mike-brown-killing-shooting-case-ferguson-police-riots-st-louis.

Linz, Juan J. & Alfred Stepan. 1997. "Toward Consolidated Democracies." Pp. 14–33. In Larry Diamond et al. eds., *Consolidating the Third Wave Democracies: Themes and Perspectives*. Baltimore, MD: Johns Hopkins University Press.

Linz, Juan J. & Alfred Stepan. 1996. *Problems of Democratic Transition and Consolidation: Southern Europe, South America, and Post-Communist Europe*. Baltimore, MD: Johns Hopkins University Press.

Lippman, Walter. 1943. *U.S. Foreign Policy: Shield of the Republic*. Boston, MA: Little Brown.

Lorenzi, Nancy M. & Robert T. Riley. 2000. "Managing Change: An Overview." *Journal of the American Medical Informatics Association*, Vol. 7 (Mar.–Apr.): 116–24.

Lovelace Jr., Douglas C. 2013. "Foreword." Pp. iii–iv. In Clarence J. Bouchat, *The Causes of Instability in Nigeria and Implications for the United States*. Carlisle, PA: Strategic Studies Institute & U.S. Army War College Press (Aug.).

Luckham, Robin. 1971. *The Nigerian Military: A Sociological Analysis of Authority and Revolt, 1960–1967*. New York: Cambridge University Press.

Lugard, Frederick J.D. 1922. *The Dual Mandate in British Tropical Africa*. London: Frank Cass & Co.

Lugard, F.D. & A.H.M. Kirk-Greene. 1968. *Lugard and the Amalgamation of Nigeria: A Documentary Record*. London: Cass.

Lui, Andrew. 2012. *Why Canada Cares: Human Rights and Foreign Policy in Theory and Practice*. Montreal, Canada: McGill-Queen's University Press.

Lund, Susan & Arend van Wamelen. 2015. "Lions on the Move: 10 Things You Don't Know about Africa's Booming Economy." Pp. 42–5. In J. Tyler Dickovick & Jonathan Eastwood, eds., *Current Debates in Comparative Politics*. New York: Oxford University Press.

Lyakurwa, William, et al. 1997. "Regional Integration in SubSaharan Africa: A Review of Experiences and Issues." Pp. 159–209. In Ademola Oyejide et al. eds., *Regional Integration and Trade Liberalization in SubSaharan Africa: Framework, Issues, and Methodological Perspectives, Vol. 1*. London: Macmillan Press Ltd.

Macmillan, Harold. 1960. Speech at the South African Parliament, Cape Town, http://www.bbc.co.uk/archive/apartheid/7203.shtml (video).

MacMillan, Margaret. 2003. *Paris 1919: Six Months that Changed the World*. New York: Random House.

"Madeleine Albright Extended Interview." 2006. *PBS* (May 19), http://www.pbs.org/wnet/religionandethics/2006/05/19/may-19–2006-madeleine-albright-extended-intreview/2838/.

Mahmood, Abba. 2013. "Nigeria's Africa Policy in Perspective." *Leadership* (Dec. 26), leadership.ng/columns/Thursday-column/343/nigerias-africa-policy-in-perspective.

Maja-Pearce, Adewale. 2014. "Nigeria Does Generate More Electricity Now than It Did 15 Years Ago." Africa Check (Nov.), https://africacheck.org/reports/nigeria-does-generate-more-electricity-now-than-it-did-15-years-ago/.

Maja-Pearce, Adewale. 2014. "Changing Nigeria's Cruel Police Culture." *N.Y. Times* (Oct. 7), http://www.nytimes.com/2014/10/08/opinion/adewale-maja-pearce-changing-nigerias-cruel-police-culture.html.

Maluwa, Tiyanjana. 2000. "Human Rights and Foreign Policy in Post-Apartheid South Africa." Pp. 250–75. In David P. Forsythe, ed., *Human Rights and Comparative Foreign Policy*. New York: United Nations University Press.

Mandara, Mairo. 2012. "Family Planning in Nigeria and Prospects for the Future." *Int'l Journal of Gynecology & Obstetrics*, Vol. 117, pp. 1–4. Feb. 20.

Mantey, Comfort Assa. 2013. Ensuring Free Border Movements in ECOWAS Integration: Challenges to National Security, M.A. Thesis, University of Ghana (Jul.).

Martinez, Michael. 2013. "Kerry: Nigeria Acknowledged Human Rights Abuses in Terror Fight." *CNN* (May 25, updated 1:49 PM ET), www.cnn/com/2013/05/25/world/africa/nigeria-kerry-human-rights.

Martinez, Jenny S. 2011. *The Slave Trade and the Origins of International Human Rights Law*. New York: Oxford University Press.

Maxfield, Michael G. & Earl R. Babbie. 2015. *Research Methods for Criminal Justice and Criminology, 7th Ed.* Stamford, CT: Cengage Learning.

Mays, Terry M. 2015. *Historical Dictionary of International Organizations in Africa and the Middle East.* Lanham, MD: Rowman & Littlefield.

Mays, Terry M. & Mark W. Delancey. 2002. *Historical Dictionary of International Organizations in Sub-Saharan Africa*. Lanham, MD: Scarecrow Press.

M'Bet, Allechi. 1999. "The CEAO and UEMOA within ECOWAS: The Road Ahead towards West African Economic Integration." Pp. 66–85. In Ademola Oyejide et al., eds., *Regional Integration and Trade Liberalization in SubSaharan Africa: Regional Case Studies, Vol. 3*. London: Macmillan Press Ltd.

McCarthy, Colin. 1999. "Regional Integration in SubSaharan Africa: Past, Present and Future." Pp. 12–44. In Ademola Oyejide et al., eds., *Regional Integration and Trade Liberalization in SubSaharan Africa: Synthesis and Review, Vol. 4*. London: Macmillan Press Ltd.

McCaskie, T.C. "Western Africa." *Encyclopedia Britannica*, http://www.britannica.com/place/western-Africa.

McElroy, Robert W. 1992. *Morality and American Foreign Policy*. Princeton, N.J.: Princeton University Press.

McFadden, Robert D. 2011. "Odumegwu Ojukwu, Breakaway Biafra Leader, Dies at 78." *N. Y. Times* (Nov. 26), http://www.nytimes.com/2011/11/27/world/africa/odumegwu-ojukwu-leader-of-breakaway-republic-of-biafra-dies-at-78.html?_r=0.

McKenna, Amy. "Goodluck Jonathan, President of Nigeria." *Encyclopedia Britannica*,http://www.britannica.com/biography/Goodluck-Jonathan.

McLoughlin, Gerald & Clarence J. Bouchat. 2013. *Nigerian Unity: In the Balance*. Carlisle, PA: Strategic Studies Institute & U.S. Army War College Press (Jun.), http://www.strategicstudiesinstitute.army.mil/pdffiles/PUB1159.pdf.

McMahon, Robert. 2003. *The Cold War: A Very Short Introduction*. New York: Oxford University Press.

"Members of the IC." Office of the Director of National Intelligence, http://www.dni.gov/index.php/intelligence-community/members-of-the-ic.

Meredith, Martin. 2011. *The Fate of Africa: A History of the Continent since Independence*, revised and updated edition. New York: PublicAffairs.

Michnik, Adam. 1990. "After the Revolution." *New Republic* (Jul. 2): 28.

Milakovich, Michael E. & George J. Gordon. 2013. *Public Administration in America, 11th Ed*. Boston, MA: Wadsworth Cengage Learning.

Miners, Norman J. 1971. *The Nigerian Army, 1956–1966*. London: Methuen.

Mingst, Karen A. & Margaret P. Karns. 2012. *The United Nations in the 21st Century, 4th Ed*. Boulder, CO: Westview Press.

"Ministry of Foreign Affairs." *ConnectNigeria.com*, www.connectnigeria.com/businesses/ministry-of-foreign-affairs-14273.html.

"Ministries of Nigeria." *Ngex!*, http://www.ngex.com/nigeria/govt/officials/ministers.htm.

Mitter, Siddhartha. 2016. "To Find Progress in Nigeria, Think Local." *Foreign Policy* (May 26, 2.54 PM), http://foreignpolicy.com/2016/05/26/to-find-progress-in-nigeria-think local/.

Mohammed, Murtala. 2013. "Africa Has Come of Age." Speech to the OAU Extraordinary Summit Conference, Addis Ababa (Jan. 11, 1976), *Africa Youth Union* (Dec. 3), https://www.facebook.com/Africanyouthunion/posts/726490580710778.

Morgenthau, Hans J. 1978. *Politics Among Nations: The Struggle for Power and Peace, Revised 5th Ed*. New York: Alfred A. Knopf.

Morgenthau, Hans J. 1977. "The Pathology of American Power." *International Security*, Vol. 1, (Winter 1977): 3–20.

Morse, Edward L. 2014. "Welcome to the Revolution." *Foreign Affairs* (May/Jun.), https://www.foreignaffairs.com/articles/2014–04–17/welcome-revolution.

Mundt, Robert J. & Oladimeji Aborisade. 2000. "Politics in Nigeria." Pp. 680–728. In Gabriel A. Almond et al., eds., *Comparative Politics Today: A World View*. New York: Longman.

Mustapha, Abdul Raufu. 2001. "Civil Rights and Pro-Democracy Groups in and Outside Nigeria." Pp. 143–83. In 'Kunle Amuwo et al., eds., *Nigeria during the Abacha Years (1993–1998)*. Lagos: IFRA-Nigeria.

Nabakwe, Ruth. 2002. "France Continues Peacekeeping Initiatives for Africa." *Pan African News Agency* (Jan. 23), https://www.globalpolicy.org/component/content/article/199/41018.html.

Naldi, Gino J. 1998. "The Aouzou Strip Dispute—A Legal Analysis." *Journal of African Law*, Vol. 33 (Spring): 72–77.

"National Interest: Meaning, Components[,] and Methods." *Dinesh International Politics*, http://www.yourarticlelibrary.com/international-politics/national-interest-meaning-components-and-methods/48487/.

"National Security Strategy, United States." 2004. *Encyclopedia of Espionage, Intelligence & Security*, http://www.encyclopedia.com/doc/1G2–3403300516.html.

Nda-Isaiah, Sam. 2014. "Is Nigeria a Poor Country of Rich Men or a Rich Country of Poor Men?" *Leadership* (Abuja) (Apr. 7; 2:39 AM), http://leadership.ng/columns/363727/nigeria-poor-country-rich-men-rich-country-poor-men.

Ndujihe, Clifford, et al. 2015. "Power Sector: Senate Probes OBJ, Yar'Adua, Jonathan." *Vanguard* (Lagos) (Aug. 14, 5:01 AM), http://www.vanguardngr.com/2015/08/power-sector-senate-probes-obj-yaradua-jonathan/.

"Niger." *One World Nations Online*, http://www.nationsonline.org/oneworld/niger.htm.

"Nigeria." 2014. *CIA World Factbook*, https://www.cia.gov/library/publications/the-world-factbook/geos/ni.html. Last updated Nov. 19.

"Nigeria." 2010. M. Paul Lewis, ed., *Ethnologue: Languages of the World, 17th Ed.* Dallas, TX: SIL Int'l. http://www.ethnologue.com/country/NG (last visited Nov. 17, 2014).

"Nigeria." 2006. Pp. 619–25. In Dilip K. Das & Michael Palmiotto, eds., *World Police Encyclopedia, Vol. 2*. New York: Routledge.

"Nigeria: Africa's New Number One." 2014. *Economist.com* (Apr. 12), http://www.economist.com/news/leaders/21600685-nigerias-suddenly-supersied-economy-indeed-wonder-s-are-its-still-huge.

"Nigeria Angry at Being Rated Second Most Corrupt." 2003. *IRIN* (Oct. 9), http://www.irinnews.org/report/46630/nigeria-nigeria-angry-at-being-rated-second-most-corrupt.

"Nigeria Becomes Africa's Largest Economy." 2014. *Al Jazeera* (Apr. 6), http://www.aljazeera.com/news/africa/2014/04/nigeria-becomes-africa-largest-economy-20144618190520102.html.

"Nigeria Becomes Africa's Biggest Economy." 2014. *BBC News* (Apr. 6), http://www.bbc.com/news/business-26913497.

"Nigeria Cedes Bakassi to Cameroon." 2008. *BBC News* (Aug. 14), http://news.bbc.co.uk/2/hi/africa/7559895.stm.

"Nigeria Independence Act, 1960." 1960. 8 & 9 Eliz., 2 Ch. 55 (Jul. 29), www.legislation.gov.uk/ukpga/1960/55/pdfs/ukpga_19600055_en.pdf.

"Nigeria—Ministry of Defense." *Global Security*, http://www.globalsecurity.org/military/world/nigeria/mod.htm.

"Nigeria Orders Arrest of Ex-Adviser over $2 Billion Arms Deal." 2015. *Al Jazeera* (Nov. 18, 08:03 GMT), http://www.aljazeera.com/news/2015/11/nigeria-orders-arrest-adviser-2bn-arms-deal-151118043340314.html.

Nigeria Population (Live). 2016. *Worldometers*. (Apr. 2016), http://www.worldometers.info/world-population/nigeria-population/.

"Nigeria: The National Intelligence Agency (NIA) at Twenty—A Tribute." *Daily Trust* (Abuja), http://allafrica.com/stories/200607200663.html.

"Nigeria Republican Act 1963." 1963. 1963 Ch. 57 (Dec. 18), http://www.legislation.gov.uk/ukpga/1963/57.

"Nigeria (Republic) Bill." 1963. H.L., Deb. Vol. 254 cc208–14 *Hansard* (Dec. 17), hansard.millbanksystems.com/lords/1963/dec/17/Nigeria-republic-bill.

Nigeria (Republic) Bill, H.L. Deb. 1963. Hansard, Vol. 245, cc208–14. Dec. 17. "Nigeria Suspended from Commonwealth." 1995. *CNN* (Nov. 11), http://www.cnn.com/WORLD/9511/nigeria/11–11/.

"Nigeria." *WorldAtlas*, http://www.worldatlas.com/webimage/countrys/africa/ng.htm.

"Nigeria's Muhammadu Buhari in Profile." 2015. *BBC News* (Mar. 31), http://www.bbc.com/news/world-africa-12890807.

"Nigeria's Technical Aid Corps for ACP Countries to Expand to Brazil, Venezuela, Vietnam." 2014. *ACP* (Sept. 10), http://www.acp.int/content/news-nigerias-technical-aid-corps-acp-countries-expand-brazil-venezuela-vietnam.

Nigerian Army Education Corps & School. 1992. *History of the Nigerian Army 1863–1992*. Abuja: Nigerian Army Headquarters.

"The Nigerian Diaspora." Nigerian Diaspora, http://www.nigeriandiaspora.com/nigerian-diaspora.php.

"Nigerian Ex-President Goodluck Jonathan Stole $2 billion via Fake Arms Deals, Current President Says." 2015. *Japan Times* (Nov. 18), http://www.japantimes.co.jp/news/2015/11/18/world/nigerian-ex-president-goodluck-jonathan-stole-2-billion-via-fake-arms-deals-current-president-says/#.Vszw_pwrK1s.

"Nigerian Military Leader Ousts Interim President." 1993. *N.Y. Times* (Nov. 18), http://www.nytimes.com/1993/11/18/world/nigeria-military-leader-ousts-interim-president.html.

"Nigerians Abroad: Secret Weapon." 2015. *Economist* (London) (June 20), http://www.economist.com/news/special-report/21654360-nigerias-diaspora-source-money-markets-skills-and-ideas-secret-weapon.

"Nigerians Living in Poverty Rise to Nearly 61%." 2012. *BBC News* (Feb. 13), http://www.bbc.com/news/world-africa-17015873.

Noble, Kenneth. 1993. "Nigerian Military Rulers Annul Election." *N.Y. Times* (Jun. 24), http://www.nytimes.com/1993/06/24/world/nigerian-military-rulers-annul-election.html.

Northedge, F.S. 1969. "The Nature of Foreign Policy." Pp. 9–39. In F.S. Northedge, ed., *The Foreign Policies of the Powers*. Westport, CT: Praeger.

Nossiter, Adam. 2015. "In Town of Missing Girls, Sorrow, but Little Progress." *N.Y. Times* (May 12), http://www.nytimes.com/2014/05/12/world/africa/in-town-of-missing-girls-sorrow-but-little-progress.html.

Nwabueze, Ben. 2015. "Corrupt Practices: Igbo Leaders' Position on Probe of Past Governments." *Vanguard* (Aug. 13, 9.05 a.m.), http://www.vanguardngr.com/2015/08/corrupt-practices-igbo-leaders-position-on-probe-of-past-govts/.

Nwanolue, Bonn O. & Victor C. Iwuoha. 2012. "A Reflection on Nigeria's Past: Africa as the Centerpiece of Nigeria's Foreign Policy Revisited," *Developing Country Studies*, Vol. 2. Pp. 78–9, http://www.iiste.org/Journals/index.php/DCS/article/view/1756/1709.

Nwanze, Cheta. "A Short History of the Nigerian Police Force." *Trent Online*, http://www.thetrentonline.com/cheta-nwanze-short-history-nigeria-police-force/.

Nwogugu, E. I. 2014. *Family Law in Nigeria.* Ibadan, Nigeria: HEBN Publishers.

Nye, Jr., Joseph S. 2008. *Understanding International Conflicts: An Introduction to Theory and History, 7th Ed.* New York: Longman.

Obaje, Nuhu George. 2009. *Geology and Mineral Resources of Nigeria*. Berlin, Germany: Springer-Verlag.

Obama, Barack. 2009. Speech in Ghana on African Development 3 (Jul. 12), http://www.voanews.com/wm/live/special-events/english-obama-ghana-event/vb.asx.

Obasanjo, Olusegun. 1987. *Nzeogwu: An Intimate Portrait of Major Chukwuma Kaduna Nzeogwu*. Ibadan: Spectrum Books.

The Obasanjo Years: His Legacy, *Lawyers Chronicle*, http://thelawyerschronicle.com/the-obasanjo-years-his-legacy/.

Obi, Emeka A. 2006. *Fundamentals of Nigerian Foreign Policy: A Study on the Role of National Interest in Foreign Policy Making*. Abingdon, U.K.: Bookpoint Ltd.

Obiagwu, Chinonye & Chidi Anselm Odinkalu. 2003. "Nigeria: Combating Legacies of Colonialism and Militarism." Pp. 211–50. In Abdullahi Ahmed An-Na'im ed., *Human Rights under African Constitutions: Realizing the Promise for Ourselves*. Philadelphia, PA: University of Pennsylvania Press.

"Obituary: President Yar'Adua." 2010. *BBC News* (May 6; 02:33 UK, updated at 01:33), http://news.bbc.co.uk/2/hi/africa/6187249.stm.

O'Cléireacáin, Séamus. 1999. "SubSaharan Africa's Trade Liberalization Experience." Pp. 50–73. In Ademola Oyejide et al. eds., *Regional Integration and Trade Liberalization in SubSaharan Africa: Synthesis and Review, Vol. 4*. London: Macmillan Press, Ltd.

Odeh, Lemuel Ekedegwa. 2010. "A Comparative Analysis of Global North and Global South Economies." *Journal of Sustainable Development in Africa*, Vol. 12 (3): 338–48.

Odinkalu, Chidi A. 2001. "The Management of Transition to Civil Rule by the Military in Nigeria (1966–1999)." Pp. 57–99. In 'Kunle Amuwo et al., eds., *Nigeria during the Abacha Years (1993–1998)*. Lagos: IFRA-Nigeria.

Odinkalu, Chidi A. 1999. "Why More Africans Don't Use Human Rights Language." *Human Rights Dialog*, Vol. 2 (Dec.), www.carnegiecouncil.org/publications/archive/dialogue/2_01/articles/602.html.

Odiogor. Hugo & Abiodun Alade. 2015. "I Cannot Rest When the World Is Being Terrorized—Prof. Ibrahim Gambari." *Vanguard* (Lagos) (Jun. 21; 1:44 AM), http://www.vanguardngr.com/2015/06/i-cannot-rest-when-the-world-is-being-terrorised-prof-ibrahim-gambari/.

O'Grady, Siobhan. 2015. "In Nigeria, $2 Billion in Stolen Funds Is Just a Drop in the Corruption Bucket." *Foreign Policy* (Nov. 18, 6:47 PM), http://foreign policy.com/2015/11/18/in-nigeria-2-billion-in-stolen-funds-is-just-a-drop-in-the -corruption-bucket/.

Ogunlesi, Tolu. 2014. "Abuja, Nigeria's Capital City, Grows and Flourishes." *Financial Times* (London) (May 4; 10:59 AM), http://www.ft.com/intl/cms/s/0/68c28016-bb16–11e3–948c-00144feabdc0.html#axzz3n50kTd6W.

Ohaegbulam, Festus Ugboaja. 1982. *Nigeria and the United Nations' Mission to the Democratic Republic of the Congo: A Case Study of the Formative Stages of Nigeria's Foreign Policy*. Gainesville, FL: University Press of Florida.

Ojameruaye, Emmanuel. "A Tentative Analytical Evaluation of President Obasanjo's Performance (May 1999–May 2007)." *Gamji.com*, http://www.gamji.com/article 6000/NEWS7024.htm.

Ojukwu, Emeka Odumegwu. 1994. "Nigeria: The Truths Which Are Self-Evident." *Sunday Magazine* (Lagos) (Mar. 6): 15–23.

Okafor, Victor Oguejiofor, ed. 2008. *Nigeria's Stumbling Democracy and Its Implications for Africa's Democratic Movement*. Westport, CT: Praeger.

Okogwu, L.E. & A. Akpuru-Aja. 2004. *Nigerian Diplomacy and the Conflict of Laws: An Insight into the Practice of Nigeria's Foreign Policy*. Abakaliki, Nigeria: WillyRose & Appleseed Publishing Co.

Okoro, Stevens. 2012. "Nigeria and the Concept of National Interest." *Daily Independent* (Lagos) (Jul.), http://dailyindependentnig.com/2012/07/nigeria-and-concept -of-national-interest/.

Olawale, Salami B. 2014. "The Preclude to Babangida Regime's Foreign Policy Initiatives." *Mediterranean Journal of Social Sciences*, Vol. 5(3): 81–85. http://www .mcser.org/journal/index.php/mjss/article/view/2120.

Oloka-Onyango, J. 2015. *Battling Over Human Rights: Twenty Essays on Law, Politics and Governance*. Bamenda, Cameroon: Langaa Research & Publishing.

Olonisakin, 'Funmi. 2000. *Reinventing Peacekeeping in Africa: Conceptual and Legal Issues in ECOMOG Operations*. London: Kluwer Law Int'l.

Olukoya, Sam. 2001. "Nigeria's Trigger Happy Police." *BBC News* (May 11, 15:33 GMT 16:53 UK), http://news.bbc.co.uk/2/hi/africa/1322017.stm.

Olusanya, G.O. & R. A. Akindele, eds. 1990. *The Structure and Processes of Foreign Policy Making and Implementation in Nigeria, 1960–1990.* Lagos: Nigerian Institute of Int'l Affairs.

Olusanya, G.O. & R.A. Akindele. 1986. *Nigeria's External Relations: The First Twenty-Five Years*. Ibadan: Ibadan University Press.

Olutoyin, Babatunde Isaac. 2004. "Treaty Making and Its Application under Nigerian Law: The Journey So Far." *International Journal of Business & Management Invention*, Vol. 3, p. 7, http://www.ijbmi.org/papers/Vol%283%293/Version-3/ B033307018.pdf.

Omotola, J. Oshola. 2010. "Elections and Democratic Transition in Nigeria under the Fourth Republic." *African Affairs*, Vol. 109: 535–53.

O'Neil, Patrick H. et al. 2012. *Cases in Comparative Politics, 4th Ed.* New York: W. W. Norton & Co.

Onishi, Norimitsu. 2015. "Nigeria's Comics Pull Punch Lines from Deeper Social Ills." *N.Y. Times* (Dec. 5), http://www.nytimes.com/2015/12/06/world/africa/nigerias-comics-pull-punch-lines-from-deeper-social-ills.html.

Onishi, Norimitsu. 1999. "What War Has Wrought: Sierra Leone's Sad State." *N.Y. Times* (Jan. 31), http://www.nytimes.com/1999/01/31/world/what-war-has-wrought-sierra-leone-s-sad-state.html?pagewanted=all.

"Operation Iraqi Freedom." 2003. *White House* (Mar. 27), http://georgewbush-whitehouse.archives.gov/news/releases/2003/03/20030327–10.html.

"Organization." Office of the Director of National Intelligence, http://www.dni.gov/index.php/about/organization.

Osaghae, Eghosa E. 1998. *The Crippled Giant: Nigeria since Independence*. Bloomington, IN: Indiana University Press.

Ostien, Philip & Albert Dekker. 2010. "Sharia and National Law in Nigeria." Pp. 555–612. In Jan Otto, Michiel, ed., *Sharia Incorporated: A Comparative Overview of the Legal Systems of Twelve Muslim Countries in Past and Present*. Leiden, Netherlands: Leiden University Press.

Owete, Festus. 2014. "Between Jonathan's National Conference and Obasanjo's National Political Reform Conference: What You Need to Know." *Premium Times* (Abuja) (Feb. 16), http://www.premiumtimesng.com/news/155237-between-jonathans-national-conference-and-obasanjos-national-political-reform-conference.html.

Oyekanmi, Babatunde. 2015. "2015 General Elections and the Role of INEC." Paper Presented at a Conference in July, http://www.inecnigeria.org/wp-content/uploads/2015/07/Conference-Paper-by-Tunde-Oyekanmi.pdf.

Ozekhome, Mike A. A. 2014. "The Nigerian Judiciary—15 Years of Democracy." *Pointblanknews.com*, http://pointblanknews.com/pbn/articles-opinions/the-nigerian-judiciary-15-years-of-democracy/ (last visited Nov. 24, 2014).

Ozoigbo, Bonaventure I. 2008. "Federal Balancing in Nigeria: A Paradigm for Democracy." *African Journals Online*. Pp. 66–84.

Papp, Daniel S. 2001. *Contemporary International Relations: Frameworks for Understanding, 6th Ed.* Upper Saddle River, N.J.: Pearson.

Patterson, Thomas E. 2008. *The American Democracy, 11th Ed.* New York: McGraw-Hill.

Patterson, Thomas E. 2008. *The American Democracy, 8th Ed.* New York: McGraw-Hill.

"Peace Corps." Boston, MA: John F. Kennedy Presidential Library & Museum. http://www.jfklibrary.org/JFK/JFK-in-History/Peace-Corps.aspx.

"People's Democratic Party (PDP)." *Encyclopedia Britannica*, http://www.britannica.com/topic/Peoples-Democratic-Party-political-party-Nigeria.

Pere, Garth le. 2008. Review of Adekeye Adebajo & Abdul Raufu Mustapha, eds. *Gulliver's Troubles: Nigeria's Foreign Policy after the Cold War* (University of KwaZulu-Natal Press, 2008), *African Journal of Conflict Resolution*, Vol. 8, http://www.accord.org.za/publications/book-reviews/638-gullivers-troubles-nigerias-foreign-policy-after-the-cold-war.

"The Perils of Liberian Peacekeeping." 2003. *BBC News* (Aug. 4; 15:35 GMT 16:35 UK), http://news.bbc.co.uk/2/hi/africa/3113009.stm.

Pham, J. Peter. 2007. Nigeria's Foreign Policy: An Inquiry into Sources and Prospects, Paper Prepared for Presentation at an Int'l Conference in Lisbon, Portugal (Nov. 8–9), www.ipri.pt/eventos/pdf/JPeterPham_paper.pdf.

Pine, Atah. 2011. "Nigerian Foreign Policy, 1960–2011: Fifty Years of Conceptual Confusion." *Modern Ghana* (Oct. 4), http://www.modernghana.com/print/354264/1/nigeria-foreign-policy-1960–2011-fifty-one-years-o.html.

Pine, Atah. 2009. "Parliamentary Diplomacy and Foreign Policy in Nigeria's Fourth Republic." *Blogger* (Jul. 1), http://atahpine.blogspot.com/2009/07/parliamentary-diplomacy-and-foreign.html.

Pitts, Chip. 2005. "'Mobilizing Shame' Can Bring Abuses Up Short." *Topeka Capital-Journal* (Mar. 11), http://cjonline.com/stories/031105/opi_pitts.shtml.

Plato. 2007. "The Myth of the Cave." Pp. 23–6. In Jonathan E. Adler & Catherine Z. Elgin, eds., *Philosophical Inquiry: Classic and Contemporary Readings*. Indianapolis, IN: Hackett Publishing Co., Inc.

Podesta, James. 1994. "Haile Selassie 1892–1975." *Contemporary Black Biography*, http://www.encyclopedia.com/topic/Haile_Selassie.aspx.

Pogoson, A.I. "Leadership Roles and Foreign Policy: A Study of President Shehu Shagari's Foreign Policy Posture." *AfricaBib*, ttp://www.africabib.org/rec.php?RID=170748693.

"Politics in the Crisis Years." In Helen Chapin Metz, ed., *Nigeria: A Country Study*. Washington, D.C: GPO for the Library of Congress.

"Political Realism in International Relations." 2013. *Stanford Encyclopedia of Philosophy* (Jul. 26, 2010, revised Apr. 2, 2013), http://plato.stanford.edu/entries/realism-intl-relations/.

"Political Transition." In Helen Chapin Metz, ed., *Nigeria: A Country Study*. Washington D.C.: GPO for the Library of Congress.

Pope Francis. 2015. Text of Address to a Joint Session of the U.S. Congress. (Sept. 24; 10:30 AM EDT), http://www.politico.com/story/2015/09/pope-francis-speech-to-congress-transcript-text-video-214016.

"Poverty in Nigeria: Rich Country, Poor People." 2013. *Poverties.org* (Mar. 2012 updated Apr. 2013), http://www.poverties.org/poverty-in-nigeria.html.

Power, Samantha & Graham Allison. 2000. "Introduction." Pp. xiii–xxvii. In Samatha Power & Graham Allison, eds., *Realizing Human Rights: Moving from Inspiration to Impact*. New York: St. Martin's Press.

"Profile: African Union." 2012. *BBC News* (Feb. 1), http://news.bbc.co.uk/2/hi/africa/country_profiles/3870303.stm.

"Profile: ECOMOG." 2004. *BBC News* (Jun. 17; 15:15 GMT 16:15 UK), http://news.bbc.co.uk/2/hi/africa/country_profiles/2364029.stm.

"Profile: Economic Community of West African States (ECOWAS)." Institute for Security Studies, https://www.issafrica.org/AF/RegOrg/unity_to_union/ecowasprof.htm.

"Protests in Biafra: Go Your Own Way." 2015. *Economist* (London) (Nov. 28), http://www.economist.com/news/middle-east-and-africa/21679210-half-century-after-war-angry-biafrans-are-agitating-again-go-your-own-way.

Przeworski, Adam. 1991. *Democracy and the Market*. New York: Cambridge University Press.

Purefoy, Christine. 2011. "Goodluck Jonathan: By Name and Nature?" *CNN* (Apr. 17; 10:36 pm EDT), http://www.cnn.com/2010/WORLD/africa/05/06/nigeria.jonathan/.

Quigley, Fran. 2014. *How Human Rights Can Build Haiti: Activists, Lawyers, and the Grassroots Campaign*. Nashville, TN: Vanderbilt University Press.

Quist-Arcton, Ofeibea. 2006. "Nigeria Rejects Term-Limit Change in Constitutions." *N[ational] P[ublic] R[adio]* (May 17, 6:00 AM ET), http://www.npr.org/templates/story/story.php?storyID=5410583.

Ralph, Jason. 2007. *Defending the Society of States: Why America Opposes the International Criminal Court and Its Visions of World Society*. New York: Oxford University Press.

Ramcharan, B.G. 2002. *The United Nations High Commissioner for Human Rights: The Challenges of International Protection*. Leiden, Netherlands: Martinus Nijhoff.

Rasiulis, Andrew P. 2001. "The Military Training Assistance Program (MTAP): An Instrument of Diplomacy." *Canadian Military Journal* (Autumn): 63–64. http://www.journal.forces.gc.ca/vo2/no3/doc/63–64-eng.pdf.

"Rectification of Names." *Cultural China*, http://www.cultural-china.com/chinaWH/History/en/165History878.html.

Redmond, Paul. 2003. "Transnational Enterprise and Human Rights: Options for Standard Setting and Compliance." *International Law*, Vol. 37: 69–101.

"Reforming Nigeria: A Conversation with Ngozi Okonjo-Iweala." 2014. *Foreign Affairs* (Mar./Apr.), http://www.foreignaffairs.com/discussions/interviews/-nigeria.

"Republic of the Congo: United Nations Operation in the Congo, ONUC (July 1960–June 1964)." *United Nations*, http://www.un.org/en/peacekeeping/missions/past/onuc.htm.

Report of the Commission Appointed to Inquire into the Fears of Minorities and the Means of Allaying Them. 1958. London: Her Majesty's Stationery Office.

"Return to Military Rule." 1991. In Helen Chapin Metz, ed., *Nigeria: A Country Study*. Washington D.C.: GPO for the Library of Congress.

Reuters. 2016. "A Year on From Nigerian Election Victory Buhari's Reforms Founder." *N.Y. Times* (Feb. 25, 6:54 AM EST), http://www.nytimes.com/reuters/2016/02/25/world/africa/25reuters-nigeria-politics.html?_r=0.

"Rioting in Nigeria Kills at Least 11." 1993. *N.Y. Times* (Jul. 7), http://www.nytimes.com/1993/07/07/world/rioting-in-nigeria-kills-at-least-11.html.

Robinson, Mary. N.D. "The Business Case for Human Rights." http://www.unhchr.ch/hurricane/huricane.nsf/0/e47d352dedc39697802566de0043b28e?OpenDocument.

Rocha, José Luís. 2010. "Cape Verde and ECOWAS: The Challenge of Regional Integration." *Portuguese Journal of International Affairs* (Autumn/Winter): 3–7.

"The Role of Non-State Entities." *Icelandic Human Rights Center*, http://www.humanrights.is/en/human-rights-education-project/human-rights-concepts-ideas-and-fora/human-rights-actors/the-role-of-non-state-entities.

Rosenau, James N. 1968. "National Interest." *International Encyclopedia of the Social Sciences*, http://www.encyclopedia.com/doc/1G2–3045000855.html.

Rosenberg, Matt. "Non-Members of the United Nations." *About.com*, http://geography.about.com/od/politicalgeography/a/nun.htm.

Rosenthal, Elisabeth. 2012. "Nigeria Tested by Rapid Rise in Population." *N.Y. Times* (Apr. 14), http://www.nytimes.com/2012/04/15/world/africa/in-nigeria-a-preview-of-an-overcrowded-planet.html?pagewanted=all&_r=0.

Ross, Will. 2015. "Nigeria Elections: Buhari Scores Historic Win." *BBC News* (Apr. 1), http://www.bbc.com/news/world-africa-32141703.

Roth, Kenneth. 2000. "Human Rights Organizations: A New Force for Social Change." Pp. 225–48. In Samantha Power & Graham Alison, eds., *Realizing Human Rights: Moving from Inspiration to Impact.* New York: St. Martin's Press.

Rotimi-John, Alade. 2015. "The Nigerian Question and Its Resolution." *Guardian* (Lagos) (Nov. 18; 4:20 am), http://www.ngrguardiannews.com/2015/11/the-nigerian-question-and-its-resolution/.

Rupert, James. 1998. "Corruption Flourished in Abacha's Regime." *Washington Post* (Jun. 9): A01, http://www.washingtonpost.com/wp-srv/inatl/longterm/nigeria/stories/corrupt060998.htm.

Saro-Wiwa, Ken. 1996. *A Month and a Day: A Detention Diary*. London: Penguin Books.

Saunders, Paul J. 2016. "The Five Most Abuses Foreign-Policy Cliches." *National Interest* (retrieved Jan. 20), http://nationalinterest.org/commentary/the-five-most-abused-foreign-policy-cliches-9978.

Sauti, Lazarus. 2013. "Thabo Mbeki's Legacy to Africa." *Herald* (Zimbabwe) (Sept. 16), http://www.herald.co.zw/thabo-mbekis-legacy-to-africa/.

Schell, Jonathan. 2003. *The Unconquerable World: Power, Nonviolence, and the Will of the People*. New York: Henry Holt & Co.

Schifferes, Steve. 2003. "U.S. Names 'Coalition of the Willing.'" *BBC News* (Mar. 18, 21:38 GMT), http://news.bbc.co.uk/2/hi/americas/2862343.stm.

Schmidt, Brian C. 1998. *The Political Discourse of Anarchy: A Disciplinary History of International Relations.* Albany, N.Y.: State University of New York Press.

Schmidt, Steffen W., et al. 2005. *American Government and Politics Today 2005–2006 Edition*. Belmont, CA: Thomson Wadsworth.

Sen, Amartya. 2006. "Democracy as a Universal Value." Pp. 171–81. In Mark Kesselman & Joel Krieger ed., *Readings in Comparative Politics: Political Challenges and Changing Agendas.* Boston, MA: Cengage Learning.

"Senate Asks Buhari to Review Nigeria's Foreign Policy." *Premium Times* (Lagos), http://www.premiumtimesng.com/news/top-news/194812-%E2%80%8Bs%E2%80%8Benate-asks-buhari-to-review-nigerias-foreign-policy.html.

Shagaya, John N. 2003. *Governance in Nigeria: The IBB Era: An Insider's View*. Lagos: Viewpoint Communications Ltd.

Sharp, Paul. 2009. *Diplomatic Theory of International Relations*. Cambridge Studies in International Relations No. 111. New York. Cambridge University Press, 2009.

Sheehan, Michael. 1996. *Balance of Power: History and Theory*. New York: Routledge.

Shikyil, Sylvester S. 2000. Human Rights in Foreign Policy: Nigeria's Experience since 1979. Doctoral dissertation, Dept. of Law, University of Jos, http://datad.aau.org/handle/123456789/42302?show=full.

Shinn, David H. Reversing the Brain Drain in Ethiopia, Address to the Ethiopian North American Health Professionals Association, Nov. 23, 2002, http://chora.virtualave.net/brain-drain8.htm.

"A Short Definition of Democracy." *Democracy Building*, http://www.democracy-building.info/definition-democracy.html.

"Sierra Leone." *Global Security*, http://www.globalsecurity.org/military/world/war/sierra_leone.htm.

Sikkink, Kathryn. 1993. "The Power of Principled Ideas: Human Rights Policies in the United States and Western Europe." Pp. 139–72. In Judith Goldstein & Robert O. Keohane, eds., *Ideas and Foreign Policy: Beliefs, Institutions, and Political Change*. Ithaca, N.Y.: Cornell University Press.

Simpkins, John. 2004. The Role of Constitution-Building Processes in Democratization: Case Study Nigeria. Sweden: Institute for Democracy & Electoral Assistance.

Siollun, Max. 2016. "Nigeria Is Coming Apart at the Seams." *Foreign Policy* (Feb. 8), https://foreignpolicy.com/2016/02/08/nigeria-is-coming-apart-at-the-seamsbiafra/.

Siollun, Max. 2009. *Oil, Politics, and Violence: Nigeria's Military Coup Culture (1966–1976)*. New York: Algora Publishing.

Sklar, Richard L. 1963. *Nigerian Political Parties: Power in an Emergent African Nation*. Princeton, N.J.: Princeton University Press.

"Slave Coast." *Encyclopedia Britannica*, http://www.britannica.com/EBchecked/topic/548212/Slave-Coast.

"Slavery Fact Sheets." *Digital History*, www.digitalhistory.uh.edu/disp_textbook.cfm?smtID=11&psid=3807.

Smith, Daniel Jordan. 2008. *A Culture of Corruption: Everyday Deception and Popular Discontent in Nigeria*. Princeton, N.J.: Princeton University Press.

Smith, Robert Charles. 1995. *Racism in the Post-Civil Rights Era: Now You See It, Now You Don't*. New York: SUNY Press.

Smith, Steve. 2001. "Foreign Policy Is What States Make of It: Social Construction and International Relations Theory." Pp. 38–55. In Vendulka Kubálková, ed., *Foreign Policy in a Constructed World*. Armonk, N.Y.: M.E. Sharpe.

Smith, William Edgett. 1971. *We Must Run While They Walk: A Portrait of Africa's Julius Nyerere*. New York: Random House.

Sodaro, Michael J. 2008. *Comparative Politics: A Global Introduction, 3d Ed*. Boston, MA: McGraw-Hill.

Soyombo, Fiyaso. 2015. "How Will Nigeria Fare under Buhari?" *Al Jazeera* (Jun. 9; 07:44 GMT), http://www.aljazeera.com/indepth/opinion/2015/06/nigeria-fare-buhari-150607105418906.html.

Soyombo, Fisayo. 2014. "Why Is Nigeria's Jonathan Worried?" *Al Jazeera* (Nov. 27; 14:39 GMT), http://www.aljazeera.com/indepth/opinion/2014/11/why-nigeria-jonathan-worried-20141123104313818965.html.

"Statehood Dates." *50States.com*, http://www.50states.com/statehood.htm#.VoL53x-UrK1s.

"State and Local Governments." *American Government*, http://www.ushistory.org/gov/12.asp.

"States of the United States." *Statoids*, http://statoids.com/uus.html;.

Sterling-Foster, Jennifer, ed. 2013. *Making Sense of International Relations Theory, 2d Ed*. Boulder, CO: Lynne Rienner.

Strayer, Joseph R. 2005. *On the Medieval Origins of the Modern State*. Princeton, N.J.: Princeton University Press.

Stremlau, John J. 2015. *The International Politics of the Nigerian Civil War, 1967–1970*. Princeton, N.J.: Princeton University Press.

Stromberg, Roland N. "Collective Security." *Encyclopedia of the New American Nation*, http://www.americanforeignrelations.com/A-D/Collective-Security.html.

Suberu, Rotimi T. 1999. *Public Policies and National Unity in Nigeria*. Ibadan, Nigeria: Development Policy Centre.

Sule, Ahmed Musa. 2013. Nigeria's Participation in Peacekeeping Operations, Thesis, Certificate-In-Training in U.N. Peace Support Operations, cdn.peaceopstraining.org/thesis/sule.pdf.

Sussman, Alison. 1993. "Babangida, Ibrahim 1941–." *Contemporary Black Biography*, http://www.encyclopedia.com/doc/1G2–2870600010.html.

Swarns, Rachael L. 2002. "African Leaders Drop Old Group for One That Has Power." *N.Y. Times* (Jul. 9), http://www.nytimes.com/2002/07/09/international/africa/09AFRI.html.

"Switzerland's Political System and Government." n.d. *All About Switzerland*, http://swiss-government-politics.all-about-switzerland.info/.

Tamuno, Tekena N. 2003. "The Nigeria Police Force and Public Security and Safety: Major Challenges and Opportunities since 1930." Pp. 119–40. In Laurent Fourchard & Isaac Olawale Albert eds., *Security, Crime, and Segregation in West African Cities since the 19th Century*. Paris, France: Karthala Editions.

"Tanzania (1961–Present)." University of Central Arkansas, http://uca.edu/politicalscience/dadm-project/sub-saharan-africa-region/tanzania-1961-present/.

Thomas, Daniel C. 2001. *The Helsinki Effect: International Norms, Human Rights, and the Demise of Communism*. Princeton, N.J.: Princeton University Press.

"The Transformation of Technical Aid Corps Scheme." 2014. *Sun* (Lagos) (Aug. 20), http://sunnewsonline.com/new/the-transformation-of-technical-aid-corps-scheme/.

Timberg, Craig. 2006. "Bid to Allow Nigerian a Third Term Hits Snag." *Washington Post* (May 13), http://www.washingtonpost.com/wp-dyn/content/article/2006/05/12/AR2006051200518.html.

Treaty of the Economic Community of West African States (ECOWAS). 1975. (May 28), http://www.internationaldemocracywatch.org/attachments/351_ecowas%20treaty%20of%201975.pdf.

"Truman Signs the National Security Act." 1947. *This Day in History* (Jul. 26), http://www.history.com/this-day-in-history/truman-signs-the-national-security-act.

Turner, Valerie. 2003. "How Many Troops Make Up a Brigade, Battalion, Company, Etc.?" *Orlando Sentinel* (Mar. 29), http://articles.orlandosentinel.com/2003-03-29/news/0303290257_1_support-troops-battalion-divisions.

Uchenna, Tony. 2010. "Osu Caste in Igboland." *Vanguard* (Lagos) (Oct. 9; 7:35 PM), http://www.vanguardngr.com/2010/10/osu-caste-in-igboland/.

Ukaigwe, Jerry. 2016. *ECOWAS Law*. New York: Springer.

Umoru, Henry. 2010. "Nigeria Lost 2,000 Soldiers, $10 bn. in Peacekeeping Operations." *Vanguard* (Lagos) (Oct. 25; 1:21 AM), http://www.vanguardngr.com/2010/10/%E2%80%98nigeria-lost-2000-soldiers-10-bn-in-peace-keeping-operations/.

Umozurike, U. Oji. 1997. *The African Charter on Human and Peoples' Rights*. Leiden, Netherlands & Boston, MA: Brill.

"UNMIL Background." *United Nations*, http://www.un.org/en/peacekeeping/missions/unmil/background.shtml.

United Nations. 2008. *United Nations Peacekeeping Operations: Principles and Guidelines*. New York: Dept. of Peacekeeping Operations.

United Nations. "What Is Peacekeeping?" http://www.un.org/en/peacekeeping/operations/peacekeeping.shtml.

United Nations. "Peace and Security," http://www.un.org/en/peacekeeping/.

United Nations Aouzou Strip Observer Group (UNASOG). 1994. (May/Jun.), http://www.un.org/en/peacekeeping/missions/past/unasog.htm.

Universal Declaration of Human Rights, G.A. Res. 217 A (III), U.N. GAOR, 3d Sess., U.N. Doc. A/810 (1948).

University of Minnesota. Human Rights Library, Ratification of International Human Rights Treaties—Nigeria, http://www1.umn.edu/humanrts/research/ratification-nigeria.html (last visited Feb. 26, 2015).

U.S. Energy Information Admin. 2013. *Nigeria* (Dec. 30), www.eia.gov/contries/and/analysisbriefs/Nigeria/nigeria.pdf.

Vasquez, John A. & Colin Elman, eds., 2005. *Realism and the Balance of Power: A New Debate*. Upper Saddle River, N.J.: Prentice Hall.

"Vienna Declaration and Program of Action." 1993. *Office of the United Nations High Commissioner for Human Rights* (Jun. 25), http://www.ohchr.org/EN/ProfessionalInterest/Pages/Vienna.aspx.

Vincent, R.J. 1986. *Human Rights and International Relations*. New York: Cambridge University Press.

"Vision 2020." ECOWAS, www.ecowas.int/about_ecowas/vision-2020/.

"Wachuku, Jaja Anucha." *S9.Com Biographical Dictionary*, http://www.s9.com/Biography/Wachuku-Jaja-Anucha.

Walker, Andrew. 2009. "The Story of Nigeria's 'Untouchables.'" *BBC News* (Apr. 7; 10:30 UK), http://news.bbc.co.uk/2/hi/africa/7977734.stm.

Walton Jr., Hanes & Robert C. Smith. 2010. *American Politics and the African American Quest for Universal Freedom, 5th Ed.* New York: Longman.

Wando, William M. 2012. Challenges, Benefits, and Recommendations for Continued Nigerian Peacekeeping, Paper for the Naval War College, Newport, R.I. (Nov. 2), http://www.dtic.mil/dtic/tr/fulltext/u2/a569419.pdf.

"What Is a 'State.'" *Global Policy Forum*, https://www.globalpolicy.org/nations-a-states/what-is-a-state.html.

"What Is the 0.7% Target?" 2002–2006. Millennium Project, http://www.unmillenniumproject.org/press/07.htm.

"What We Do." United Nations Human Rights Office of the High Commissioner, http://www.ohchr.org/EN/AboutUs/Pages/WhatWeDo.aspx.

Weissbrodt, David, et al. 2009. *International Human Rights: Law, Policy, and Process, 4th Ed.* San Francisco, CA: LexisNexis.

"Welcome to the Directorate of Technical Aid Corps." Directorate of Technical Aid Corps, http://www.dtac.gov.ng/DTAC/dtac/aboutDTAC#.

Wendt, Alexander. 1999. *Social Theory of International Politics*. New York: Cambridge University Press, 1999.

Wendt, Alexander. 1992. "Anarchy Is What States Make of It: The Social Construction of Power Politics," *International Organization*, Vol. 46: 391–425.

"Western Sahara." *CIA World Factbook*, https://www.cia.gov/library/publications/the-world-factbook/geos/wi.html.

"Western Sahara Profile." 2014. *BBC News Africa* (Jan. 7), http://www.bbc.com/news/world-africa-14115273.

"What Is the Difference between Humanitarian Law and Human Rights Law?" International Committee of the Red Cross, https://www.icrc.org/eng/resources/documents/misc/5kzmuy.htm.

"When Rape Becomes Genocide." 1998. *N.Y. Times* (Sept. 5), http://www.nytimes.com/1998/09/05/opinion/when-rape-becomes-genocide.html.

Whisky, Ayakeme. 2014. "The South-South Position: A Stitch in Time Saves Nine." *Vanguard* (Lagos) (Jun. 5), http://www.vanguardngr.com/2014/06/south-south-position-stitch-time-saves-nine/.

White, Theodore H. 1982. *America in Search of Itself: The Making of the President 1956–1980*. New York: Harper & Row.

The White House, Office of the Press Secretary. 2014. "Remarks by President Obama in Address to the United Nations General Assembly." (Sept. 28), www.whitehouse.gov/the-press-office/2014/09/24/remarks-president-obama-address-united-nations-general-assembly.

"Who Said, 'Charity Begins at Home?'" 2010. *Bible or Not* (Apr. 24), http://bibleornot.org/who-said-charity-begins-at-home/.

Williams, Alabi. 2016. "It's Time to Review Nigeria." *Guardian* (Lagos) (Jun. 12 3:47 a.m.), http://guardian.ng/opinion/its-time-to-review-nigeria/.

Wilson, Frank L. 1996. *Concepts and Issues in Comparative Politics: An Introduction to Comparative Analysis*. Upper Saddle River, N.J.: Prentice Hall.

Wilson-Keenan, Jo Anne. 2015. *From Small Places: Toward the Realization of Literacy as a Human Right*. New York: Springer, 2015.

"Wind of Change" Speech, *About.com*, http://africanhistory.about.com/od/eraindependence/a/wind_of_change1.htm.

Wittkopf, Eugene R., et al. 2008. *American Foreign Policy: Pattern and Process 7th Ed*. Belmont, CA: Thomson Wadsworth.

"World Conference and the Vienna Declaration." *BBC World Service*, http://www.bbc.co.uk/worldservice/people/features/ihavearightto/four_b/treaties_vienna.shtml.

"World Conference on Human Rights, 14–25 June 1993, Vienna, Austria." *United Nations Human Rights Office of the High Commissioner*, http://www.ohchr.org/EN/ABOUTUS/Pages/ViennaWC.aspx.

Yokota, Yozo & Chiyuki Aoi. 2000. "Japan's Foreign Policy towards Human Rights: Uncertain Changes." Pp. 115–45. In David P. Forsythe, ed., *Human Rights and Comparative Foreign Policy*. New York: United Nations University Press.

Yusuf, Hakeem O. 2013. "Human Rights Violations Investigations Commission, the Oputa Panel (Nigeria)." Pp. 161–65. In Lavinia Stan & Nadia Nedelsky, eds., *Encyclopedia of Transitional Justice*. New York: Cambridge University Press.

Zakaria, Fareed. 2011. "Are America's Best Days Behind Us?" *Time* (Mar. 3), http://content.time.com/time/magazine/article/0,9171,2056723,00.html (last visited Mar. 14, 2016).

Zakaria, Fareed. 1997. "The Rise of Illiberal Democracy." *Foreign Affairs* (Nov./Dec.), http://www.foreignaffairs.com/articles/53577/fareed-zakaria/the-rise-of-illiberal-democracy.

Zane, Damian. 2015. "Nigeria's Goodluck Jonathan: Five Reasons Why He Lost." *BBC News* (Mar. 31), http://www.bbc.com/news/world-africa-32136295.

Index

Note: Page references for figures and tables are italicized.

About the Author

Philip C. Aka is professor of political science at Chicago State University and adjunct professor of law at Indiana University Robert H. McKinney School of Law at Indianapolis. He earned six academic degrees, including an S.J.D. in law and a Ph.D. in political science. Dr. Aka also holds an Illinois law license.

Lightning Source UK Ltd.
Milton Keynes UK
UKOW02n0801161216
290117UK00001B/22/P